TASTES OF THE DIVINE

COMPARATIVE THEOLOGY: THINKING ACROSS TRADITIONS

Loye Ashton and John J. Thatamanil, *Series Editors*

This series invites books that engage in constructive comparative theological reflection that draws from the resources of more than one religious tradition. It offers a venue for constructive thinkers, from a variety of religious traditions (or thinkers belonging to more than one), who seek to advance theology understood as "deep learning" across religious traditions.

TASTES OF THE DIVINE

Hindu and Christian Theologies of Emotion

MICHELLE VOSS ROBERTS

Fordham University Press NEW YORK 2014

Fordham University Press also publishes its books in a variety of electronic formats. Some content that appears in print may not be available in electronic books.

Library of Congress Cataloging-in-Publication Data is available from the publisher.

Printed in the United States of America

16 15 14   5 4 3 2 1

First edition

for Anya Devi

CONTENTS

ABBREVIATIONS

ABh	*Abhinavabhāratī* of Abhinavagupta
BhP	*Bhāgavata Purāṇa*
BhRS	*Bhaktirasāmṛtasindhu* of Rūpa Gosvāmin
CSI	Church of South India
DhĀ	*Dhvanyāloka* of Ānandavardhana
Loc	*Locana* of Abhinavagupta
NŚ	*Nāṭya Śāstra* of Bharata
NBCLC	National Biblical, Catechetical, and Liturgical Centre (Bangalore)
NRSV	Bible: New Revised Standard Version
REDS	Rural Education for Development Society (Tumkur, Karnataka)
Serm.	[Sermons] *On the Song of Songs* of Bernard of Clairvaux
Sg.	Song of Songs
UN	*Ujjvalanīlamaṇī* of Rūpa Gosvāmin

SANSKRIT PRONUNCIATION GUIDE

Pronunciation suggestions are adapted from Robert P. Goldman and Sally J. Sutherland Goldman, *Devavāṇīpraveśikā: An Introduction to the Sanskrit Language*.[1] I have omitted characters that do not appear in this work. Diacritics are used for Sanskrit, but not for modern Indian languages or Sanskrit words that have entered the English language. I do not amend diacritics in direct quotations.

a	like the *u* in "but"
ā	like the *o* in "mom"
i	like the *i* in "bit"
ī	like the *ee* in "beet"
u	like the first *u* in "suture"
ū	like the *oo* in "pool"
ṛ	like the *ri* in "rig"
e	like the *a* in "gate"
ai	like the *i* in "high"
o	like the *o* in "rote"
au	like the *ou* in "loud"
k	like the *k* in "skate"
kh	like the *k* in "Kate"
g	like the *g* in "gate"
gh	like the *gh* in "dig hard"
ṅ	like the *n* in "sing"
c	like the *ch* in "eschew"
ch	like the *ch* in "chew"
j	like the *j* in "Jew"
jh	like the *djeh* in "hedgehog"

ñ	like the *n* in "cinch"
ṭ	like the first *t* in "start"
ṭh	like the first *t* in "tart"
ḍ	like the *d* in "dart"
ḍh	like the *dh* in "red-hot"
ṇ	like the *n* in "tint"
t	like the first *t* in "start," but with the tongue against the teeth
th	like the first *t* in "tart," but with the tongue against the teeth
d	like the *d* in "dart," but with the tongue against the teeth
dh	like the *dh* in "red-hot," but with the tongue against the teeth
n	like the *n* in "tint," but with the tongue against the teeth
p	like the *p* in "spin"
ph	like the *p* in "pin"
b	like the *b* in "bin"
bh	like the *bh* in "rub hard"
m	like the *m*'s in "mumps"
y	like the *y* in "yellow"
r	like the *r* in "drama"
l	like the *l* in "lug"
v	between the *w* in "wile" and the *v* in "vile"
ś	like the *sh* in "shove"
ṣ	like the *sh* in "crashed"
s	like the *s* in "so"
h	like the *h* in "hope"
ṃ	like the *m*'s in "mumps," but before certain consonants like the *n*'s in "bingo," "punch," and "mint"
ḥ	echoes the preceding vowel; aḥ is pronounced like "aha"

PREFACE

Mahler's soaring resurrections and gentle cynicism. Bach's intelligent intricacy. Bruckner's majestic block chords. Grainger's whimsy. Mozart's perfection. When all factors come together—the tuning of the instruments, the skill of the performers, the vision of the composer, the insight of the conductor, and the attention of the audience—music is pure bliss. During my college years, the conductor of the Calvin College orchestra referred to such conjunctions as "goose-bump moments." Whether sitting in the French horn section or in the audience, my heart and body still stir at these moments of aesthetic transcendence.

My mind-body-spirit also knows these goose-bump moments through religious experience. Although my musical tastes have changed over time, the moments have arrived through hymns in four-part harmony, heartfelt praise choruses, protest songs, *kīrtana*s, and simple Taizé chants. I have looked around me and observed that others feel it too: closed eyes, raised hands, shouts of "Hallelujah," silent tears. Even the "frozen chosen" in the Reformed churches are not immune to the thaw of the heart.

Sometimes it is difficult to tell where aesthetic experience ends and religious experience begins. From the humble sanctuaries of the American Midwest to Eastern Europe's history-laden churches, our orchestra's tour venues gave our music a religious cast. We sang tunes from the Genevan Psalter in Hungarian, striking the chord of a shared heritage spanning continents and centuries. The electric charge of beauty and spirit intensified in proximity to the handsome trumpet player two seats over. Our courtship and breakups were narrated to the soundtrack of some of the world's most stirring music. Some alchemy of aesthetic bliss, a shared spiritual search, hormones, and true love ignited a world of meaning and value.

What creates a moment of transcendence? The apostle Paul, Saint Augustine, and John Wesley attribute such experiences, especially those with clear religious content, to divine grace. They are correct; but as a musician, I also know something about the "works" side of things. Even when the pinnacle of the experience seems rapturously disembodied, I do not forget the hours of scales, etudes, rehearsal hours, and lessons. I bear in my body the pre-performance butterflies, the self-conscious trembling of my legs during a recital, the technique, the sounds resonating in my ear drums, and the goose-bumps themselves. The hairs on my arms do not arise of my own volition: A community of composers, audiences, and fellow musicians collectively call them to attention. All of this points me toward the embodied disciplines, worship practices, and communities at work in the creation of religious experience.

Once we get specific about the components that combine to create religious and aesthetic experience, we also notice its specific emotional quality. It, too, is marked by particularity. The cathartic grief of Bach's "St. Matthew Passion" differs from the energetic solidarity when members of a multi-racial Atlanta church link arms to sing "We Shall Overcome." The terror of Fate's wheel evoked at the beginning and end of Orff's "Carmina Burana" differs markedly from the bawdy eros of the middle. Each one thrills the listener, but the dispositions are not identical.

This book pursues three sentiments for their aesthetic, spiritual, and ethical value: the transcendence of a soul at peace, the passion of a heart in love, and the liberating energy of fury at injustice. Peace, love, and fury compete for prominence in religious communities past and present. In an aesthetic of peace, art and meditation offer an escape from the demands of daily life. Momentarily tranquil and still, the soul emerges refreshed. In an aesthetic of love, sacred and secular music enkindle desire toward divine and human lovers. Rather than soothing the spirit, this art awakens us to pursue these relationships passionately, sometimes to the neglect of all else. In an aesthetic of fury, the lived realities of our embodied lives caution against the temptations of escapism offered by the other two modes. We are furious at injustice, as well we should be. The following chapters explore these tensions as they are created and mediated aesthetically along religious avenues.

Aesthetics and Interreligious Inquiry

The beauty and wisdom of Hindu traditions excite me for many of the same reasons as the monumental works of Western classical music. The peace of meditation resonates with the bliss of absorption in a great work of art. The intimacy of devotional love in the *bhakti* traditions touches some of the same affects and desires. And whenever I find myself deep in conversation with learned Hindus, I find myself asking the same urgent ethical question: What do inner peace and love for the divine have to do with peace in our world and love of the other?

The philosophical, religious, and aesthetic traditions of India have helped me begin to formulate answers regarding the relation of the religious and the aesthetic. The inward benefits of meditation draw me, as do the sensory aspects of Hindu devotion. (Bright goddesses, incense, and bells were decidedly missing in the Calvinism of my youth.) In response, I wonder anew about the capacity of beauty to awaken a sense of the divine. I also wonder about the physical means of production that give rise to those feelings. My attraction to the religious traditions of India has been deeply aesthetic in nature. It is felicitous that India's aesthetic theory would help me to understand that attraction.

The theory of *rasa*, aesthetic "tasting" of emotion, postulates that aesthetic rapture is produced by the combination of determining factors or excitants (*vibhāva*s), consequent responses or indicators (*anubhāvas*), and complementary or transitory emotional states (*vyabhicāribhāvas*). This theory is formulated in an ancient drama manual, the *Nāṭya Śāstra* (*NŚ*), attributed to Bharata.[2] In intricate detail, Bharata works out the means of evoking specific emotions in an audience. Everything from the stage setting to the movement of the actor-dancer's eyebrows is laid out with great care. The result of these efforts is a complex vocabulary of hand gestures, facial expressions, and poetic idioms that have delighted cultured audiences of dance forms such as *bharatanatyam* for centuries. It has also spawned a tradition of literary theory and philosophy that explores the religious significance of these means of producing emotion.

These speculations are worth considering in a Christian theology of emotion. As Francis Clooney notes of his interest in the hymns of Śrīvaiṣṇava Hindus, emotions resist the reductions of reason: People cannot always account for their loves and interests, including the reasons they might study another faith tradition alongside their own. Although "in theory the comparative process is flawed, the learning incomplete, and the consequences illogical and unwarranted," reflection on the role of affective connection to religious traditions "may help us to develop richer and more adequate theologies about the intellectual and emotional dimensions of interreligious exchange, and about what is to be gained from actual comparative study."[3] Although my choice of traditions in this book may be no more complex than the fact that I find them deeply interesting, I wager that this attraction bears fruit: *Rasa* allows theologians to account for the transcendence of religious experience, the embodied means that evoke it, and the tensions between transcendence and the demands of justice.

The Postcolonial Situation and the New Comparative Theology

Only a few pages into this work, the antennae of savvy readers are abuzz. Why should a Christian theologian turn to Hindu sources for inspiration? Doesn't her own tradition have everything it needs? If she draws on other sources of wisdom, does her theology cease to be Christian? The Christian tradition has always drawn from surrounding cultures—Jewish, Hellenistic, imperial Roman, Indian, North American—to articulate its identity and embody its practices. No religion or culture can claim to be self-contained. A question from another direction concerns me more urgently. What kind of power does a scholar ensconced in the Western, Christian academy exert when she engages in this work?

Third-world intellectuals following Edward Said have called attention to the imbalance of power that allows first-world scholars and colonial officials to define and represent third-world cultural realities. The knowledge of colonized people has been treated as a resource to be exploited. Their own resources are appropriated in service of subordinating them.[4] In the academic or "comparative" study of religion, claims of objectivity, universality, and science have served as a guise for Christian apologetics.[5] An ongoing debate in cultural anthropology and related disciplines weighs the validity of scholarship by a culture's outsiders (an etic perspective), in contrast with that by insiders or participants (an emic perspective); and the former is now viewed by many in the formerly colonized world as a continuing legacy of oppression. In these dangerous waters, is my Christian interest in *rasa* theory yet another act of appropriation?

One response to such problems has been for the academic study of religion to distance itself from *comparison* as a method. Comparison has a long history of entanglement with the academic study of religion. In the early nineteenth century, comparison was touted as an objective method that would promote religious tolerance and respect. As Hugh Nicholson has demonstrated, this approach arose out of a liberal Christianity that endeavored to escape politics, dogmatism, and exclusion through a search for common elements (already shared by liberal Christians) lying beneath divisive creeds.[6] Using this comparative method, scholars could appropriate other traditions to argue for what they already knew to be true. In response, some contemporary scholars argue that no normative conclusions can be drawn from comparison, and that religious traditions should be studied as discrete units. Postliberal theologians following George Lindbeck liken religions to languages or cultures, and some go so far as to argue that translation or comparison between them is impossible.[7]

As scholars of religion have endeavored to identify and eliminate bias, a second strategy has been to distance their work as much as possible from *theology*. Twentieth-century scholars of comparative religion, such as Joachim Wach, Mircea Eliade, and Joseph Kitagawa, reacted against the normative Christianity of the discipline and attempted to treat religions in a purely descriptive manner. Arvind Sharma, a contemporary scholar who defends comparison as a method, reflects this effort to purify the discipline of theology: He dismisses without much comment the "elementary consideration" that "the study of religion should not be confused with religion" and states that such study should be "disengaged from the religious nature of the content."[8] To this effect, Sharma's crucial intervention in comparative method is that it should go two ways: each side illuminates something about the other. Whereas he sees theology as an insider discourse that pronounces on the other, he wants the voices of both insiders and outsiders to be heard. This quest for objectivity is a fundamentally modern approach to the study of religion. Nevertheless, critics such as Nicholson have observed that those who deny theological investment often harbor unacknowledged hegemonies. A "crypto-theology" hides in the work of the Wach and others.[9] One suspects that the endeavor to become more scientific yet again reifies Western epistemological method.[10]

By identifying myself as a comparative theologian, I distance myself from neither comparison nor theology. I align myself with a postmodern approach to the theological study of religions that recognizes the "ambiguity of classic liberalism" as well as "the inescapability of the political."[11]

In this approach, a theologian may criticize the history of her discipline and openly acknowledge her situatedness in a tradition, but she may also identify and defend the norms she brings to her work. Comparison can be a useful tool for pursuing these tasks. As Sharma argues, traditions are mutually illuminating.

> Reciprocal illumination, as a method, respects the integrity of each tradition. It allows it to speak for itself, and the other tradition to hear for itself. It allows each tradition to be studied on its own terms, yet at the same time it renders such a respectful study of one tradition meaningful for another, in terms of the other tradition.[12]

John Dunne describes this process as "passing over" to less familiar territory, so that when one "passes back," the learning obtained in the process becomes a new set of lenses for viewing the familiar.[13] Each of these metaphors reflects something of the interstice where the comparativist resides (and, arguably, where all traditions reside) in the work of conversing with new interlocutors and responding to new situations. With a chastened sense of itself as a discipline in process, theology can retain comparison as both a tool and a goal.

The discipline of comparative theology has been revitalized by theologians such as James Fredericks and Francis Clooney in light of postcolonial critiques of religious studies.[14] Comparative theologians do not feign objectivity but acknowledge their starting point within particular religious traditions. They endeavor to understand another religious tradition by reading its texts, often under the tutelage of practitioners or commentaries, and often in original languages. The comparative moment happens when they consider these sources of wisdom—which might also include practices, rituals, or aesthetic objects—alongside those of their home traditions. The categories and questions of the other tradition provide new lenses for viewing materials that were once familiar. Often, things that initially appear similar turn out to serve quite different functions, or vice versa, and this can be the impetus for further inquiry.[15] On this model, the finality of doctrinal judgment is deferred in favor of ongoing exploration and interplay.[16]

Comparative theology offers a method to engage other religions in a spirit of friendship that is chastened by a history of Christian hegemony.[17] Christian knowledge of the world's religious traditions is inevitably embroiled in the colonial impulse to appropriate, consume, exploit, and market other cultures. Christian theologians must be cognizant of their implication in these power dynamics, for theological judgments, however partial and contingent, assert authority. My choice to begin with an Indian category (*rasa*) could be read either as an act of appropriation or as an attempt to take Indian thought seriously. In my view, when Western theologians avoid engaging the ideas of others, they perpetuate the imperial assumption that only Western ideas are rational or can adequately explain how the world works.[18] A project such as this strives toward what José Cabezón calls "theory parity": Hindu texts not only present data for a Western scholar of religion to analyze: they are sources of theory as well.[19] In a deviation from Western epistemological hegemony, the Christian theology of the emotions developed here *begins* with categories that originate in Indian aesthetic theory. This borrowing does not replicate the original theory but considers its relevance in other contexts.

Dialogical processes have always been a part of how human beings think. In these processes, power does not only flow one way but forms a complex circuitry of current and resistance. There is an imbalance when Christians appropriate symbols from vulnerable minority traditions such as Judaism or Native American religions. Christianity is not dominant everywhere, however, and the flow of power shifts in other contexts. In India, should Christians, a numerical minority, appropriate the language and symbols of dominant Western forms or embrace Indian religious idioms? Either approach contains difficulties *vis-à-vis* the Hindu majority. The former strategy marks Christians as foreign, in collusion with the forces of global capitalism and Western imperialism; but after centuries of symbolic association between Christianity and the West, the latter approach is often dismissed as a cynical missionary ploy. Different power dynamics inhere outside of India, where Hindu minorities might on the one hand desire that others appreciate the beauty and richness of their tradition, but on the other hand might closely guard its proper interpretation by outsiders.

For theology, these shifting global contexts mean that the comparative process is never final. Postcolonial theory describes the circuitry of power and resistance in terms of the abrogation and appropriation of language. Colonial powers attempt to set the terms of discourse, but colonized people abrogate this power when they refuse to play by these rules. Colonial power appropriates resources; but through acts of counter-appropriation, the colonized exercise power for themselves, molding dominant symbols and language to express differing cultural realities. What sets such appropriation apart from mere acquiescence to hegemonic norms is the prior moment of abrogation, the "refusal of the categories of the imperial culture, its aesthetic, its illusory standard of normative or 'correct' usage, and its assumption of a tradition and fixed meaning 'inscribed' in the words."[20] Comparative study subtly reroutes the circuitry of the discipline of Christian theology. Hindu categories are not simply something for Western Christian scholars to consume and appropriate; rather, thinking with these categories destabilizes dominant Christian modes of thinking. As more voices join the dialogue, Christian theological loci are exposed to critique, revision, and refinement, as well as to counter-appropriation by others.

This messy matrix of politics, culture, and religion points past older essentialized notions of religion and culture. Religions and cultures are not self-contained wholes but sites of engagement, internal debate, and consensus building. Particular cultural features are not essential boundaries between groups of people but are elements that are put to work in different ways. Kathryn Tanner uses the metaphor of *style* to describe these distinctive manners of engagement: Culture is the "process of taking over and making one's own what one finds."[21] Accordingly, *rasa* is a malleable concept that has been put to work in a variety of styles by Indians of various backgrounds and religious temperaments, by Hindus and Christians, and by contemporary scholars, including myself. The appropriations and counter-appropriations of *rasa* documented and performed in this book are thus a microcosm of larger processes of culture, religion, and identity.

Given its ineffable divine subject matter, theology is always provisional and under construction. I find this especially true when I do this work in diverse company. Guided by philosophical and theological treatments of *rasa*, this book is written on the wager that Christians have much to learn from Indian theory on the emotions. The process of working with the original language (when the language is Sanskrit) and providing my own translations has impressed me with gratitude for what I have learned from religious others as well as a sense of humility in the face of all I still have to learn from them.

Norms Guiding this Study

My location in the discipline of comparative theology is conditioned not only by the revitalized possibilities of comparison but also by the norms of liberation theologies, for which the importance of identifying the scholar's positionality is nothing new. Feminist theologians, for example, assist the larger discipline of theology by pointing out that Christian scripture and theology has largely been produced by men, about men, and for men. When women add their voices to the discipline, some of its patriarchal norms begin to crumble. The same process happens when biases of race, class, sexual orientation, ability, and cultural location come into focus. The lesson to be learned is that *all* intellectual and spiritual work happens from particular locations. This fact should encourage theologians to notice their locations, attend to power imbalances, and enter into dialogue across many markers of difference—including religious difference.

Because normativity cannot simply be disavowed, postcolonial and feminist scholars endeavor to name their locations and commitments as clearly as possible. My Protestant roots, my feminist critique of those roots, my interreligious practices of yoga and meditation, my affinity with liberation theologies, and my identity as a non-celibate laywoman all shape my encounter with the materials in this study. These factors incline me toward theological biases of justice and flourishing, especially for those on the margins. My faith in Jesus—a teacher and healer who cared and advocated for persons rejected by the powers of his day, and who in turn was executed by those powers—undeniably shapes these commitments. In view of these values, commitment to understanding is not the same as uncritical acceptance. Awareness of marginalized bodies, individuals, and communities serves as the critical principle for my provisional assessments of *any* tradition's vision of truth. This book therefore explores tensions in religious theories of emotion that play out *within both Hindu and Christian traditions in complex ways.* Comparative study grants depth of insight unavailable through studying these traditions in isolation.

Because of these liberative commitments, my work differs somewhat from the "patient deferral of issues of truth" exemplified in the early work of Clooney and others.[22] Like them, I engage in sustained readings of particular texts and figures, but each section of this work comes to a critical juncture in which I employ a practical ethical criterion for theology's truth and efficacy. As Paul Knitter describes this norm,

> For Christians participating in a globally responsible religious dialogue, what decides between true or false, good or bad, better or worse among the different beliefs and practices is not whether followers of a religion believe in only one God, or whether they acknowledge Jesus as Savior, or

whether they evidence some kind of baptism of desire, but whether a particular religious belief or practice is able to bring about greater peace and justice and unity in the world.[23]

Judgments about the redemptive efficacy of a belief or practice must be accountable to experience, particularly the experience of persons at the margins of traditions. I ask, therefore: As Christian and Hindu traditions have cultivated particular religious emotions, what has been occluded, and who has been excluded from its consummation? These questions are essential if religions are to be forces for justice, reconciliation, and compassion in the world.

As Jonathan Z. Smith states, comparison is not done for its own sake. Rather, the rectification of scholarly (here, theological) categories emerges from the process.[24] The convictions the comparativist brings to her work should be responsive to this learning. For instance, my critical principle of the flourishing of those on the margins developed over the course of this project. During the early stages, I was interested in how *rasa* theory could deepen Christian understanding of the theological and ethical dimensions of religious emotion, but I had not intended to focus on the furious sentiment or upon the Dalit Christian communities of South India. This shift was suggested to me by a colleague at the United Theological College in Bangalore, Joseph Prabhakar Dayam, and confirmed by the Bangalore artist Jyoti Sahi, whose work deeply informs this book. The move from classical, Sanskritic texts to contemporary texts and performances by Dalits has sharpened my thinking about emotion and religion in ways I had not anticipated. My theological norms have taken on new dimensions as a result of interfaith inquiry.

It should be clear to the reader that I share the liberal goals of interreligious tolerance and appreciation that have been part of the comparative endeavor since the nineteenth century. In contrast to earlier attempts to escape politics through objective comparison, however, the trajectory of this project arcs *back* into the political questions of difference and solidarity. It is risky and vulnerable work, but this risk is the price of a theology that is both open and accountable to religious neighbors.[25]

Intersections in the Study of Emotion

This book arises not only from a peculiar intersection of loves but also at the intersection of a number of academic disciplines and theoretical approaches. Leading postcolonial theologians observe that the historical moment is ripe for border-crossing exploration:

> The task of a postcolonial theology will not be to shore up the barriers between the Christian and the non-Christian, the holy and the profane, the church and the world, the ethical and the immoral, even the Creator and the creation. Nor will it be simply to demolish them. We will want instead to pay careful attention to what happens in all these in-between places. What refuses enclosure? What *crosses* over? What revels and reveals itself in the many tongues of many peoples? What is dis/closed in the shifting borderlands?[26]

In the spirit of attending to shifting in-between places, this book crosses multiple borders: between aesthetics and religion, between the mystical and the prophetic, between Hinduism and Christianity, between insider and outsider (emic and etic) perspectives to these traditions, between center and margin, between various historical moments, and between comparative and normative approaches.

Because of its emphasis on the local and particular, comparative theology is ideally suited to traverse multiple terrains with care. Like many comparative theologians, I find my way forward through the close reading of texts. I move back and forth between the texts of Christian and Hindu traditions to discern what new questions and insights they raise for one another. I begin each section with reflection on a different work of art, which I treat as embodied texts to read for their theological and emotional force. Other disciplines help to illumine this path: Art critics help me to analyze how aesthetic techniques evoke particular feelings, and ethnographers teach me the importance of performative context.

Various subdisciplines of Christian theology, including epistemology, revelation, the status of religious pluralism, and the holistic nature of the human being illuminate this study.[27] As one of the chief investigators on the topic of emotion has noticed, however, most theological studies of emotion "are less concerned with specific emotions than with . . . the attempt to define emotion *per se*, and to place it within theological constructions of the self."[28] By contrast, because I begin with the Indian category of *rasa* rather than with one of the traditional loci of Christian theology, my focus remains on the theological significance of particular emotions. If we stay with *rasa* and do not move too quickly to reframe it in terms that have traditionally governed treatments of emotion in Western Christianity (such as the relation of the *affectus* and *intellectus*), we gain a closer focus on the phenomena of specific religious emotions. The fulcrum of *rasa* then allows the theologian to reconsider the traditional loci.

Scholarship on the emotions is inherently interdisciplinary. Biologists and neuroscientists explore the role of chemical and other physiological phenomena associated with emotion. A burgeoning group of philosophers, literary critics, and social scientists has begun to focus on the role of cognition and belief in shaping emotion. This field houses a lively debate on whether human emotion has an essence shared within the species, or whether its experience and expression are culturally relative. Neuroscientists who posit a common physiological core to the experience of emotion find allies in universalist philosophers and theologians. On the relativist or constructivist side, ethnographers and historians point to differences across time and place in how people evoke, experience, and express emotion. Within these poles, evolutionary biologists from Charles Darwin to Paul Ekman observe emotional responses that appear to be stable across the species; linguists such as Anna Wierzbicka note similar semantics about emotion in multiple languages; and structuralists including Emil Durkheim, Victor Turner, and Claude Levi-Strauss observe the performance of emotion across cultures. Philosophical and theological foundationalists such as Rudolph Otto and Friedrich Schleiermacher root our deepest aspirations in emotion.[29]

Into this interdisciplinary mix, *rasa* theory carries important implications regarding the evocation of emotion. The universalist-constructivist divide is becoming less polarized as more scholars locate themselves in the middle. John Corrigan reports, "[M]ost researchers continue to embrace, in some measure, the notion that certain aspects of emotional life are consistent across cultural boundaries. Such a position should not be confused with an orthodox universalism but appreciated rather as an openness to discovering what aspects of emotionality are shared."[30] Even if there is a broad similarity across cultures in many aspects, culture contributes to the meaning and significance people attribute to emotions. *Rasa* theory invites attention to sensory and behavioral modes of feeling that are widely shared, even as this theoretical frame has developed in specific cultural contexts.

The interdisciplinary study of the emotions also raises the question of normativity. While philosophers often discuss how to *assess* and *govern* the emotions through reason, Charles Altieri faults such scholars for imposing the standard of their discipline (reasonableness) upon the subject.[31] He argues that feelings, like works of art, often resist rational or ethical assessment. Martha Nussbaum, the primary target of Altieri's criticism, inquires how emotions enable human beings to make decisions. Contrary to those who would pit reason against emotion, she argues for the reasonableness of the emotions. In her holistic approach, she rehabilitates the body's role in emotions in a way that attends to the integrity of other people. Nussbaum wrestles with aesthetic treatments of love that "repudiate daily life" and instill shame and disgust at ordinary embodied reality. As compelling as literary lovers' ascents may be, the best treatment of emotion will "[ask] us to climb the ladder and yet, at times, to turn it over, looking at a real person in bed or on the chamber pot. . . . Only in that way do we overcome the temptation, inherent in all ideals, to despise what is merely human and everyday."[32] Nussbaum's goal is not far from that of Altieri, who also wants to give an account of emotions "compatible with immediate and sustained attention to the situations of other human beings."[33] Despite their differences, then, Altieri and Nussbaum both operate with a *norm* of attention to embodied particularity.

Normative judgments in theories of emotion seem unavoidable, and unavoidably theological. Like Nussbaum and Altieri, I worry when aesthetic-cum-religious goals of beauty, peace, and love are transposed beyond particular bodies. I, too, draw criteria from my own discipline. First, Christian affirmation of the body finds its apex in the incarnation of divinity in Jesus Christ. The best of Christian theological anthropology and Christology insists on the integration of human somatic, conative, cognitive, and relational faculties. Jesus specifically embodies a second criterion: love for the other (cf. Matt. 7:12, Lk. 10:29–37). Theologians fall short of these norms when they privilege intellect over affect or the individual soul over bodies-in-community. Bodies, including embodied emotions, matter. Divinity longs for the flourishing of creatures. The following chapters theorize how emotions that participate in this longing for wholeness are tastes of the divine.

ACKNOWLEDGMENTS

The foremost emotion that arises at the completion of a scholarly endeavor is gratitude. When I recall the conversations and material support that produced this book, I am flooded with it. I am grateful for time away from the classroom that enabled me to do research in India in 2010. This travel was funded by a Pre-Tenure Summer Grant from the Wabash Center for Teaching and Learning, a Creative Advance Planning-Mellon Study Leave from Rhodes College, and a Faculty Development Endowment Grant from Rhodes College. The Lindsay Young Visiting Faculty Fellowship from the Marco Institute for Medieval and Renaissance Studies at the University of Tennessee (Knoxville) in 2011 enriched my research on Bernard of Clairvaux. I could not have completed this project without the generosity of my hosts at Jai Singh Ghera in Vrindavan; Nav Sadhana Kala Kendra in Varanasi; Tamilnadu Theological Seminary in Madurai; and United Theological College and the National Biblical, Catechetical, and Liturgical Centre in Bangalore.

Different people helped to cultivate the emotions discussed in this book. No one helped me think about peace more than Jyoti Sahi, who not only hosted me several times in Bangalore but was also a superb correspondent on the entire manuscript. For conversations on devotional love, I am grateful to Urmila Sharma, Acyut Lal Bhatt, Srivatsa Goswami, David Mason, Katherine Zubko, Madan Mohan Mohini Dasi, Jayadvaita Swami, Francis X. Clooney, Gloria Hernandez, and the participants in the Song of Songs Conference at Harvard University in 2013. Friends in India (Joseph Prabhakar Dayam, Christopher Duraisingh, Mohan Larbeer, and M. C. Raj) and colleagues at Wake Forest School of Divinity (John Senior, Derek Hicks, Clinton Moyer, Angela Yarber, Jarrod Whittaker, and Tanisha Ramachandran) provided sounding boards for the section on fury. I am indebted to Manjunath Shamanna for his help with the Kannada language in that section. Emily Holmes, Jon Paul Sydnor, and the participants in the Symposium on Women and Interreligious Dialogue at Boston College in 2012 deepened my consideration of wonder. The Comparative Theology Group at the American Academy of Religion and the Society for Hindu-Christian Studies provided venues to develop my comparative framework: Special thanks are due to John Thatamanil, Tracy Sayuki Tiemeier, Barbara Holdredge, Kristin Kiblinger, and Holly Hillgardner. The fingerprints of my talented research assistants—Melissa Kessler, Molly Bolton, and Lindsey Mullen—are also evident here, especially in the glossary and index. I am grateful for Seema Janga, Lacey Hudspeth, and Ashley Sims, who gave me time to write. Helen Tartar, Thomas Lay, and the editorial staff at Fordham University Press were invaluable in shepherding this work to completion.

I remain mystified by the temporal and spatial balancing act that Brian Roberts and I have performed over the years. I dedicate this book to our daughter, Anya Devi Voss Roberts, who experienced India with us as an infant, and who will forever bear the imprint of India's song and dance.

Take away all love and hatred, all hope and fear, all anger, zeal and affectionate desire, and the world would be, in great measure, motionless and dead; . . . As in worldly things, worldly affections are very much the spring of men's [sic] *motion and action; so in religious matters, the spring of their actions is very much religious affections.*

—JONATHAN EDWARDS[34]

Deliverance is not for me in renunciation. I feel the embrace of freedom in a thousand bonds of delight.

Thou ever pourest for me the fresh draught of thy wine of various colors and fragrance, filling this earthen vessel to the brim.

My world will light its hundred different lamps with thy flame and place them before the altar of thy temple.

No, I will never shut the doors of my senses. The delights of sight and hearing and touch will bear thy delight.

Yes, all my illusions will burn into illumination of joy, and all my desires ripen into fruits of love.

—RABINDRANATH TAGORE[35]

TASTES OF THE DIVINE

Introduction

RASA

Prior to its use as a term for aesthetic delight, *rasa* had basic meanings of taste, relishing, or the essence of a thing. *Rasa* denotes juice or sap, as well as a special concoction of various ingredients that yields a unique flavor distinct from any one of the ingredients. The word *rasa* also applies to each of the six flavors—sweet, bitter, sour, salty, pungent, and astringent—which impart unique gustatory experiences.[1] *Rasa*'s use as a technical aesthetic term derives from the Indian tradition of dance-drama in Bharata's *Nāṭya Śāstra*, where it denotes emotional states savored by spectators of the drama.[2] As in the culinary sense of *rasa*, the process of refining emotion transforms physical elements into an experience that is greater than their sum. Bharata lists eight such sentiments: the erotic (*śṛṅgāra*), the comic (*hāsya*), the pathetic (*karuṇa*), the furious (*raudra*), the heroic (*vīra*), the terrible (*bhayānaka*), the odious (*bībhatsa*), and the marvelous (*adbhuta*). A ninth, peace (*śānta*), was added to the list after debate among later theorists. As a work of art balances and blends various ingredients, it grants an emotional "taste" that is savored inwardly by the audience.

A myth of the origins of Bharata's manual underlines the metaphysical significance of aesthetic experience. As the *Nāṭya Śāstra* itself tells it, during the decline of one of the cosmic ages, the gods approach the creator, Brahmā, to ask him for a diversion, visible as well as audible, which will be accessible to all classes of society (*varṇas*). In response, Brahmā combines the essence of the four canonical Vedas into this text, a treatise on dance-drama that will educate human beings, inspire them to fulfill their duties, and offer to all classes the fulfillment offered by other religious texts. Brahmā marks this text's significance and authority by declaring it the "fifth Veda" (*NŚ* I.7–18, pp. 6–10), a claim that has similarly been made to elevate other non-canonical texts including the Purāṇas and the Mahābhārata epic.

Readers familiar with the self-laudatory nature of ancient Sanskrit treatises might dismiss this myth as simple prolegomena, but Susan Schwartz argues that the religious origins and contexts of India's performing arts should not be ignored.[3] Her book *Rasa: Performing the Divine* recognizes that religion is not just a common theme in Indian performing arts. She argues for "religion *as* performing arts in India."[4] The arts have a divine source and are elevated to Vedic status because of their capacity to evoke transcendence: "Like the elaborate rituals described in the Vedic texts, the theatre offers in microcosm a representation of the greater, macrocosmic realities, and in so doing, allows those prepared to understand a path to transcendence."[5]

The *Nāṭya Śāstra* bears multiple ties to religion. The text may have its roots in drama, dance, and song that were performed in honor of deities and then expanded into performances for religious festivals and popular entertainment.[6] Procedures for theatre construction resemble those of temple architecture (*NŚ* II). Many of the preliminary rites for a play incorporate elements of worship, including *pūjā* to the gods of the stage (*NŚ* III) and a ritual to purify the performer (*NŚ* V.59–170, pp. 190–212). The text predicts eternal rewards for those who perform these preliminaries and execute the production well (*NŚ* V.175–179, pp. 213–214). It equates the goal reached by an attentive audience member with that of religious activities such as mastering the Vedas, performing sacrifices, and giving gifts (*NŚ* XXXVI.79, p. 1483). Each *rasa* also has a presiding deity (*NŚ* VI.44–45, p. 245).

Commentators on the *Nāṭya Śāstra* frame the aesthetic experience in philosophical terms. A performance parallels the creation of the world: Both are *māyā*, artifice. The actor is to the spectator as the supreme spirit (*paramātman*) is to the individual soul (*jīva*): The actor retains her identity yet engrosses audiences susceptible to the illusion (*māyā*) of the shadow world of literature.[7] Audiences become so engrossed in this world that they fail to notice the technique by which they are been lured there. Meditation on a drama suspends ordinary notions of propriety: Whereas onlookers might be uncomfortable watching lovers in person, the fourth wall of the stage permits an audience to be captivated by their love play. Because the experience of *rasa* takes the audience beyond the concerns of the ego, it offers a fleeting taste of the goal of spiritual discipline. Ascending beyond the ordinary constraints of space, time, and sensory limitation, spectators savor the bliss of the infinite. This transcendent experience affords a glimpse of the unity of reality and the harmony underlying the world of conflict.[8]

Tastes of the Divine

The Taittirīya Upaniṣad describes *brahman* in terms of *rasa*: "That which is Self-made is a flavor (can be tasted), for only after perceiving a flavor can any one perceive pleasure" (1.2.7).[9] As a sensory metaphor for both taste and emotion, *rasa* offers Indian theorists a subtle framework for elaborating the analogy between aesthetic and religious experience. The famous tenth-century philosopher and literary theorist Abhinavagupta invokes the language of enjoyment or relishing (*āsvādana*): The taste of *rasa* (*rasāsvāda*) can prepare one for the taste of the ultimate reality (*brahmāsvāda*) (*Loc* 2.4). For some worshippers of Kṛṣṇa, *rasa* is merged into devotional experience (*bhakti*). The Gauḍīya Vaiṣṇava's "devotion is a fundamentally aesthetic one, in which the development of *bhakti* toward the Lord involves a gradual refining and intensifying of emotion through repeated encounters with the eternal drama of Krishna and his close associates."[10] For these devotees as for Abhinavagupta, both of whom will be central to this work, there is no sharp dichotomy between aesthetics and religion. If we attend to the relation between emotional tastes (*rasāsvāda*) and the taste of the divine (*brahmāsvāda*), each of the nine emotional tastes in *rasa* theory offers a taste of the divine that becomes fruitful material for theological reflection.

Theologians do not interpret scripture, appropriate tradition, or exercise reason in a vacuum. Embodied interactions with the world, other persons, and the holy not only give rise to theological insight but also serve as an important means of testing it. In the Christian tradition, pietists, revivalists, and mystics have been at the forefront of such inquiries, sometimes demanding experiential verification—a "heart strangely warmed," a sense of assurance, or some other physical or emotional response. By giving authoritative weight to such accounts, I employ a theological paradigm in which experience is a source of theology alongside scripture, tradition, and reason.[11]

In the texts I study here, theologians and religious leaders deem certain emotional experiences religious. Starting with this deeming allows me to take seriously the accounts of the Hindu, Christian, and subaltern persons who describe emotions as spiritually significant. Ann Taves advocates attribution theories of emotion, which attend not only to scientific explanations of events but also to the beliefs of people experiencing the events about what happened. On this model, "religious experience could be understood as an experience (state of arousal) coupled with a (religious) attribution."[12] Both cognitivist/constructivist and perennialist/essentialist approaches thus retain explanatory power for emotions deemed religious. Unlike causes that can be verified in the natural sciences, however, divine grace as a cause of religious experience is not strictly falsifiable. Deeming experiences as divine does not determine whether there actually is a divine source behind them. We can observe how religious cultures prescribe and generate the emotions they deem important, as well as how these processes generate power and authority, but the nature of the question prevents definitive answers.

What, then, are tastes of the divine? In answering this question, I do not reignite the old Christian debate over the philosophical ideal of divine *apatheia* and its relation to scriptural testimony that God loves, grieves, or becomes enraged. My interlocutors in this work differ regarding whether and how divinity experiences emotion. For Abhinavagupta, we taste the peace of the divine nature when we transcend the flux of our individual and momentary feelings and rest in blissful equanimity. By contrast, the Christian artist Jyoti Sahi affirms the divine capacity for suffering. For Rūpa Gosvāmin and Bernard of Clairvaux, love is the nature of God, and we participate in that nature by loving God. And for Dalit liberation theologians, human beings tap into the prophetic fury of the biblical God when they rage against unjust systems. Despite differences regarding divine feeling, the idea that a person might "taste" one emotion or another as a way to partake of the divine is present in each of these figures.

As tastes of the divine, emotions open us to experience God. This claim goes beyond a weak sense of religious emotion in which "an emotion becomes religious by referring to God or something else transcendent: thus joy in the Lord, fear of the Lord, awe before Being, reverence for Life, and so on."[13] In this definition, according to Robert C. Roberts, God can be related to emotion in any number of ways—as its object, but also in love "*for the sake of* Christ," "a devout terrorist's hatred of the infidel . . . *out of devotion to* Allah," and a Pentecostal's sorrow "*about his or her offenses against* God."[14] By contrast, to taste the divine in the strong sense examined later on is not only to have feelings about, toward, or in relation to God but to participate in the nature of divinity.

My constructive stake in this conversation arises out of the contingent cultural processes of constructing emotion and, in particular, the power dynamics therein. Throughout this study, I highlight the "positive" dispositions of contentment, love, and compassion that can be generated through aesthetic and religious experience, but I also observe the tendency of these feelings to obscure the material foundations on which they depend. *Rasa* theory helps us to unpack this dynamic. Its formula for the production of *rasa* draws attention to the conditions, effects, and accompanying emotions that combine to create the blissful taste of the divine. Following this thread, I attend to the circumstances, bodily states, and non-elites that are elided in the construction of religious experience. I also deem important "negative" emotions such as anger, and I ask how theology differs when the elided elements are valued. This deconstructive, feminist, liberationist question becomes the basis for my return to the nine common emotions of *rasa* theory in the last sections of the book.

Emotion

Emotion resides somewhere between sensation and belief on a spectrum of affective phenomena that includes feelings, moods, and passions.[15] These distinctions may be illustrated by imagining a fledgling attempt at meditation. When the novice sits down to meditate, physical sensation is the most salient feature of the experience. After a few minutes, her back begins to ache, and it is not long before she must stretch her legs. Her teacher may direct her to notice the sounds of air conditioning, traffic, and other people around her, or sensations of clothing on skin, air entering the nostrils, and the floor beneath her. Just when she congratulates herself for not responding to these ambient stimuli, an itch absolutely demands scratching. At this point on the spectrum, sensation has not yet developed into affect, let alone belief.

As the novice sits a bit longer, she begins to notice the activity of her mental and emotional apparatus (a faculty called *manas* in Sanskrit). She notices that she has been engaging the *sensations* and developing *feelings* about them: discomfort, contentment, excitement. She may notice a particular *mood* (a diffuse sort of feeling) settling over her: a general sense of anxiety manifest in tense shoulders, an atmosphere of shame that blankets her as the voices of her past become audible in the silence, a depression that lulls her into sadness or apathy, or a wave of contentment. Distinct *emotions* begin to form as she interprets particular sensations and feelings: worry about failure, anger at the inability to sit still, pleasure at her progress. She finds affirmation of her *passions*, the emotions in which she invests her sense of identity, such as her desire to be a peaceful or compassionate person.

Emotions are just one part of a spectrum of affective states that differ in terms of precision, object, and intensity. Emotions arise as we process sensations and feelings at the point when we make judgments about them. Theorists who wish to rehabilitate affective states from their denigration as irrational animal passions tend to emphasize this feature. They focus on the role of emotions in reason, the reasonableness of the emotions, and the relative reliability of emotions in making assessments about the world. This approach has its limitations. Altieri, for instance, argues against Nussbaum's monumental *Upheavals of Thought* for the affective nuances he thinks she misses when she uses a definition of emotion as a kind of assessment to analyze particular aesthetic works; and he demands closer attention to the affects, feelings, and moods that escape or defy rationality.[16]

Rasa theory holds in tension the semiotic aspects of affect with their development into the heights of religious emotion. The spectator in this theory oscillates between the particular and the universal so that she can attend to the particular situation at the same time as she may be inspired to do, think, or feel something else. In this theory, emotion (*bhāva*) "is a powerful force which is at the same time subtle and delicate, invisible to the senses yet capable of generating physical expressions, associated with perception, intuition, and realization. There is no sharp distinction between emotion and cognition."[17] In its development in devotional (*bhakti*) contexts such as the North Indian Vaiṣṇavism examined here, *bhāva* is also an experience of ecstasy that can be shared with the deity and with other devotees.[18] These multivalent concepts unsettle customary dichotomies of reason and emotion, mind and body, and private and shared experience.

How *Rasa* Works

Rasa arises in the spectator of a drama through "the combination of excitants, indicators, and transitory emotional states" (*NŚ* prose after VI.31, p. 227).[19] This brief statement, known as the *rasa sūtra*, encapsulates how *rasa* works.

Excitants + Consequents + Transitory Emotional States = *Rasa*

We may use the erotic sentiment (*śṛṅgāra rasa*) as an example and unpack this aphorism.[20]

The first ingredients in *rasa* are excitants or contextual markers (*vibhāvas*). In the case of the erotic mood, the setting might include a garden, the full moon, ornaments and garlands, seeing the beloved, and hearing his or her voice. These excitants include sensations like smelling flowers or perfume as well as more complex things like the company of a loved one (in the case of love in union) or remembrance (in the case of love in absence).

The second ingredient, *anubhāva*, is the physical action that results from an encounter with these stimuli. A character must display the appropriate indicators to communicate to the audience that he feels the emotion the scene intends to convey. Sidelong glances, delicate movements, and sweet words are appropriate for love in union, whereas anxiety, indolence, or jealousy might convey love in absence. In the dramatic context, these are not the behaviors of the observer but of the character experiencing the emotion.

The third ingredient in the rasic mix consists of emotional states that accompany the primary emotion. These are known as *vyabhicāribhāva*s, emotions that move or change, because they are transitory. They are also sometimes called *sañcāribhāva*s because they "nurture" or complement the main sentiment. Thus passing states of discouragement, dreaming, or pretending to be with the beloved might contribute to the aesthetic experience of love. Some complementary states such as weakness, intoxication, agitation, sleep, epilepsy, and sickness border on sensation. Others such as apprehension, discouragement, envy, arrogance, and contentment might be classified as feelings, intentional states with an object that have not fully developed into emotions. This set of affective states illustrates a range of ways the mind and the body are related to emotions. These categories are flexible, and many conditions that appear in lists of *vyabhicāribhāva*s also appear on lists of *vibhāva*s and *anubhāva*s. Their designation depends on their role in developing the *rasa* at hand. *Rasa* is the subjective experience that takes place in a spectator when all of these factors come together in a work of art.

Other important concepts do not appear in the *rasa sūtra* but are important for understanding how *rasa* works. *Sāttvikabhāva*s are involuntary states experienced with emotion, such as blushing, sweating, goose-bumps, and tears. Although these appear to be merely physical, the term *sāttvika* indicates effort of the mind.[21] An actor must concentrate in order to produce or imitate them realistically (i.e., produce tears without feeling sadness). The *Nāṭya Śāstra* advises actors how to pretend to perspire, blush, and cry (*NŚ* VII.101–106, pp. 309–310). These *sāttvikabhāvas* may be "simply a kind of *anubhāva*," or response, but they are singled out as being particularly difficult to feign.[22]

Each aesthetic taste is rooted in an ordinary emotional state (*sthāyibhāva*):

Rasa	*Sthāyibhāva*
The erotic sentiment (*śṛṅgāra*)	Affection (*rati*)
The comic sentiment (*hāsya*)	Laughter (*hāsa*)
The pathetic sentiment (*karuṇa*)	Sorrow (*śoka*)
The furious sentiment (*raudra*)	Anger (*krodha*)
The heroic sentiment (*vīra*)	Energy (*utsāha*)
The terrible sentiment (*bhayānaka*)	Fear (*bhaya*)
The odious sentiment (*bībhatsa*)	Disgust (*jugupsā*)
The marvelous sentiment (*adbhuta*)	Astonishment (*vismaya*)
The peaceful sentiment (*śānta*)	Pacification (*śama*) or World-weariness (*nirveda*)[23]

Because human beings experience the ordinary emotions on a regular basis, these emotions are called durable, stable, or foundational (*sthāyi*) states. *Sthāyibhāvas* are like receptors lying within every spectator: When we view a drama or work of art, the excitants, consequents, and transitory emotional states in that work act on these receptors to make *rasa*.[24] *Sthāyibhāvas* are not listed as a component of *rasa* in the *rasa sūtra*, but they lie in the background of aesthetic experience.

Indian theorists argue about how the *rasas* relate to one another. Bharata indicates that the eight sentiments can be reduced to four: the erotic, which the comic mimics; the furious, which leads to the pathetic sentiment; the heroic, which leads to the marvelous sentiment; and the odious, which leads to the terrible sentiment (*NŚ* VI.39–40, pp. 242, 244). Others posit one primary emotion as the source of all the others: Abhinavagupta identifies peace as the basis of all emotion, while Bhoja and Rūpa Gosvāmin view all emotion as variations of love.[25] Because some *rasas* harmonize with one another and others stand in opposition, Bharata instructs poets not to impede the evocation of a drama's primary *rasa* with contrary elements. For example, it is not fitting to depict disgusting, pathetic, or dispassionate themes within the context of love in union (cf. *NŚ* prose after VI.45, p. 252).[26]

This line of thought develops into a science of propriety (*aucitya*) in drama which aims to specify the obstacles and faults that destroy *rasa* or lead to its mere semblance (*ābhasa*). In addition to the combination of emotional states, the poet must consider factors such as the time of performance, the scale and meter of accompanying music, costuming, social class of characters, and the harshness and sweetness of diction. All of these factors and more can either enhance or impede *rasa* in an audience.

With its infinite combinations of factors, *rasa* theory reflects the complex and varying ways that individuals experience emotion: not only love in general, but also shades of jealousy, ambivalence, embarrassment, satisfaction, and so on. The *Nāṭya Śāstra* lists forty-nine emotional states (*bhāvas*): eight foundational emotions (*sthāyibhāvas*), eight involuntary states (*sāttvikabhāvas*), and thirty-three transitory emotional states (*vyabhicāribhāvas*) (*NŚ* VI.14–23, pp. 222–224). If we add the innumerable conditions that might evoke these emotions (*vibhāvas*) and the manners of responding to them (*anubhāvas*), there is no limit to the nuance with which emotion might be treated. This is a real advantage of *rasa* theory, in contrast to the Western philosophical accounts that Altieri criticizes as sacrificing subtlety for the sake of conceptual clarity. At the same time as *rasa* theory develops emotion to its fullest normative significance, it contains ample room for feelings that defy rationality, lie in tension with one another, and have no telos.[27]

Rasa and Ordinary Emotion

Not every emotion is an aesthetic experience. Abhinavagupta insists upon a distinct break between ordinary emotion (*bhāva*) and *rasa*. He reasons that *sthāyibhāva* (the basic emotion upon which each of the nine *rasas* is based) does not appear in the *rasa sūtra* because aesthetic emotion is fundamentally different from it.[28] The basic emotion is ordinary (*laukika*). By contrast, *rasa* is *alaukika*, non-worldly, transcendent, or sublime.

Certain conditions must be met for the blissful experience of *rasa* to arise. For this reason, Abhinavagupta says, only the spectator of a work of art experiences *rasa*. Neither the artist, nor the characters, nor the actors experience *rasa*.[29] Most artists will confess that a great deal of ordinary, uninspired work goes into creating the conditions for aesthetic appreciation to arise in other people. This work is only occasionally infused with the blissful contemplation that might be described as *rasa*.[30] Characters in a play experience emotion directly, as their own, as *bhāva*. The actor may experience emotion, as when she brings to mind something sad in order to convey sadness, but this, too, is only *bhāva*. The excitants, resulting behaviors, and accompanying emotions have their effect on the spectator alone.

One of the reasons for the discontinuity between ordinary and aesthetic emotion is that we ordinarily experience emotion in particular, ego-bound ways. Sorrow, terror, and love in separation are painful; but in the theatre, when these feelings are refined into *rasa*, they are pure bliss. *Rasa* is independent of beauty. Not only pleasant feelings but the odious and other unpleasant sentiments evoke it as well. Dhanañjaya's *Daśarūpa* says, "Delightful or disgusting, exalted or lowly, cruel or kindly, obscure or refined, (actual) or imaginary, there is no subject that cannot evoke *rasa*."[31] Aesthetic delight abstracts from the emotion with which we, as particular subjects, encounter sensory stimuli in real life. In the realm of art, we lose this quality of "me and mine" and relish the sentiment in its pure and universal form, stripped of the coloring of individual personality and circumstance.

The *Nāṭya Śāstra* lacks clarity regarding the precise distinction between *rasa* and *bhāva*. Bharata is enigmatic. At one point he tells us that *rasa* arises organically from *sthāyibhāva* as flowers from a tree and a tree from a seed. He then switches tack and states that psychological states and their aesthetic enjoyment interact and mutually cause one another (*NŚ*, prose after VI.37, pp. 240–242). Some theorists take this ambiguity as a warrant to claim that *rasa* does not break from ordinary emotion but intensifies it. This perspective supports the personal investment (*mamatā*, or "myness") that we will see in our later discussion of devotional love.[32]

Rasa and Human Nature

If drama generates *rasa* through the generalization (*sādhāranīkaraṇa*) of emotion, then human beings must share some element of their emotional experience in common. Bharata explains, "The *rasa*s arise from them when they are joined with the quality of universality [*sāmānya*]" (*NŚ* prose after VII.6, p. 279).[33] For him, a shared human nature (*lokasvabhāva*) accounts for this commonness or universality (*NŚ* prose after VII.5, p. 278). One commentator posits an analogy: Just as a lamp illuminates what is already there, drama lifts a veil of ignorance so that we can see our true self (*ātman*).[34] Because everyone has had some experience of the basic emotional states, their soliciting factors, and common responses, art can appeal to spectators from many walks of life. It is why art works.

We might object that a coward has no experience of heroism and a king no experience of ascetic detachment. How then can they appreciate the heroic or peaceful sentiments? Indian theorists appeal to past lives to account for a shared emotional repertoire. Each of us, in one life or another, has undergone every possible fluctuation of emotion. These life experiences leave unconscious traces (*vāsanā*s) on the soul that are awakened to consciousness when we encounter poetry. The ideal spectator is called a *sahṛdaya*, one whose heart (*hṛd*) is fully attuned to the range of emotion. Abhinavagupta describes the sympathetic response of such a viewer as a "heart conversation" (*hṛdayasaṃvāda*).[35] Full appreciation of the arts requires refinement of the heart, but even the most unsophisticated audience member can be drawn in by a good story through latent traces from past lives.

According to Bharata, everyone can delight in drama because of their store of emotional experiences, and everyone can also benefit from it. Kings are entertained and sorrowful and anxious persons soothed. Audience members from all walks of life are refreshed and encouraged in their pursuits. Because aesthetic experience deals with all possible subjects, everyone can receive instruction through it (*NŚ* I.108–118, pp. 32–35). Even ascetics benefit from art, either through the equanimity of the peaceful *rasa*, or through amusements that "strengthen their spirit of renunciation."[36] In order to account for the educative aspect of art within the teaching that *rasa* is transcendent (*alaukika*), Abhinavagupta explains that instruction and delight are not opposed; they are ultimately one if they arise from the same cause (in this case, art). Art can teach us about the four ends of life (pleasure, material success, duty, and liberation). Young princes may not warm to instruction in history or good governance, but they can learn through skillful storytelling: through the heart rather than the head (*Loc* 3.10–14f, pp. 437–438). Enjoyment of art is also conducive to spiritual liberation. It is like honey that disguises the bitterness of medicine: Even if a person finds philosophy tedious, she can approach the taste of *brahman* through art.[37]

Some *rasa* theorists assiduously deny an "aesthetic hedonism" that would reduce art to the mere gratification of the senses.[38] They appeal to the transcendent nature of aesthetic feeling to assert its utter discontinuity from sensory experience. For example, K. S. Ramaswami Sastri invokes the theory of the five sheaths (*kośa*s) to posit that emotion and aesthetic delight occur in the mental sheath, which is closer to the essence of the self than the dense physical sheath, which obscures the self's nature as truth and bliss.[39] Reminding their readers that in aesthetic experience negative emotions such as grief and horror never cause pain, these theorists argue that the production of *rasa* is unlike ordinary cause and effect and "should, therefore, be distinguished from the experience of natural feelings and from all natural experience of life."[40] This strict separation, which ignores or devalues the sensory and material aspects of art, is debated within the tradition; and it is a position with which I shall take issue as well.

Christian Engagement with *Rasa* Theory

A poet cannot simply name an emotion and expect an audience to feel it. *Rasa* must resonate from a subtle combination of factors. Ānandavardhana calls *dhvani*, the art of resonance or suggestion, the soul of poetry (*DhĀ* 1.1). Aesthetic delight comes not from the literal meaning (the body of poetry) but from the suggested meaning (the soul). Three categories of things can be suggested—a bare fact or idea (*vastu*), a figure of speech (*alaṃkāra*), or an emotion (*rasa*). The success of the best poetry depends on the suggestion of emotion (*rasa dhvani*). Although a skilled poet wields many techniques of suggestion, the process happens imperceptibly for the audience member, who is unaware of the transition between the expressed and the suggested sense.[41] This resonance interplays with the subjectivity of the individual spectator; and unlike direct expression, the meaning of *dhvani* cannot be fixed.[42]

The concept of *dhvani* has proven useful for Indian Christian readers of scripture. Christian exegetes of scripture have long realized that the Bible speaks on many levels: literal, historical, moral, allegorical, anagogical, and so on. Christian theologians have also professed that words can never exhaust the wondrous depths of divine mystery. *Dhvani* resonates with these insights.

In a 1979 issue of the Indian Biblical Quarterly *Biblebhashyam*, Indian Christian scholars demonstrate *dhvani* as a method in which a reader "steadily and systematically learns to attune" herself to scripture. The reader moves beyond "the primary and the secondary meanings" to "the atmosphere that they create. . . . What is really of importance in it will be conveyed through *dhvani*."[43] The contributors attend to the resonances of several New Testament passages. Francis X. D'Sa discovers that as the Lord's Prayer

(Mt. 6:25–33) instructs the reader not to be anxious, its language suggests a sense of divine care. George Soares Prabhu finds that the story of Jesus' stilling of the storm (Mk. 4:35–41) evokes the terror of existence, the peace of trust, and awe in the presence of the miraculous. Matthew Vellanickal reads the conversation of Jesus with the Samaritan woman (Jn. 4:4–26) as an exhortation for both the woman and readers of the story to look beyond the literal.[44] The essays join the narrative theology movement of the time in pointing out the limitations of historical-critical method, but they also offer a mechanism for analyzing how a text produces its effects. *Dhvani*'s distinct contribution to the traditional Christian hermeneutic strategy of reading scripture on various levels is its sensitivity to the emotional resonances of the text.

Dhvani has philosophical as well as hermeneutical implications. Because the term denotes 'inner Significance' or the 'poetic Significance' or 'Meaningfulness,'" Jesuit thinker Anand Amaladass works with *dhvani* to elaborate "a particular world-view" including a theory of language, a hermeneutics, an epistemology, a psychology, and an ontology.[45] What is important for Amaladass is not narrative but the wider functioning of symbols; and although he does not attempt to articulate a Christian theology in terms of *dhvani*, this emphasis on symbol has found application in Christian art.

Jyoti Sahi argues that the Indian concept of *dhvani*, "with its concept of multiple layers of meaning to be found in the art work, has enshrined a principle of the respect for the Other."[46] Art resonates at different frequencies for different people. Religious fundamentalists violate this principle when they dictate or nail down the meaning of scriptural narratives. Art engages the other—the artist, the artwork, and interpreters. For Sahi, aesthetic experience offers a model for dialogue in which people tell and retell their stories and "see the world imaginatively through the eyes of the other."[47] *Dhvani* embraces uncertainty. It creates space to criticize traditions and evoke new meaning.[48]

Caroline MacKenzie, an artist associated with INSCAPE, Jyoti Sahi's art ashram, channels the evolving Christian interest in *dhvani* to her creative process. She finds "strong resonances" between *dhvani* and the theories of Ricoeur and Gadamer that stress the importance of the reader's situation for the reception of an image. Diversity "allows for a whole variety of valid interpretations, which enrich the meaning of the text and broaden the horizon of our understanding."[49] Drawing from her Catholic roots, she employs the Ignatian method: She places herself within a scriptural story to generate ideas for her painting. Her position as a woman from the United Kingdom with significant immersion in Indian religious culture inspires her to imagine herself in the position of the injured traveler in the story of the Good Samaritan:

> As a woman in a desacralized consumer society, I have been robbed of my basic dignity and self-worth. I have been made into an object of sexual desire. I experience the establishment religion as passing me by, being largely unconcerned with my injuries. Then, in India, I find there is a sense of the sacred feminine. I experience a profound sense of healing in relation to the Indian culture and Indian Christianity. I feel genuinely understood as a woman by an Indian sister who is a guru. Thus in my picture, the person injured is a woman and the unexpected help comes from an Indian woman.[50]

As in biblical and philosophical studies, *dhvani* inspires Christian artists to make meaning in their Indian context.

Dhvani, the literary theory that emerges from an earlier notion of *rasa*, has thus received attention in terms of Christian hermeneutical and creative method. Because *dhvani* works well in the slippery and multivalent realm of symbol, the concept also illuminates the process of comparative reading. When I read the texts of two traditions together, they suggest things to me as a reader that they would not if read alone. They resonate together and strike chords within me, but there is no rule to determine how this will happen for me or for anyone else.

Although Christians have explored *dhvani* as a helpful theological concept, *rasa* itself remains largely unexplored. One exception lies in a short book of meditations on the Psalms, in which woodcuts by Sahi are accompanied by narrative and theological reflections by Martin Kämpchen. The two men interweave themes of the seasons, the elements, the Indian countryside, and the nine emotions (*rasa*s) as they explore the meaning of the Psalms for the rural Indian context.[51] In the following chapters, I explore *rasa* further as a helpful rubric for discussing the emotional content of art and religion.

Toward a Holistic Theology of Religious Emotion

The arc of the following sections is broadly comparative. I place the dominant religious themes of peace and love (parts I and II) alongside criteria of liberation expressed in the prophetic fury of marginalized groups (part III) in order to move toward a holistic theology of the emotions (part IV). Focused comparisons within this larger arc explore the texture of each emotion. Each of the three sections should be read as a unit. An opening vignette evokes an aesthetic work that unites the chapters in each section through a shared emotional tenor.

Part I, "Peace," begins with a chapter on the great literary theorist and Kashmir Śaiva theologian Abhinavagupta, who makes the case for peace (*śānta*) as the most important aesthetic taste (chapter 1). For him, this *rasa* most closely resembles the union of the self with the absolute. He argues that the experience of a great work of art is akin to the blissful state experienced by the yogi absorbed in meditation. Both experiences are transcendent, not of this world (*alaukika*). This theory opens itself to theological critiques of an aestheticism that elides concrete, material realities and the demands of justice. The aestheticizing tendency comes to full flower in inheritors of the tradition, but I argue for a return to Abhinavagupta's dynamic Kashmir Śaiva theology that contributes to a more grounded notion of *alaukika*. Chapter 2 observes the expression of these tensions in the context of post-Vatican II Catholicism in India. Jyoti Sahi's art and theology serve as the focal point. Sahi's work demonstrates an effort to find spiritual peace that is responsive to physical reality, aided by the centrality of the incarnation and suffering of Jesus Christ.

Part II, "Love," compares two theologians of love: Rūpa Gosvāmin (chapter 3) and Bernard of Clairvaux (chapter 4). The theme of propriety (*aucitya*) frames the tensions within their work. Their respective scriptures—the story of Kṛṣṇa and his *gopī* lovers and the biblical Song of Songs—evoke a highly erotic subject matter; but each guards against inappropriate eroticism in devotees through reading strategies that discourage readers from physically experiencing or imitating it. In chapter 5, I observe that each thinker also uses these strategies to marginalize particular groups of people and to reinforce conventional notions of gender and social standing. This critical comparison inspires me to reread Bernard using Rūpa's aesthetic categories in order to reinvigorate a Christian notion of the spiritual senses and develop a holistic theology of devotional love. I also retrieve a place for *aucitya* in the context this holistic theology.

The temptations of an otherworldly (*alaukika*) religious peace and an appropriate (*aucitya*) love encourage a turn to voices on the margins of both Hindu and Christian traditions. Part III, "Fury," focuses on the Paraiyar Dalits of South India. I argue that viewing Dalit drumming and dancing through the lens of *rasa* theory offers important correctives to the dominant aesthetic and theological traditions. Rather than blaming the aestheticizing tendencies on aesthetics itself, I argue for the religious value of suppressed emotions such as fury. Chapter 6 defends the application of *rasa* theory to Dalit arts. I develop aspects of the theory that resist otherworldly tendencies, trouble the notion of propriety, and incorporate communal experience in order to accommodate non-elite religious and aesthetic traditions. Chapter 7 explores arts and liturgies developed at the Tamilnadu Theological Seminary that express fury against injustice and empower the community for action.

Part IV, "Tastes of the Divine," develops a holistic theology of emotion within this interreligious context. In chapter 8, the ethical criterion that emerges from the comparative exploration of peace, love, and fury is applied to each of the nine *rasa*s of classical Indian theory. I consider how responsiveness to bodies, the material world, and marginalized persons creates a place for each sentiment in the religious life. This series of brief reflections sheds light on the cultural construction of these emotions within a shared set of human faculties for perceiving and expressing them. The final chapter, "Wonder," reflects theologically on the aesthetics of religious pluralism; I suggest that wonder is both a religious orientation and a posture toward religious others, that Christians can become sympathetic spectators (*sahṛdaya*s) of other traditions, and that these traditions can contribute to Christian spirituality as accompanying or nurturing emotional factors (*vyabhicāribhāva*s).

The issue of how to discern authentic religious emotion is not new for Christian theology. It preoccupied Jonathan Edwards during the Great Awakening. Convinced that "true religion, in great part, consists in holy affections," he wanted to discern which signs reliably indicate the work of divine grace.[52] He rejected intensity, number, bodily effect, and order of emotions as proof of the authenticity of the experience. He found similarly unreliable a person's talk of religion, facility with quoting scripture, time spent in worship, confidence, and ability to convince others of the genuineness of the experience. The sure and reliable markers of saving grace resemble the fruits of the spirit: love, joy, and the persistence of Christ-like virtues and conduct. In my theological assessment, Edwards' instincts hold up well today. Emotions have a particular kind of intelligence; yet we are now more aware than ever of the human capacity to be manipulated by strong emotion, not least in political and religious contexts.[53] We are right to be disciplined in our assessment of emotions. As with Edwards, the criteria I employ throughout these chapters have much to do with love and joy; but justice for the marginalized other, shaped by a vision of Christ's suffering on the cross, is equally essential.

This critical principle is basic to Christianity's prophetic impulse, and it is basic to *rasa* as well. Hindu theologian Rita Sherma retrieves the ethical significance of *rasa* for Hindu *dharma*. She asserts that "[*r*]*asa* is fundamentally evocative of relationality, engagement with the other—whether in passion or compassion." Although art ideally moves the sensitive viewer into communion with the other, this experience does not always translate into ethical engagement: "The poignancy of the experience of *rasa* is overwhelming in its intensity, and powerful in its arousal of the sense of divine presence. But it can too easily be subsumed in the peace of a self-indulgent interiority unless the ethics of engagement . . . are imprinted on the heart of the experiencer."[54] In opening *rasa* for Christian theology, I find a strong affinity with this constructive Hindu theology.

Through comparison we recognize that tensions between the aesthetic and the aestheticizing are present across diverse contexts, and that diverse religious cultures have much to teach one another. In this exchange, let us taste the divine in new and familiar recipes and in delightful rasic combinations.

PART I

Peace

Crossing the threshold into the Saccidananda Chapel at the National Biblical, Catechetical, and Liturgical Centre in Bangalore, India, we instinctively become quiet and attentive. We have left our shoes behind us on the steps and now tread on holy ground. The space is a kind of *axis mundi* or cosmic tree, planted where the vertical and horizontal dimensions meet. A central column rises as the focal point: earth, water, fire, air, and ether, continuing up into a seven-tiered tower that blossoms at last into a six-petaled lotus. The column replicates the yogic scheme of the body, each of the lower chakras represented by one of the elements, ascending to the opening above the crown of the head where one tastes union with the divine. Ensconced in the space of the heart is the tabernacle containing the Eucharistic host: word made flesh, descended to dwell among humanity.

On the horizontal axis, the chapel marks a square, a symbol of fullness and the basic orienting scheme for Hindu temples. The lines crossing the room provide a mandala for meditation: they represent the space of the cosmos, which is replicated within the space of the heart. The windows in each of the nooks hold grilles with imagery resonant across Indian religious traditions: a monk in a yogic posture of meditation next to Mary praying with Jesus in the cave of her heart; the four stages of life (*āśramas*), together with the four gospels; the *upanāyana* initiation ceremony, side by side with symbols of the Christian sacraments; and the Buddha receiving hospitality as a beggar, with Abraham and Sarah welcoming divine guests unaware. In addition to these many details, designed by Indian Christian artist and theologian Jyoti Sahi, traditional Indian symbols of devotion—oil lamps, garlands of fresh flowers, and a lotus altar—accentuate a feeling of peace.[1]

1 The Bliss of Peace

The peaceful feeling of transcendence palpable in the NBCLC chapel is *śānta*, the *rasa* of peace. *Śānta* won a place as the ninth *rasa*, in addition to the eight enumerated by Bharata, after long debate. Abhinavagupta (tenth century), possibly India's greatest literary theorist, champions *śānta* as the ninth and most important *rasa*, the one into which all other aesthetic emotions eventually resolve. We shall consider Abhinavagupta's notion of *śānta* as it evolves in his works of literary criticism: the *Locana* (*Loc*), a commentary on Ānandavardhana's *Dhvanyāloka* (*DhĀ*);[2] and the *Abhinavabhāratī* (*ABh*), a commentary on the *Nāṭya Śāstra*.[3] As not only a great reader of poetry and drama but also a practitioner of tantric meditation in the Hindu tradition of Kashmir Śaivism, Abhinavagupta interprets aesthetic experiences and religion in light of one another.[4] The imagery that Jyoti Sahi's chapel uses to evoke a meditative mood draws upon symbols of tantric mandalas and the yogic body with which Abhinavagupta was intimately acquainted.

Śānta is the religious emotion *par excellence* in India's contemplative traditions, and, as such, it has several shades of meaning. Ānandavardhana uses the word in the sense of "an intense experience . . . of detachment that comes from reading or witnessing a work of art depicting ruin, impermanence, the transitory character of worldly existence, and the futility of ambition."[5] This momentary disillusionment with the world is conducive to liberation (*mokṣa*), especially as sought by those who renounce worldly life. Abhinavagupta expands the meaning of *śānta* to include a characteristic of aesthetic experience more generally: In the unobstructed experience of *rasa*, one tastes the tranquil bliss of the pure self. As Abhinavagupta combines these two senses of the term,

> [t]he peaceful *rasa* may be characterized as the full development into aesthetic enjoyment of a certain type of happiness (*sukha*) occurring as a

> basic emotional state. This happiness consists in the dying off, that is, the complete cessation, of desires, that is, yearnings for objects of sense, and may be called an indifference to worldly things (*nirveda*).[6]

Śānta, then, evokes the peaceful repose of the self in *brahman*, which grants the momentary cessation of conscious thought and the transcendence of subject-object duality. For Abhinavagupta, the spectator's absorption in the drama is akin to the deepest contemplation. In a later development, which we will explore in part II, proponents of devotional religion (*bhakti*) further expand this contemplative calm to include a kind of mute awe in the presence of a deity.

Christian theologians, too, have observed the power of art to evoke something of the divine. The great twentieth-century Protestant theologian Paul Tillich writes of an encounter with a Botticelli painting that "produced an ecstatic feeling of revelatory character." The experience merged art and philosophy in his mind as both being intimately related "to being itself, to the ground and the power of being."[7] The influential Catholic theologian Karl Rahner writes of the ability of art to help "to bring about, through a sensory experience of transcendence . . . that properly religious experience of transcendence."[8] Both find in aesthetic experience the power to evoke a transcendental encounter with the divine ground of being.

Despite these attractions, the ascent proffered by the realm of art is ethically ambivalent insofar as it lures the spectator away from the material realm. Among Christian theologians, none have probed the ambiguities of the intersections between religious and aesthetic experience more fully than Hans Urs von Balthasar. In his five-volume "Theo-Drama," the first volume, *Seeing the Form*, strives to develop a theological aesthetics that, in his words, does not "deteriorate into an 'aesthetic theology' by betraying and selling out theological substance to the current viewpoints of an inner-worldly theory of beauty."[9] That is, von Balthasar resists reducing religious experience to either the merely attractive or a serene inner world.

It is with this second reduction that we are concerned here. The peaceful sentiment beckons away from the world of messiness and conflict to the repose that belongs to the divine life itself. This allure shines through accounts like those of Tillich and Rahner. Yet Balthasar holds theological aesthetics accountable to the *form* of revelation. For him, the beauty of the divine life is Christoform: It includes the formlessness, humiliation, and ugliness of the cross.[10] It challenges religious persons not to lapse into a sedate mystical complacency that ignores the demands of injustice, suffering bodies, and material reality.

One does not need a Christocentric starting point to make this critique. A basic commitment to the well-being of sentient beings and the earth cautions against the otherworldly escapism that art sometimes offers. With this ethical criterion, we may embark on an exploration of the peaceful sentiment. *Śānta rasa* will serve as a testing ground for a theology of religious experience that reckons with the emotive power of the aesthetic without thereby becoming an aestheticizing theology.

This pair of chapters considers the place of the peaceful sentiment in the *rasa* theory of Abhinavagupta and in the later Indian Christian context represented by Jyoti Sahi. Our comparison centers on the extent to which *rasa* is extraordinary, non-worldly, or transcendent—the Sanskrit term for this is *alaukika*, which is derived from *loka* ("world") with the privative *a*. If aesthetic experience is akin to religious experience, particularly in the peaceful sentiment, what does this imply about the material realm in which art is rooted?

Extraordinary Emotion

Rasa's nature as *alaukika*—non-worldly, extraordinary, or transcendent—provides one important link to the theological import of *śānta*. Abhinavagupta writes, "This aesthetic relish, whose soul is supernormal (*alaukika*) wonder and whose breath is the tasting of the excitants (*vibhāvas*), etc., found in poetry, should not be vitiated by identification with memory, inference, and the like."[11] This statement sets aesthetic experience apart from real life. As Abhinavagupta explains, *rasa* does not work like ordinary processes of feeling and thinking. It is *sui generis*.

Rasa differs from the ordinary emotions (*sthāyibhāvas*) that underlie aesthetic feeling. Love (*rati*), for example, is the basis of the erotic sentiment (*śṛṅgāra*), anger (*krodha*) of the furious sentiment (*raudra*), and so on. These foundational emotions are produced directly, as in the joy that arises when someone receives happy news, or inferred, as when one apprehends what another person is feeling. By contrast, *rasa* can only be produced indirectly through the combination of evocative elements in an aesthetic context.[12] The foundational emotions play no role in this process; they operate on the worldly plane.

For similar reasons, Abhinavagupta differentiates aesthetic experience from ordinary means of knowledge and perception: "[T]his relishing does not arise because of some other means of knowledge, because perception, etc., do not function in super-normal (*alaukika*) [experience]."[13] Again, *rasa* arises through a unique process of suggestion (*dhvani*) and is not directly perceived or produced by the memory or inference. This is why the *vibhāvas*, *anubhāvas*, and *vyabhicāribhāvas* of the *rasa sūtra* are not called "causes" (*kāraṇas*) and "effects" (*kāryas*): They do not operate like ordinary causes.[14] The awareness *rasa* produces is also unique because it lacks the obstacles inherent to other kinds of knowledge. Unlike ordinary knowledge, it does not lead to desires; unlike the knowledge of imperfect yogis, which lacks vividness, it is crisp and vibrant; and unlike the knowledge of perfect yogis, it is not so overpowered by union that it impedes apprehension of beauty.[15] In this latter respect, *rasa* is superior even to the realization of *brahman*.

Aesthetic emotion is also distinct from ordinary emotion because even the "negative" *rasas* such as terror, fury, disgust, and pathos are experienced as bliss. In real life, these can be painful; but when relished in an aesthetic context, they only bring pleasure. Mundane things are transformed through the poet's imagination and the spectator's participation in it. Audiences do not share in the grief (*śoka*) of the characters in a play—if they did, theatres would be empty—but savor the idealized emotion of compassion (*karuṇa*).[16]

Furthermore, in ordinary life, emotions are related to individuals: We experience emotion as subjects, and emotion usually has something as its object. We rejoice in our own happiness, sympathize with our friends, and despise our enemies. But in *rasa*, the spectator does not experience the sentiment as her own. *Rasa* is *alaukika* because it is idealized, depersonalized, or universalized (*sādhāranīkṛta*). On the one hand, the spectator relates to the situation without the personal investment one would have if it were happening to oneself, one's friend, or one's enemy. On the other hand, one's engrossment in the situation prevents the opposite emotional response of indifference or detachment.[17]

This feature of generalization (*sādhāranīkaraṇa*) allows Abhinavagupta to elaborate upon the analogy of Bhaṭṭanāyaka, an earlier theorist, between aesthetic relishing (*rasāsvāda*) and the taste of the divine (*brahmāsvāda*). "We admit," he writes, "that the relishing of *rasa* bears a family resemblance to the relishing of the ultimate brahman."[18] Both are *alaukika*, not of this world. In the theatre, as in deep meditation, one becomes completely engrossed. One forgets oneself and loses track of ordinary space and time. An extraordinary sense of wonder or mystic delight overtakes the mind of the spectator.[19] The same sorts of obstacles apply to both experiences: If a person is too immersed in his own condition to the exclusion of others, distracted by his own bodily sensations or desires, or unable to identify with the states of consciousness of others, he can fully enter neither meditation nor the realm of drama.[20] As Kulkarni characterizes the ideal state of absorption,

> Being altogether divorced from reference to personal interests, one's own or those of others, aesthetic experience is free from all the limitations of ordinary pleasure, arising out of narrow attachment, such as envy, desire or aversion; and the *sahṛdaya* [sensitive audience member] becomes almost unconscious of his private self. He rises above the duality of pain and pleasure, love and hatred and enjoys through disinterested contemplation absolutely pure joy or delight.[21]

The spectator of a work of art thus arrives at the same goal as the contemplative, but by different means.

A Ninth *Rasa*?

The special relation of the peaceful sentiment to the non-worldly nature of *rasa* highlights its importance for Abhinavagupta as a philosopher and religious practitioner.[22] He explicates his position in his *Abhinavabhāratī*, a commentary on the *śānta* portion of the *Nāṭya Śāstra*. This text is extant only in fragmentary and corrupt form. The discussion that follows relies on the translations by J. L. Masson and M. V. Patwardhan (1969) and by Edwin Gerow (1994).

Abhinavagupta seems aware that manuscripts with only eight *rasa*s were "older and more genuine," and that the section on the peaceful sentiment is most likely a later interpolation.[23] He is aware of objections to its inclusion, as well as of other contenders for inclusion in the list of basic emotional states.[24] Because of the absence of the peaceful sentiment in Bharata's *Nāṭya Śāstra*, Abhinavagupta must defend its status as a *rasa* in its own right.

Abhinavagupta faces a number of problems in making his case for *śānta*. For example, there are very few examples of *śānta rasa* as the predominant *rasa* of a classical drama.[25] He counters this problem with reference to the great Indian epic, the *Mahābhārata*. Although this vast work contains episodes in which all of the other *rasa*s are prominent, its mighty heroes end in tragedy. The epic as a whole creates a sense of world-weariness (*vairagya*) and a desire for liberation (*mokṣa*). The other *rasas* are thus subordinated to the overarching feeling of *śānta*, which is artfully suggested (i.e., conveyed through *dhvani*) in the accumulation of narratives.[26]

Some opponents of *śānta* as a distinct *rasa* subsume it under the heroic sentiment (*vīra*), which has several subtypes, including heroisms of compassion (*dayāvīra*), religious duty (*dharmavīra*), and generosity (*dānavīra*). Abhinavagupta follows Ānandavardhana's reasoning that these characteristics can only be called *śānta* if there are no traces of egoism; otherwise they are simply varieties of the heroic.[27]

Critics also raise questions about the existence of *śānta rasa* because it is essentially a negative state: the absence of desire. This negation of mental activity cannot be regarded as an emotion, which is by definition a positive mental state. Abhinavagupta deftly makes a technical distinction to counter this objection: there are two types of nonexistence, that of something that has never come into being and that of something which once existed but has been destroyed. The negative mental state of *śānta* is the latter. All persons come into the world with desire, but when desire ceases, the mind returns to peaceful equanimity.[28] *Śānta* is a state of mind that is not particularized by any of the other moods, a mode of awareness from which those other moods have melted away.

The question still remains whether a negative definition of *śānta rasa* (the cessation of activities and desires) allows for stage representation. The spiritual realization that lies at its core is an internal event; it is a state of fullness and pacification that leads to the end of all striving. The critics argue that this interiority undercuts the educative value of the drama: How can the spectator attain knowledge of the truth by observing a state of inactivity?[29] Abhinavagupta grants that *śānta rasa* cannot be represented in its culminating state, but this is true of other *rasas* such as love and its culmination in sexual ecstasy as well.[30] Furthermore, one manuscript of the interpolated passage in the *Nāṭya Śāstra* states, "It should be portrayed onstage by *anubhāvas* such as yogic restraints and disciplines (*yamas*, *niyamas*, etc.), meditation on the Self, concentration, worship, compassion for all beings, wearing religious markers, etc."[31] In other words, although the final state of *śānta* cannot be portrayed, the activities that lead to it, such as the eight limbs of yoga or acts of compassion, can.

In order to fit the criteria of a *rasa* according to the *rasa sūtra*, the peaceful sentiment must arise from the combination of particular elements: *vibhāvas*, *anubhāvas*, and *vyabhicāribhāvas* (*NŚ* prose after VI.31, p. 227).[32]

The *Abhinavabhāratī* names excitants (*vibhāva*s) such as the fear of the cycle of rebirth and the indifference to worldly things exemplified by renouncers and ascetics. Such characters display indicators (*anubhāvas*) such as contemplating religious texts on final liberation. They may exhibit other accompanying emotions (*vyabhicāribhāvas*) like world-weariness, contentment, piety, or devotion.[33] Elsewhere Abhinavagupta lists "*vibhāva*s such as contact with persons devoid of desire and with esoteric texts on the supreme spirit, the favor of the highest God, and the ripening of one's previous good deeds," and cites outward symptoms of the liberated such as performing yogic disciplines or ruling wisely.[34]

Every *rasa* must have a foundational emotion (*sthāyibhāva*), yet even the theorists who accept *śānta* disagree about what that emotion might be. Some offer *śama*, which is basically synonymous with *śānta*, and argue that its excitants are ascetic practices, Vedic recitation, and the like. Abhinavagupta cites the objection that because these activities do not always lead to peace, they cannot be called its causes.[35] Others say that *nirveda*, world-weariness arising from knowledge of the truth, is the foundation. This position leads to some circularity, for knowledge can also be seen as the cause of detachment from worldly things.[36] Still others posit that the foundational emotions of each of the other *rasa*s can be refined to the point of undisturbed bliss: Love (*rati*) can be directed toward the Self, humor (*hāsa*) can help one to see the oddity of the world, sorrow (*śoka*) helps one see it as lamentable, anger (*krodha*) can be directed against the spiritually harmful aspects of existence, effort (*utsāha*) can be used to overcome delusion, disgust (*jugupsā*) for the sources of desire and fear (*bhaya*) of the objects of the senses can lead to liberation, and astonishment (*vismaya*) accompanies realization of the Self. Abhinavagupta counters that these different ways to reach *śānta* negate one another as contenders for its unique foundational emotion. So many different ways to reach the state of *śānta* would imply an infinite number of *śānta rasa*s, not one.[37]

In light of this debate, Abhinavagupta designates knowledge of the truth (*tattvajñāna*), or even the Self (*ātman*), as *śānta*'s foundation. He argues that although knowledge of union with the ultimate self can mingle with other emotional states, as when a person emerges from deep meditation, it can be experienced in its pure form. As the interpolated passage of the *Nāṭya Śāstra* states, "The emotions arise from peace, each through its own cause, / And when the cause is withdrawn, each dissolves back into peace."[38] The pure taste of the nature of the self is unique to *śānta* as a *rasa*. Abhinavagupta likens the Self (*ātman*) to a wall on which the foundational emotions each appear in the presence of their causes, and then disappear again. Knowledge of the truth is unique in its stability; all the other states of mind, including the other eight *rasas*, become transitory feelings (*vyabhicāribhāvas*) in relation to peace.[39] In another analogy, knowledge of the Self is like a white thread that shines through the jewels strung on it, even as the jewels tinge it with their various colors.[40]

Śānta as Religious Experience

Abhinavagupta's arguments for the priority of the peaceful sentiment ultimately revolve around its proximity to religious experience: "Because this [*śānta*] yields the highest aim of humanity, with the fruit of *mokṣa*, it is preeminent among all the *rasas*."[41] He must answer a final potent objection to *śānta*'s status as a *rasa*. In theory, *rasas* resonate with audiences because every person has had some experience of each of the emotional states, but not everyone is disposed to the experience of *śānta* as they are to the other *rasas*. *Śānta* is quite exceptional in real life, and only a few extraordinary individuals actually reach final liberation. Masson and Patwardhan are not convinced by Abhinavagupta's suggestion that people can imagine the cessation of desire based on their own experience of hunger and satiation.[42]

> There seems to us no doubt in reading through the objections made against *śāntarasa* that the objectors had a real point. There is something about [*śānta*] that forces it apart from all the other *rasas*. . . . Truly to be able to enjoy it, one must be religious . . ., and if the *śāntarasa* experience truly takes place during a drama, it must change our lives. It is not like the other *rasas*, which simply enrich us, provide great scope for our imagination, refine our sensibilities, in short do all the things that great literary experiences are supposed to do. It is not that it demands a suspension of judgment as do the other *rasas*, a momentary identification with different emotions. It means a complete reversal of our personality.[43]

Abhinavagupta's stronger argument is that the taste of meditative bliss is something to which all persons would have been exposed at least once in their many lifetimes.[44] *Śānta*'s association with *mokṣa*—one of the valid ends of human life (*puruṣārthas*) alongside pleasure, wealth, and duty (*kāma*, *artha*, and *dharma*)—means that it may be rare in day-to-day life, but it remains part of the common store of human experiences.

The objection nevertheless encourages Abhinavagupta to clarify the scope of the analogy between the taste of *rasa* (*rasāsvāda*) and the relishing of the divine (*brahmāsvāda*). Numerous similarities obtain between aesthetic and contemplative experience. Both are transcendent, blissful, and conducive to rest. Both states of consciousness transcend pain. Immersion in both experiences erases our ordinary sense of subject and object, of time and space, and of the finite self. Each experience removes the veils from our deepest nature so that we can perceive it. Preparation is necessary, in the form of external aids such as music and dance on the one hand and religious practices on the other. These means are not the goal in themselves but are merely the lamp that illuminates the object.[45]

In true analogical fashion, the taste of *śānta rasa* and the taste of *brahman* differ in important ways as well. As Masson and Patwardhan note, the latter is life-altering (a rather "top-heavy" goal for a night at the playhouse), and the preparation for religious realization is much more stringent than for an audience member.[46] In Abhinavagupta's analysis, the differences between *brahmāsvāda* and *rasāsvāda* have to do with the relative purity and permanence of the former. Aesthetic experience, though superior to ordinary happiness, is still inferior to mystic bliss. It is truly just a taste of the divine: "[T]he taste of *rasa* is only the reflection of a drop of the bliss (*ānanda*) . . . of repose in the highest God."[47] Unlike knowledge of *brahman*, which is unconditioned by worldly objects, concrete elements (a beautiful woman, a lovely garden, etc.) lead to the perception of *rasa*.[48] All of our worldly experience, including our experience of art, also bears traces of our individuality and is mixed to various degrees with suffering. We call upon our own experiences so that we can enjoy the emotional shadings of a work of literature. Impressions accrued over many lifetimes allow for this range of enjoyment, and these slight tinges of past experience color our enjoyment of the aesthetic object.[49] *Brahmāsvāda* is pure and unconditioned by the traces that accrue to *rasa*.

Abhinavagupta's arguments for the ultimacy of *śānta* in relation to the ultimate human goal won the day. Indeed, his position seems to capture something of our enchantment by the theatre, absorption in good novel, and rapture of listening to a Bach cantata or an exquisite bhajan. Many people experience this holy state in the presence of soaring cathedrals, the interior of a temple, solemn words, rich harmonies, or simple silence. The emotions rendered well—whether beautifully or not—transport us beyond ourselves. We are momentarily still.

Aesthetics as Religion

In the nineteenth century, the Romantic poets, artists, and musicians of Europe turned to art for the noumenal experience they called divine. Prominent literary figures such as Schelling, Schlegel, and Novalis turned to Sanskrit literature to find its purest expression. Indian artists in the Swadeshi movement that led to Indian independence similarly extolled the art of the subcontinent as a uniquely spiritual tradition. These perspectives shape Abhinavagupta's legacy in India.

To understand contemporary interpretations of the Indian aesthetic tradition, one must come to grips with the work of Ananda Coomaraswamy (1877–1947). Coomaraswamy, born in Sri Lanka, was raised and schooled in England, where he moved with his English mother after his father died when he was a small boy. His life's work, represented by the large collection of Asian art he donated and managed at the Boston Museum of Fine Art, was devoted to art criticism and philosophy. His influence on contemporary aesthetic theory in India is unparalleled.[50]

Coomaraswamy draws together his extensive knowledge of Western and Eastern art and philosophy to propose a *philosophia perennis* that reframes Abhinavagupta's influential analogy between the aesthetic and the religious realms. Although he does not directly cite Abhinavagupta, whose texts were likely not available to him, he is deeply immersed in a tradition of literary criticism that bears Abhinavagupta's fingerprints. His discussions of *rasa*, which quote from the *Nāṭya Śāstra*, Viśvanātha's *Sāhitya Darpaṇa*, and Dhanamjaya's *Daśarūpa*, demonstrate familiarity with the classical Indian tradition.[51]

In an important shift, Coomaraswamy equates what Abhinavagupta treats as analogous. He concludes his essay, "Hindu View of Art," by stating, "[R]eligion and art are thus names for one and the same experience—an intuition of reality and of identity."[52] Coomaraswamy decries the separation of the functional and spiritual in art that he witnesses in modern art criticism.[53] In order to retrieve the unity of art and religion, he calls upon his vast knowledge of Western art and philosophy. He notes that the experience of art as religious "is not, of course, exclusively a Hindu view: it has been expounded by many others, such as the Neo-Platonists, Hsieh Ho, Goethe, Blake, Schopenhauer and Schiller."[54] He also points to contemporary Indian practices, such as the dancer's prayers before a performance, as evidence that there is no inherent "distinction of sacred from secular."[55]

In Coomaraswamy's view, this philosophical position accords perfectly with the nondual Advaita Vedānta school of Indian philosophy that has come to represent Hinduism to the West. This school teaches the oneness of the self (*ātman*) with the ultimate (*brahman*). Coomaraswamy writes, "The theory of *rasa* set forth according to Viśvanātha and other aestheticians, belongs to totalistic monism; it marches with the Vedānta."[56] He finds a Vedantic view of the self at the heart of traditional views of the anonymity of the artist. In contrast to the contemporary emphasis on individual artistic genius, the traditional artist is anonymous; she is "only the instrument of the 'self,'" the inner controller that is *brahman*.[57]

For Coomaraswamy as for Abhinavagupta, the relation of *rasa* to religious realization implies the priority of *śānta* among the *rasas*. Coomaraswamy declares that "[t]he 'nine rasas' are no more than the various colorings of one experience." He appeals to the *alaukika* nature of this sentiment, which evokes bliss regardless of the subject matter.[58] For both theorists, *rasa* is a state of enjoyment achieved through contemplation, "the intuition of things as they are on higher than empirical levels of reference."[59] This kind of intuition is the *śānta* of the yogis and mystics.

Critical Intervention

Coomaraswamy goes further than Abhinavagupta when he entrenches within art experience the feeling of nondual awareness attained by the mystics. *Śānta rasa*, the interloper in Bharata's original list of basic emotional tastes, seems to have taken it over completely. Coomaraswamy's broad influence on this point has been contested in Indian scholarship in recent years. The debate today is not whether *śānta rasa* exists but whether art is essentially a non-worldly (*alaukika*) and/or religious (read: nondual, *śānta*) experience.

Several contemporary theorists contest the idea that *rasa* is "supernormal" or "in a class by itself (*alaukika*)."[60] K. Krishnamoorthy claims that *rasa* belongs entirely to the realm of normal experience of subjectivity and intuition. Although *rasa*

> is to be discovered or intuited within by an inward directed process, which is non-empirical and hence called *alaukika* or *lokottara*; these terms should not be interpreted as super-normal because intuitive apperception is quite a normal feature in all aesthetic contemplation. . . . *rasa* as explained by Bhaṭṭa Nāyaka and Abhinava does not exist outside the percipient.[61]

R. B. Patankar notes that the universalization or generalization (*sādhāranīkaraṇa*) of emotion in rasic experience does, in fact, happen in worldly experience other than art. Most notably, universalization is the condition of empathy and moral agency. He also notes that it is technically not *sui generis* if it arises only in the presence of its causes (the *vibhāvas*, etc.). And it does not, in fact, have a special ontological status that is not subject to ordinary categories of perception, for Abhinavagupta maintains that *rasa* is conducive to the four ends of human life (*puruṣārthas*). Furthermore, the spectator compares characters to real people and recognizes the verisimilitude, thus cycling back toward the real world.[62] T. S. Nandi adds that although Abhinavagupta excludes unhappiness from the blissful experience of *rasa*, many other theorists—including, possibly, Bharata—seem to think that a mixture of pleasure and pain endures in art.[63] By challenging the *alaukika* nature of *rasa*, these voices also implicitly dethrone *śānta*'s philosophical claim as the basis of the other eight.

Coomaraswamy's unequivocal emphasis on the religious character of Indian art has also prompted theoretical backlash. Here we must invoke our criterion of responsiveness to the body and to particularity. Rekha Jhanji argues that art is not essentially a spiritual activity but a sensuous experience that resides first and foremost in the realm of materiality and form. She notes that because Abhinavagupta and Coomaraswamy approach art from the perspective of the spectator rather than the artist, they easily slide into discussing the ideal form created in the spectator's mind rather than attend to the artist's creative manipulation of physical materials.

For Jhanji, Coomaraswamy's borrowing of Abhinavagupta's parallel between aesthetic and religious ecstasy is unhelpful in two ways. First, Coomaraswamy tends to exaggerate instructions in the ancient manuals for artists to meditate on a divine form before creating. These can be read as simple exhortations to single-mindedness. Secondly, and more to the point, Coomaraswamy makes too much of the similarities between the bliss of aesthetic and mystical experience. Jhanji locates the transcendence inherent in art experience entirely within the realm of the mundane ends of human life (*puruṣārthas*): *kāma* (pleasure), *artha* (material well-being), and *dharma* (right interpersonal relations). "[A]mongst the treatises devoted to the four pursuits of human existence (*puruṣārthas*), arts are classified under *Kāmasūtra*. *Kāma* is defined . . . as the disposition to feel pleasure in the experience of the five senses of hearing, touch, vision, taste, and smell."[64] Jhanji thus indexes the arts to pleasure rather than to the fourth end of life, *mokṣa*.

In Jhanji's view, art is created and enjoyed primarily for the pleasure of the senses. Its surface lies entirely in the realm of *kāma*, but for her this sensory pleasure is demarcated from egocentric desire:

> In the creation and appreciation of art works, sensuous experience is extolled for its own sake, and not for fulfilling or generating any desires. Wherever sensory experience is used to excite and titillate the senses and thus generate desire in the beholders, it has generally led to vulgarity and sensationalism, and not to aesthetic enjoyment. . . . A distinctive feature of aesthetic enjoyment is freedom from desire and detachment from any personal involvement with the object appreciated.[65]

This position does not exclude functions such as moral exhortation from art, but these are secondary. Jhanji thus unlinks religion from the experience of art.

Jhanji grants that aesthetic experience is *sui generis* (*alaukika*) because of the joy that arises from a desireless contemplation. The sensitive audience member enjoys emotion through generalization (*sādhāraṇīkaraṇa*): The situations portrayed do not derive from the spectator's particular experience. Yet Jhanji emphasizes that this "*sui generis* character . . . stems from the peculiar role the surface qualities of the art work play in aesthetic enjoyment."[66] The connoisseur derives her primary pleasure from the sensory forms presented, but in a special way: Because she lacks desire related to these experiences, she can encounter each of the *rasa*s—including the terrible and the disgusting—with a feeling of joy.

Returning to Coomaraswamy, we observe a struggle with the centrality of materiality in aesthetic experience. As an art collector and historian, he does not want to denigrate the material. He that claims a nondualist (*advaita*) understanding "is inconsistent with a view of the world as absolute *māyā*, or utterly unreal." Rather, it "implies that through the false world of everyday experience may be seen by those of penetrating vision (artists, lovers and philosophers) glimpses of the real substrate."[67] Despite this caveat, Coomaraswamy shares the temptation of Advaita Vedānta in India and Platonism in the West to denigrate the material realm as less real. The denigration of the physical senses comes through most clearly in his frequent dismissal of the "aesthetic." Coomaraswamy would discard the term "aesthetic," he says, "for these arts were not produced for the delectation of the senses." If they had been produced for the senses, art would be nothing but "reaction to external stimuli," a lower function we have in common with animals and plants. The sensations are closely related to the passions to which we are passively subject, and which we must resist through rational judgment in moral society. He concludes, "Art is an intellectual, not a physical virtue. . . . We take account, in other words, of the *form* of the work. 'Form' in the traditional philosophy does not mean tangible shape, but is synonymous with idea and even with soul."[68]

Coomaraswamy's position reflects the idealizing tendencies of both nondual Hindu philosophy and the premodern Platonisms he admires. This otherworldliness is a temptation endemic to *śānta*, a *rasa* often depicted in a character with closed eyes. (The Yoga Sūtras name withdrawal of the senses, *pratyāhāra*, as one of the eight limbs of yoga.) Jhanji's critique of Coomaraswamy and Abhinavagupta invites a rereading of the classical theory. Because Coomaraswamy's writings have colored Abhinavagupta's legacy in Indian scholarship, we must attend more closely to what Abhinavagupta does and does not wish to claim with his analogy between aesthetic and religious experience. This rereading will keep *rasa* anchored in this world but also challenge Jhanji's dichotomous treatment of pleasure and religious ends.

Abhinavagupta, Revisited

Following Coomaraswamy, many contemporary discussions of the religion-aesthetics analogy call upon the philosophical system of Advaita Vedānta, the school that cultivates nondual awareness of *brahman*.[69] Important contributions to *rasa* theory have come from this school: Bhaṭṭanāyaka, a Vedantin, first introduced the notion of generalization (*sādhāraṇīkaraṇa*), drew parallels between aesthetic experience and the pure experience of *brahman*, and observed similarities between the illusion created by drama and the illusion (*māyā*) of existence.[70]

We should recall, however, that Abhinavagupta is a proponent of a Kashmir Śaiva worldview, which distinguishes itself from Advaita Vedānta in important ways.[71] Many of Abhinavagupta's texts have only been rediscovered and edited after Coomaraswamy imparted his legacy to the study of Indian art traditions;[72] and some of Abhinavagupta's most important texts, including his Tantrāloka, remain untranslated today. It is, therefore, worth revisiting his views of the religious nature of *rasa*, and of *śānta* as the root *rasa*, in light of what we know about his religious worldview.

Abhinavagupta's philosophical context allows him to preserve the sensory aspects of art experience that Jhanji worries are lost in latter day theorists such as Coomaraswamy. While the Vedantic view asserts the absolute identity of the one and the many, Abhinavagupta achieves his experience of totality through a metaphysics of stages. One discovers in his *Īśvara Pratyabhijñā Vimarśinī* that, unlike the relatively static *brahman* of Vedānta, the universal divine consciousness in Kashmir Śaivism is self-conscious, dynamic, and manifest in the world of experience.[73] Pure consciousness (Śiva) differentiates itself in thirty-six increasingly limited gradations (*tattvas*), ranging from the first conscious awareness of subject and object all the way to the organs of sensation and action and the subtle and gross elements. Creation is indeed artifice (*māyā*), but it is not for that reason utterly illusory. All of reality shares the nature of Śiva's consciousness.

Because human consciousness replicates divine consciousness at the microcosmic level, human beings can experience its many gradations of subject-object duality. There is a place for unity: The unity of consciousness, called the "void" (*śūnya*) in tantric texts, can be perceived in the transitions between mental states, as in the initial moment of intent before a thought, action, or utterance.[74] The *Vijñānabhairava Tantra* prescribes a number of meditations that allow a person to taste the void of consciousness at the heart of reality. Some practitioners come to it instantaneously, and some receive it through divine grace, but this text recommends practices that attend to the subtle mental and physical processes that replicate the vibration of consciousness.[75]

Practices related to sensory and aesthetic experience fall among these latter means. As outlined in *Vijñānabhairava Tantra* verses 66–73, anything that throws us into a state of awe or delight can serve as a suitable object of meditation. Viewing a magic show, enjoying sexual intercourse, reuniting with a long-lost friend, savoring a delicious meal, or listening to beautiful music can lead to this state of mind: "When, because of the expansion of the mind, a yogi unites with the relishing of song and other sense objects, his essence becomes that same enjoyment by being absorbed in it."[76] Jaideva Singh comments that aesthetic delight is a "greater source of the experience of the spiritual self" than purely physical delights, for in the Kashmir Śaiva system "there can be aesthetic rapture only when the person experiencing that rapture has *samid-viśrānti* i.e. when his mind is withdrawn from everything around him and reposes in his essential Self."[77] In other words, aesthetic experience, which borders mediated and unmediated means of grace, finds a central place within Kashmir Śaiva spiritual discipline.

Abhinavagupta discusses of a number of tantric practices that put the microcosm of human consciousness in contact with the macrocosm of Śiva's all-pervading awareness, including mantras, mandalas, and esoteric sex rites. His commentary, *Parā-trīśikā-Vivaraṇa*, describes the element of *ojas*, "vital energy," that lies within each person. Singh explains that "[w]hether it is the enjoyment of good food, beautiful scenery, sweet music, entrancing poem, the embrace of a dear one, everywhere it is this energy that is at play. It is the representative of the divine energy . . . on the physical plane."[78] Abhinavagupta explains that when *ojas* is awakened in sensory and emotional experience, it pulsates creativity just like Śiva's own power of consciousness. It is the power that enables each of the human faculties to expand to their full capacity for delight. Liberation comes from recognition that this power in us is identical to the divine power (*śakti*), which rests in union with Śiva but is also impelled to expand outward in creation.[79]

This context reframes Abhinavagupta's analogy between *rasāsvāda* and *brahmāsvāda*. When we are deeply moved, we experience our deepest nature. Both types of experiences catapult us into a kind of awareness unlike our everyday interaction with the particular details of worldly life. We become conscious of the very conditions of consciousness—of the *ātman* which provides the stable base for the colorings of particular emotional experience, and of Śiva, whose divine awareness reverberates through our own.[80] This awareness does not negate the particularities but reveals them as grounded in the unfolding dynamism of divine consciousness.

As Kapila Vatsyayan avers, "Both Ānandavardhana and Abhinavagupta develop a theory of aesthetics on the premise that 'art' is another path for experiencing, if not permanently attaining the absolute freedom of universal and unmediated . . . consciousness."[81] Because individual consciousness is a microcosm, its experience of aesthetic objects is *analogous* (not strictly identical) to divine consciousness. When Śiva becomes aware of external objects, he creates. The one becomes many through the limitations of time, space, and individuality. In aesthetic experience, the spectator reverses the process of creation, as it were, to shed these limitations and taste the unity of divine consciousness at the heart of reality.[82] Although human beings cannot shed all limitations in this life, we can glimpse the ultimate unity of consciousness through the workings of our own awareness in such situations.

Abhinavagupta does more than posit his analogy ("this enjoyment is *like* the divine bliss") and then immediately back away from it in apophatic denial (i.e., "but *brahman* is *so much more* unconditioned, transcendent, etc."). Bettina Bäumer notes,

> [T]he simile is not merely a pretext for explaining the inexplicable (as in *Vedānta*), because the play is a real play of delight even for the yogin. The senses are here not denied, but they assume the role of spectators of the world drama that is reflected in the inner consciousness, on the interior stage. Interiority . . . is not opposed to playful manifestation[;] it is rather the condition for the fullness of aesthetic delight.[83]

Aesthetic experience fits into a program of training in which we come to see that all of reality shares the nature of the divine Self. The experience of enjoying a work of art is a microcosm of the movement of divine consciousness and thus can become a part of that training.

We have seen that Abhinavagupta's privileging of the peaceful *rasa* as the quintessential religious emotion raises questions about the importance of materiality in his aesthetics—or in any aesthetic system. As Masson and Patwardhan observe, "*Rasa* is after all not an objective 'thing' in the real world. It is a private experience. This is perhaps why later writers tend to compare it to religious experiences[,] for ecstatic experiences are essentially private inner happenings more or less invisible to a third party."[84] *Rasa* is private, subjective, and interior. For Abhinavagupta, the technique and materials are relatively unimportant, as long as the well-trained spectator picks up on the cues that launch him or her into a state of transcendental bliss.

For Abhinavagupta, the senses and ordinary emotions also lose their importance, for attachment to them impedes the savoring of *śānta* and the other *rasa*s that rise from and merge back into it. *Rasa* is based in sensory experience (hearing the prose and seeing the gestures of the drama, for instance) but unlike ordinary perception (it is *alaukika*). *Rasa* as emotion is unique, generalized, and savored without individuality or desire. If *rasa* in general and *śānta rasa* in particular are entirely inward, transcendent experiences, and if such experiences are the highest human end, then why should artists (or theologians) concern themselves with the body—its suffering, its difference from other bodies?

These questions were not Abhinavagupta's driving concerns as they are for many today, when the problems of environmental depredation, class exploitation, and gendered dualisms reside in the forefront of our consciousness. We have seen, however, that his Kashmir Śaiva metaphysics can help to account for difference through its nuanced cosmology. The union of the void is not the sole destination for the practitioner, for she also learns to view the world of difference as mirroring the movement of divine consciousness. In such a worldview, aesthetic experience affirms embodied existence as a microcosm of the whole.

Jyoti Sahi wrestles even more vigorously with this problem for, unlike those who would strike an easy dichotomy between religious ends (*mokṣa*) and the world of the senses (*kāma*), he must account for the incarnation and suffering of Christ.

2 Suffering and Peace

In the work of Jyoti Sahi, a contemporary Indian Christian artist who resides near Bangalore, the peaceful sentiment has a special place among the *rasas*. Much of Sahi's work explores the interplay of opposites in relation to Indian culture and religion. His book *The Child and the Serpent*, for example, looks for symbols of unconscious structures (the serpent) and their birth into consciousness (the child). His use of Jungian psychology grounds his keen interest in Hindu art and mythology in pre-Aryan themes and rituals, so that he draws inspiration both from high Sanskritic culture and from Dalit and Tribal folk art.[1]

For Sahi, *śānta* is a state of equilibrium between opposing emotions, the pivot between the positive and negative *rasas*. As he explains it, the attractive feelings of erotic love, joy, courage, and compassion are balanced by the repulsive feelings of disgust, sadness, fear, and anger. The peaceful sentiment resolves these contradictory moods:

> Thus by attaining a balance between erotic attraction, and disgusted separation, or Joy as opposed to pain and sadness, a state of balance or "Saumya" could be discovered which we experience as Peace. In Indian aesthetics Peace is a state of indifference, when the "oceanic" state associated with spiritual bliss is reached, beyond the temporal states of opposing feelings.[2]

Art explores all aspects of human emotions, but it also has the capacity to resolve these emotions into a state of "spiritual bliss" that resides "beyond the temporal states." This peace offers a taste of divine equilibrium beyond our ordinary consciousness of pleasure and pain. As with Abhinavagupta, some aspects of Sahi's religious context mobilize this sentiment toward an otherworldly spirituality, though crucial elements in his work resist this tendency.

The NBCLC

If we are to understand the importance of *śānta* in the Saccidananda Chapel described at the beginning of part I, we must understand the context of the National Biblical, Catechetical, and Liturgical Centre (NBCLC), the campus on which the chapel resides as its focal point. Following the Second Vatican Council, churches around the world were encouraged in the project of inculturation, that is, the project of expressing the Christian faith in idioms native to particular contexts. The NBCLC was founded following the Council to continue the initiative that was already under way in projects such as the Christian Ashram movement in India. During this period, the Centre produced writings, liturgies, and art that embraced many symbols from India's religious traditions. The NBCLC's early art and architecture were replete with the meditative ideals of brahmanical philosophy. The liturgy, too, reflected upper-caste ideals: It held a weekly "Indian Mass," conducted primarily in Sanskrit, and later established a company of classically trained dancers to promote the gospel through classical *bharatanatyam* dance.

This creative period in the institution's history reflects the ongoing desire of the Indian church to define its identity as simultaneously *Indian* and *Christian*. Thomas Thangaraj explains, "In forming their sacred life Indian Christians seek to be distinct from their Hindu and Muslim neighbors. Therefore, the use of Western music, Gothic and Roman church architecture, and other such Western Christian practices functions to highlight their difference from their Hindu neighbors. At the same time, Indian Christians are keen to locate their sacred life squarely in the cultural ethos of India and therefore see themselves as different from Western Christians."[3] If early- to mid-twentieth-century Catholic leaders in India leaned upon the latter side of this balance, then it should not be surprising that their efforts met resistance from the other side.

Hindus as well as Indian Christians have come to view Christian experiments in liturgy, art, and ashram-style communities with skepticism. Indian Christians react negatively to the imposition of religious forms that their community rejected when it accepted Christ. For many, their religious identity has been forged in contrast to Hinduism, as being "not that." This deeply embedded and embodied response stands as an obstacle to the aesthetic success of the Saccidananda Chapel. In light of such controversies, NBCLC leaders have moved away from the language and methods of inculturation in recent years.[4] For their part, many Hindus view inculturation efforts as "Christians' attempt to 'proselytize' through fraudulent and coercive means," a wolf-in-sheep's-clothing strategy to convert Hindus.[5] There has been a strong push from some political parties to make this perceived duplicity (and proselytization in general) illegal. Cynicism and suspicion stand in the way of aesthetic appreciation.

Has this chapel failed in its aesthetic objective because a properly attuned audience cannot be found? The ideal spectator, the *sahṛdaya*, must be prepared to receive and experience a set of aesthetic cues in such a way that *rasa* will arise. Contextual markers, not only within a work of art but also its setting in time and space, influence its reception. If the Saccidananda Chapel evokes feelings of revulsion or anger instead of the intended transcendent religious experience, then perhaps the building's religio-political context irreparably impedes the flourishing of *rasa*.

The fact that a work of art evokes certain responses in certain spectators, however, is not all that can be said about it. Culture and its artifacts are modes of discourse. Representations are recycled and redeployed. They make meaning in numerous modes of creativity, struggle, and resistance. Trinh Minh-ha describes exclusionary reifications of culture as "at best no more than a form of reactive defense and at worst, an obsession with the self as holder of rights and property—or, in other words, as owner of the world." She continues,

> In the renewed terrain of struggle and of deterritorialized subjectivities, no moon-lovers can really claim possession of the soft light that illuminates towns, villages, forests, and fields. . . . The one moon is seen in all waters; and the many-one moon is enjoyed or bawled at on a quiet night by people everywhere—possessors and dispossessed.[6]

A postmodern comparative theology rejects ahistorical, reductive, and unimaginative cultural essentialisms that claim to own the moon, or that fix form and language in time and place. For the purposes of comparison with Abhinavagupta's aesthetic theory, therefore, my inquiry is not about the validity of inculturation in general or of the NBCLC's work in particular but about the character, evocation, and implications of the peaceful sentiment. I invite the reader to adopt the position of the *sahṛdaya* and become momentarily absorbed in Sahi's vision of religious peace.

Śānta in a New Key

Peace (*śānta*) receives sustained attention in the writings of the NBCLC's founder and first director, D. S. Amalorpavadass (also known as Swami

Amalorananda). Dressed in the ochre robes of the *sannyāsin*, Amalorpavadass also served as the guru-*sannyāsin* of the Anjali Ashram in Mysore. The director expresses a metaphysical vision of union in which the peace of "integration and interiorization" is the goal of Asian Christianity.[7] His approach to inculturation draws heavily on the wisdom (*jñāna*) ideal of Hindu philosophical schools, the union of *ātman* with *brahman*, and the goal of interior peace.

Amalorpavadass' last speech before his death offers a summary of the principles that governed the early period of the NBCLC's ministry. He begins the speech with the Gāyatrī Mantra and ends it with the Śāntiḥ Mantra (peace mantra),[8] both of which are used in the Mass for India at the Centre.[9] In his concluding remarks, he states,

> The sadhana [practice] which will cause an experience of integration at an emotional level, which will spring up from our depth and permeate our whole person, this entire assembly, and the whole universe is the chanting of the santi mantra. Thereby we shall send vibrations of peace to all and everything, and in him we shall also receive the peace of everything and everybody.[10]

The liberation (*mokṣa*) that accompanies the sentiment of peace begins on the interior or "emotional level" for persons with a discipline of meditation, who then extend goodwill to all people.[11]

Amalorpavadass denies that this contemplative spirituality is "evasive and escapist" and insists that social justice (*dharma*) flows from interior integration.[12] Nevertheless, he opines that liberation movements that concentrate on systemic, institutional, or economic oppression miss the essential point of liberation: that "inner freedom can be affected and lost only by ourselves."[13] His emphasis upon the transcendent, universal, and unitive nature of religious and aesthetic experience potentially ignores embodied and socially situated particularities. Sahi's work wrestles with this tension.

Sahi worked closely with the NBCLC in its early years, and his family owned a residence adjacent to it. The art he generated for the Centre retains the primacy of the peaceful religious sentiment at the same time as it addresses today's ecological and social concerns. Sahi concludes his artistic autobiography, *Stepping Stones*, with a reflection on the centrality of *śānta* in this work:

> I tried to express [humanity's] longing to live in peace and harmony with creation. Ultimately I feel that Christian art aspires to a new heaven and

> a new earth. The theme of Peace is a central theme of Christ oriented art—not just a passive peace, but a creative dynamic peace, which hopes for the restoration of all things in Jesus, in whose body, which is the real and spiritual Church, all creation is bound together.[14]

In this statement, we begin to hear the theme of *śānta* in a new key. Peace is the quintessential religious longing, but it is not solely an *alaukika*, otherworldly affair. This peace cannot come at the expense of relations with material creation and the people around us.

Sahi's work within an Indian aesthetic, informed by his training in both England and India, evinces a concern for the spiritual dimensions of art in relation to the earth. He says that "what has attracted [him] to Hinduism has not been its metaphysical speculations, but rather a sense that this religion has arisen slowly and organically out of a long experience of the physical realities of India."[15] He calls upon on the Indian understanding of *dhvani* to draw together the internal and external aspects of religious experience:

> Where I feel that Indian aesthetics could contribute to a proper theology of art, is by its understanding of *Dhvani*, or resonance. . . . Faith is not just something inward looking, it is a new way of looking at the external world, a way of seeing it as a "sign" or resonance of a spiritual world beyond.[16]

Rather than transcending the world of experience, art and faith imbue that world with significance. The bodies of the art form, of the dancer, and of scripture suggest more than themselves, even as their feet are planted in the material realm.

For Sahi, art's prophetic role lies in its ability to bring together two main features of religion in India: movement or activity (dance, pilgrimage, procession) and inner transformation (calm contemplation, yoga). Elijah on the mountain, listening to God as a still, small voice (I Kings 9:12), is the exemplary prophet of *śānta* in the Bible. Sahi writes, "The prophet, however, was not only the inspired dancer, he was also the man of deep inner searchings. He was a man who went into himself to try and find in the cave of his own heart the image of God . . . and find his rest in Him."[17] In this key, the peaceful sentiment resists some of the critiques leveled against it in the previous chapter.

Art in the Ashram

The Christian ashram movement in India exercised profound influence on Sahi's aesthetic. In 1963 he met Fr. Bede Griffiths, the founder of the

Kurisumala ashram in Kerala, who became a guru figure for him. Griffiths, who was in contact with disciples of Coomaraswamy who had founded a small community of artists in England, encouraged the idea of founding a center for Christian art and contemplation in India.[18] Other Christian ashrams devoted to the arts already existed, such as the Gyan Ashram, founded by Fr. George Proksh for Christians to study dance, music, and singing; and Snehasadan, founded by Fr. Matthew Lederle for dialogue and the study of Indian culture. Sahi established his art ashram outside Bangalore in 1983. Throughout the years, the ashram has hosted the "Indian School of Art for Peace" (INSCAPE), served as a retreat center, and become the primary residence for various artists.

The word "ashram" carries within it a reference to the four stages of life (*āśrama*s) for males within caste Hinduism, and its contemplative focus has firm roots in brahmanical institutions. Hindu texts speak about the ashrams of Hindu sages, such as the forest retreat of Valmiki where Rāma stayed during his exile. This communal way of life was resurrected by the Hindu reform movements of the nineteenth and twentieth centuries. Figures such as Keshub Chander Sen, Debendranath Tagore, Sri Aurobindo, and, later, Mohandas K. Gandhi treated the ashram as a place of learning, hospitality, and healing.

For Sahi, residence in such a community depends on neither religion, nor caste, nor celibacy. He sees the ashram as "an inspiration for the renewal of Indian society by offering a model of selfless service to the community and a willingness to sacrifice all personal ambition in order that the whole society might find a new sense of purpose."[19] He follows the Hindu reformers in redefining the ashram as a place where people of all vocations can engage in a spiritual search and establish a new order (*rām rājya*) set apart from the values of worldly society.[20]

Art is the central spiritual practice (*yoga*) in Sahi's ashram. Citing Coomaraswamy's suggestion that "every form of art is a yogic Sadhana, or spiritual search," Sahi describes art as a process of incarnation, the birth of Christ as a child in the heart.[21] He views icons, mandalas, and Hesychastic prayer as training for a new way of seeing that goes beyond all images, a "yoga of the heart."[22] Through art, he explores archetypal images such as the cosmic cross, the snake, and the guru or friend who resides at the center of the heart. Art can probe the mystery of the relation between unity and duality and open the "third eye" of extraordinary perception. In one striking application of this theory, he depicts the stations of the cross as a series of yogic postures (*āsana*s) that foster the goal of *śānta*: "The function of the image then will be to lead the human being inwards and to help in the establishment of a quietness in his heart."[23] Sahi views this yoga as a process that is open to all.

On Christian Peace

The Saccidananda Chapel that Sahi designed for the NBCLC invites calm contemplation. An element of verticality is inscribed in the central pillar's ascending system of the chakras, and iron window grates depict persons seated in meditation and other symbols from India's religious traditions. The chapel's invitation to contemplation has not, however, always been accepted; and the theological and sociological obstacles to the search for distinctly Indian modes of expressing Christianity have come to the fore in controversy over the building.[24] Sahi takes up three main objections to the chapel, each of which bears upon *śānta*'s place in the Christian life.

First of all, Indian Christians sometimes view yogic concepts and practices as theologically dangerous. They detect a world-denying Gnostic mysticism in the focus on interiority and contemplation. Because of such suspicions, Protestant ashrams in India have focused on social action and service (*karma yoga*) rather than meditation (*dhyāna yoga*). Sahi's ashram leans toward the meditative ideals of earlier Catholic ashrams, and his response to Christian fears arises out of the experience of meditation. For example, the process of drawing and contemplating geometric designs called mandalas is a standard meditation technique in India, but Sahi experienced anxiety as well as external criticism when he began to work with them. He reflects, "[T]he Mandala should really be a symbol of peace and integration, and not of conflict and fear, as I seemed to experience."[25] Rather than abandon the practice, however, he delved more deeply into Christian contemplative practices. He rediscovered the Jesus Prayer alongside other practices based in India such as *nam jap* (repetitive utterance of divine names), to practice in conjunction with mandalas for a calming effect.

A second objection is that the formal texts and institutions of yoga are immersed in upper-caste, Sanskritic culture. Dalits excluded from caste Hinduism have been loath to embrace the signposts of its culture. Contemplative practices also demand respite unavailable amid hard labor. Sahi acknowledges that virtually none of the modern Hindu contemplative monks have come from tribal or low-caste backgrounds. He counters, however, that the roots of yoga and tantra likely lie in aboriginal shamanistic practices and that the intent of *sannyāsa*, the renouncer stage of life, is to "go beyond caste."[26] For him, these symbols speak to the Indian cultural situation to challenge rather than perpetuate caste hierarchies. His work has increasingly focused on tribal forms and mythologies, as evidenced by the open air stage erected just outside the Saccidananda Chapel (more on this in part III). Its mosaic background depicts tribal origins myths and the dancing of tribal women, and its position next to the chapel emphasizes the multivocality of Indian culture.[27]

Sahi often returns to archetypal images such as the square, the tree, and the elements, forms he sees as universal and familiar to all cultures. The central pillar in the chapel is not only a yogic body. It is also an *axis mundi*, connecting earth and heaven, representing both the body (the chakras) and the elements of earth, water, fire, air, and space. Sahi writes of a "cosmic covenant," whereby Christians can use "natural symbols while investing them with a new meaning . . . stressing the new dimension which Christianity has discovered in these age-old signs."[28] In a novel way, the chapel echoes the idea that *rasa* is shared or generalized (*sādhāraṇya*) emotion: It inspires contemplation rooted in the earth and bodily experiences common to all.[29]

Thirdly, Sahi wrestles with the live tension, embedded in architectural forms, between inward religion and religion concerned with social justice. The Hindu temple moves inward, toward the dark womb (*garbha gṛha*) where the image of the deity resides. Although one might view the font of Christian baptism as such a space, the movement in Christianity has been outward: One is born from the waters, Christ is resurrected from the grave. Gothic cathedrals embody principles of height and light, not depth and interiority. Furthermore, the message of Christianity encourages the outward spread of the gospel to all nations and to the poor.[30] Beyond a view that seeks peace solely as an unwavering inner calm, the Bible envisions "peace in its fullness when God blesses the righteous . . ., protects the orphans and the poor, when all of them—the whole people—'conquer the land'. And this leads us to the meditation on the Earth, by which is the land given to all of us by God."[31]

The Saccidananda Chapel refuses to separate the inward and outward movements into what Sahi calls "an unnecessary polarization . . . of contemplation from action that is totally un-Christian."[32] Especially in the original design, the structure joins the vertical and the horizontal as well as interior and exterior dimensions. The main area was to be not an enclosed structure but an open-pillared assembly hall (*maṇḍapa*) on the plan of the Vedic fire altar. An open horizontal space would suit the Indian climate; as in the courtyards of many temples, it would welcome pilgrims to gather freely and offer a place to celebrate festivals and dance.[33] Instead of the window grilles depicting parallels between Hindu and Christian themes, which overdetermine the meaning of the space, Sahi would have embedded symbols in the pillars "representing the evolution of nature towards Christ" so that the "temple" would be "a symbol of nature striving towards the Incarnation."[34]

Sahi's vision of art as contemplation has strong affinities with both Abhinavagupta and Coomaraswamy. He responds directly to the critiques of the transcendent peaceful sentiment that have dogged this vision. For him, art is a discipline not only of divine contemplation but of seeing the human condition. The canons of Indian aesthetics dictate that nothing ugly or imperfect may be depicted, but much in the human condition thwarts the blissful repose of *śānta* or, indeed, of any *rasa*.[35] Life is cruciform; and the cross, an instrument of torture and cruel death, is the central Christian symbol. If the canons are correct, then the Christian attention to suffering stands as a major obstacle to *śānta*.

Christianity and Suffering in Art

The cross bears similarities to other archetypal symbols: the pillar, the *axis mundi*, the lamp, and the tree; but most fundamentally, the cross stands as a reminder of human injustice and suffering.[36] As Sahi wrestles with its significance for Christian art, he calls upon the tradition's central theological categories: incarnation, crucifixion, and resurrection.

For Sahi, the task of the Christian artist is bound up with the incarnation. Art moves from spirit into the material realm in particular ways amid history and diverse cultures. The Word becomes flesh in the specificity of a first-century Palestinian Jewish man. Christ continues to meet the church in the sacraments, in encounters with those who bear his image, and in art. Sahi views creation, revelation, and incarnation as ongoing realities; the artist is a "priest" with a mediating role that embodies grace in particular times and places.[37] Regardless of the history of the term, this is the meaning of inculturation as well: "[I]ncarnation is returning to the roots of a people's history." For groups that have been dominated culturally and politically, this rediscovery can be painful, especially if "they have . . . been taught to despise [it] as superstitious, primitive, [or] ugly."[38] Sahi describes Christ as a pilgrim who visits "all nations and all cultures as a new dimension of His Incarnation" to share their "joys and sorrows."[39] God's assumption of the human condition entails participation in its struggles.

Incarnation leads to crucifixion. Amid the pulls of the glorification of suffering on the one hand, and the sentimentalism of much Christian art on the other, Sahi contemplates the best way to depict the cross. He admits, "For me the theme of the Cross has always been a difficult one."[40] Several Indian images help him explore the crucifixion: the *sannyāsin*, who suffers through ascetic renunciation; the yogi, whose body is transformed through physical strain; or the cross of light, which grants new vision.[41] The cosmic significance of redemption appears in Sahi's treatment of the beams of the cross as the warp and woof of the cosmos, upon which the primal person (*puruṣa*) is sacrificed at the time of creation. Here, the cross becomes a mandala at the foundation of the church, the cosmic temple.[42] In other depictions of the cross as a tree, Christ's suffering entwines with nature's suffering and redemption.[43]

Perhaps the most controversial of Sahi's crucifixion scenes depict Christ as Lord of the Dance (*nāṭarāja*), with the cross as a moment in the dance of death and life.

> Some have felt scandalized by this figure of the dancing figure of Jesus upon the tree of life. Perhaps the objection could be made that by representing Christ on the Cross as a dancer our recognition of his suffering might be minimized, and also the historical reality of his Passion would become less credible, for after all the torture and death of the Jesus of history was a horrible, human fact, which such a symbolic or mythological rendering might tend to obscure.[44]

Sahi has been accused of Christological heresy on both sides: that he downplays Christ's humanity in a Docetist stance toward suffering, and that he impugns Christ's divinity by making him subject to physical passions. For Sahi, however, the divine dancer reveals the glory and joy (*ānanda*) of God, inviting people into the dance of liberation.[45] Christ enters into solidarity with those who suffer, but Christianity does not find glory in suffering as such. "Here lies the theological secret of the Cross," he writes, "fusing both the Passion and the Resurrection[,] the suffering and the joy."[46] Christ dances the step that transgresses the space between death and life. (Because of its powerful imagery of stepping across religious boundaries through aesthetic experience, one of Sahi's *Nāṭarāja* paintings, "Lord of the Dance as the Risen Christ," adorns the cover of this book.)

The resurrection, for Sahi, becomes a way to comprehend the suffering of Christ and of all of humanity. Sahi explores the Garden of Gethsemane and the Garden of the Resurrection as "two aspects of the same ashrama." Here, the peaceful bliss (*śānta*) of the resurrection must be infused with the *rasa* of compassion (*karuṇa*).

> Christ, meditating alone in the garden of olive trees, with his disciples near at hand asleep, confused and worn out, experienced through His compassion *their* agony as His own agony, *their* confusion as part of His own self awareness. This was his *karuna*; not just pity, but empathy; that is, he identified himself with the confusion of all creation, down to the last insentient blade of grass. . . . This is the *karuna*, or compassion of the enlightened one, that He forgoes his own liberation until all are liberated.[47]

It is difficult to maintain the resurrection as a mode of consciousness. Perhaps it comes as a flash of insight that soon fades. It resists codification in dogma: "How to say, without blaspheming, that the suffering of the Lord is also His Joy?"[48]

For Sahi, the *śānta* of Christianity is a convergence of opposites that holds the cross and resurrection together. The incarnation drives toward crucifixion but also toward resurrection. Something more lies beyond the suffering on the road. Aesthetic experience offers a taste of this "something more" that Sahi calls the resurrected body:

> This hope of the Resurrection of the body gives us a way of understanding aesthetics in a new light. In this belief we see that the world available to our senses is not just simply gross and external, but is essentially linked to the life of the spirit. By the Resurrection of the body we understand that the physical senses can themselves be entrances to the spiritual. In our Indian tradition we speak of *ananda*, or bliss. This religious joy is beyond mere speculation—it is a living experience of truth which includes the aesthetic. In our joy in the aesthetic we have a glimpse of this spiritual joy, which, though it is infinitely greater than the kind of joy which we can experience with our senses, is nevertheless mirrored, or partly experienced, by those who experience the joy of what is beautiful. Art points to the realization of this joy. In that sense also the category of beauty which art testifies to is the hope of a Resurrected body.[49]

For this Christian artist and theologian, as for the tradition of Indian aesthetics from Abhinavagupta to Coomaraswamy, art tends toward spiritual bliss. Yet art evokes this bliss not by transcending the world of everyday joy and sorrow but by journeying with the incarnate, crucified, and resurrected Lord toward a liberation that is, for all its concreteness, nevertheless extraordinary (*alaukika*).

Comparison

The assertion that *rasa* is *alaukika* in Indian aesthetics highlights what is so transporting about a good novel, a riveting film, or an exquisitely rendered string quartet. The experience of art uniquely moves us out of ourselves. We momentarily lose sight of our own pain and desire. We are absorbed, enraptured. It is bliss.

Claims for the non-worldly nature of aesthetic experience are paradoxical because of art's grounding in sense experience. Color, sound, texture, form, and movement point beyond themselves, but to forget about the idea's grounding in the material realm is to risk alienation from worldly realities that should not be forgotten. This aestheticizing tendency threatens to minimize suffering—as in the prettified crucifixion scenes that appall Sahi or in "big picture" theodicies that posit that a little evil here and there is like the shadow in a painting that makes it all the more beautiful. Too much emphasis on the *alaukika* can be ethically compromising.

An Indian tradition stretching from Abhinavagupta through Coomaraswamy has emphasized *śānta*, the peaceful sentiment of the accomplished yogi absorbed in the Absolute, as the ultimate aesthetic experience. All *rasa* has the potential to move a person beyond herself into a state of mind that transcends subject-object duality. Because *śānta* is this very state of mind, the other *rasa*s find their culmination in *śānta*. Rekha Jhanji objects to this transcendent ("religious") approach to art criticism because it ignores the experience of the artist and the material condition in which she works. Other theorists take issue with the exceptional status given to *rasa*, pointing out that it is quite rooted in worldly ways of encountering the world.

Abhinavagupta and Sahi each push back at charges of aestheticizing approaches to art forms, but in different ways. Their contexts and approaches contain distinctive contributions to a contemporary theology of religious emotions.

I have argued that Abhinavagupta's Kashmir Śaivism counters the charge that he simply wants art to launch the spectator into undifferentiated union with divine consciousness. Rather, for the tantric practitioner, aesthetic experience enters into a program of training to view the world in all of its many shades of unity and diversity. The taste of the divine that one receives through the transporting nature of art is a taste that remains on the palate, as it were, to condition ordinary experiences of duality.

Sahi resists the aestheticizing tendency even more vigorously, even as he retains the priority of *śānta*. His understanding of the function of the ashram in society refuses to separate contemplation from social concern and action. His art operates under the incarnational principle that divinity encounters the world in embodied forms. He boldly asserts the religious significance of art under this doctrinal rubric: "God is incarnated not only in the person of the historical Jesus but through the built forms where the divine presence continues to inspire devotion, leading individual worshippers to an experience of the continuing intervention of the divine within human cultures."[50] The material is an avenue for divine-human encounter, for the incarnation of the palpable presence of God.

Here, Sahi speaks back to *rasa* theory by exploring, as an artist, the sensory aspects that evoke it. He writes of "sacramentalizing the body" through architecture.

> The church building reflects not only an attitude towards the body but also serves the process of sacramentalizing the body. The church building is even understood as the body of Christ. The built form helps the worshipper to discover a new dimension of being present in the body and ultimately finding the Lord enshrined within the "cave of the heart." All sacred architecture ultimately points back to the incarnation of God into the physical being of the worshiper. In a way, the building serves as a door through which divine reality is experienced as entering first into the cosmos, and then through the cosmos and nature as we experience it with our bodily senses into the very heart and physical self-awareness of the worshipper. The external form of the building, its use of materials, its sacralizing of space and time, intensifies the senses of the worshipper, so that ultimately God is experienced as incarnated into the life and physical being of the worshipper.[51]

I quote at length to show the many bodily layers that can be present in a theological aesthetic that tends toward the peaceful sentiment. The art form is homologous with both the body of the spectator and the divine body of Christ. Participation in one becomes participation in all, and Christ is incarnated once again in the believer.

Embodied apprehension of divine consciousness is possible in Abhinavagupta's tantric context, yet he does not draw it out in his works of literary theory. In contrast to critics who would exclude ultimate ends from the work the sensory can accomplish, Sahi treats incarnation and redemption as ultimate ends *and* as worldly matters. As he puts it, "True religion is not something which affects the mind or the spirit alone. The body, and all that the body implies in the sense of physical awareness and the use of the senses, also constitutes an essential aspect of being human and fully alive."[52]

Sahi does important comparative theological work in his Indian context, as strands of yogic, Hindu, and Buddhist thought inform his Christian theology. His apprehension of the importance of *śānta* recognizes in the moment of nonduality a redemptive bliss (*ānanda*) that can be tasted in and through art. He risks painting the Lord of the Dance, even on the cross, for Christ is not limited to his suffering. Sahi will not minimize the reality of human suffering, but for him redemption must ultimately move toward joy.

In this risky paradox, Sahi might draw even more deeply on Abhinavagupta's *rasa* theory. Sahi admits to being more interested in the theory of *dhvani*, poetic resonance, than in *rasa per se*.[53] His emphasis makes perfect sense, for the aural metaphor of resonance not only points to the spectator's role as interpreter but also roots the artist's thinking on art and theology in the physical senses. It is in keeping with his incarnational focus that Sahi does not emphasize *rasa* as non-worldly (*alaukika*). What is more worldly (*laukika*) than incarnation? Yet if the incarnate Christ is divine as well as human, and if divinity and humanity are transcendent as well as immanent, a constructive theology of *rasa* may also ask what a taste of Christ's divinity contributes to aesthetic experience.

Abhinavagupta's analysis of the ways that *rasa* is *alaukika* offer some hints for a constructive theology of *rasa*. In *rasa*, we feel emotion in a unique way. The analogy with mystic wonder implies that there is something akin to the redeemed state in aesthetic experience. Abhinavagupta asserts that *rasa*s differ from ordinary emotions (*sthāyibhāva*s) because *rasa*s are emotions relished in their pure state. Could this purity be a foretaste of passions redeemed, a vision of heaven where humanity does not rise above intense emotions but experiences them in their vividness and complexity like never before? Our egoism and unhealthy attachments often cloud our day-to-day emotional judgments. We cannot savor another's joy because of our jealousy and resentment; we cannot grieve another's loss because other matters clamor for our attention. In the redeemed state, which we begin to inhabit in this world, emotional depth and color shines like a newly polished jewel.[54]

In this vision of redemption, even fear and anger have the fullness of bliss—a bliss born of the generalization or universalization (*sādhāranīkaraṇa*) that gets the ego out of the way. Christ incarnated this egoless relation to the world around him, but this did not entail a passionless existence. He drove out the moneychangers in righteous anger, he feared the human cruelty that would ultimately put him to death, and he grieved the suffering he saw when he surveyed Jerusalem. Sahi's exploration of elements, vegetation, and the seasons evokes a rasic universality as well: We all share the tactile experiences of the natural world, and we share a common ecological plight. *Śānta* encompasses redemption on all planes; and the embodied, human, ecological element of fulfilled longing can be tasted as belonging to us all.

Abhinavagupta insists that *rasa*s are evoked in a unique way, not directly through ordinary causes that prompt our reaction but indirectly, through particular means (excitants, indicators, etc.). In this sense, art is sacramental, a means of grace. The material presentation of wood, paint, cloth, bodies, sound, and light becomes a "cause" (*vibhāva*) that resonates through multi-tiered "effects" (*anubhāvas*) in body, soul, and spirit. The wonder and repose of contemplation offers a foretaste of the unfettered contemplation of the divine.

When *rasa* as a modality of feeling takes over, the usual divisions between this world and the next, between ethics and aesthetics, and between body and soul cease to function in their ordinary way. Bambang Sugiharto explains how *rasa* as a way of knowing structures Javanese mentality. This "multi-layered concept of *rasa*" lacks exact Western parallels:

> [*R*]*asa* in the sense of the mysterious ultimate inner connection with the Divine and even as the vehicle of life (in the form of male and female semen) can hardly be found in the tradition of western philosophy. While it may sound promising to elaborate, the problem with the latter meanings of *rasa* is that in such [a] profound level of human existence verbal-conceptual discourse does not play the most important role any longer. It may serve to lead one's consciousness towards more profound levels of understanding, yet the understanding itself, that is, the enlightenment, is achieved not by the discursive mode. It is achieved, instead, through concrete practices and exercises. What is gained is not so much knowledge as *gnosis*.[55]

The person who savors *rasa* does not only relish beauty internally but also refines her emotions, senses, and actions in the world. The peaceful sentiment informs "concrete practices and exercises" in response to the world of suffering.

What we experience in aesthetic bliss is not the soul devoid of characteristics but the commonality of human and ecological concern. Saccidananda Chapel both ascends toward heaven and roots the divine-human encounter in the elements of this earth and in the vital centers of the body. *Śānta* becomes a foretaste of a liberation that enfolds all of material existence, a veritable "touch of transcendence."[56]

In the peaceful sentiment, *rasāsvada* is akin to *brahmāsvāda*. The taste of divinity in aesthetic experience is a phenomenon that both engages the senses and reaches beyond them. We have tested to what extent this "non-worldly" experience must transport us away from this world and discovered that aesthetics need not be aestheticizing. Art can attend to the reality of suffering. We engage this matter in another register in the next section: If we experience God as love, what becomes of the eroticism of human bodies?

PART II

Love

It is the festival day of Holi in Vrindavan, the dusty North Indian village that is the locus of the Hindu god Kṛṣṇa's childhood sojourn on earth. The stage of the Jai Singh Ghera ashram is decked in red, gold, and green garlands and flowers for the performance of the *rāsa līlā*. To the tune of a devotional hymn, the curtain rises to reveal two actors, both boys, dressed as Kṛṣṇa and Rādhā, the divine lovers. Additional boys appear, dressed in saris as the *gopī* cowherd women, the supporting cast for the divine love story. They circle lamps to honor the couple, much as a priest would do before temple images.

The ensuing drama plays out in a series of scriptural episodes that offer the audience access to Kṛṣṇa's famous boyhood exploits. He steals butter, teases young women, and generally wins the hearts of all the denizens of Vrindavan. The performance culminates in a dance, in which the charming young Kṛṣṇa dances with the *gopī*s in a great circle. Ankle bells jingle in time with their rhythmic steps. Kṛṣṇa, wearing a fan of peacock feathers, steals the show with a sequence of rapid spins upon his knees.

At various moments in the dance, Kṛṣṇa and Rādhā pause to pose together in stylized *jhanki* poses. He holds his iconic flute; she entwines her arms with his. The audience contemplates the posed tableau as if it were a sacred icon. Some take photographs. Devotional love (*bhakti rasa*) swells in their hearts as they imaginatively enter the drama.[1]

3 The *Rasa* of Love Incarnate

The followers of the medieval *bhakti* saint Caitanya, known as the Gauḍīya Vaiṣṇavas, cultivate love for Kṛṣṇa by contemplating scenes from his life. Among the favorite scenes for contemplation are the five chapters of the Bhāgavata Purāṇa that narrate the story of the *rāsa līlā*, the dance Kṛṣṇa performs with his beloved *gopīs*. In this celebrated passage, Kṛṣṇa calls the cowmaidens to him with the sound of his flute. They abruptly leave home in the middle of their activities (getting dressed, applying makeup, milking cows, nursing babies) to go to him. After enjoying themselves with him for a while, the women's pride in their good fortune causes Kṛṣṇa to disappear. Disconsolate, they roam the forest looking for him. Their minds become so absorbed with him that they begin to imitate his appearance and actions, and they enact scenes from his childhood. They discover that he has gone off with one favored lover (the Gauḍīya Vaiṣṇavas later identify her as Rādhā), but he leaves her as well. As the women mourn his absence, he suddenly reappears. They dance a circle dance in which Kṛṣṇa multiplies himself so that each woman believes she is dancing with him alone.

This contemplative tradition has spun off a style of drama, called *rāsa līlā*, that generates devotional sentiment through depictions of these stories. The drama consists of two parts: the *rāsa*, reenacting the round dance, and the *līlā*, a play depicting a scene from Kṛṣṇa's early life in Vraja, the part of north India along the banks of the Yamuna River that includes the towns of Vrindavan and Mathura. The *rāsa līlā* is not to be confused with *rasa*, aesthetic emotion, although the two inevitably become entwined in the experience of the devotee. As one scholar observes,

> Often during a *līlā* the devotees are visibly affected, expressing their emotional participation in the events being enacted by laughing, shouting

> formulas of praise, thrusting their right arms upwards in moments of joy, or weeping openly during scenes of separation. In a performance of the *līlā* representing Yaśodā's grief at Kṛṣṇa's departure for Mathurā, . . . the emotional response of the audience grew so intense that the *līlā* was somewhat abruptly cut short. Afterwards I was informed that the *gosvāmī* presiding over the occasion feared that the devotees watching the *līlā*, who had been weeping profusely throughout, would not be able to bear any more grief. It is such an experience of total absorption in the eternal *līlā* of Kṛṣṇa, of complete self-forgetfulness through communal participation in intense emotions toward the Lord like those expressed on the stage, that is the cherished goal of this form of Kṛṣṇa devotion.[2]

Such dramas place demands on spectators to become ideal viewers (*sahṛdaya*s) through a well-trained religious imagination that savors the refinement of the erotic sentiment (*śṛṅgāra-rasa*) embodied in Kṛṣṇa and Rādhā.

Viewing the staged plays in Vrindavan is only one way that Gauḍīya Vaiṣṇavas participate in Kṛṣṇa's eternal play. The *gopīs*' imitation of Kṛṣṇa in their lovesick madness provides the example for devotees to imitate the *līlā* (divine sport) of Kṛṣṇa.[3] In the writings of one of Caitanya's principal disciples, Rūpa Gosvāmin, devotees are encouraged imaginatively to inhabit one of the roles in the drama of divine love. Participation in the eternal drama makes devotion come alive in "an aesthetic foretaste of and powerful incentive for further pursuit of [Kṛṣṇa's] world."[4]

As I discuss in the next chapter, the love poetry of the biblical Song of Songs similarly inspired an interior drama for the medieval Christian monastic tradition. As they read the Song, the monks in their all-male community took the stage as the Bride of God. The Cistercian abbot and reformer Bernard of Clairvaux gave one of the most enduring performances.[5] Both the Cistercian and the Gauḍīya Vaiṣṇava traditions encourage practitioners to inhabit scripture in such a way that they imagine themselves as lovers of God. I am not the first to observe these aesthetic and affective resonances. June McDaniel has compared the salvific role of erotic emotion in Gauḍīya Vaiṣṇavism and Catholic mysticism. She notes, "Envisioning the realms of the divine is important in both traditions, involving the spiritual senses and an ascetic way of life."[6] Imagination, emotion, and above all, love, are central to both traditions.

The idea that practitioners must become female in relation to the divine lover expresses much of the sweetness and intimacy that is integral to these devotional and mystical movements. It also creates a potential disjunction within the heterosexually normed or celibate male subject. To what extent should one imitate the female lovers of God? What are the limits of bodily expressions of divine love? What are the implications of these limits for the inclusiveness of the religious community?

Scholarship on these questions has been polarized in various directions. While McDaniel celebrates the interpenetration of the spiritual and physical senses in the Gauḍīya Vaiṣṇava tradition, Sushil Kumar De objects that its aesthetic orientation "borders definitely upon sense-devotion, and leans perceptibly and dangerously towards the erotic passion."[7] As for the Cistercian tradition, some see in Bernard the repression and sublimation of sexual desire: As Stephen Moore writes, "Allegorical exposition of the Song . . . replicates the deadly struggle of male celibacy itself. What must be overcome in either instance is the sexual, the sensual, the fleshly, the female."[8] Others argue vigorously against the idea that "monastic theologians beckon us down a path of unswerving domination of the weak and repression of the body."[9] Bernard and Rūpa are read alternately as repressed or perverse, as overly sensual or the epitome of body-soul integration. Contemporary readers approach their texts with their own models of healthy sexuality, which are not, of course, the categories of the medieval traditions. A focused comparison will delve into the texts' ambivalences surrounding the body, the senses, and the feminine, with a view toward a constructive retrieval of the notion of the spiritual senses.

Reading Bernard of Clairvaux side-by-side with Rūpa Gosvāmin and his followers alerts us to the discursive dynamics surrounding the role of the body in each tradition. Comparison draws out the complexity of the mechanisms each uses to situate the devotee's body within the erotic narrative of scripture. Each theologian expresses ambivalence about the relation of the devotee's body to the eroticism of scripture. Attending to their thought can help us to locate these devotional bodies within a matrix of scripture, narrative, imagination, and contemplative practice. Ligatures between the *experiential* and *exegetical* notions of the spiritual senses will be central to this analysis. I will argue that traditional claims about the allegorical nature of the divine-human love relationship attenuate the liberative social potential of a devotion centered on the sentiment of love.

The first section of this book investigated a tradition of art criticism, stretching from Abhinavagupta to Coomaraswamy to Sahi, which opened a door to viewing religious experience in aesthetic terms. Gauḍīya Vaiṣṇava theologians accepted this invitation long ago and developed their theology with direct reference to *rasa* theory. In this chapter, I first consider the avenues for participation (one meaning of *bhakti*, usually translated as devotion) created by the use of this theory, as well as the Gauḍīya Vaiṣṇava tradition's caution regarding the appropriateness (*aucitya*) of bodily imitation of the divine drama of love. In the next chapter, I return for comparison to Bernard of Clairvaux's Christian exegesis of the biblical love poem, the Song of Songs.

For the Love of Krsna

In the Gauḍīya Vaiṣṇava tradition, Kṛṣṇa does not appear as the supreme, awe-inspiring deity that he is in the Bhagavad Gītā. Although he *is* the supreme deity, he does not desire the respectful worship due to a sovereign Lord. Instead, he longs for the intimacy of human love. For this reason, he veils his full majesty from human beings so that he can live among them as a child, a friend, or a charming lover. In one famous scriptural episode, his foster mother Yaśodā, suspecting he has been eating dirt, demands that he open his mouth. In the mouth of that child, she gains a paralyzing glimpse of his totality. Kṛṣṇa graciously causes her to forget so that she can again coddle him as her baby (*BhP* 10.8.32–45).[10] This motherly love is tender and sweet, but for the Gauḍīya Vaiṣṇava community, the highest love of the devotee for God is embodied by Kṛṣṇa and his lover Rādhā.

The origins of this community lie with the ecstatic devotee of Kṛṣṇa, Caitanya (1486–1533), who has been described in aesthetic terms as "*rasarāja* and *mahābhāva* . . . in one *rūpa*." In other words, Caitanya's followers came to view him as the appearance of Kṛṣṇa, the King of Rasa (*rasarāja*), and Rādhā, the Supreme Emotion (*mahābhāva*), united in one body.[11] Kṛṣṇa wanted to know, from the inside, the love experienced by Rādhā, his favorite *gopī* lover in Vrindavan, and so Kṛṣṇa took on the form of Caitanya in order to savor the erotic sentiment (*śṛṅgāra*) in full.[12] Caitanya showed human beings how to savor this love as well. He inspired the rediscovery of the sacred places of Vrindavan that now grant devotees access to the eternal divine *līlā*. They, too, can participate in the divine realm by cultivating the emotions of its inhabitants. *Rasa* thus links the temporal and the eternal realms.[13]

Caitanya attracted a large following in Bengal, including five disciples known as the Gosvāmins, who left their posts in the Muslim court at Gauḍa to join him. (Various names for the movement, including Gauḍīya

Vaiṣṇavism and Bengal Vaiṣṇavism, derive from this geographical origin). Caitanya charged the Gosvāmins to go to Vrindavan to find the sites of Kṛṣṇa's *līlā* and resuscitate these places as centers of devotion. These erudite men were also given the task of elaborating the theology and practice of the movement. Rūpa Gosvāmin was the systematic theologian of the group.

Rūpa defines the highest devotion (*bhakti*) as "constant service to Kṛṣṇa, done suitably, without a wish for anything else, unimpeded by the religious goals of knowledge (*jñāna*) and proper action (*karma*)" (*BhRS* 1.1.11).[14] This definition sets the path of devotion apart from other approaches to liberation—*karma*, the path of right action (especially sacrifice), and *jñāna*, the path of philosophical insight. It questions the aim of liberation (*mokṣa*), which in prominent Indian systems denotes freedom from the cycle of rebirth and union with the Absolute. By contrast, *bhakti*, the loving service of the Lord, is its own goal (*BhRS* 1.1.13–15). One seeks neither one's own pleasure (*bhukti*) nor liberation (*mukti*), but *bhakti*. Rather than merging into God, one desires to remain separate so as to serve God in this and future lives.

Rūpa defines two basic practices or paths (*sādhanas*) toward building a foundation of devotional emotion (*bhāva*). The first, *vaidhī bhakti*, is impelled by scriptural injunction and characterized by sixty-four practices that include initiation by a guru, living in sacred places, and replacing ordinary pleasures with sensory experiences related to devotion. Physical stimuli such as reciting hymns, eating sacred food, smelling the incense used in worship, touching and gazing upon the divine image, and listening to stories about Kṛṣṇa (*BhRS* 1.2.6, 74–92) aim for "a bodily experience of a transcendent reality."[15]

Rūpa devotes the majority of the *BhRS* to describing the second path, *rāgānugā bhakti*, in which a devotee is impelled by passion (*rāgā*) to imitate the devotion of the residents of Vraja through a particular emotional relationship such as that of Kṛṣṇa's parents or lovers (*BhRS* 1.2.270–273). This path has three stages. First, the devotee's true spiritual identity is uncovered through the practices of *vaidhī bhakti*. The devotee then advances to a second stage, *bhāva bhakti*, in which the sprout of the foundational emotion (*sthāyibhāva*) of that relationship is cultivated. When this emotion fully flowers, he or she enters the highest experience, known as *prema bhakti* (*BhRS* 1.3.2, 1.4.1).[16]

Many scholarly commentators have noted a positive view of the senses in the tradition stretching from the Sanskrit dance-drama manuals to their application in Gauḍīya Vaiṣṇava spirituality. The *Nāṭya Śāstra* evinces the capacity of the arts to draw together all aspects of life—physical, psychic, ethical, and spiritual—through the refinement of the senses. Susan Schwartz, one of the definitive scholars of *rasa* in the West, maintains that this is not a tradition that denigrates sensuality and sexuality. Rather, "the very senses responsible for the deception [of *māyā*] may be used to surmount it. . . . Artistic experience *through* the body may enable the attainment of the highest spiritual goals."[17]

The use of the body to achieve spiritual goals is at the center of Kṛṣṇa's worship (*bhakti*), which Rūpa defines as "service with the senses to the Lord of the senses" (*BhRS* 1.1.12).[18] In contrast to ascetic paths that encourage the withdrawal or transcendence of the senses, Rūpa's sensory theory includes such moments within the aesthetic framework of the *rasa sūtra*. For example, realization of a vision of Kṛṣṇa may result in a variety of involuntary physical reactions, including disinterest in sensory objects, stupefaction, or the temporary loss of the senses (*BhRS* 1.3.30–31; 2.3.24; 2.4.92–98). These, too, are counted among the sensory responses to sensory stimuli, alongside trembling, goose bumps, and tears. The use of the senses to open oneself to such extraordinary experiences is the norm. The sweet sounds of Kṛṣṇa's flute, his extraordinary fragrance, and the beauty of Vrindavan's forest groves awaken physical responses of love. In worship, sensory experiences such as the smell of incense and flower garlands are said to purify the senses and release the devotee from the bondage of sins (*BhRS* 1.2.163–164).

Despite these vivid physical means to cultivate devotional feeling, Rūpa's definition of *bhakti* contains the seeds of a tendency to distance the devotee from the direct experience of Kṛṣṇa's love. For him, devotion (*bhakti*) should be oriented solely toward the Lord's pleasure and not the devotee's enjoyment (*bhukti*). In order to observe this trajectory, I first lay out Rūpa's aesthetic approach to devotional love and then tease out its implications for the body as developed in Jīva Gosvāmin and other later theologians.

Rūpa's Five-Fold *Rasa* of Divine Love

Gauḍīya Vaiṣṇava scriptures revel in the divine couple's erotic encounters and their mutual longing in separation. Rūpa promotes aesthetic enjoyment of the divine love play by designating religious experience as the ultimate taste of *rasa*. His major work, *Bhaktirasāmṛtasindhu* (*BhRS*), imports categories directly from aesthetic theory to frame his theology, from the excitants, responses, and accompanying emotions to the impediments to *rasa*'s development.

Rūpa accomplishes his task through several modifications to classical aesthetic theory. First, whereas Abhinavagupta prioritizes peace (*śānta rasa*) as paramount in the religious life, Rūpa views all devotional sentiments as varieties of love. Its foundational emotion (*sthāyibhāva*) is affection for Kṛṣṇa (Kṛṣṇa-*rati* or Kṛṣṇa-*prema*). Second, due to the personal nature of *bhakti*, the devotee loses the disinterestedness essential for the ideal spectator (*sahṛdaya*) in the theatre. Kṛṣṇa's playful manifestation in the world invites human beings into intimate loving relation with him, and he, too, enjoys the resulting *rasas*.[19] Devotional emotion is not generalized or abstracted as in Abhinavagupta's principle of *sādhāraṇīkaraṇa*. No longer asked to bracket feelings of "I, me, and mine" that impede the savoring of *rasa* in classical dramatic theory, the devotee cultivates a feeling of "myness" (*mamatā*) in relation to a personal deity. Third, unlike Abhinavagupta, for whom the non-worldly (*alaukika*) nature of aesthetic experience renders aesthetic emotion (*rasa*) discontinuous from ordinary feeling (*bhāva*), Rūpa sees *rasa* as an intensification of the foundational emotion (*bhāva*, *rati*). In modifying *rasa* in this more personal direction, Rūpa weighs in on a debate within aesthetics over the relation of *rasa* to *bhāva*. He comes down on the side of Bhoja, Bhaṭṭa Lollaṭa, and Daṇḍin, all of whom see *rasa* as the intensification or culmination of *bhāva*.[20]

The greater continuity of *rasa* with ordinary emotion in Rūpa's thought offers a non-dichotomous way of viewing emotion. Whitney Sanford therefore advises against translating his use of "*laukika* and *alaukika* . . . as 'profane' and 'sacred'" because of their associations "with western concepts of the relationships between spirit and material." She explains that Vaiṣṇava practitioners experience these designations less as "ontological" than "perspectival," and that any experience of the world can be *alaukika* if related to Kṛṣṇa.[21] The material realm is thus enlivened with Kṛṣṇa's presence through the senses—the experience of hearing of his activities, being in Vraja, and performing divine service—and the exhibition of physical symptoms in the devotee are thus deemed more appropriate than in other aesthetic contexts such as theatre. The aesthetic mode thus enables Rūpa, in many respects, to incorporate the sensory and emotional aspects of devotion into a transcendent religious experience.

Rūpa's major modification to *rasa* theory is to elaborate the aesthetic emotion of love (*śṛṅgāra rasa*) into five subtypes, which he calls *bhakti rasas*.

These five—peaceful love, respectful love, companionable love, parental love, and erotic love—are based on the primary modes of relating to Kṛṣṇa found in scripture.[22] *Bhakti* is a form of love or enjoyment; its root (*bhuj*) connotes participation. Devotees participate in a loving relationship with Kṛṣṇa through these five modalities. The five relationships of devotional love offer increasing levels of intimacy, from a distanced worshipper or a respectful servant, to a friend, parent, or lover. The highest degree of intimacy occurs within the total absorption and self-abandonment of Kṛṣṇa's lovers. Each of these *bhakti rasa*s includes the ones preceding it, so that the *gopī*s and devotees that imitate them experience aspects of all five.

Peaceful love. The implications of Rūpa's modifications of classical aesthetic theory are perhaps most evident in his treatment of *śānta*, which he incorporates as the lowest form of devotional love. The *rasa* of peaceful devotion (*śānta bhakti rasa*) includes many aspects of the traditional *śānta* surveyed in part I. It is the *rasa* of the yogis and all those who pursue liberation (*mokṣa*) through merging with the Absolute. As a form of love, however, it undergoes modifications in Rūpa's theory. Its foundation is not the self (*ātman*) or indifference (*nirveda*) but *śānta-rati*, love in a peaceful modality.[23] Unlike the classical *śānta*, there is a trace of emotion in *bhakti rasa*, a love that makes this relation to Kṛṣṇa more complete than that of the yogis (*BhRS* 3.1.5, 46). Peaceful love relates not to the impersonal *brahman* but to personal forms of Kṛṣṇa considered by Gauḍīya Vaiṣṇavas to be higher than it, such as the awe-inspiring, four-armed Viṣṇu. This form of devotion is also called *aiśvarya*, related to the supreme power and majesty of the Lord. The yogi therefore "moves beyond the realization of the undifferentiated Brahman and the meditative state of objectless consciousness to an encounter with some form of Kṛṣṇa as the object of an astonishing love."[24] Rūpa classifies this emotion under the rubric of "nondistinct" love. Peaceful love is characterized by the cessation of the mind's fluctuations as in yoga, a sense of tranquility, and an absence of "myness" (*mamatā*). This last feature makes the *rasa* of peaceful devotion inferior to the other *bhakti rasa*s, which cultivate personal tastes of love for God in response to his divine play (*BhRS* 2.5.16–22, cf. 3.1).

Respectful love. The devotional sentiment of respect (*prīti* or *dāsya bhakti rasa*) is a slightly more intense and personal mode of love than peaceful devotion. In this mode, devotees consider themselves inferior to Kṛṣṇa, and their love takes the form of honor for a respected elder (2.5.27). Their scriptural models include Kṛṣṇa's attendants, servants, and sons, and other kings who appear later in Kṛṣṇa's life, when he leaves Vraja to become king in Dvārakā. In his childhood, the younger cowherd boys, persons who resort to him for help, and the pantheon of lesser deities also love him with this kind of devotion (*BhRS* 3.2).

Companionable love. Those who savor the *rasa* of companionable devotion (*sakhya* or *preyo bhakti rasa*) enjoy the lack of restraint associated with close friendship (*BhRS* 2.5.30). The scriptural exemplars include the cowherd boys and, later, the fellow warriors who consider themselves Kṛṣṇa's equals. The boys joke and play with him, even as he miraculously saves them from the attacks of his enemies. They assist him in arranging his trysts with his favorite *gopīs* (*BhRS* 3.3). A charming example of the devotion of friendship occurs in a verse cited by Rūpa: "I [Kṛṣṇa] had gone off desirous of seeing the flowering forest. When I returned, those boys—whose hearts are broken from just a moment of separation from me—saw me from a distance, and with their hair standing on end, played a game to see who could run and touch me first" (*BhRS* 2.5.31).

Parental love. *Vatsalya bhakti rasa*, parentally affectionate devotion, derives its name from the relationship of a mother cow to its calf (*vatsa*). It is not limited to Kṛṣṇa's biological parents; in fact, its exemplar is his foster mother Yaśodā. Anyone else, male or female, who feeds and dotes on Kṛṣṇa in his form as an adorable baby becomes a kind of surrogate mother to him.[25] It reverses the hierarchy of age in the *rasa* of respect, and it is the only personal love relationship that does not diminish when unreciprocated (*BhRS* 3.4.79). In the narratives, even when Kṛṣṇa is older, Nanda and Yaśodā only see him as a little baby, and Yaśodā often experiences the involuntary response (*sāttvikabhāva*) of leaking breast milk when she witnesses his mighty deeds. Donna Wulff notes that because his parents can only see him with these eyes, they never suspect his dalliance with the *gopīs*, which sometimes makes them seem a bit foolish in Rūpa's version of the drama.[26] Any of Kṛṣṇa's elders in the narratives might relate to him in this way.

Erotic love. The amorous sentiment (*madhura bhakti rasa*) is characterized by great sweetness (*mādhurya*) and mutual pleasure (*BhRS* 2.5.36). Rūpa provides only a brief introduction to it in the *BhRS* for, as he states, its deeply esoteric nature is difficult to understand (*BhRS* 3.5.2). This sentiment can encompass a wide range of experiences because it includes both love in union (*sambhoga*) and love in separation (*vipralambha*). The degrees of love in separation range from the stage prior to the lovers' first meeting, to indignant sulking at some offense, to the longing of physical separation (*BhRS* 3.5.25–33).

After Rūpa sets out this five-fold *śṛṅgāra rasa* as primary devotional emotions, he describes how the other eight *rasas* of classical theory can function as secondary devotional emotions (*BhRS* 4.1–7). Humor, wonder, heroism, compassion, fury, dread, and disgust enhance the devotee's love of Kṛṣṇa. These function as temporary *vyabhicāribhāvas* in relation to the more stable primary emotions of devotional love (*BhRS* 2.5.45). Anger, for example, can be directed at Kṛṣṇa's enemies or at Kṛṣṇa himself in the conflicts of love (*BhRS* 2.5.63–66), but it ultimately fosters the *rasa* of love.

In order to account for the great variety of possible emotional responses to Kṛṣṇa's play, Rūpa outlines excitants, indicators, and involuntary responses for each of the *bhakti rasas*.[27] Each factor has a number of subtypes, and each can receive support from any of the thirty-three transitory emotions of classical dramatic theory (*BhRS* 2.4).

Excitants. Devotional sentiment awakens through two kinds of excitants or stimuli (*vibhāvas*), which Rūpa elaborates with detailed illustrations in order to facilitate the devotee's meditation. Among the "substantial excitants" (*ālambana vibhāvas*) are Kṛṣṇa and his infinite wonderful qualities (as the "object" of love) and the inhabitants of Vraja (as its "vessels"). The "enhancing excitants" (*uddīpana vibhāvas*) include attendant physical circumstances, from the setting in the beautiful land of Vraja to Kṛṣṇa's ornaments (*BhRS* 2.1).[28]

Indicators. The indicators (*anubhāvas*) of devotional love in Kṛṣṇa's *līlā* strike the reader with their physicality: "dancing, rolling around, singing, crying out, contorting the body, roaring like an animal, yawning, panting, disregarding worldly people, salivating, laughing loudly, shaking, and hiccupping" (*BhRS* 2.2.2).[29] Several of these indications are explicitly tied to a kind of holy madness seen first in the *gopīs* and others in the Bhāgavata Purāṇa and later in the ecstasies of Caitanya.

Involuntary Responses. An additional set of eight emotional-physical responses (*sāttvikabhāvas*)—stupefaction, tears, perspiration, change of color, loss of consciousness, goose bumps, trembling, and broken voice—cannot be willed, imitated, or feigned but only arise from a genuine state of emotion (*BhRS* 2.3.16).[30] These responses manifest in a gradation of intensity (from "smoldering" to "blazing") depending on how long they last, how completely the body is affected, how many occur at once, and whether they can be concealed. Rādhā alone (and, by extension, Caitanya) experiences all eight responses in blazing intensity as *mahābhāva*, the great emotion (*BhRS* 2.3.64–81).

Erotic Devotion

Rūpa's *Bhaktirasāmṛtasindhu* is a broad map of devotional experience in his spiritual tradition. He divulges a detailed cartography of erotic devotional love to advanced practitioners in the *Ujjvalanīlamaṇī* (*UN*). Whereas the *BhRS* is for all devotees, the *UN* is generally studied only after mastery of the scriptures. People whose religious orientation is knowledge-based (*jñānīs*) are unlikely to understand the ecstatic feelings of this text or to look favorably upon Kṛṣṇa's affairs with married women (*UN* 5.3–5). Devotees concerned with correct action (*karma*) might confuse the text's eroticism with gross physicality, or, as in the case of the Sahajiyā Vaiṣṇava sect that developed among Caitanya's followers in Bengal, they might attempt to imitate Kṛṣṇa's love play in religious rites involving sexual intercourse.[31]

As in the *BhRS*, in *UN* Rūpa examines the experience of divine love under the rubric of excitants, indicators, and so forth. It provides a series of steps toward greater intimacy with Kṛṣṇa, exploring the many shades of the love between him and his various lovers. Many characters populate the *UN*, including different classes of heroes and heroines, Kṛṣṇa and Rādhā's many friends and messengers, and various rivals and factions. For example, lovers of Kṛṣṇa are classified as *svakīya*—those married to Kṛṣṇa, his wives at Dvārakā, and the *gopīs* who pray to have him as a husband—and *parakīya*—unmarried girls or the wives of others. The love of these women is graded according to intensity, with the love of the *parakīya* women, who pursue Kṛṣṇa and risk the penalties of adultery, as the highest.

Rūpa delineates six stages within the highest grade of love (*UN* ch. 14): "This stable emotion of love, *prema*, may be raised by degrees: it can be *sneha*, *māna*, *praṇaya*, *rāga*, *anurāga*, and *bhāva*, in the manner that rock candy is prepared gradually from the cane, juice, lump sugar, molasses, candied sugar, and refined sugar" (14.59–61).[32] These six phases include a wide range of sensory and emotional experiences determined by the capacity of the devotee's faculties. Translation of these terms presents a problem to English speakers, for each means "love" but with different shades of meaning which I outline here. Rādhā serves as the preeminent exemplar, but her rival *gopī*, Candrāvalī, is often invoked to denote other shades of these loves for Kṛṣṇa.

Sneha. The condition of *sneha* is a melting quality that can be associated with butter or honey. Candrāvalī's deferential attitude resembles butter, which must be combined with another flavor (i.e., the emotion of respect) in order to be enjoyed. Rādhā's love is sweet in itself, like honey, because of her confidence and sense of "myness" in relation to Kṛṣṇa.[33]

Māna. When *sneha* becomes acute, the play of *māna* evolves as a kind of self-conceit, pride, wounded sense of honor, indignation excited by jealousy, and feigned anger with the beloved. Because there is no real chance of Kṛṣṇa not returning love, this anger only enhances the mood of love. Whereas Candrāvalī is easily appeased, Rādhā develops the full intensity of *māna*.

Praṇaya. When one has become established in the previous two stages, *praṇaya*, a feeling of deep longing, bursts forth along with the knowledge that even quarrels can never separate the lovers.

Rāga. One may then become "colored" by love in the next condition, *rāga*, which has various shades and degrees of permanence: that which can fade (*nīlīrāga*) and that which dyes permanently (*māñjiṣṭharāga*). Kṛṣṇa's relationship with Candrāvalī exemplifies the first type, while his relationship with Rādhā is always increasing.

Anurāga. Next, *anurāga* is a kind of resonance of *rāga*, an attachment that has no desire for one's own pleasure but only wants to enhance the pleasure of the other.

Bhāva. *Bhāva* is the uppermost stage of the emotion of *prema*; and only the *gopī*s, whose ecstasy in the *rāsa* dance completely overwhelms them, enjoy its highest pitch (*mahābhāva*). Ordinary devotees do not reach this level.[34]

These six phases of love intermingle with an alternating sense of divine presence and absence. Much of the longing of Kṛṣṇa and his lovers occurs in their separation (*vipralambha*). Rādhā sees Kṛṣṇa in a dream or has heard about him in a song and is unable to sleep. She becomes confused, emaciated, agitated. After they meet, she becomes jealous of his engagement with her rivals. Even when they are together, she fears their separation and feels apart from him. When he moves to Dvārakā to become king, she meditates on him constantly, and her love takes on a tinge of pathos (*karuṇa*). Kṛṣṇa, too, longs for his beloved and exhibits many of the same symptoms (*UN* 15).

The Gauḍīya Vaiṣṇavas also explore love in union (*sambhoga*) from every angle. The waxing and waning of the moon is an apt metaphor, for this eroticism is not oriented toward a single sexual climax. The lovers exchange glances, embrace, and play in the water. Their bodies bear evidence of love bites and scratches from fingernails. They admire the loveliness of the other's form, ornaments, scent, and voice. They liken each other to the beautiful elements in nature. They tease and play games of thievery, hide-and-seek, and disguise. Kṛṣṇa delights the agitated *gopīs* by appearing suddenly after a brief absence. This love pleases of all the senses, and the sum of these pastimes together gives the women even greater pleasure than direct union. As for the union between "Hari, expert in the festival of love, with Rādhika, whose murmurs of passionate agitation fill the forest bower," the *UN* says simply that "the half-[moon] of their sexual pastime expands" (*UN* 15.252).[35]

These elaborate meditations on erotic scenes can be read as positive celebrations of the beauty of language and sensual pleasure. The earlier poetic tradition of Jayadeva's *Gītagovinda* certainly develops in this direction,[36] yet many Gauḍīya Vaiṣṇava devotees deny that Kṛṣṇa and Rādhā ever consummated their passion and insist that their affair is strictly allegorical and should be enjoyed as such.[37] To understand how this is possible given the literary tradition to the contrary, we must explore in more detail how traditional exegetes handle the erotic content of these narratives. The classical category of *aucitya*, fittingness or appropriateness, will help us to parse the delicate matter of eroticism in devotional life.

Rasa and Propriety

Appropriateness (*aucitya*) is a well-developed category of analysis in Sanskrit literary theory. Ānandavardhana considers it of the utmost importance for successful literature: "There is no other means of ruining *rasa* than impropriety; the greatest secret of *rasa* is the bounds set by propriety" (*DhĀ* III.10–14a).[38] Related to older notions of "felicity of expression," the principle of *aucitya* encompasses all of the factors in a work of art that foster or hinder the refinement of aesthetic emotions in the audience.[39] Raghavan observes a basic principle of harmony at the root of the concept of *aucitya*: Everything must be in its proper place in order for a work of art to succeed. When ornaments are misplaced—as when an anklet is worn as a necklace, or when a woman pining for her lover appears fully decked out in jewelry—they strike the audience as incongruous. The same goes for poetic ornaments: Improper treatment draws attention away from the totality of the aesthetic experience.[40]

The sole test of *aucitya*, a context-sensitive and adaptive guideline, is whether it helps or hinders *rasa*. There are no hard and fast rules.

Techniques that would be faults in one setting are excellences in another. Much of the discussion in the dramatic context hinges on technical details: what gestures, words, clothing, dispositions, meters, and times of performance are suitable for conveying the intended mood. A plot must intensify and relax the *rasa* at suitable points so that the delicate flower of emotion will neither wilt nor be crushed. Other emotions must be kept subordinate, and obstructive *rasa*s should not appear in immediate proximity to one another. For example, factors evocative of *śānta rasa* (which entails the quelling of desire) impede the erotic sentiment, as do the *rasa*s of fury (*raudra*) and disgust (*bībhatsa*).[41]

Different conventions also apply to different sorts of characters, depending on their country, caste, culture, age, wealth, and gender. According to the *Nāṭya Śāstra*, the heroic sentiment belongs by nature to superior persons; the comic, fearful, and disgusting sentiments to inferior persons; and the furious sentiment to demons. All of the sentiments can apply to others as the occasion demands. The expression of each emotion varies by type. For example, sorrow (*śoka*) belongs by nature to "women and inferior persons" who display it through weeping and lamentation. By contrast, when "superior and middling" persons experience sorrow, they react with fortitude and restraint (*NŚ* 7.14, p. 282).[42] How characters of different classes smile, walk, move their eyes—all of this bears on whether their performance will be able to evoke *rasa*. Actions inappropriate to a character's station impede the spectator's absorption in the mood.

Breach of *aucitya* gives rise to obstacles (*vighnas*), as when qualities of language or style are unsuited to the intended *rasa*. For example, harsh sounds that might be appropriate for evoking the *rasa* of fury are out of place in a scene designed to evoke the delicate erotic *rasa*, where sweet and assonant sounds are more appropriate.[43] A love scene can be impeded by inappropriate vessels for the emotion, as when the villain Rāvaṇa abducts and professes his love for the divine Sītā. There can be no real sentiment of love, only its semblance (*rasābhasa*). What arises instead of love is humor—for all his earnestness, Rāvaṇa's emotion only makes us laugh. Abhinavagupta says that *anaucitya* (impropriety) is the root of the humorous sentiment (*hāsya*). Indeed, if the humorous sentiment is intended, it might be entirely appropriate to place a necklace on a foot, for a person to imitate someone of different social standing, or for an emotion to appear in an unlikely setting.[44]

A number of activities are barred from stage representation because they block *rasa*, although each injunction also contains an escape clause for the rare case in which it might be appropriate. For example, although it is improper for an actor to sleep onstage, the scene can then be cut off if it is necessary for a character to fall asleep. It is more important, though, not to depict couples in bed engaged in erotic activities such as "kissing, embracing, and things that should be private like love bites, scratching with fingernails, loosening the woman's skirt, and squeezing her breasts." Bharata is attributed with the dictum that "[o]ne should not allow anything of this kind to be portrayed that causes embarrassment, such as enjoying food or love play in the water. Because a play is seen by father, son, daughter-in-law, and mother-in-law, all these things are diligently to be avoided" (*NŚ* XX.295–299).[45] The embarrassment that might be caused by seeing such activities with one's parents is a definite impediment to *rasa*.

Ānandavardhana similarly cautions against improprieties in relation to the erotic sentiment. This *rasa* must be treated suitably according to the three classes of human beings (i.e., superior, middling, and inferior). Love between the gods must be portrayed as it would be for characters of the superior upper classes. Vulgarity is neither permitted nor necessary in relation to these characters. As he notes, love in union can be depicted by markers other than sexual intercourse, such as amorous glances (*DhĀ* 3.10–14b).

A crucial debate over depiction of sexual encounters hinges around whether Kalidāsa's epic poem *Kumārasambhava*, which describes the lovemaking of the divine couple Śiva and Pārvatī, transgresses the boundaries of propriety. Does such a scene hinder the development of *śṛṅgāra rasa*? Kṣemendra, who classifies minute improprieties down to the use of prepositions and particles of grammar, rules against Kalidāsa.[46] After all, to witness (or imagine) the lovemaking of the God and Goddess, the mother and father of the universe, would be just as indecent as seeing one's own parents having sex. Yet Ānandavardhana opines that Kalidāsa's skill as a poet is so great that this passage is an exception to the rule. The viewer is so enraptured by the beauty of the poetry that the impropriety is imperceptible.[47]

Abhinavagupta follows the latter train of thought. He acknowledges that ordinarily, there is no aesthetic pleasure in watching a couple make love: "Because one becomes preoccupied . . . with one's own mental moods that arise, such as embarrassment, disgust, or even sexual desire, we cannot say that this is an aesthetic experience."[48] Abhinavagupta relates the notion of *aucitya* to the *alaukika* quality of art discussed in the last chapter, which removes art from the limitations of ordinary life.

In art, the spectator is so absorbed in the aesthetic experience that she is not conscious of the artificiality or the imitative nature of the situation, or of the sequence of the factors leading from the dramatic gesture to the production of *rasa*. For Abhinavagupta, in works of literary genius, this total absorption also enables the spectator to view dramatic situations that in ordinary life would be considered indecent or obscene. Ordinary notions of propriety do not apply.[49]

This brief explanation of the concept of *aucitya* shows how the aesthetic issue of "fitting" techniques for evoking *rasa* slides into the moral question of appropriate thought and action. Rūpa and his commentators address both sorts of concerns.

Aucitya and the Erotic

If in aesthetic theory *aucitya* is concerned with how most fittingly to evoke *rasa* in the spectator, Rūpa must consider which factors are appropriate to fostering the *rasa* of devotional love. These considerations arise out of his engagement with both the actual stage and the internal stage of the devotee's meditation. In keeping with the stipulations for the theatrical context, Gauḍīya Vaiṣṇava dramas do not directly depict the union of Rādhā and Kṛṣṇa. Rūpa himself crafts verses that "suggest to the audience or reader the intimate forms of expression of Rādhā's and Kṛṣṇa's love that may not, according to Sanskrit dramatic convention, be explicitly represented on the stage."[50] Suggestion is the key to evoking *rasa*.

Rūpa concludes the *BhRS* with an extended consideration of matters of *aucitya* in the evocation of *bhakti rasa*. He notes that although each of the many kinds of *bhakti* is a form of relation to the divine, not all are compatible with one another. The combination of incompatible *rasa*s is like throwing salt into a sweet drink (*BhRS* 4.8.53). The amorous sentiment can be accompanied by humor or friendship; but the *rasa*s of disgust, peace, fury, and terror are incompatible with it (*BhRS* 4.8.7). The combination of the amorous sentiment with the sentiment of parental affection is extremely detrimental to *rasa* (*BhRS* 4.8.60); the taboo against incest strongly prohibits the same character from inhabiting both kinds of love for Kṛṣṇa.[51]

Certain transitory emotions (*vyabhicāribhāvas*), such as Arjuna's fear in response to Kṛṣṇa's theophany in the Bhagavad Gītā (*BhRS* 2.4.213), can also impede love for Kṛṣṇa. Fear or awe in the face of Kṛṣṇa's majesty (*aiśvarya*) is one of the most detrimental emotions for devotional love.

Kṛṣṇa's parents, friends, and lovers can only enjoy intimacy with him if they think him to be a playful, charming youth.

As he reflects on scriptural narratives, Rūpa observes that *bhakti rasa* can also fail because of deficiencies in the characters, improprieties that lead to the mere semblance (*ābhasa*) of *rasa*. *Bhakti rasa* sometimes appears to manifest in people who are not pure devotees. Rather than being completely absorbed in Kṛṣṇa, they harbor other desires—for worldly pleasure (*bhukti*) or for liberation (*mukti*). Their enjoyment is but a pale reflection of the bliss of devotion, and their fickleness causes the *bhāva* to wane (*BhRS* 1.3.42–56, cf. 2.3.82–96). Rūpa lists several subtypes of semblances: *bhakti rasa* is absent when the emotions lack a connection with Kṛṣṇa (*anurasa*), when they belong to an enemy of Kṛṣṇa (*aparasa*), or when inappropriate excitants, responses, or accompanying emotions are present (*uparasa*). The vessels of the amorous sentiment must be worthy. Anyone other than young, beautiful women (i.e., plants, animals, old women) is ineligible for the erotic sentiment. The women must display actions considered normal for someone in love, such as being jealous when betrayed. They must not be vulgar or impudently solicit sex (*BhRS* 4.9.18–22).

The same shading into the moral realm as I noted in the classical aesthetic tradition occurs in Rūpa's work. As he teaches advanced practitioners how to meditate on the erotic content of scripture, he considers: What constitutes appropriate behavior for devotees—or, for that matter, for Kṛṣṇa himself? How is it that the highest deity can engage in behavior that is so conventionally unacceptable? And to what extent can the devotee (*bhakta*) "participate" (*bhuj*) in this play?

Aucitya and Krsna: The Two Loves Doctrine

Is Kṛṣṇa's sexual dalliance with the *gopīs* ethical? Although some Vaiṣṇava texts revel unapologetically in his erotic exploits, the Bhāgavata Purāṇa itself takes steps to defend his behavior as compatible with conventional morality. This concern is reflected in Rūpa's *BhRS*, which has been described as a commentary on the Bhāgavata Purāṇa,[52] and is amplified in commentaries on the *BhRS* by other Gauḍīya Vaiṣṇava theologians such as that of his younger contemporary, Jīva Gosvāmin. The result of these commentarial discussions is a gradual distancing of divine from human love.

The primary strategy of the Bhāgavata Purāṇa is to deny or downplay the element of sexual union. According to the verse that concludes the *rāsa līlā*, Kṛṣṇa and the *gopīs* "set aside sexual enjoyment" and "take refuge in the *rasa*" evoked by the beauty of nature and their dance (*BhP* 10.33.26).[53] As the Lord of the Universe, Kṛṣṇa is eternally self-fulfilled. The *gopīs* are content merely to touch his limbs (*BhP* 10.33.1).[54] When the Bhāgavata Purāṇa puzzles how Kṛṣṇa, "the teacher and executor who has protected the boundaries of dharma, has done the opposite and touched the wives of others" (*BhP* 10.33.28),[55] it concludes that Kṛṣṇa, as the highest God, is exalted above *karma*, is free from its effects, and has the power to act as he pleases (*BhP* 10.33.30–35). The *gopīs*' secret tryst with their divine lover is highly unconventional behavior. When they arrive, Kṛṣṇa ostensibly tries to dissuade them from acting against their *dharma* as wives and mothers. Although this passage has been read as upholding ordinary notions of duty, each of these verses is a double entendre that can give exactly the opposite meaning (*BhP* 10.29.19–27).[56] Later, the text takes a different tack when it explains how there is no actual impropriety from the perspective of the women's husbands. Kṛṣṇa's divine power of *māyā* ensures that the men never discover their wives' absence: Kṛṣṇa creates a double of each woman to remain by her husband's side through the night (*BhP* 10.33.38).

These playful strategies are not entirely convincing. Later Gauḍīya Vaiṣṇava texts invent additional theological defenses. The *Govindalīlāmṛta* styles the *gopīs* as Kṛṣṇa's own powers (*śaktis*, a feminine term in Sanskrit), personified. In their game, Kṛṣṇa makes love to himself or, to put it another way, plays with his own reflection.[57] The drama of Vrindavan thus takes place eternally within God. Indeed, everything in the world that Kṛṣṇa creates as external to himself is one with him—human beings as his *jīva śakti* and the external world as his *māyā śakti*. The *gopīs* and all of Vrindavan are essentially the same as Kṛṣṇa; they are his own form (*svarūpa śakti*). Rādhā is Kṛṣṇa's power of pure bliss (*hladinī śakti*), which Kṛṣṇa, as the supreme enjoyer, savors eternally.[58]

Extending this metaphysical reading, commentators also read the erotic play as a metaphor for the union of the self with the Absolute. Sexual metaphors are the closest that our language and our sensory experience can get to the ineffable play of the one and the many. Even celibate saints and poets such as Sūrdās (who was both celibate and blind from birth) naturally turn to the language of human coupling when they experience the interplay of unity and difference (*acintyabhedābheda*). Erotic language is an apt metaphor for this relationship, even if there is nothing physically sexual about it.[59] As for the adulterous nature of these relations, the love of "another's" spouse (*parakīya*) serves as a metaphor for the total risk involved in the highest love.

In the face of appearances of impropriety, Jīva Gosvāmin backs away from the *parakīya* doctrine that is so central to Gauḍīya Vaiṣṇava theology. Despite the metaphorical nature of the relationship, he goes a step further to exonerate Kṛṣṇa. Because Kṛṣṇa is the supreme self, who indwells all living things (cf. *BhP* 10.33.35), the *gopīs* are not really married to their husbands. Kṛṣṇa is their true spouse.[60] Jīva further argues that either adulterous relations or improper contact would be inappropriate for Kṛṣṇa according to the cannons of *rasa*. The *gopīs* at home are illusory forms, and their relationship with their husbands is likewise illusory. When they go to the forest, they receive pure spiritual bodies that are never tainted by contact with other men. So, whenever Kṛṣṇa refers to the worldly husbands, it can only be in jest. Otherwise, the women's neglect of their children, not to mention their husbands, would present a major impediment to *rasa*.[61]

Appeals to the illusory nature of Kṛṣṇa's *līlā*, aesthetic arguments regarding the impropriety of the love of paramours, and the reasoning that Kṛṣṇa and the *gopīs* were actually married to one another (*svakīya*)—all of these discussions emphasize the transcendent nature of divine love. Jīva argues that "[b]ecause it embodies a kind of love distinct from ordinary desire, therefore there is no fault" (*Prīti Sandarbha* 143).[62] Kṛṣṇa's *līlā* is a tale not of worldly passion but of a love that, when offered to devotees, calls them to renounce worldly desires. Worldly love is associated with the kind of attachments and enjoyment (*bhukti*) that impede rather than aid spiritual progress. If sex implies a concern with one's own pleasure, sex has no part in Kṛṣṇa's *līlā*, where his lovers think only of him. Kṛṣṇa disappears when the *gopīs* become overly pleased with themselves. His love cannot flourish unless demands of the self—whether sensory or egoistic—are displaced.

The difference between divine and worldly loves receives dramatic form in *rāsa līlā* performances in Vrindavan. John Stratton Hawley reveals how the sixteenth-century addition of Kāmadeva, the god of erotic love, into the *rāsa līlā* narrative makes the allegory explicit.[63] Kāmadeva, who ordinarily acts as a kind of Cupid by firing arrows to enamor his victims, arrives at the *rāsa līlā* dance only to be smitten by Kṛṣṇa. The circle dance becomes a battle between two incompatible kinds of love: *kāma*, sexual desire, and *prema*, the pure love of Kṛṣṇa. The *gopīs* leave *kāma* behind, with all the pleasures, duties, and results that come with the love of husband

and children, for the pure play of Kṛṣṇa devotion. The two forms of love cannot coexist. Kāmadeva loses consciousness and dies.[64] Popular treatments of the Kṛṣṇa narrative thus contribute to the widening distance between ordinary sensual relationships and the divine love embodied in his love play with the *gopīs*.

Aucitya and Devotees: The Two-Bodies Doctrine

The devotional life outlined by Rūpa calls devotees toward ever greater degrees of participation in Kṛṣṇa's *līlā*, yet Rūpa's community has placed clear boundaries on the development of devotional love. Unlike the *gopīs*, whose *bhakti* apparently transcends social norms, devotees are afforded little room for socially transgressive behavior. Whereas the *gopīs* effectively abandon their previous lives through an illusory double, practitioners develop devotional service in two bodies: the practitioner's body in the world (*sādhaka rūpa*) and an eternal, perfected form in Kṛṣṇa's realm (*siddha rūpa*).

The term here used for "body," *rūpa*, is a multi-tiered concept. Divine and human beings can inhabit several kinds of "forms," sometimes simultaneously. Some of these bodies are temporal, concrete, and material, while others are eternal, mental, or created in meditation. Gods, for example, have unblemished eternal forms, take body in temple images (*mūrtis*), and "descend" to appear on earth in various *avatāras*. All are "bodies." We must, therefore, resist imposing a simple spirit/body dichotomy on the two-body doctrine.

I will be arguing that the *materiality* of these bodies, the degree of contact with matter (*prakṛti*), is gradually attenuated as the Gauḍīya Vaiṣṇavas work out the implications of Rūpa's two-bodies doctrine. The impact of the aesthetic framework is diluted as the excitants, indicators, and accompanying emotions are removed several degrees from the devotee's experience: Concerns with the appropriateness of the devotee's behavior dictate that the devotee should not participate directly in the Kṛṣṇa-*līlā* by imitating its original characters.

In the process of initiation to the *rāgānugā* path, devotees discover their true relationship to Kṛṣṇa as a servant, friend, guardian, or lover. This identity is a person's *siddha rūpa*, or perfected body, which resides in the eternal realm of Kṛṣṇa. Through a process of mentally remembering Kṛṣṇa's pastimes, devotees progressively shift their identities onto that body. David Haberman likens the resultant "total identification with and absorption" in one's devotional identity to contemporary acting techniques developed by Constantin Stanislavski: "At first, the practitioners merely copy the character they are striving to become. But the successful practitioner's goal is to become so totally identified with a character in the Vraja-līlā that he or she *really is* that character."[65]

Rūpa says that in order to effect this transformation of identity, one should visualize oneself playing an active role in Kṛṣṇa's drama and perform service to Kṛṣṇa in both the practitioner's (*sādhaka*) and perfected (*siddha*) bodies (*BhRS* 1.294–295). The stage seems to be set for the identification with the major characters in Kṛṣṇa's *līlā*, yet this instruction raises numerous questions about the relation of the two bodies. Which characters are suitable for imitation? If male practitioners want to imitate the *gopī*s, or if female practitioners want to imitate Kṛṣṇa's male attendants, how far should this imitation express itself in their daily lives? Should men dress the part of a *gopī* in their ordinary, *sādhaka*, body? Should they cease to perform their caste, professional, and familial duties? And is it really appropriate for human worshippers to aspire to erotic enjoyment of the deity?

Conflicts of interpretation arise among later Gauḍīya Vaiṣṇavas around the imitation of exemplars. Rūpa states one clear boundary on imitation: "One must behave in one's thoughts like a *bhakta*, not like Krishna. This is the settled rule of the devotional manuals. . . . As with Śiva drinking poison churned from the ocean, one who is not God perishes by foolishly acting this way, even mentally" (*UN* 3.24, 3.26).[66] Kṛṣṇa's activities, undertaken out of mercy for his devotees, are dangerous for ordinary mortals. One should instead follow saints or scriptural exemplars and focus on serving Kṛṣṇa rather than imitating him.

How, then, should one imitate scriptural devotees? On the one hand, some protest that Rūpa does not use the word "imitation" (*anukāra*), but "following after" (*anusāra* and *anuga*); but the latter terms are broad enough to include imitative action.[67] On the other hand, some rare groups have interpreted Rūpa's hint about service in both the *sādhaka* and *siddha rūpa*s as an invitation to live as a *gopī* in their external lives, dressing in women's clothing.[68] According to legend, the great god Śiva was prevented from entering the circle dance until he became a *gopī* in physical form. Miraculous stories even from the present day suggest that the eternal form of a fully realized saint can become perceptible in this world. Disciples might meet a beautiful adolescent girl only later to realize that it was their teacher's *siddha rūpa*.[69]

Theoretical justification for practices such as cross-dressing may have been provided by Rūpa Kavirāja, who opined that the physical body, the *sādhaka rūpa*, undergoes an ontological transformation imperceptible to the uninitiated. One's meditation on Kṛṣṇa's *līlā* becomes so complete that the behavior of this transformed body will "in all ways" be the same as that of the *siddha rūpa*. The practitioner's body becomes free from ordinary social rules and the injunctions of the preliminary stages of devotional practice (*vaidhī bhakti*).[70] This radical interpenetration of the two bodies of the devotee has not been common, however, and Rūpa Kavirāja was excommunicated by a Vaiṣṇava synod at Jaipur in 1727.

The solution to the two-bodies doctrine that has prevailed institutes a separate set of practices for each body. Viśvanātha Cakravartin's commentary on Rūpa Gosvāmin's *BhRS* refutes the interpretations of Rūpa Kavirāja. Viśvanātha stresses the necessity for all devotees to follow the sixty-four injunctions of *vaidhī bhakti* with the practitioner's body (*sādhaka rūpa*). Devotees at every stage of their practice must submit to a guru, study scripture, sing devotional songs, chant the holy names, worship images of Kṛṣṇa, and so forth.[71] The *siddha rūpa* should be engaged mentally: One participates in Kṛṣṇa's eternal *līlā* solely in meditation. Viśvanātha writes, "Following the likes of Śri Rādhā [and other *gopī*s] one should perform service mentally with one's *siddha rūpa*. But one should perform service in the corporeal body, with the *sādhaka rūpa*, by following those who live in Vraj like Śrī Rūpa and Sanātana."[72] The last clause is significant. It limits imitation of the scriptural exemplars to the mental realm, but it offers the Gosvāmins as exemplars for the empirical realm.

Viśvanātha also answers objectors who claim no need to follow a guru, observe fasts, or worship sacred stones or plants because the *gopī*s did not do these things. Although the *siddha rūpa* should imitate one of the *gopī*s or another exemplar from Kṛṣṇa's realm, the *sādhaka rūpa* must imitate Rūpa and the other original Gosvāmins, who were also exemplary individuals in Vraja. Their models for imitation have been passed on through a succession of gurus. In this way, institutional injunctions as well as conventional gender guidelines prevail: A male brahmin should continue acting like a male brahmin, regardless of his spiritual identity, and engage in the kinds of service followed by his guru. A woman should imitate the guru only insofar as it does not violate her traditional *dharma* as a daughter, wife, mother, or widow.

In effect, a dichotomy between the physical (*sādhaka*) and spiritual (*siddha*) bodies crops up in a theological system that otherwise evinces a great deal of permeability between the temporal and eternal. Practitioners assert that the body in the eternal Vraja is more real than their current physical form, but the perfected spiritual body is not physical or material in any ordinary sense of the word.

This distancing from the physical body is even greater in the later tradition. Love's fullness must wait until after death; and the insertion of multiple heavenly realms delays it further. *Prakaṭa* Vraja is the material world (*prakṛti*) where Kṛṣṇa manifests his *līlā*, which is always occurring in some universe. *Aprakaṭa* Vraja is the ongoing existence of this *līlā* when it has disappeared from the material realm. After death, a fortunate devotee might be born to a *gopī* and meet Kṛṣṇa in a *prakaṭa* (material) realm. Only after that life will he or she serve Kṛṣṇa fully with all the other *gopī*s in his *aprakaṭa* (transcendent) realm.[73]

In these developments, worries about appropriate behavior in the practitioner's body narrow possibilities for participation in Kṛṣṇa's *līlā*. As Donna Wulff observes, "Rūpa's own theory seems to be more flexible than the interpretations of his successors."[74] As a result of internal disputes, the devotional body is decorporealized and dematerialized, and the guru becomes an intermediate paradigm for imitation.

Not a Lover but a Servant of a Friend

One final aspect of devotional distancing occurs in the perfected body of Gauḍīya Vaiṣṇava practitioners. One might surmise from reading Rūpa's works that contemplative participation in Kṛṣṇa's drama means imagining oneself in the role of Rādhā, Yaśodā, or one of the other scriptural characters. The examples Rūpa gives for the five devotional loves and their subvarieties draw from this cast of characters, but Rūpa's followers tend not to take them as exemplars. Let us examine how this discontinuity emerges in relation to the erotic variety of devotion.

Rūpa offers the direct love of Kṛṣṇa as one of two options for participation in the amorous sentiment, the "desire for love in union" and the "desire for various emotions" (*BhRS* 1.2.298).[75] In the first option, a devotee might take the *siddha rūpa* of a lead *gopī* (*nāyikā*) and aspire to enjoy Kṛṣṇa's love play directly. In the second, the devotee imagines himself or herself as one of the subordinate friends (*sakhī*s or *mañjarī*s) of a lead *gopī*. In the latter model, practitioners aspire not to the unmediated love of Kṛṣṇa but to the vicarious enjoyment of the erotic sentiment. Rather than participating in the love play, they witness it as privileged servants or subordinate friends. These minor characters perform tasks to serve Kṛṣṇa and Rādhā such as fanning them, feeding them betel nut, and fetching their clothing.

Although Rūpa holds out both options, Jīva's and Viśvanātha's commentaries on *BhRS* 1.2.306 both emphasize the indirect mode of amorous devotion. Jīva imposes an important caveat for devotees who want to foster the direct loving sentiment of a parent, friend, or lover of Kṛṣṇa: They must never think oneself identical with one of the original characters such as Rādhā.[76] Here, he applies a central Gauḍīya Vaiṣṇava principle, *acintyabhedābheda*, the inexpressible difference-in-union enjoyed by Kṛṣṇa and his devotees. Neither difference nor union may be compromised. Lovers are irreducible to one another, even as they enter into a loving relationship. Devotees must be distinct from divinity, even in union; and if the eternal characters in Kṛṣṇa's drama are aspects of him, then the devotee must remain distinct from them as well.

Notably, a rival sect, the Sahajiyā Vaiṣṇavas of Bengal, views the difference between the human being and God as ultimately illusory. This philosophy permits not only direct identification with Rādhā and Kṛṣṇa but also imitation of their union through an esoteric sexual rite. In their interpretation of *acintyabhedābheda*, they "read the images the other way."[77] The Sahajiyās believe that the difference between Rādhā and Kṛṣṇa makes possible the expression of their essential *union*. The Gauḍīya Vaiṣṇavas, by contrast, view their relationship as a metaphor for the *difference* of the human being and God. For Gauḍīya Vaiṣṇavas, the union of the self and the divine never melts into complete monism, and the Sahajiyās' heterodox rites remain outside the range of permitted practices.

To hedge against any hint of heterodoxy, many Gauḍīya Vaiṣṇava practitioners maintain that the indirect method of relating to Kṛṣṇa is the superior path. Jīva debases the more direct option that Rūpa offers as belonging to characters such as Kubjā, a somewhat comic character who directly asks Kṛṣṇa for sex.[78] *Rasa* from the vicarious enjoyment of Kṛṣṇa's love play is said to be sweeter than if one had to rely on one's own merits to achieve it. As Haberman puts it, "[I]n the first option, the direct approach, the *bhakta* must rely on the depth of his or her own vessel while experiencing the religious emotions of the Vraja-līlā. By contrast, in the second option, the indirect approach, the *bhakta* relies on the vessel of his or her chosen inhabitant of Vraja, usually Rādhā, whose emotional vessel or *āśraya* by definition is infinitely deep."[79] Devotees in the latter model love Rādhā even more than Kṛṣṇa; they aim for total absorption in the feeling tones of her experience rather than developing these feelings on their own.

Rūpa Gosvāmin's own devotional identity is said to be of this indirect sort, a *sakhī* named Rūpa Mañjarī. This *siddha rūpa* has become an exemplar of the distanced devotional mood. Rūpa Mañjarī is imagined as a thirteen-and-a-half-year-old girl with a dark yellow complexion, dressed in a sari patterned with peacock's feathers. She is Rādhā's intimate friend, whose role in the *līlā* is to serve betel nut to the lovers.[80] Rūpa and others would imagine themselves in such a role or, as has become common in his lineage, they invent new roles as servants of Rūpa Mañjarī. Their devotional sentiment participates in the erotic mood, but from several removes from the main action. They neither love Kṛṣṇa directly as Rādhā nor savor Rādhā's love in close proximity as one of her attendants. Rather, they become servants of a friend of the lover of Kṛṣṇa.[81]

The trajectory of the steps taken to mitigate the sensuality of Kṛṣṇa's love for his devotees may here be summarized. The strictures of *aucitya*, that which may appropriately be depicted in art, are extended to religious practice. The love of God is allegorized, carefully separated from ordinary desire (*kāma*). The devotee's participation in this love is circumscribed in the imagined eternal body, the *siddha rūpa*, so that the body of religious practice, the *sādhaka rūpa*, bears no trace of eroticism. Finally, even the imagined body is cautioned against direct participation in sex with Kṛṣṇa. The persona of the *mañjarī*, the attendant in Rādhā's entourage, becomes the preferred mode of devotion. As Wulff concludes,

> It is difficult not to see in the practice of *mañjarīsādhana* a greater sense of distance between these characters and the ordinary human *bhakta* than Rūpa's . . . theory [seems] to require. Rūpa's view of the superiority of more intimate relations between the devotee and the Lord, as articulated in the *Bhaktirasāmṛtasindhu*, is a radical and daring one, and it is hardly surprising that elements of *aiśvarya*—in a new guise—have reemerged with the passage of time.[82]

In short, the intimacy of love retreats toward the devotional sentiment of peace (*śānta*), the *bhakti rasa* that Rūpa's theory holds in the least esteem.

The Aesthetics of Love at a Distance

In working out the details of how a devotee should imagine himself in Kṛṣṇa's play, the Gauḍīya Vaiṣṇava tradition has wrestled with how to combine Rūpa's aesthetic framework with the basic tenet of *bhakti* as participation. On the one hand, *bhakti* removes the curtain and levels the stage. The devotee is invited to become an actor in the drama, to identify with one of the characters, and to develop feelings of "myness" (*mamatā*) toward the leading divine character. These are no longer the generalized (*sādhāraṇīkṛta*) sentiments of classical aesthetic theory. On the other hand, *rasa* is in the dramatic context a depersonalized sentiment aroused by the combination of excitants, responses, and accompanying emotional states depicted onstage. *Rasa* occurs in the spectator, not the actor. Rūpa's later followers, who identify with the *sakhī*s or *mañjarī*s (spectators of Kṛṣṇa's love) lean toward this classical view. Wulff notes, "Not surprisingly, the discontinuity is most apparent in the highest and most intimate mode of relating to Kṛṣṇa."[83] The specter of sexual impropriety causes the religious tradition to retreat to a less personal, more distanced stance for the devotee.

The discontinuity of devotional and erotic love might be unremarkable if the tradition were not rooted so firmly in narratives of Kṛṣṇa's illicit dalliances with the cowherd women and in poetry and art depicting these scenes. The various exegetical strategies and fences erected around the imitation of the *gopī*s reveal this tension. The erotic sentiment arouses concerns with appropriateness (*aucitya*). Kṛṣṇa's behavior must not be unworthy of God if it is to foster *rasa*. A series of attenuations of the devotee's participation in Kṛṣṇa *līlā* prevent inappropriate behavior. The claim that divine love (*prema*) is not like worldly love (*kāma*) attenuates Rūpa's linkage between emotion (*bhāva*) and aesthetic sentiment (*rasa*). The true devotional identity is then relegated to a mental form, where one receives a new body; the physical body must imitate the guru rather than the exemplars in the *līlā*; and even in the spiritual body it is best to imitate the servant of a friend of Rādhā and Kṛṣṇa.

The theologians' caution around imitation of the *gopī*s draws attention to some of the blurry areas in Gauḍīya Vaiṣṇava application of aesthetic theory. Many of the excitants (*vibhāva*s) of *bhakti rasa* can be encountered not only in meditation on the Kṛṣṇa narrative but also in the course of everyday devotional practice. For example, when one visits a temple or performs worship at home, one sees and hears of Kṛṣṇa's alluring qualities. Should the practitioner not then exhibit the appropriate responses (*anubhāva*s) and attendant emotions (*vyabhicāribhāva*s) of this experience? Or should she only meditate on these responses in the exemplary individuals in scripture so as to enhance her own experience of *rasa*?

Jīva's response to this question demonstrates the overlap between the two realms, which in other ways he tries to keep apart. Haberman summarizes Jīva's distinction between experiential consequents (*anubhāvas*) and practice (*sādhana*):

> [T]he same act can be either an *anubhāva* or an act of *sādhana*, depending on its motive. If it is a spontaneous and natural expression of an inner emotion, it is an *anubhāva*; if it is an intentional act designed to acquire an inner emotion, it is *sādhana*. However, the two (*anubhāva* and *sādhana*) take the same physical form.[84]

In other words, a practitioner might imitate the *anubhāvas* of the *gopīs* as a practical means (*sādhana*) to generating the appropriate devotional emotions. When Rūpa lays out, in great physical detail, the indications of devotional love, he both describes and prescribes. His descriptions of devotees in scripture help present-day devotees to craft vivid mental pictures of scriptural scenes. Yet many of the indications of *bhakti* are also appropriate to the practice of any devotee, as when he lists the *anubhāvas* of the devotee at the stage of *bhāva bhakti* as "patience, profitable use of time, freedom from passion, absence of pride, hopefulness, yearning, a desire for always singing the divine names, commitment to telling the divine qualities, and pleasure in the places where he lives" (*BhRS* 1.3.25–26).[85] When Rūpa describes these qualities in scriptural characters, he inspires devotees who mediate on them to embody them as well.

The problem, it seems, comes with the development beyond the "sprout" of *bhāva* into the full-blown amorousness of *prema*. The *BhRS* and the *UN* describe indicators (*anubhāvas*) including dancing, rolling on the ground, shrieking, twisting the body, and laughing loudly and additional involuntary responses (*sāttvikabhāvas*) such as perspiration, goose bumps, trembling, tears, and loss of consciousness. By the reasoning applied in relation to the preliminary stage of *bhāva bhakti*, the devotee might then undertake a devotional discipline of rolling on the ground or fainting (cf. *BhRS* 2.2.15–17). Instead, devotees insist that the physical manifestations of *bhakti* occur in the exemplary individuals, but not in practitioners. Practitioners should meditate on the example of these individuals in scripture. The *BhP* functions as a drama: When one "sees" the play of Kṛṣṇa in meditation and in festival plays, the foundational emotion of Kṛṣṇa-*rati* builds, which Kṛṣṇa can transform and intensify into *bhakti rasa*. When the indicators occur among devotees, they are treated as a sign of grace that can be neither feigned nor concealed.[86]

Significant tensions regarding the value of the material realm emerge from this theorizing. On the one hand, the lush sensuousness of the Kṛṣṇa story lends itself to sensory and aesthetic enjoyment. On the other hand, certain physical responses, including imitation of physical eroticism, have been deemed improper and indicative that the devotee is overly attached to sense enjoyment. Participation in Kṛṣṇa's love story is to occur primarily in the inner/other-worldly (*alaukika*) realm, an emphasis that has had a socially conservative function with regard to gender and caste. A parallel set of mechanisms exists in Christian erotic mysticism. I turn now to one of its major Christian proponents, Bernard of Clairvaux, to examine how the eroticism of the scriptural Song of Songs generates a similar ambivalence toward the sensory experience of love.

4 A Dilemma of Feeling

Like Rūpa Gosvāmin, the medieval Christian theologian Bernard of Clairvaux (1090–1153) elevates love over all other emotions in the devotional life. He finds ample material for the devotional sentiment of love in the biblical Song of Songs. He writes no fewer than eighty-six sermons on the first chapters of this short book of Hebrew wisdom literature, which consists of a series of poetic exchanges between two lovers. Bernard ranks "reverence" and its attendant emotions of "horror or stupor or fear or wonder" (characteristic of *śānta* in Rūpa's system) far below the intimacy of love (Serm. 83.3).[1] For him, nuptial love is superior to other forms of love, a "bond . . . stronger even than nature's firm bond between parents and children" (Serm. 83.3, cf. 83.5). It is also the most mutual of emotional experiences of the divine. God's emotions are not ordinarily met in kind—the proper response to God's anger, for example, is fear and repentance—but "when God loves, he desires nothing but to be loved, since he loves us for no other reason than to be loved" (Serm. 83.4). In these preliminary features—love's mutuality and its superiority to reverence and familial love—this Christian love of God invites comparison with the Vaiṣṇava love of Kṛṣṇa.

Bernard, a celibate monk and abbot, lifts up the eros of the Song of Songs as a model for divine love. He does this in the theological context of the twelfth century, which saw an unprecedented emphasis on Christ's humanity and the devotee's affective relation to it. Mystical and Eucharistic practices increasingly gave visibility to the corporeal presence of Christ. The importance of feeling—both sensory and emotional—rose to prominence in the theology of Bernard's contemporaries.[2] In Bernard's symbolic, the deity is male, and the lover of God, like the lover in the Song he designates the "Bride," is imagined as female. We follow his imagery, though other gendered readings are possible.

In this context, like Rūpa and the other Gosvāmins, Bernard faces what Denys Turner has called a "dilemma of feeling" in dealing with the erotic content of scripture.[3] Bernard preaches a more direct identification with the scriptural Bride than the Gosvāmins allow. He follows a long tradition of Jewish and Christian exegetes before him in interpreting the erotically charged verses of the Song as allegories for God's relationship to God's people.[4] Even so, the dilemma of how members of a celibate monastic community should imitate the Bride's passionate desire leads to the emphatic foreclosure of physical eros as an avenue of expression for this love.

Many Christian exegetes, including Bernard, arrive at their theological reading of the biblical Song through a multi-tiered notion of scripture based in a neo-Platonic model of the human being as body, soul, and spirit. The body of scripture consists of the literal meaning—the sense of the words and the facticity of the historical events reported. The soul of scripture is its moral (tropological) meaning, which encourages readers to live rightly. The spirit of scripture refers to its capacity for allegorical interpretation, as when Christians read passages in the Hebrew Bible as references to Christ.[5] As we shall see, this movement toward allegorization yields results similar to the metaphorical reading of Kṛṣṇa's love play in the Vaiṣṇava tradition.

Bernard's forerunner, Origen of Alexandria (second century), is the first exegete both to articulate this method systematically and to apply it to the Song of Songs. Origen opens his commentary on the Song with the explanation that "this little book is an epithalamium, that is to say, a marriage-song, which Solomon wrote in the form of a drama."[6] His discussion of each verse begins with "a simple record of events," in other words, the literal or bodily meaning. For example, he writes of the opening verse, which proclaims, "Let him kiss me with the kisses of his mouth,"

> Reading it as a simple story, then, we see a bride appearing on the stage, having received for her betrothal and by way of dowry most fitting gifts from a most noble bridegroom; but because the bridegroom delays his coming for so long, she, grieved with longing for his love, is pining at home and doing all she can to bring herself at last to see her spouse, and to enjoy his kisses.[7]

After setting the stage, Origen moves on to the "spiritual interpretation," in which "the appellations of Bride and Bridegroom denote either the

Church in her relation to Christ, or the soul in her union with the Word of God."[8] The characters in the drama hold deeper theological significance.

For Origen, scripture is strewn with verses that have no literal meaning. God has placed these verses as "stumbling-blocks" or "impossibilities" that impel readers to search for their true meaning.[9] The Song of Songs is such a text. Origen places a strong caution in the prologue to his commentary on the Song, calling it "difficult," "dangerous," and liable to misuse by perverse persons "to foster vicious longings and the secrets of sinful love." Readers unprepared to understand the spiritual meaning behind the text's passionate declarations of love will be tempted "to rush into carnal sins and down the steep places of immodesty, either by taking some suggestions and recommendations out of what had been written. . . or else by using what the ancients wrote as a cloak for their lack of self-control."[10] As in Vaiṣṇava interpretations of the *rāsa līlā*, carnal love is the antithesis of the true meaning of the text. To the skilled reader who encounters the love story in scripture, it should be self-evident that it is really about something else.

For Bernard, too, the meaning of the text goes beyond the letter of its alluring poetry. His first sermon on the Song alerts readers that there is more to this scripture than meets the eye. The unusual phrasing of the verse, "let him kiss me with the kiss of his mouth," demands deeper reflection (Serm. 1.5). Why not simply, "Let him kiss me"? There is more to discover here. The text is describing no ordinary relationship, for the Bridegroom here is God. The bodily or literal meaning—particularly when it refers to actual bodies—is inadequate. Certainly, Bernard assures us, God does not have a mouth—"he has no need of bodily instruments"—but such figures of speech "represent certain modes of our encounter with him" (Serm. 4.4–5). The kiss is metaphorical. There are other kisses: the humble kiss of the feet, the supplicatory kiss of the hand, and finally the unitive kiss of the mouth (Serm. 3), each of which is a step in spiritual growth. It will be our task to discern how far beyond the physical body Bernard intends to take his readers.

In contrast to Origen, Bernard and his medieval contemporaries affirm divine love as the perfection rather than the antithesis of human affect (*affectus*). Human feelings can be purified and directed toward God as their object.[11] Despite this continuity between human and divine love, however, Bernard's manner of framing the first and last sermons evinces the same discomfort with the erotic content as Origen expresses. The Song is not a text for beginners. Bernard notes in the first sermon,

> The novices, the immature, those but recently converted from a worldly life, do not normally sing this song or hear it sung. Only the mind disciplined by persevering study, only the man whose efforts have borne fruit under God's inspiration, the man whose years, as it were, make him ripe for marriage—years measured out not in time but in merits—only he is truly prepared for nuptial union with the divine partner. (Serm. 1.12)

The final sermon, written shortly before Bernard died, describes the bed of this union by emphasizing the importance of modesty. The reader would be mistaken to interpret the bed of the Songs as a bed for literal lovemaking, for it symbolizes the solitude of prayer (Serm. 86).

The approach by which Bernard arrives at the chaste bed of prayer signals one of the central means by which he neutralizes the erotic content of the biblical Song. The meaning of the bed is that monks must pray at the appropriate place and time, avoid wickedness, and not seek "praise or ostentation" (Serm. 86.2). Astonishingly, according to Bernard this (and not the drama of the lovers) is the *literal* meaning of the text. After explaining the bed as a reference to prayer (for him, the literal meaning), he offers "to examine further the privacy of the bed and the time, to see if there is *any hidden spiritual meaning*" (Serm. 84.4; emphasis added). As we shall discover, this curious literalization of the moral and allegorical meanings (i.e., what monks should do, and how they are wedded to Christ) enables Bernard to avoid the temptations inherent in the letter of the text.

An examination of Bernard's treatment of the "body" or literal sense of the text will demonstrate an effort to distance Christian monastic practice from the physical aspects of the erotic sensibilities, an effort which runs parallel to Gauḍīya Vaiṣṇava discourse. The following reading of *On the Song of Songs* shows that in almost every case, Bernard moves swiftly from the literal to the moral and spiritual senses of the text, often eliding the literal altogether. He also explicitly rejects impulses toward physical eroticism—a rhetorical move which, I argue in the next chapter, contributes to his resistance to other devotional communities: Jews, Muslims, women, and "heretics."

No Literal Song?

For Bernard, who shares Origen's method of reading scripture, the kiss, the breasts of the Bride and Bridegroom, the ointments on their bodies, and their bed present the reader with a "difficult task," for "the words that describe these visions or images seem to refer to bodies or bodily substances, yet they are means of conveying spiritual truths to us, and hence there must be a spiritual character to our enquiry into their causes and meaning" (Serm. 32.1). The "moral teaching" takes precedence over any "historical sense" the text may contain (e.g., Serm. 23.3–5, 80.1). These tropological readings are always couched within the spiritual allegory in which the Bridegroom and his Bride are God and the Church—or, to a greater extent in Bernard than many of his predecessors, God and the individual Christian soul.

Bernard's allegorical focus dismisses the literal meaning as unworthy of God's Bride. Following the Pauline tradition of contrasting letter with spirit and law with gospel, Bernard derides the literal as "the portion of the Jews," "barren and tasteless . . . its taste brings the savour of the flesh, and to swallow it brings death, but its hidden meaning is of the Holy Spirit" (Serm. 73.1–2). This dismissal becomes imperative when the letter of the text evokes bodily pleasure. For example when the Bride is described as "keeper of the vineyard" (Sg. 1.5),[12] Bernard denies the "direct meaning" of this verse because vineyards "produce the wine that ministers to wantonness." "In a spiritual sense," he tells us, the vineyards must be churches and souls the grapes (Serm. 30.2, 6).

More commonly, Bernard omits the literal sense altogether. Unlike Origen, who systematically sets the stage with the amorous exchange between the lovers, Bernard moves directly to the allegory. Allegory displaces—becomes—the literal sense of the text. One example will illustrate this process. Sg. 1.6 reads, "Tell me, you whom my soul loves, where you pasture your flock, where you make it lie down at noon." This verse appears to refer to the female lover's desire to see her beloved's favorite locales for herding sheep, but Bernard interprets it as the soul's desire to see God as God truly is, a form hidden to humans in this life. Bernard undertakes a long explanation of the various guises in which Christ appears in order to adapt to the needs of individual souls (Serm. 31, 32). It appears as if Bernard has leapt over the literal meaning of the text, but he concludes these sermons with the claim, "So far I have been dealing with the obvious meaning of the words. But for the spiritual meaning that lies hidden beneath, you must await a new sermon" (Serm. 32.10). Here, and in other places, the allegorical framework swallows the literal meaning of the text, so that it becomes *literally* about the God-soul relationship.

Ann Astell calls this move a "reliteralization" of the text for Bernard and his fellow monks. Earlier Christian allegorical readings fuse with the text, eliding the original context. Astell explains,

> [W]hen the literal narrative incorporates its own gloss, the poet obviates the need for the reader to discover the philosophical/dogmatic meaning and displaces the allegory itself as the "hidden" or "spiritual" sense. The original allegory . . . becomes part of the face value of the text; the allegorical Other becomes rhetorically present.[13]

The resulting "two-in-oneness of the Song's letter and gloss" allows the dangerous eros of the text "to be sublimated into the love of God and neighbor."[14] This rhetorical strategy nicely fits Bernard's context, in which the new Cistercian order recruited largely from the ranks of adult men, many of whom had been married or were familiar with the ideals of secular courtly love literature. While the imagery of the Song might resonate with such experiences, it poses no real threat to their chastity because it is always already about spiritual experience.[15]

When the Song becomes literal in this new way, embodied in the moral lives of Christians, the literal love story all but disappears. Medieval exegetes do not *deny* a historical relationship behind the text (by tradition, the marriage between Solomon and Pharaoh's daughter), but that relationship attains significance only as a figure of the ecclesiastical and mystical marriages yet to come.[16] I submit that something crucial is lost when the soul and spirit are allowed to elide the body of the text. The reader is encouraged to forget the physical human body and the created goodness of its eros. To borrow Rūpa's terminology, the indicators and attendant emotions (*anubhāvas* and *vyabhicāribhāvas*) of erotic love are rendered impotent in the devotional sentiment.

Bernard's Decorporealized Devotional Love

The critique I am pursuing takes me to contested ground. Other readers praise Bernard for his richly sensuous language; and although I aim to discern the limits of this language, I concur that his imagery offers fertile soil for Christian reflection on embodiment, sexuality, and aesthetics. Bernard's principal defender, Jean Leclercq, responds to readers who would criticize Bernard for his repression and sublimation of sexual desire:

> If there was any sublimation it seems very likely that it went on beforehand, once and for all. It was not the result of an effort which had to be renewed

> each time a new image or an expression liable to an erotic meaning cropped up. There are symbols which can rouse sexual echoes but which an author—and the readers he had in mind—can sufficiently "sublimate," and use without any complexes.[17]

I have no interest in arguing that Bernard suffers from pathological sexual repression, but I do find that a careful reading of his sermons evinces great care to distance the reading of the Song from corporeal eroticism.

For instance, *On the Song of Songs* does not develop a theology of marriage, which would certainly be one way to justify the Song's place in the scriptural canon.[18] Bernard treats sexual relations and married life obliquely in the Sermons. He views these as the condition of humanity without the gospel (Serm. 59.8), as a source of trials that warrant repentance (Serm. 60.2), and as a preferable alternative to certain heretical temptations (Serm. 65–66). This rhetoric regarding sex and marriage is suited to Bernard's monastic context, in which he and his fellow monks resist sexual urges in order to fulfill their vows of celibacy.

Other than these few references, Bernard largely bypasses the implications of the Song for married love and reads it on another level entirely. He writes, "If these are incidents in a human marriage, and the love spoken of is physical love, as a superficial reading might imply, then I must leave the matter to those it concerns; but if my task is to give an answer which will satisfy, as far as I can, the minds and affections of those who seek the Lord, then I must draw from Holy Scripture . . . something of vital spiritual importance" (Serm. 75.2). The physical is the "superficial" level of the text, whereas those who "seek the Lord" will seek what is "spiritual" in it.

Bernard lays the groundwork for this argument in early sermons that emphasize the metaphorical nature of the text. He imagines his auditors objecting to the notion that God has a body: "This poses a problem for you? God is spirit, his simple substance cannot be considered to have bodily members, so then, you say, show us what you mean by the hands and feet of God; explain to us the kiss of these hands and feet" (Serm. 4.4). He answers, "I allow of course that God does not have these members by his nature, [but] they represent certain modes of our encounter with him" (Serm. 4.4). As a metaphor, the erotic is summarily removed from physicality on God's part and, by extension, on the part of the monks as well.

To be sure, Bernard does not view the body as evil. God both created it and took it up in the incarnation (Serm. 6). Monks should not be excessively abstinent with regard to its needs (Serm. 64.5, 66.6–7). The soul, not the body, is to blame for sin (Serm. 24.6, 56.3). Even so, bodily limitations are like the dark "tents of Kedar" (Sg. 1.4) that "deprive the soul for a while of the vision of the infinite light" (Serm. 26.1). The "sensuality of the body" is one of the walls behind which the Beloved stands obscured (Sg. 2.9). Even if one avoids building up additional walls by submitting to sin, sensual desire remains as long as human beings are in the body (Serm. 56.5–6; cf. 72.8–9).

Because erotic desire is apt to pose a strong temptation for the monks, Bernard handles the content of the Song with great care, superimposing the tropological and allegorical sense over the body of the text wherever possible. For example, the lush praises of the Bride's body are quickly transmuted into something more edifying: Her neck signifies the soul's intellect, by which she is nourished; her ears signify the importance of hearing the gospel; and her breasts are the preaching by which she suckles beginners (Serm. 41). The breasts of the Bride are not erotic but maternal, transmuted into the evangelical act of preaching:[19] They fill with divine grace and "flow in the preaching God's word" (Serm. 9.8). In the statement, "Your breasts are better than wine" (Sg. 1.2), wine denotes "carnal pleasures." Just as the grape is dry after pressing, the flesh is forever drained of pleasures after death (Serm. 9.10).

As we have already seen, the bridal bed is similarly deeroticized: It is not a place of lovemaking but of prayer. This prayer does not excite the senses but is an imageless, contemplative repose, "safe from the jarring turmoil of carnal desires, from the restless intrusion of sensible images" (Serm. 14.5). To emphasize the distance of this love from ordinary love, Bernard describes the Song's maidens, who must wait outside the doors, as former prostitutes addicted to lust, who "are now at last filled with the shame that urges them to rid themselves of that deformity" (Serm. 14.5). Bernard gets carried away by the contrastive rhetoric: In such passages, physical love is prostitution, and the body has nothing to do with the divine embrace.

Bernard consistently redirects Christian love from the physical to the incorporeal. The incarnation plays an ambiguous role in this process. Bernard recalls the injunction to love God with the whole heart, soul, and strength (Deut. 6.5). He writes, "Notice that the love of the heart is, in a certain sense, carnal, because our hearts are attracted most toward the humanity of Christ and the things he did or commanded while in the flesh" (Serm. 20.6). Carnality, then, relates to physicality (*carne*, meat).

The incarnation allows God "to recapture the affections of carnal men," to lure them with human love, "and then gradually to raise them to a spiritual love" (Serm. 20.6). He states the case even more strongly: "The measure of such love is this: its sweetness seizes the whole heart, and draws it completely from the love of all flesh and every sensual pleasure" (Serm. 20.7). The love of Christ's humanity must completely replace other affections: "But that carnal love is worthwhile since through it sensual love is excluded, and the world is condemned and conquered" (Serm. 20.9).

Even Bernard's richly evocative descriptions of mystical experience downplay the physical dimension. He cautions, "[W]henever you hear or read that the Word and the soul converse together, and contemplate each other, do not imagine them speaking with human voices nor appearing in bodily form." Their mode of conversation is spiritual in nature (Serm. 45.7). Many people perceive God within creation, and some meet God in visions or dreams; but Bernard counsels that one should not be content with these sensory experiences. The soul as Bride "wants to have the one she desires present to her *not in bodily form but by inward infusion, not by appearing externally but by laying hold of her within.* It is beyond question that the vision is all the more delightful the more inward it is, and not external" (Serm. 31.6; emphasis added). Bernard describes this interior experience as akin to sleep, closer to death than to the mere lulling of the senses:

> For it is a genuine sleep that yet does not stupefy the mind but transports it. . . . [T]he soul is drawn out of itself by a thought that is both powerful and holy . . . it so separates itself and flies away from the mind that it transcends the normal manner and habit of thinking. . . . This kind of ecstasy, in my opinion, is alone or principally called contemplation. Not to be gripped during life by material desires is a mark of human virtue; but to gaze without the use of bodily likenesses is the sign of angelic purity. (Serm. 52.3–5)

The highest mystical ecstasy is far beyond bodily perception. It refines and then transcends the mental capacity. Physical desires, images, and sensations are left far behind.

In light of Bernard's consistent transmutation of the eroticism of the Song and the experience of the Christian mystic away from the physical, we must ask: Where are the boundaries of the senses and emotions? Can the experience of devotional love ever become palpable, or does it affect only the inner life? Is the incarnation a mere enticement to the love of

God through the flesh, or can it also be an affirmation of the goodness of the body and its affections? The previous chapter illustrated the presence of such tensions in the Gauḍīya Vaiṣṇava tradition. With a view toward a more holistic view of the erotic sentiment, and the "spiritual senses" more generally, the following critical comparison retrieves elements in both Rūpa and Bernard that invite an expansive vision of the body in the erotic devotional sentiment.

Parallel Reading Strategies

The parallels between these two scriptural traditions are so striking that Graham Schweig has argued, "The love poem of the Rāsa Līlā could easily be regarded as the 'Song of Songs' of ancient India."[20] Schweig notes that the *rāsa līlā* chapters of the Bhāgavata Purāṇa, like the Song, are viewed as the paramount revelation of divine love, and both have exerted broad influence in their respective religious cultures. Here, I extend his comparison to include the commentarial traditions, especially the role of metaphor and allegory in the reading strategies designed to distance devotees from the physical eroticism evoked in the text. For both, considerations of the appropriateness (*aucitya*) of the erotic content for religious communities lead to a devaluation of the body's sensuality.

In both the Gauḍīya Vaiṣṇava and Cistercian traditions, the ideal reader of the scriptural love song imagines himself or herself as the feminine lover of God. The cow-herding *gopī* women become exemplars of love for Kṛṣṇa, and the female lover in the Song serves as a model for individual Christian souls. The delicate transition from scriptural poetry to devotional practice impels both Bernard and Rūpa to warn against the study of these texts by insufficiently prepared seekers. The moral pitfalls are readily apparent: Kṛṣṇa dallies with thousands of lovers, many of whom are married to other men. The Song of Songs celebrates erotic love between a single couple, but despite their designations in the commentaries as "Bride" and "Bridegroom," their marital status is unknown. The language of sensual delight is replete throughout both texts. Bernard and Rūpa both worry that readers will take the eroticism of scripture in too direct or physical a sense. To avoid inappropriate imitations of these textual characters, four general strategies emerge. Reading the commentators together, we see that they 1) circumscribe the reading of the text through allegory; 2) limit the degree to which devotees imitate the scriptural lovers; 3) impose degrees of separation between the physical and devotional bodies; and 4) conceive of indirect ways of loving God.

Allegory. Both Rūpa and Bernard appeal to an allegorical reading of scriptural narrative to contrast divine love with ordinary sensory experience. Sexual desire is the best metaphor human beings have for devotional love, but the two experiences of longing and ecstasy are merely analogous. Rūpa's tradition distinguishes two kinds of love, physical sexual desire (*kāma*) and pure affection toward God (*prema*). Love for Kṛṣṇa is purely the latter type, as exemplified in the dramatic defeat of Kāmadeva, lust personified; yet erotic language strives toward expression of the inconceivable unity-in-difference (*acintyabhedābheda*) that is the nature of reality. Rādhā and Kṛṣṇa, the self and God, you and I all are expressions of the Absolute, but inexpressibly so. If one gets mired in the language of sexual union, one misses the unity of all reality.[21] For his part, Bernard views love as a single quality, but one that must be turned away from lower physical objects toward the higher spiritual reality. He cautions readers to think of this love in spiritual, not carnal, terms. The allegorization of the text attains the status of a kind of exegetical science in Bernard, who moves so swiftly from the literal (the body) to the spirit of the text that the allegory *is* the literal meaning for the well-trained reader.

Imitation. The individual's true identity in each tradition is typically that of a female lover of God. Both traditions must explain how devotees are to imitate the scriptural lovers. Vigorous debate over imitation (*anukāra*) versus following (*anusāra*) occurs in Rūpa's tradition. Every initiate takes on the persona of one of Kṛṣṇa's companions in his eternal play, but the mainline interpretation is that this must occur in the *siddha rūpa*, the internal body, and not in the flesh. What one must do in the *sādhaka rūpa*, the external practitioner's body, is to imitate one's guru rather than the *gopī*s. Something similar happens in the Cistercian tradition. Only in contemplation does the monk cross over into the female persona. Furthermore, as Astell demonstrates, when Bernard "reliteralizes" the love story as tropology, breasts, ointments, kisses, and beds become first and foremost symbols for moral and monastic virtues. It is these virtues that Bernard holds up for imitation. Bernard, like the guru, holds up his own conduct and experience as exemplary: "I have applied these things to myself for your sake, that you may do likewise. Be my imitators" (Serm. 43.9, cf. 1 Cor. 4.6).

Body. The upshot of the spiritual and perfected bodies, as well as of the injunction to imitate exemplary devotees rather than the Bride or *gopīs*, is that the physical body experiences little of the erotic relationship between the individual and God. *Bhakti* denotes devotion as "participation," but the teachings of these two traditions erect numerous fences to exclude the body's sensuality. The erotic body is sublimated, transposed from the physical to the transcendent realm. This fact does not necessarily entail pathology or unhealthy repression, as participants in these traditions rather defensively point out. However, the mechanisms that distance the physical body from the experience and expression of the erotic dimensions of mysticism invite a closer look at what such sublimation entails. The Gauḍīya Vaiṣṇava tradition, which is not celibate or even ascetic, does not fear the body or blame it for sin in the same way as the Christian tradition often does. Its concerns with propriety (*aucitya*) in this case have more to do with social conventions of bodily display: Ordinarily, one should not roll about on the ground, cry out inarticulately, and the like. The tradition instead enumerates another set of appropriate physical responses (*anubhāva*s and *vyabhicāribhāva*s) that the devotee should both expect and cultivate in relation to Kṛṣṇa. Bernard's discussion of the body is more cautious, perhaps because he has not fully worked out the implications of a "spiritual" body in his denials of carnality. Most of his treatments of the devotional body relate to the discipline of desire and participation in the larger community.

Indirect love. Union with the divine lover is detached from human experience in both commentators. The greatest intimacy with God is withheld. No one may aspire to the role of Rādhā, Kṛṣṇa's favorite and eternal divine counterpart. Although Rūpa's texts appear to hold open the possibility of identification with one of the other *gopīs*, he himself chooses the role of a *mañjarī*, one of Rādhā's friends or attendants; and many of Rūpa's followers imagine themselves as a servant of such an attendant. The paradigm of loving the lover of Kṛṣṇa, and of enjoying their erotic play as a bystander, spectator, or minor participant, becomes the standard for later Gauḍīya Vaiṣṇavas. For them, the *rasa* of devotional love is best savored from afar. Although Bernard makes it clear to an unprecedented degree that any Christian may describe herself as a Bride of Christ, it is primarily the Church that holds this place. Individual Christians can strive to attain this status, but they remain imperfect in this life. For this reason, Bernard states, "[W]e shall be lovers of the bride [the Church] and loved by the Bridegroom Jesus Christ our Lord" (Serm. 24.8).

Experience of divine love is possible, but no one should claim to have tasted it in full.

These four mechanisms enable the Gauḍīya Vaiṣṇavas and Cistercians to inhabit their scriptural stories imaginatively without embarrassment. Allegory, circumscribed models of imitation, theological delineations of the devotional body, and an ideal of indirect love all distance devotees from scripture's eroticism so that they will avoid inappropriate feelings and behavior. Although the comparative similarities in these reading strategies are striking, readers from these traditions will be unsurprised by the patterns of spiritualization that result from them. I argue in the next chapter, however, that the religious emotion of love is impoverished by this sensibility, especially insofar as it serves to define the boundaries and margins of religious communities.

5 Love, Bodies, and Others

The four distancing strategies discussed in the last chapter set fences around appropriate devotional feeling, but they also set the devotional community apart from persons suspected of inappropriate love for God. This dynamic is most clear with regard to rival religious groups. Bernard of Clairvaux projects perverse practices upon heretical groups, and later church officials view with profound suspicion unauthorized women who claim Christ as their lover. These moves anticipate the Fourth Lateran Council's careful circumscription of the real presence and body of Christ to the institutional Church and its sacraments.[1] The rivalry of Gauḍīya Vaiṣṇavas with other sects around Vrindavan (such as the Sahajiyās) similarly stems from disagreements over how to embody the love of Kṛṣṇa. Rhetorically, these others symbolize a mentality that the lover of God must leave behind. Not only the male practitioner's physicality, but whole persons, especially women, are excluded from full participation.

This claim is paradoxical on its face. Commentator Edwin Bryant calls the Bhāgavata Purāṇa "radical" in its immediate context for "its validation of female spirituality, its undermining of caste by birthright, the extent of its elevation of low-caste devotees, and its implicit criticism of *brāhmaṇical* orthopraxy." He highlights the way these features reshaped the ideals of subsequent Hinduism: "[T]he Bhāgavata provided—and still provides—significant resources for potentially revolutionary social change."[2] One would expect the position of women to be stellar among devotees. Although the narrative context of the Bhāgavata Purāṇa offers much support for an embodied devotion that would celebrate the erotic and subvert conventional relations, it is far from clear that this subversion has taken place on the institutional level in the Gauḍīya Vaiṣṇava community.

The elevation of the feminine in Rādhā and the *gopīs* changes little for the status of most flesh-and-blood women.[3]

Bernard's affective mysticism elevates the Bride as a feminine principle and shifts away from earlier speculative approaches to mysticism that emphasized the intellect. One might thus expect the body, emotions, and women (viewed as "more" physical and emotional) to play a greater role in Bernard's new form of Christian spirituality; but as Grace Jantzen observes, "[T]he emphasis on love and will were often conjoined with an actual despising of bodiliness and sexuality, and, inevitably, of women."[4] She explains,

> The vocabulary of erotic yearning, the hunger for the presence of the beloved and for sexual consummation, of bliss and contentment is the weft on which Bernard's sermons are woven. . . . But if the weft of his sermons is the vocabulary of erotic love, the warp is a sharp denial of the body as having any part of it. . . . Time after time, when Bernard begins with a theme set in an erotic key, he transposes it into a spiritual meaning which leaves out the physical and the sensual.[5]

As another scholar puts it, "[T]he problem is not so much that the female or the feminine defines women in restrictive or negative terms. On the contrary, the problem is that the feminine is detached from women and that it floats freely on a textual level."[6] Again, woman as symbol has little to do with actual women.

Two stories about the figures we have been studying illustrate this disconnect between positive feminine symbolism and the treatment of women. Bernard's contemporary, William of St. Thierry, relates an anecdote in which Bernard refused to see his sister Humbeline, "hating and loathing her as if she were a snare of the devil set on luring souls." When she complained about this, their other brother Andrew, doorkeeper of the monastery, "rebuked her with being a parcel of dung."[7] A story is told about Jīva Gosvāmin in which the great devotee Mirabai came to join the community in Vrindavan, and he, too, refused to see her. "He had undertaken a vow to think only of Krishna and never, therefore, to have concourse with a woman, since that would be apt to distract him from his holy thoughts." Mirabai countered with a theological argument: "[A]s far as she could see there was only one male in all of [Vrindavan] and it wasn't [Jīva]."[8] Jīva relented, and Mirabai attained a large following of devotees in Vrindavan. Despite the different outcomes of these tales, both episodes suggest that the first inclination of the founders of these religious communities is to exclude women.

Each of these stories is hagiographic and doubtful, therefore, in terms of historicity. The first is told in order to extol the extent of Bernard's renunciation of worldly temptations, here personified by his sister. The second is told to support Mirabai's reputation as a devotee of the highest order. Both kinds of narratives are commonplace in their respective traditions. Within Christianity, "such scenes are part and parcel of the legendary themes from antiquity onwards and are meant to illustrate the fact that monks were to break with their families."[9] Within the Hindu *bhakti* movement, similar stories are told of Mahadeviyakka and Lalleshwarī debating with holy men.[10] The stock-in-trade nature of these tales may have led to them being attached to Bernard and Jīva without historical basis.

Despite the real possibility that these episodes did not happen as reported, they do offer a window into the challenge that women's devotion poses to traditions that encourage a feminine persona in relation to the divine at the same time as they uphold contemporary views of actual women. Even if Bernard and Jīva do not turn away women outright, their system of feminized devotion is primarily crafted by and for men. For example, Caroline Walker Bynum has documented how Bernard's use of maternal imagery for Christ and for himself as abbot creates a system of authority within his all-male community. His feminine imagery is explicitly directed toward other men.[11] Meanwhile, the women's branch of the Cistercian order experienced considerable difficulty getting established. The men's houses resisted association with them because of the burden of providing priests and spiritual directors for them.[12]

The acceptability of women participating fully in this feminized mode of spirituality is questionable. Bernard does not specify how women might inhabit his affective, experiential mysticism; but as Jantzen vividly narrates in her history of the gendered nature of mysticism, the next several centuries flesh out its implications. Bernard's popular mode of exegesis prompted imitation, not only in other commentaries on the Song, but also in secular love poetry and the devotional writings of women. Beguines such as Mechthild of Magdeburg and Hadewijch of Antwerp did not quote the Song directly. Instead, they narrated vivid scenes of love inspired by it. They rooted their authority in experience rather than in the education or ecclesiastical office denied to them. Jantzen succinctly describes this lineage of female spirituality: "Such subversion of male authority could not go unchecked. . . . Visionary women generally were increasingly suppressed from the time of the rise of clericalism in the twelfth and thirteenth centuries until the atrocities of the witch hunts in the early modern period."[13] Women found ample room within the Song of Songs tradition to develop their identities as lovers of Christ, but their visionary and experiential modes of doing so were increasingly treated with suspicion by church authorities.

The challenge represented by visionary women offers a counter tradition to Bernard's denials of the body—both the body of scripture (the literal sense) and the physical body. Jantzen argues that several of the female mystics offer a more holistic imitation of the incarnate Christ as well as a healthy model for a devotional sentiment of eros. For example,

> Erotic mysticism for [the thirteenth-century beguine] Hadewijch is passionate, embodied mysticism; the erotic is not merely metaphorical, but rather is a focus for integration. Unlike in Bernard, there is no need to put aside the things of the body; indeed, the things of the body must emphatically not be put aside, since it is the body, not a disembodied spirit, which performs the mighty works of justice.[14]

Bodies, materiality, and women reveal themselves as much more than impediments to religious love.

The social potential of Gauḍīya Vaiṣṇava devotion has also been curtailed in exegesis and practice by a number of strategies that keep the body, the feminine, and the erotic in check. Leena Taneja attributes this unrealized potential to a temptation toward the unitive aspects of *rasa*. She notes that the doctrine of "simultaneous oneness and difference" (*acintya-bhedābheda-tattva*) evolved in such a way that it

> pays only lip service to the concept of difference. Although difference is given voice to in this doctrine, the force of difference is minimized as an "effect of identity" or a figment of "perception" that in reality does not really exist. For the Gauḍīya Vaiṣṇavas difference is, if not totally absorbed, at least made subordinate to identity.[15]

In short, gender difference is said not to matter, because everything is an aspect of Kṛṣṇa and enters into union with him. This solution, which Mirabai takes, does not subvert the ordinary functioning of gender and caste rules. As a woman who had renounced her husband's home, her place and authority in the community were the exception, not the rule. Taneja proposes a theological remedy to this elision of embodied difference, which would retrieve the importance of *bhāva*, emotion as personally savored, alongside the blissful dissolution of the self that occurs at the pinnacle of rasic experience. The subjective and universal elements of devotional practice might then enter into a dialectical relationship, so that the tradition might practice both an "opening towards the other (*rasa*) and a closure from the other (*bhāva*)."[16] In this vision, the experience of divine love could alter the community's treatment of embodied differences.

Although I have focused here on the implications of the devotional sentiment of love for women, we may also ask which other lovers of God it excludes. Even as his texts open themselves to queer readings, Bernard denigrates homoeroticism (Serm. 66.3). He not only associates Jews with spiritual blindness and the mere literal reading of scripture; he was also one of the major proponents of the Second Crusade, which unleashed horror on Jews, eastern Christians, and Muslims. Bruce Holsinger has noted the political force of Bernard's interpretation of the Bride's statement that she is "black but beautiful" (Sg. 1.4, Serm. 25). Through Bernard's exploration of "the somatic and ethical significance of skin color . . . [he instills] a militaristic will in his readers to overcome the alterity that the Bride's blackness comes to represent."[17] This feminized blackness is first of all to be conquered within the monks; but combined with his rhetoric of white skin as representing the Christian ideal, it bolsters the Crusaders' mission against dark-skinned others.

Bernard's erotic mysticism is hedged about with exclusions of those who do not love God properly—Jews and Muslims, but heretics in particular. A leader often consulted for advice about irregular individuals and groups, he famously butted heads with the early scholastic theologian Peter Abelard and took a leading role in Abelard's condemnation at the Council of Sens in 1140. In Sermons 65 and 66, where he responds to the request of Everwin of Steinfeld to address the problem of new religious groups, the linkage between heresy and Bernard's view of women emerges most clearly.

Everwin identifies two communities with heretical tendencies: "those with ancient roots who practice the laying-on-of-hands as their sacrament and live openly with women (proto-Cathars) and those who reject infant baptism and ecclesiastical authority (proto-Waldensians)."[18] Bernard conflates the two groups in his interpretation of the "little foxes that spoil the vines" (Sg. 2.15). Among the various errors of the heretics is the fact that they attempt to live as celibates in mixed communities of men and women. He writes,

> To be always in a woman's company without having carnal knowledge of her—is this not a greater miracle than raising the dead? . . . Every day

> your side touches the girl's side at the table, your bed touches hers in your room, your eyes meet hers in conversation, your hands meet hers at work—do you expect to be thought chaste? (Serm. 65.4)

Here, woman is a temptation, a sure downfall to the man aspiring to celibacy. These sermons preach marriage as preferable to such a perilous chastity: "Take from the Church the honorable estate of marriage and the purity of the marriage-bed, and you will surely fill it with concubinage, incest, masturbation, effeminacy, homosexuality—in short, with every kind of filthiness" (Serm. 66.3). Bernard is obviously speculating about the practices of these purportedly heretical groups, but his comments reveal that in his mind "heretics are capable of any sort of behavior that Bernard viewed as sexual pollution."[19] His worries about inappropriate eroticism—the hetero- and homosexual versions of which both dance enticingly around his own rhetoric—emerge in full force when he projects deviant practices on groups outside his own religious community.

In both traditions, hermeneutical mechanisms to avoid inappropriate physical feelings and behaviors vitiate the devotional sentiment of love. The transcendence of the body, coupled with a feminine symbolism oriented entirely toward men, carries the seeds of misogyny and violence. The neglect of embodied differences in Gauḍīya Vaiṣṇava hermeneutics, at very least, fails to challenge the social practices of the community; the rhetoric of the Christian exegetical tradition, at its most insidious, stokes the fire of a crusade. Both groups' projections of sexual deviance onto outsiders block alternative visions of loving the divine.

Toward an Aesthetic Hermeneutic of Love

By and large, modern commentators on the Song have shifted their interest to include the literal, historical sense of the text. At the extreme end of this shift, André LaCocque argues that the Song should not be allegorized, and that it actively resists allegorization. In his reading, the author is a woman, and she rejects the common erotic metaphor for divine-human relations.

> The "trajectory" of the text might be traced as follows: first of all, we could say, the author of the Song de-metaphorizes the language of the Prophets when describing the relationship between Israel and God. In a fashion, the Song thus restores the language to its first and original meaning, making that language once again available to describe the love between a man and a woman. Second, the author goes even further. In her poem

> she magnifies luxury, nature, courtship, eroticism, all things which the Prophets and sages found objectionable. . . . Language has gone full circle, from literal sense to metaphorical to nonfigurative again.[20]

For readers like LaCocque, the Song's glorification of love takes place in a secular, even "irreligious" setting.[21]

Somewhere in the middle of the exegetical shift, a new wave of commentators is working to restore the plain sense of the text as one of several, non-hierarchically related ways of reading it. In response to LaCocque, Paul Ricoeur demurs from a contrast between "naturalistic" and allegorical readings that would divest the latter of spiritual authority. Instead, he proposes "a multiple, flowering history of reading," in which the text is "open to a plurality of interpretations, among which allegorical readings, which are themselves multiple and even contrary to one another, would find a place."[22] Rather than hierarchizing the senses of scripture, the reader moves fluidly between them.

The theological significance of this approach should not be underestimated. Christian theologian Stephanie Paulsell observes that although "critical focus on the historical, literal meaning of the Song has made it impossible to ignore its celebration of erotic desire, sexual pleasure, and the beauty of the human body," the reduction of the text to a mere love poem strips it of its allure as a text of devotion.[23] By contrast, Paulsell holds the various senses of scripture together, arguing that Christians "need the Song because of the reverence for embodied life that shines through every verse."[24] Here, the spiritual meaning does not replace the physical meaning, but intersects it. As Ricoeur argues, "It is the power of love to be able to move in both senses along the ascending and descending spiral of metaphor."[25] Love in one realm holds significance for love in others. Love of human partners mutually informs the love of God.

A comparative perspective offers additional intervention into the retrieval of the erotic in the two scriptural traditions we have been discussing. The following retrieval of the aesthetic elements in Rūpa and Bernard works toward a holistic vision of the spiritual senses that does not elide the body, women, and others in favor of the spirit but re-values the bodily and emotional aspects of eros. Using Rūpa's aesthetic framework, I ask how far Bernard's thought can be stretched toward valuing the body and what foundations he might offer for moving beyond the exclusions of his immediate context. Can we locate *rasa*, or something like it, in Bernard of Clairvaux?

Rasa in Bernard of Clairvaux

An understanding of Gauḍīya Vaiṣṇavism may serve as a new set of lenses with which to view the Christian tradition. Rūpa Gosvāmin's genius is the systematic application of theory from the realm of Sanskrit drama to the devotional life. He meticulously analyzes the components that create the devotional sentiment of love (*śṛṅgāra bhakti rasa*) in the heart of the devotee. Beginning with the *rasa sūtra*, which states that *rasa* arises in the conjunction of certain factors, he describes the physical stimulants of devotional love and the signs that indicate the presence of this love. These categories allow us to revisit Bernard's sermons with an eye to the aesthetic elements of his rhetoric and to consider their potential for a reinvigorated notion of the spiritual senses.

Excitants. Although I have noted how quickly Bernard transmutes the erotic setting of the Song (its excitants or *vibhāvas*) into its moral and allegorical significance, it is hard to deny that the process of reading the text of the Song of Songs is an aesthetic experience. The grace of the original poetic utterance glimmers beneath a heavy overlay of scholarly and pastoral commentary. Descriptions of the pastoral environment (the garden, the fields) set the stage. The lovers praise one another's bodies with extraordinarily sensual comparisons to fruit, wine, and the natural world. The pair enacts a drama of longing: She desperately roams the streets in search of him, and he comes to her in the secrecy of night. Such rich imagery and sensuous language are among the basic stimuli for the *rasa* of love. As Bernard himself notes, the attractive language of the Song delights the reader. Bernard seems to revel in this language, or at least uses it to sustain the interest of his audience and to entice people to the mystical life. As one contemporary reader observes of the first eight sermons, "[B]y repeating the 'kiss' image Bernard developed the erotic nature of his sermon through prolongation of the sensual."[26]

Indicators. The responses of characters in the drama to the stimuli just described are called indicators (*anubhāvas*); and these, too, constitute part of the formula for *rasa*. The Vaiṣṇava tradition teaches that many of the indicators of love can be imitated as spiritual practice, especially the moral goodness that accrues through loving Kṛṣṇa. For Bernard, too, the Bride in the text and the reader as Bride attain a "beauty and brightness" that first fills the heart and then permeates the body with moral luster:

> It shines out, and by the brightness of its rays it makes the body a mirror of the mind, spreading through the limbs and senses so that every action, every word, look, movement, and even laugh (if there should be laughter) radiates gravity and honor. So when the movements of the limbs and senses, its gestures and habits, are seen to be resolute, pure, restrained, free from all presumption and license, with no sign of triviality and idleness, but given to just dealing, zealous in piety, then the beauty of the soul will be seen openly. (Serm. 85.11)

The works of justice and piety are the primary indications of this intimate love, not only as a response to proximity to the divine lover but also as a practice to strengthen love.

Involuntary Responses. Bernard is at the forefront of a burgeoning Christian mysticism concerned with the experiential dimension of devotion. Although later mystics would develop it further, Bernard includes reflection on involuntary physical and emotional responses, such as weariness, restlessness, stupefaction, and tears, that can be called *sāttvikabhāva*s in Rūpa's terminology (*BhRS* 2.3). He describes the process of reading the Song as reading "the book of our own experience" (Serm. 3.1) and peppers the sermons with accounts of his own experience. Note, for example, his striking evocation of the feeling of grace as the let-down reflex of a nursing woman:

> Men with an urge to frequent prayer will have experience of what I say. Often enough when we approach the altar to pray our hearts are dry and lukewarm. But if we persevere, there comes an unexpected infusion of grace, our breast expands as it were, and our interior is filled with an overflowing love; and if somebody should press upon it then, this milk of sweet fecundity would gush forth in streaming richness. (Serm. 9.7)

The effusion of milk is one of the responses of the women of Vrindavan when they gaze upon Kṛṣṇa's adorable childhood activities (*BhRS* 3.4.45). It is an involuntary physical expression of love, and Bernard's use of this metaphor for the monk's (almost?) physical sensation of overflowing grace signals a tipping point toward embodied expression that exceeds regimented moral discipline.

Rasa. Is there *rasa* in Bernard's sermons? In other words, do they evoke an aesthetic experience through the combination of the poetic excitants, their effects on the lover/devotee, and the attendant physical responses? My reading suggests that Bernard's notion of an internal sense activated by faith can be developed in that direction. After a long, fairly typical, excursus on the deceptive nature of the physical senses (Serm. 28.7–8), Bernard grants the existence of such a sense:

> With the power to understand invisible truths, faith does not know the poverty of the senses; it transcends even the limits of human reason, the capacity of nature, the bounds of experience. Why do you ask the eye to do what it is not equipped to do? And why does the hand endeavor to examine things beyond its reach? What you may learn from these senses is of limited value. . . . *And yet he could be touched, but by the heart, not by the hand; by desire, not by the eye; by faith, not by the senses.* (Serm. 28.9; emphasis added)

This internal sense borders on the physical. Faith makes possible a spiritual experience that is not quite physical in our ordinary manner of speaking but is best expressed using the language of sensation.

Bernard moves fluidly between the five senses to speak of the mystical encounter with God. Christians touch God with "the finger of desire" and see God with "the mind's eye" (Serm. 28.10). Bernard also grants priority to the sense of hearing: As scripture states, "faith comes from hearing" (Rom. 10.17). Humans may open their *ears* in this life so that the gospel will prepare them to *see* God in the next: "How I wish the Lord would open my ear, that the word of his truth would enter into my heart, cleanse my eye and make it ready for that joyful vision" (Serm. 28.6, cf. 31.2).

In a manner reminiscent of Rūpa's exploration of the five devotional loves, Bernard employs the vocabulary of taste to describe God's activities not only as Bridegroom but also as a physician, fellow traveler, father, or king: "For the various desires of the soul it is essential that the taste of God's presence be varied too, and that the infused flavor of divine delight should titillate in manifold ways the palate of the soul that seeks him" (Serm. 31.7). Elsewhere, Bernard describes the aesthetic effect of wisdom (*sapientia*) on the way one savors (*sapor*) scripture. The "taste for goodness . . . drives out the taste for evil. . . . [It] makes the carnal sense taste flat, it purifies the understanding, [and] cleanses and heals the palate of the heart" (Serm. 85.8).

The refinement of taste in reading scripture enlivens the other senses. Bernard savors the fragrances of the perfumes and lilies in the Song. To invoke Rūpa's terminology, not only the *rasa* of love but also its excitants or *vibhāvas* (the qualities of the Bridegroom) cause Christians to "run in the odor of [his] ointments" (Sg. 1.3). The events of Christ's life—his birth, teachings, passion, and resurrection—as well as his manifold virtues give off fragrances to be savored. As they run after the ointments (an indicator or *anubhāva*), Christians also become excitants (*vibhāvas*) of devotional delight for others. They become redolent for others to enjoy, giving off the scent of good character (Serm. 71.1).

Are these sensory images "mere" metaphors? Through an aesthetic lens, we need not choose. The sensory aspects of Bernard's rhetoric contribute to the aesthetic experience of his readers (as *vibhāvas*), and they indicate how prayerful reflection on the Song might result in particular behaviors (*anubhāvas*) and sensations (*sāttvikabhāvas*) in the faithful Christian.

It is not until an odd sermon on belching, an involuntary physical occurrence (*sāttvikabhāva*), that Bernard fully lays out his notion of feeling (*affectus*). Sermon 67 considers the utterance of the Bride: "My beloved is mine and I am his" (Sg. 2.16). To Bernard, this outburst seems to come out of the blue. It is one of the first indications of what the Bride *feels*.

> It is the *affectus*, not the intellect, which has spoken, and it is not for the intellect to grasp. What then is the reason for these words? There is none, except that the Bride is transported with delight and enraptured by the long-awaited words of the Bridegroom, and when words ceased she could neither keep silence nor yet express what she felt. (Serm. 67.3)

The Bride gushes forth with an unrestrained expression of emotion, an ecstatic eruption, a torrent of words subject to neither rational thought nor will.

> The *affectus* have their own language, in which they disclose themselves even against their will. Fear has its trembling, grief its anguished groans, love its cries of delight. Are the lamentations of mourners, the sobs of those who grieve, the sighs of those in pain, the sudden frenzied screams of those in fear, the yawns of the replete—are these the result of habit? Do they constitute a reasoned discourse, a deliberate utterance, a premeditated speech? Most certainly such expressions of feeling are not

> produced by the processes of the mind, but by spontaneous impulses. So a strong and burning love, particularly the love of God, does not stop to consider the order, the grammar, the flow, or the number of the words it employs, when it cannot contain itself. . . . [I]mpelled by love she does not speak clearly, but bursts out with whatever comes into her mouth. (Serm. 67.3)

This verse is one of the few places in the text where Bernard does not rush to the moral or allegorical meaning but allows the emotional force of the text to stand.

What, then, should a reader do with such a passage? For Bernard, the nearly inarticulate nature of the Bride's cry recalls for Bernard the Psalmist's contented declaration: "My heart has belched a goodly theme" (Ps. 44.2 [Vulgate], Serm. 67.4). Sanskrit aesthetic theory uses gustatory relishing (*rasa*) and aural resonance (*dhvani*) as sensory metaphors for aesthetic reading; Bernard here resorts to taste and smell. Bernard proposes that we savor this outburst as we would a delightful fragrance or taste—as when one belches after a delicious meal. He writes, "I shall sense the fragrance of every Psalm, not merely of every Psalm, but of every Psalm, every verse, every belch, more fragrant than any perfume" (Serm. 67.7). The apostles, gospel writers, and Christ himself belched forth truths that remain hidden to us, but we may nevertheless scent something of their beauty and long all the more ardently for them. So, too, the Bride here allows us to "catch the fragrance of the mystery which through our unworthiness or weakness she sees we are not fit to taste" (Serm. 67.7). Smelling is a precursor to tasting, which remains the privilege of those who have fully attained the status of Bride.

On occasion, readers of the text may also experience such an outburst of their own. What the Bride experiences is available in some small part in religious ecstasies. Because God is intangible, Bernard cannot describe exactly how God comes to him in such moments:

> I perceived his presence, I remembered afterwards that he had been with me; sometimes I had a presentiment that he would come, but I was never conscious of his coming or his going. . . . The coming of the Word was not perceptible to my eyes, for he has no color; nor to my ears, for there was no sound; nor yet to my nostrils, for he mingles with the mind, not the air; he has not acted upon the air, but created it. His coming was not tasted by the mouth, for there was no eating or drinking, nor could he be known by the sense of touch, for he is not tangible. (Serm. 74.5)

Bernard "perceives" God's presence not through the physical senses but through something like a *spiritual sense*. This would be paradoxical if spiritual and physical were strictly antonyms; but as with the body, soul, and spirit senses of scripture, these faculties are intimately related, depend upon each other, and can even be said to interpenetrate one another.

Bernard can sense the divine presence because God comes to the human being as the power of life itself: God first awakens the soul; then "stirs and soothes and pierces" the diseased, stone-hard heart; weeds, plants, and waters it as a garden; and palpably warms it like the sun (Serm. 74.5). Feelings of being awakened, enlivened, and enlightened alert him to God's work. These experiences are followed by symptoms of holiness including knowledge of one's own faults, subjection of one's ordinary desires, and the amendment of one's life. The bliss of union, as in the unitive love in Rūpa's tradition (*sambhoga śṛṅgāra*), "is sweet intercourse, but it lasts a short time and is experienced rarely" (Serm. 85.13). Although Bernard pays less attention to the feelings attending divine absence (*vipralambha śṛṅgāra*) than Rūpa or even later Christian mystics, he acknowledges that "all these spiritual powers become weak and faint and begin to grow cold" and that he feels "sorrowful" during periods of separation (Serm. 74.7).[27]

In sum, traveling subtly beneath the surface of Bernard's frequent denials of the embodied senses, a rasic sensibility stirs the feelings—both emotional and physical—of the practitioner. Bernard concedes that "*even in this body* we can often enjoy the happiness of the Bridegroom's presence, but it is a happiness that is never complete because the joy of the visit is followed by the pain at his departure" (Serm. 32.2; emphasis added). God's sweet embrace as well as God's apparent absence can be perceived and emotionally felt, *even in this body*. The "spiritual sense" of scripture speaks to the corresponding senses of the reader.

A Holistic "Spiritual Sense"

In this set of chapters, I have troubled the allegorical solutions to the dilemma of feeling in two traditions of devotional love. Both Bernard of Clairvaux and Rūpa Gosvāmin connect exegesis and embodiment, the activities of reading and being in a body. Both worry that devotees will read the eroticism of their scriptures in an inappropriately physical way, and both insist upon the discontinuity of this love from ordinary sensory experience. Both traditions devise mechanisms by which the spiritual body and its ecstatic experiences are discontinuous with the body of ordinary practice. The erotic text is largely blocked from bodily expression. These moves divert the potency of desire in the religious context, with negative implications for the body, the feminine, and religious others. A robust notion of the spiritual senses, however, may take its cue from elements of both traditions.

By borrowing Rūpa's terminology, we have seen more clearly where Bernard's exegesis stimulates the aesthetic sensibilities as well as where the limits of bodily sensation lie. Today's readers are not be bound by the physical or communal boundaries he defends. Contemporary holistic sensibilities can inform a new appreciation for the erotic. The field is ripe for retrieval of religious idioms of the body: Phenomenologists have alerted us to the non-dichotomous functioning of the "lived body," social scientists and philosophers have theorized the complex techniques by which bodies attain identities, and gender theorists have criticized the power relations inherent in dualistic treatments of the body.[28] New scriptural commentaries are beginning to explore this complexity, and we may similarly revisit Rūpa and Bernard to read against the grain of their dichotomies.

Bernard's notion of the *affectus* offers one site for reclamation. He names four main affects: love, joy, fear, and sadness. *Affectus* arises within the ambivalence of embodied life. It is fundamentally relational. Stemming from the verb *afficere*, "to do something to someone," it is "the state produced in the recipient of . . . influence" from another. *Affectus* is also a holistic concept, with its seat in the soul, mind, or heart. The whole person experiences it.[29] These feelings express themselves in various virtues and vices. The affections of the sinful "flesh" are incapable of following God's law, but the higher, rational affections can be regulated and directed toward God. As Julia Kristeva observes, this "duality, that characterizes human experience and of which love is the dramatic expression," is the locus of "the composite, heterogeneous, and subterraneously conflicting nature of incarnational Christianity."[30] The messy affective dimension of experience arises precisely at the place where we are most human, and where God meets us in the flesh.

Contemporary theology similarly emphasizes the relational and holistic nature of the human person. Mind, body, soul, heart—all of these faculties are so deeply interrelated that it is often impossible to separate where one begins and another ends. Embodied experiences give rise to the categories in which we think. Our ideas give interpretive form to sensory experience. Feelings are physical, emotional, and cognitive all at once. Furthermore, other people, the natural environment, and social institutions all make their mark on these dimensions of experience. The experience of scripture enters into this matrix. The whole person encounters the literal sense, expresses the moral sense, and embodies the spiritual sense of the love it inspires. When things get spiritual, the body does not cease to participate.

The notion of the spiritual senses recurs throughout the Christian tradition. When Origen pioneered the method of reading scripture according to the spiritual (or allegorical) sense, he connected the capacity for this kind of reading to the human sensory apparatus. He writes, "[T]here are other senses in [the human person] besides these five bodily senses; these other senses are acquired by training, and are said to be trained when they examine the meaning of things with more acute perception."[31] Subsequent theology—Bernard of Clairvaux's notion of the *affectus*, the contemplative itinerary of Bonaventure, the imaginative methods of visualization in Ignatius of Loyola's *Spiritual Exercises*, and modern Catholic thinkers as diverse as Hans Urs von Balthasar and Karl Rahner—outlines the training necessary to access the spiritual senses.[32] The spiritual senses are not only spiritual, but sensory. As one contemporary Jesuit scholar puts it,

> [T]he concept of "spiritual senses" should be taken primarily to refer to the renewed understanding and perception of ordinary reality which flows spontaneously from the acceptance of grace. One neither can nor should postulate a range of distinct objects which can only be perceived "spiritually," nor a second set of sense-faculties in the human person somehow at once separate from, and yet analogous to, those of every day.[33]

The Christian doctrine of the incarnation and the devotional techniques it has inspired insist upon the centrality of the body in the spiritual sense. The value of the human body now seems more commonsensical than problematic.

Scholars of Gauḍīya Vaiṣṇavism have similarly described a heightened, disciplined, and transformed set of senses in the ideal devotee. *Bhakti* denotes a capacity to enjoy or participate in the deity with all of one's being, and the Gauḍīya Vaiṣṇava tradition invites participants to identify fully with their "double" in Kṛṣṇa's eternal play. Whitney Sanford describes how the devotional poetry in temple practice uses one sense (sound) to evoke another (sight). This synaesthesia—the experience of one sense in terms of another, as when musicians apprehend sound in terms of color—reconfigures the perceptions of the devotees. They "see" differently, both literally and metaphorically: They attain a vision of Kṛṣṇa's divine play and come to comprehend him in a new way.[34] This transformed sensory apparatus remains physical in nature. It perceives the same world, but through a heightened set of senses.

Both traditions imply continuity among the human perceptive faculties, and these models are worth retrieving in the contemporary theological context. In a holistic approach to devotional love, human and divine beings love with all of their faculties; whatever purification of these faculties means, it does not mean their quiescence. Bodies participate in devotional love. They can be trained to express and perceive the signs of the love of God. The love we know in other forms—with lovers, children, parents, revered authorities, members of our religious communities, animals, or nature—is caught up in our ultimate concern. In these loves, we know something of divine bliss; and in loving, we love God. This holistic view resonates with contemporary retrievals of eros in recent Christian theology. The dichotomous view of love as focused either on the self (eros, *kāma*) or on the other (*agape*, *prema*) fosters a severely truncated view of eros. Eros is a love that spills over, flows out, and cannot be contained. It is the irrepressible divine love that creates a world entirely to play the game of love within it.

The Propriety of *Aucitya*

I have aimed to disrupt the anti-body and misogynistic roots of the fear the erotic in two religious subtraditions. Although ideals of appropriate imitation of scriptural exemplars play a central role in these fears, I do not wish to jettison the notion of propriety entirely, for it has unique resonances in a comparative aesthetic context.

The classical Indian concern with propriety (*aucitya*) in aesthetics is two sided. On one side, when coupled with *rasa* theory, it allows the spectator to set aside conventional worries of the sort that bother Bernard and Rūpa. Sanskrit theorists observe that the aesthetic absorption afforded by beautiful poetry and moving drama allows mothers and sons, fathers-in-law and daughters-in-law, to experience a love story without embarrassment. To be caught up in the love story of scripture is to become fully absorbed. The spectator checks her scruples at the door so that she can be swept away by its drama. A bit of this suspension of moral rigor might be appropriate in light of the profligate love of God.

The other side of *aucitya* relates to what can properly be portrayed onstage so as not to hinder the intended *rasa*. In keeping with this aspect of the principle, we should take seriously the obstacles and semblances (*vighnas*, *ābhasas*) to robust religious experience that the theory of appropriateness brings to light. The notion of *aucitya* remains important in light of genuine obstructions to the religious experience of love.

If we view worship as an aesthetic performance (which it is, but as liturgists will tell us, it is also many other things), considerations of *aucitya* have implications for worship. *Aucitya* relates to the relationship between sense, sight, sound, and emotion.[35] If the right pieces are in place, a liturgical performance can elicit a range of emotions through these factors. Liturgists and religious artists can create the appropriate devotional mood for the occasion or, conversely, they can mar it through extraneous factors, monotony, or excessive length.

Rasa theorists identify a number of obstacles (*vighnas*) to realizing *rasa* that are relevant to their task. An analysis of these factors sheds light on the components of a successful communal religious experience.[36] If the "performance" in any way lacks credibility, for instance, devotees may fail to perceive divine love. If leaders do not conduct themselves as persons who love God, some indicator (*anubhāva*) will likely go missing. If there is any doubt about one of the ingredients (do tears signify sadness? pain? bliss?), the participants may fail to taste the devotional sentiment in full. Transitory emotions such as humor or jealous anger can foster love of God; but if such factors become predominant, love will no longer be the primary devotional mood. Divine love can be perverted into anger or disgust, and the jealous God of divine judgment can become an abusive lover.

Religious leaders, artists, and liturgists thus carry a large responsibility for appropriately fostering the devotional experience of love. Because art can manipulate the emotions, artists must also consider the ethical dimensions of their influence. Contemporary audiences are bombarded with emotional manipulations—cinematic features in campaign ads, militaristic patriotic music in church services, sentimental gimmicks that enforce conventional notions of family. Even if persons responsible for designing the worship experience do not claim to produce religious experience, they are often alert to the power of music, space, and words to elicit it.[37] The ends toward which the arts are put therefore require faithful discernment.

Audiences are usually fairly competent judges of an artistic performance. Indian theorists note that lack of evidence causes an aesthetic experience, like an argument, to fail. Direct experience is the most powerful evidence.[38] If, therefore, divine love as evoked in the words and images of a religious performance does not feel like love but wrath, shame, or some other incompatible emotion, then the practitioner's experience might guide them to move away from what can only be a semblance (*ābhasa*) of love.

Other obstacles to *rasa* stem from the devotee. Rūpa notes that the largest impediments to robust devotional feeling are the intrusions of other religious paths—particularly the paths of knowledge (*jñāna*) and work (*karma*) (*BhRS* 1.1.11). The devotional sentiment thrives in the realm of the heart, imagination, and play. An overly intellectual approach can kill the mood, as can a busy attitude that is absorbed with what must be done. Devotional love can arise imperfectly, in various semblances of itself, because of the presence of some defect. For example, a competing desire for material or other religious ends can thwart devotional love (*BhRS* 1.3.43). The sentiment may also fail to flower if it arises in association with things other than God, in persons who are otherwise in opposition to God, or mixed in with contrary elements such as a suggestion of the peaceful sentiment (*BhRS* 4.9).

Rasa arises in persons who have become skilled in cultivating an aesthetic perspective. It fails if the spectator is absorbed in her own immediate situation. On the one hand, it is impossible to rest one's consciousness on another object if one is overpowered by one's immediate feelings of excitement, discomfort, or anxiety. The aesthetic excitants of devotional love—liturgy, scriptural poetry, images, or *rāsa līlā* performances—cannot capture a distracted spiritual imagination. On the other hand, only a semblance of *rasa* will emerge if the audience member clings to experiences of a successful performance—if she tries to perpetuate pleasurable sensations, to escape from unpleasant feelings, or think about how to express or hide them. Overly personal identification with the drama, which can occur if she ignores the contextual markers of space, dress, and liturgical movement, may result in the related problem of being unable to distinguish oneself in some degree from the sacred story.

All of these possible failures of aesthetic experience attend the sentiment of devotional love. As with the preceding analysis of peace, this section on love has drawn a parallel critique of the aesthetic temptation to transcend the physical world. Absorption in a spiritual relationship with God can become the very kind of self-focused love that is the antithesis of the spiritual virtue. Insofar as it abstracts from the physicality of human love, it can be tempted to ignore embodied difference in favor of the internal, imagined world. It can even be perverted into relations of domination, anger, and fear. For all the richness and beauty of peace and love, we must now turn to the prophetic strand of fury and face these temptations head-on.

PART III

Fury

Eight women take the stage against a backdrop depicting a rural Indian village. Each holds a *parai*, the round, flat hand drum with which their "untouchable" ancestors announced the deaths of members of the wider community. They step, kick, and stomp their feet in identical choreography, ankle bells jangling, punctuating their dance with calls of "Hey! Hey!" as a wake-up call to their audience. As they weave among one another in two lines, they beat complex rhythms on their drums, posture erect, smiling broadly.

After an extended period of vigorous, exuberant dancing and drumming, a middle man, who arranges labor for a rich landowner, arrives. He waves his arms and calls the drumming to a halt. He surveys this group and reports to his boss that he has found people to work, but they seem unwilling to serve him. The landowner comes onto the scene. He, like the middle man, wears a band tied around his head to signify authority, but he also carries a long staff and a whip. The dancers huddle together, visibly afraid and confused. Immediately, the landowner begins giving orders. He makes one of the dancers get down on her hands and knees so that he can use her as a chair. He orders two others to dance and swings his whip until the others join in. The women's backs are now bent low in fear. Their beat loses its complexity. Their feet shuffle rather than dance.

As they move, the women organize themselves into pairs, indicating that a response is growing. Before long, one of the dancers stands up. She plants her feet hip distance apart and waves her drum stick emphatically as she speaks her defiance. They will not work for free. They are not his servants. But the man with the whip yells back and beats not only her but the entire group. They all fall to the ground, hiding their terrified faces from him. He laughs and jabs his weapons into the air above him, triumphant.

The women then start a slow beat. Their leader declares that they cannot face such forces alone but need to band together. They stand and surround their task master. As the dance resumes, he is trapped in the middle of their circle. Now he is afraid. Unable to run, he falls to the ground. The choreography expands so that the dancers step on him, in time with the beat. He lies still on the ground and does not get up.

The women smile once more as they dance in victory. As the piece ends, several performers construct a pyramid so that they stand tall over the vanquished oppressor. One drummer rests with her knee on his back.[1]

6 Dalit Arts and the Failure of Aesthetics

The Rural Education for Development Society (REDS) in Karnataka, South India, produces the piece of street theatre just described. The organization works for the promotion of Dalits, the current preferred name for the group formerly known as Untouchables or Harijans. REDS works in over one thousand villages, with pro-Dalit projects ranging from the organization of democratic community councils (Panchayats) to the construction and distribution of solar-powered lamps to families without electricity. There are seventy-seven Dalit groups in the South Indian state of Tamilnadu alone, and these groups include a variety of professions, religions, and ideological approaches to Dalit liberation. In the following pair of chapters, I concentrate primarily on the Paraiyars, who constitute the majority of Dalits in Tamilnadu,[2] and by extension the activism in Tamilnadu and the neighboring state of Karnataka that has arisen around the drum from which the group takes its name.

The lowest classes of people in the Indian social system have gone by many names. In Sanskrit texts written by the priestly caste, the Brahmins, these groups fall below even the Śūdras, the lowest of the four castes (*varṇas*). They are named by their "impure" professions (such as Paraiyars, who work with leather to make drums) or, in Sanskrit literature, by their imagined habits (such as "Śvapakas," dog cookers). The British called them Untouchables or Scheduled Castes. Gandhi designated them Harijans, children of God. Contemporary activists from these groups prefer the name "Dalit," meaning crushed, broken, or oppressed.[3]

Rather than frame a specific textual comparison as I did in the first two parts of this work, I now focus on Dalit activism as an answer to some of the challenges raised by the religio-aesthetic emotions of peace and love. This focus provides one case study in the applicability and critique of *rasa* theory, but it holds implications for justice in relation to other oppressed and marginalized groups. The focus is apt because Dalits are religiously diverse (Hindu, Muslim, Christian, Sikh, etc.), and because the activists I study here focus on challenges of poverty, ecology, and gender violence that are experienced across the globe. In this chapter, I consider the preliminary question of whether Dalit arts can be analyzed in terms of *rasa*. The next chapter considers the religious import of Dalit expressions of fury, particularly in Christian contexts. Part IV of the book takes a cue from the holistic approach to emotion in Dalit arts and sketches theological possibilities for all nine of the traditional *rasa*s.

Drumming as Protest and Identity

Integral to the Dalit movement is the effort to reclaim Dalit culture as a source of pride. The performance described earlier does this in several ways. First, the drum (*parai*, from which comes the caste name Paraiyar and the English cognate "pariah") is the symbol of the community. Within the system of caste Hinduism, this drum is a symbol of pollution. The Paraiyars construct the drum out of leather and play it on the occasion of death. In the past, upper-caste Hindus relied on this service at the same time as they devalued it to the extreme. Today, Dalits beat the drum with pride. They often refuse to perform funeral services and prefer to drum on auspicious occasions. The intricate rhythms and footwork are a living cultural resource, learned even by children. The beat is so vibrant and enlivening, REDS organizers say, that a person cannot help but join in, begin to dance, or pick up a drum, and will continue to drum even if his hands are bleeding.[4] The drum communicates life, empowerment, and community.

Second, although the REDS performance contains elements common to other Indian dance traditions (ankle bells, long hair braided down the back, and a particular style of tying and tucking the sari to facilitate movement), important elements set it apart. The dancers have no accompanying orchestra but provide their own music by drumming and shouting. Their costumes are local, signifying menial labor and rural identity. Unlike upper-caste "classical" dance forms with their angular propriety, this folk style encourages fluid bodily motion: shoulders move, hips shake. Folk art forms such as this are integral to Dalit identity and to the critique of the dominant aesthetic tradition.

Third, the drama narrates a Dalit view of history. Originally, the community was happy and danced together with joy. When others came to oppress them, it caused confusion, fear, and subservience. Together, however, they will stand tall in a unified front and defeat their oppressors. The dancers' spirited movements bespeak the effort necessary for the community to rise up; and the concluding pyramid symbolizes that if everyone lends a hand, a leg, or a shoulder, everyone will gain confidence to exhibit strength.[5]

The method of Dalit uplift arises out of Dalit spirituality. REDS director M. C. Raj enumerates the features of this spirituality (his term is "cosmosity"): It denies a matter/spirit dichotomy; is centered on the earth, woman, ancestors, body, and community; and operates according to principles of non-violence and harmony with the cosmos. According to him, these qualities make the Dalit community inherently resilient, inclusive, magnanimous, welcoming, peaceful, and freedom-loving.[6] In this context, the fact that the drummers are women also holds significance. The ashram associated with REDS is called Bhooshakthi Kendra, "Mother Earth Center," in accordance with the traditional Dalit values of the feminine and the land. By training women in this art form, the organization asserts a social structure counter to that of dominant society.

The protest embodied in this performance has much in common with the protest we have leveled against spiritual traditions focused on peace or love, a protest against the temptation to retreat to an other-worldly realm of emotional bliss and to ignore the demands of the body and of the vulnerable in the community. Raj levels the charge even more pointedly, drawing connections between the dogmas of the "dominant religions" and their violent propensities to subjugate matter, women, the land, and the Dalit people.[7]

For reasons we shall explore later on, folk aesthetic forms and protest genres have not been widely received in the Indian Christian church. They are gradually emerging, however, in places such as the Tamilnadu Theological Seminary in South India. I will argue that viewing Dalit drumming and worship through the lens of *rasa* theory offers important correctives to the dominant aesthetic tradition and to dominant forms of Christianity.

Dalit arts and their reflection thereupon serve as the "textual" sources for this section. In making this choice, I enter into complicated territory. As a multiply privileged person (Euroamerican, educated, employed, with access to academic and publishing institutions, etc.), I cannot hope to represent the Dalit subaltern in the full sense of the term. Even a well-meaning academic who opposes colonial and neo-colonial structures participates in and benefits from those structures. Following Gayatri Spivak, who helpfully theorizes this paradoxical complicity, I therefore attempt to "listen to that other constituency" and learn "to speak in such a way that [I] will be taken seriously by that other constituency."[8] I am, therefore, grateful to my Dalit interlocutors, especially those at REDS, the Dalit Resource Centre in Madurai, and United Theological College in Bangalore. Following the norms of comparative theology that govern this work, I write in the hope that what I say here can be corrected through ongoing conversation.

Beyond Religious Borders

My choice of the REDS street theatre performance to begin this consideration of fury highlights something important about the Dalit contribution to this discussion of emotion in religion: Many in the Dalit consciousness movement forge their identity in opposition to (or with indifference to) Hinduism and Christianity, the two religious traditions I have been comparing thus far. Dalit identity takes precedence over the various religions of the Dalit people. The title of the dance-drama described previously, *Neeli Suria* ("Blue Sun"), paints the community with the Dalit color blue rather than the colors associated with Hinduism (saffron), Christianity (white), or Islam (green). Dalit identity and categories arise out of lived experiences of oppression and liberation.

Dalits activists are united by their experience of oppression and their solidarity in their work to overcome it. The religious implications vary. Raj has received training as a Shaman and rejects both Hinduism and Christianity. For his part, Christian theologian Arvind P. Nirmal redefines Christianity such that the Christian gospel is only Christian if it attends to the realities of oppression. He writes,

> In such a theological venture the primacy of the term "dalit" will have to be conceded against the primacy of the term "Christian" in the dominant theological primary. What this means is that the non-dalit world will ask us "What is Christian about Dalit theology?" Our reply will have to be: "It is the *dalitness* which is 'Christian' about Dalit theology."[9]

Such criteria lend themselves to "an inter-religious approach" that benefits from engagement with "historical liberation movements in other religions like [Hindu] Bhakti and Buddhism."[10] Some Indian theologians use the term "Dalit" to refer to any oppressed group.

Dalit Christianity

Although some of the earliest modern missionaries to India encouraged a radical break from existing religious forms, others attempted to express Christianity in local cultural idioms. One of the first Jesuit missionaries to the subcontinent, Roberto de Nobili (1577–1656), strategized that the best way to introduce the gospel to Indians was through a positive appeal to the priestly class. He styled himself as a "Roman Brahmin," lived an ascetic life complete with the ochre robes of a *sannyāsin*, and entered into scholarly debate through appeals to the Bible as the "fifth Veda" (a claim, we have noted, that has been made to bolster the status of other texts, including the *Nāṭya Śāstra*). Brahmabandhab Upadhyay (1861–1907), a convert, later founded ashrams that adapted Christianity to the nondualist Indian philosophical school of Advaita Vedānta; and the first half of the twentieth century witnessed a surge of similar experiments in Christian ashrams.[11]

The promise of dignity and improved social status associated with these elite cultural forms encouraged a series of large-scale conversions of Dalit groups to Christianity from the 1860s to the 1930s. As a result of these conversions, Nirmal conservatively estimates that "between 50% and 80% of all the Christians in India today are of Scheduled caste origin."[12] Despite the numerical majority of Dalit Christians, most positions of church authority have continued to be held by men from the higher castes. The theology and liturgy of the church have also reflected the hegemony of these castes. Sanskrit terminology and elite forms of local languages have predominated as native religious leaders have endeavored to cultivate an Indian identity for the mainstream denominational churches. At the same time as some Dalits have seen Christian identity as a significant form of protest against Hindu caste politics, then, they have also found it necessary to hold church leaders accountable for discrimination within the church. The persistence of caste discrimination among Christians in matters such as church membership, marriage, and commensality led to the rise of Dalit consciousness and Dalit liberation theology in the church in the late 1970s and 1980s. Dalit liberation theologians push toward theological changes and political representation in the church but also toward greater affirmation of their cultural differences.

Dalit liberation theology can be placed against the backdrop of the liberation theologies that emerged in Latin America and the United States in the mid-twentieth century, which claimed God's preferential option for the poor and oppressed. Like these movements, Nirmal's germinal essay roots Dalit liberation theology in the Exodus narrative: the experience of being "no people," the need for community consciousness, attention to the people's suffering, and the goal of liberation. In these ways, Dalit liberation theology mirrors other liberation movements, but there are important differences as well. Nirmal cautions his contemporaries against the seduction of "yet another imported theology" that does not reflect the Indian situation—particularly the factors of caste and caste-related violence in India.[13] He calls for greater theological attention to Dalit activism in the arts and politics.[14] "The historical dalit consciousness in India depicts even greater and deeper *pathos* than is found in the Deuteronomic Creed," he writes. "My dalit ancestor did not enjoy the nomadic freedom of the wandering Aramean."[15] The history of Dalit oppression runs deeper, he argues, for Dalits have been denied their basic humanity for millennia. Nirmal therefore proclaims the goal to be "realization of our full humanness or conversely, our full divinity, the ideal of the *Imago Dei*, the Image of God in us."[16] The servanthood of God and of Jesus Christ in scripture signifies a radical identification with the servant classes in India. These themes have not historically received attention in the Indian Christian church.

What began as a protest against hegemony within the church is now becoming an institutional focus of the church. The contemporary context of Hindu nationalism, in which the Hindu right has claimed Dalits as Hindus and called for them to "reconvert" away from "foreign" religious traditions like Christianity and Islam, has had a galvanizing effect on Christian denominations. As David Mosse describes the recent shifts, "[R]adicalizing its message and making itself 'more Dalit' allows the church to claim a mass support base, which enhances its political significance and appears to offer a safeguard against the incursions of a pro-Hindutva state."[17] A complex web of social, political, and religious forces has led to tactical alliances between Christians and Dalit activist groups.

The Problem of Aesthetics

Before we can address the aesthetic role of emotion in Dalit dancing and other arts, we must state the obvious objection: Is not aesthetics part of the problem that theologians of liberation want to address? The transcendent function of aesthetics abstracts from daily life, we have charged, and permits connoisseurs to become insensate to suffering and injustice.

The previous two parts of this book subjected the peaceful and erotic *rasas* to a critique of an aestheticizing tendency that has little use for the real world. Abhinavagupta posits the peaceful sentiment (*śānta*) as the paramount aesthetic feeling because, in his view, every emotion experienced in the aesthetic realm ultimately gives way to peaceful repose. One abstracts from one's own situation, forgets about one's own pleasure or pain, and savors emotion in its purest form. For him, this peace is the religious feeling *par excellence*. The soul's stillness in the moment of aesthetic enjoyment borders on the ultimate religious experience of union with *brahman*. As important as bodies, differences, and individuality are in other aspects of his philosophy, in this vision of the apex of spiritual experience, external reality melts away. So, too, with love. Rūpa Gosvāmin wants to help devotees to feel devotional love (*śṛṅgāra bhakti rasa*) for Kṛṣṇa based on the kinds of love exemplified by devotees in scripture. As his recommendations are interpreted by his successors, however, the intense eroticism of the *gopīs*' love is gradually diluted. A series of distancing strategies ensure that devotees will not mistake devotional love for anything related to the physical realm. The result is an other-worldly spiritual life with socially conservative implications. We found similar aestheticizing strategies in the Christian tradition. Bernard of Clairvaux's sermons on scriptural love poetry allegorize love to the extent that actual bodies—especially female bodies—are left far behind. The fear of the body, sex, and women runs like a red thread through the Christian theological tradition.

Dalit and Western philosophers alike have challenged the "elevated place" of aesthetics "in theories whose chief purpose is to negate or trivialize historical-political questions." The endeavor to push the discipline from this "aestheticist" effect toward a critical and political stance moves toward a politically responsible view of *rasa*.[18] Martha Nussbaum's retrieval of the role of the emotions in the moral life, for example, draws heavily on works of art and literature. She ranges through Plato, Spinoza, Proust, Augustine, Dante, Emily Brontë, Whitman, and even Mahler's Second Symphony in pursuit of an account of love that can "preserve love's energy and beauty while purifying it of deforming excesses," only to find that all of them "repudiate daily life."[19] To the extent that these enduring aesthetic examples remain trapped in an otherworldly longing, reject ordinary human passion, and evince shame and disgust at embodied human reality, they come up short in teaching us how to love in this life.

In this vein of critique, tribal theologian Manmasih Ekka argues that "for a pro-dalit, poetry as a general class of aesthetics will be of secondary importance. . . . A dalit poem is simple, direct, forceful, and writing of it is not a joy-ride in aesthetics but . . . [a] long-drawn cry for socio-economic change for liberation from suffering." If we are to treat Dalit arts as aesthetic objects, Ekka contends, it must be in a manner distinct from "mainstream" habits of considering art. [20]

Nussbaum offers several criteria for keeping the religious import of emotion rooted in the realities of the world, of bodies, and of politics. Love should foster social compassion—a feature lacking in Platonic ascents that "treat earthly need and longing as so much 'mortal rubbish.'"[21] Compassion is easily lost both in the partiality of love and in love's philosophical refinement. Nussbaum observes of the Platonic case,

> [I]nsofar as the ascending lover does become or remain involved in politics . . . she will not be inclined to relieve hunger, to heal the sick, to oppose persecution, or in general to do any of the things we usually think of under the rubric of fighting for justice. Or if she does them, she will do them, at best, . . . with a little bit of contempt, and even disgust, for those who are distressed at their lot.[22]

Unlike the Platonic lover who "looking at the whole array of the good . . . hardly sees individual persons at all," lovers must respect the individuality, agency, and difference of others.[23] These criteria are relevant as we investigate Indian aesthetic traditions in relation to subjugated communities.

The Aesthetics of Indian Christianity

The problems with the peaceful meditative ideal have come to a head in the contemporary Indian Christian context, where laypersons now question the sociological implications of dominant Indian philosophies. Nirmal observes that attempts to fashion an Indian Christian theology have taken dominant philosophical systems such as Advaita or Viśiṣṭādvaita Vedānta as their starting point.

> The result has been that Indian Christian Theology has perpetuated within itself what I prefer to call the "*Brahminic*" tradition. This tradition has further perpetuated [an] intuition-interiority-oriented approach to the theological task in India. One wonders whether this kind of Indian Christian theology will ever have a mass appeal.[24]

The dominant voices in *rasa* theory have claimed the mood of interiority fostered by these philosophical-theological systems as the goal of all aesthetic endeavors.

As discussed in chapter 2, the Indian Catholic church has attempted to harness the peaceful aesthetic-cum-religious ideal in art, liturgy, and Christian ashram initiatives. These efforts implicitly engage *rasa* theory when they incorporate Indian art forms into the life of the church. In one explicit engagement with the *rasa* tradition, the National Biblical, Catechetical, and Liturgical Centre founded a dance ministry, Nrtyavani ("voice of dance"), in 2001 to employ dancers trained in the classical dance form of *bharatanatyam* to teach dance and perform religious and social themes on the Bangalore campus. Their portrayal of the *rasa*s can be viewed in the videos for sale in the NBCLC's bookstore.[25]

Responses to these ministries have been varied. A major strand of Hindu piety appreciates the universal or shared aspects of religion, but others worry that these arts are not only used for Christian edification but can also be used in proselytization. Among the latter voices are those who claim Hindu ownership of Indian symbols, ideas, and art forms. For example, Rajiv Malhotra and Aravindan Neelakandan devote part of their book-length treatment of these issues to the "Christian denigration" and "appropriation of Hindu dance" and charge that Christian dancers and choreographers want to strip *bharatanatyam* of its Hindu identity.[26]

Some Indian Christians also object to Christian experimentation with "Hindu" forms. For example, a series of Christian mandalas by Sahi "were criticized by Sr. Genevieve, a fellow artist working in India, because she saw in them Tantric symbolism, which she felt was not suitable for Christian mandalas," and their publication was delayed for several years. Despite Sahi's efforts to explicate these themes as an elemental spirituality common to India's religions, he still receives criticism of this work as "New Age."[27] Christian critics of the NBCLC's dance ministry make similar arguments. Some find the *bharatanatyam* dance form too secular (sensual) for Christian worship, while others find it too Hindu because of its origins in South Indian temple worship.[28]

Because the majority of Indian Christians are Dalits, forms of ministry derived from upper-caste models have come under serious critique. According to Selva Raj, such attempts to adapt Christianity are ineffectual because they have been imposed as in a top-down ecclesiastical model—"adaptation from above"—and do not arise from the devotional lives of the people.[29] Even for persons cognizant of the fluid and hybrid nature of culture, the NBCLC's ministries have fallen short because they draw upon genres and styles that do not reflect the lives of the laity. Sometimes the negative response is as simple as indifference. The Sanskrit mass at the NBCLC, for example, has become a curiosity mainly attended by visiting foreigners. At other times, programs have been met with hostility. Sahi, who has been affiliated as an artist with the NBCLC since its inception, narrates several such incidents, the most notable of which was a failed campaign to tear down the Saccidananda Chapel because it calls upon religious symbols that are seen as brahmanical.[30] This politicized environment lies in the background of a recent leadership shift at the NBCLC, the downsizing of its dance ministry, and efforts to phase out of the Sanskrit mass.[31]

Dalit Christian *Rasa*?

Given the controversy over forays into classical Indian art forms, it is legitimate to ask what place *rasa* theory can have in Christian theology. Is *rasa* a uniquely Hindu concept? Does reference to *rasa* impose high-caste culture upon Dalit Christians? I venture to answer "no" to both questions. Though the theory originates in the context of a predominantly Hindu culture and has been developed through art forms that some Hindus today claim as uniquely theirs, *rasa* cannot be uniquely claimed by Hindus. As Fr. Anthony Kalliath of the NBCLC explains, the aesthetic dimension is fundamental to human beings. "[*R*]*asa* is more experiential than rational, and this experience comes through art."[32] The styles of human feeling that *rasa* engenders broadly characterize Indian culture. *Rasa* can therefore account for a variety of emotions across a variety of religious settings. M. C. Raj supports such a conclusion. For him, although the classical tradition of "*rasa* does not belong to Dalits . . . the meaning of *rasa* is very much alive in us." Dalit art forms express the full, vibrant spectrum of emotion, without being constrained by theory. Nine *rasa*s may not be enough, he explains: "[O]ur culture always breaks out of these boundaries."[33]

The founding myth in the *Nāṭya Śāstra* stipulates that this text and the arts it governs are for all *varṇa*s to enjoy (*NŚ* I.12, pp. 7–9). Sahi revives the link between Dalits and the aesthetic tradition by acknowledging that Dalit craftsmanship supports the entire edifice with work in materials such as clay, cloth, iron, and leather. For him, the notion of the "fifth" (*pañcama*) unites Dalits (the "fifth caste") and the arts (recall that the *Nāṭya*

Śāstra refers to itself as the "fifth Veda"): "[E]ven the rich tradition of dance drama, and all the cultural life associated with the performing arts in India, . . . is in some way a concession made by the gods to those who had been denied access to the other four Vedas."[34] The *rasa*s are also formulated with reference to various classes of people. For example, the *Nāṭya Śāstra* states that the furious sentiment (*raudra*) belongs properly to "Rākṣasas, Dānavas and violent men"; the comic sentiment (*hāsya*) "is seen chiefly joined to women and men of inferior nature"; and the heroic sentiment (*vīra*) belongs to persons of "the most elevated character."[35]

This latter classification reflects the values of the elite class that formulated it, but it also opens a rupture within the classical theory and creates space for critique. The idea that certain *rasa*s belong more properly to certain classes of people contradicts the pivotal idea that aesthetic emotion is transcendent or otherworldly (*alaukika*). While Bharata may have limited his classification to the kinds of characters that can be *depicted* exhibiting each emotion, Abhinavagupta's commentary goes further. Abhinavagupta states that only spectators who are like the characters (women, low-class persons, etc.) can fully *sympathize* with the emotions they depict. Masson and Patwardhan observe, however, that if only people who are like demons can relish anger, and only women and children fully enjoy the comic,

> then [Abhinavagupta's] whole theory of *rasa*s being *alaukika* will be partially damaged. For it means that we are feeling everyday emotions in the theatre and thus only certain people will like *krodha* [anger]. The whole point of the *alaukikatva* doctrine is that we need not ourselves feel the emotions we are watching in order to sympathize with them.[36]

Abhinavagupta elsewhere teaches that human beings can enjoy the theatre because everyone retains mental impressions (*vāsanā*s) of all the emotions from experiences in previous lives. This common human experience is what allows us to appreciate a good performance.[37] Even within Abhibavagupta's rather transcendent theory of *rasa*, then, the relevance of lived experience comes into play. On both sides of these tensions, *rasa* theory is formulated with a view to experiential differences in characters and audiences.

Rasa transcends caste boundaries in both classical theory and contemporary emotional sensibility. Dalit expressions of emotion participate in a common emotional milieu, even as they take up emotional expressions that are devalued in classical theory. Barbara Rosenwein calls shared emotional matrices "emotional communities," or communities that share a set of values and norms regarding emotion and its expression.[38] *Rasa* theory marks a sensibility shared across a broad Indian emotional community and, in some respects, across the broader human community as well. Because *rasa* operates in a variety of Indian subcommunities, we shall, therefore, continue with *rasa* as a template, with a view toward widening its scope in relation to the Dalit community and the religious realm.

The Matter of Form

If *rasa* as an aesthetic mode of feeling is exempted from the charge of upper-caste hegemony, the same cannot be said so easily of the art forms that have traditionally expressed it in Indian churches. In light of a lingering preference for Western and classical (karnatak) music in the Church of South India (CSI), James Theophilus Appavoo calls for a turn to folk music. His compositions for the church draw directly on the forms, rhythms, and instruments of village Dalits. His lyrics are vehicles of protest, easy for ordinary people to remember and sing.

Appavoo protests the effects of classical music on the church's ability to act in solidarity with the oppressed:

> We can not change society without agitation or protest. . . . Which music will initiate this protest? [Here, he makes a pun on karnatak lyrics which mean "be at peace and don't be angry."] When [high-caste people] beat and rape our women, should we watch and not get angry? Are you kidding? What does this music do? It quiets and calms us down, not just the content of the song, the music itself is like that. The musical sound or effect of classical music . . . quiets, soothes the mind and the person becomes tame. As soon as we sing, the listener will become drugged . . . like taking alcohol. Western music is like whisky. Tamil music like *Sa Ni Da Pa* is like arrack [cheap alcohol]. . . . There is not much difference between the two. Karnatak music is not fit for the struggle. . . . [I]t is too melodious.[39]

The courage and anger necessary for Dalit activism, Appavoo believes, cannot be evoked through the music of the dominant classes. Classical music, regardless of the *rasa*s evoked, tends toward transcendence. It functions as an opiate of the masses insofar as it pacifies Christians when they should be roused to bold action. Like many Dalit activists, Appavoo turns instead to folk forms.

Folk art in India has generally been dismissed as lacking in aesthetic value. It ranks lowest in the common classification of classical (*mārga*), regional (*deśī*), and folk art forms. Musicologist P. Sambamurthy writes that "the themes of folk song are never serious . . . but primarily entertainment," and that, by contrast, classical music has the higher purpose of the "creation of *ānanda rasa* (emotional joy)."[40] Zoe Sherinian's ethnographic study of Dalit Christian employment of folk music challenges this purported lack of agency and purpose. As she describes Appavoo's folk music, it aims to spur people to action, transform emotion, and communicate the experiences of persons without access to mainstream media. The value of folk music lies in its efficacy in these realms: "Thus the basis for evaluating musical worth shifts from complexity or aesthetic delight to the ability of the music to be a medium of purposeful communication that will attract the listener to hear the message, contextualize it (possibly changing it in the process), and retransmit it."[41] In this vision, folk dance with a drum that belongs to the people outstrips classical Indian musical forms in appeal and efficacy.

Others, such as Kuruvilla George, have turned to innovative performance media for the church. Working in the Church of South India (CSI) in Kerala, George has experimented with people's theatre, a participatory form of drama that aims to bring oppressed people to consciousness, as a model for the Christian liturgy. In the West, people's theatre has evolved under the influence of figures like Bertolt Brecht, Paulo Friere, and Augusto Boal, who aimed to motivate audiences for social change. The REDS program I described at the beginning of this chapter participates in this movement insofar as the organization employs theatre for development, tells a story of the community's oppression, involves people from the community as actors in telling that story, and builds awareness and a sense of identity. The drum works in the context of people's theatre to call for an active response to a concrete historical situation.[42]

It would seem that REDS, Appavoo, and George have moved a great distance from classical aesthetic theory; however, Sherinian contests "the implication is that there is no 'aesthetic delight' [*gana rasa*], complexity, or religiosity in folk music." She points to folk drumming that is used for rites of passage and the induction of religious trance as evidence that "folk music is both purposeful (for political protest) and transformative (spiritually and psychologically)."[43] There is *rasa* in folk music, for it moves the soul to experience emotion in a deep and spiritually transformative manner.

Despite its resistance to the pacifying effects of classical art forms, Dalit protest drama partakes in classical Indian theory in a number of ways.

The notion that the theatre should instruct is already present in the *Nāṭya Śāstra* (*NŚ* I.108–115, pp. 31–33); and despite Ānandavardhana and Abhinavagupta's theory that the ideal audience member abstracts from personal experience to savor a general feeling of *rasa*, they agree that *rasa* imparts moral benefits for the individual. Furthermore, we have observed that over time the role of the audience in *rasa* theory has evolved toward greater identification with the protagonists. Devotional notions of participation (*bhakti*) encourage personal identification with religious narratives, even if this participation takes place in the interior or transcendent divine realm. Street drama breaks down the fourth wall of the theatre, and audience members become actors. REDS empowers young women by training them to dance, drum, and act; and these performances inspire activity in those who witness them. Here, the "myness" encouraged in the earlier devotional imagination becomes total identification between what one sees on stage and what one experiences in the day-to-day external world. The drama motivates by giving voice to a community's emotions.

As in classical theory, Dalit arts express religious and theological ideals, especially when they incorporate the drum. Sathianathan Clarke describes trained drummers as religious functionaries and explains that the *parai* drum has numerous spiritual functions in communal life. The drum is prominent in processions during auspicious events such as festivals and weddings. It is an instrument that bestows divine grace during life-cycle rites. It invokes divinity and inspires possession during sacrifices and festival events. It serves a protective role during inauspicious occasions such as funerals when it drives away demonic forces. It also brings the community together when it announces events.[44] Putting the drum's role in theological terms, Clarke states,

> An imaginative and thematic recapitulation of the drum in the collective religious life of the Paraiyar will contain at least the following three components: drum as medium of divine-human communication (invokes, contains, and dispenses power); drum as an instrument of linking the subalternity of communities for resistive and emancipatory ends (call to fight invading troops, evil forces, and colonizing caste forces); and drum as a symbol of exemplifying and managing communal subaltern suffering.[45]

The REDS street drama evinces these roles. The celebratory mood of the women's dance reminds the viewer of the drum's auspicious, grace-bestowing aspect. Its protective and summoning role enables the women to organize themselves and to drive out their oppressor. The drum's power to invoke the divine and empower devotees is implied as well.

I have argued that the educative, personal, and religious aspects of Dalit arts invite reflection on how *rasa* functions in them. In turn, their subtle departures from classical uses of *rasa* invite new theorization of the category.

Redefining *Rasa*

As we have considered non-elite voices, the conception of *rasa* has migrated and expanded. Three shifts take place when we attend to Dalit aesthetic forms, each of which corresponds to the major points of tension identified in our investigations of peace and love as religious emotions: the transcendent (*alaukika*) nature of the peaceful sentiment, the role of the appropriate (*aucitya*) in the erotic sentiment, and the individualistic nature of both.

First, our critique of the peaceful sentiment has centered upon the issue of the transcendent aim of art. Aesthetic experience, according to Abhinavagupta, enables the spectator to escape her ordinary life and temporarily stop identifying with her own emotions. She is absorbed in the enjoyment of emotion in its most abstract form. Aesthetic experience is not of this world (*alaukika*). We notice by contrast how very *laukika*, or this-worldly, the liberation is that occurs through the transmission of folk music. According to Appavoo,

> 1) people reflect on and include their experience in the music, 2) they develop self-esteem by proudly reclaiming folk Dalit culture and identity, 3) they resist the tendency to internalize the hegemonic Brahmanical and Western cultures, and 4) they struggle together (in ritual, action, and performance) against multiple oppressions.[46]

This model of art retains a place for transcendence insofar as the production and enjoyment of the people's art creates a sense of self-esteem not granted elsewhere; but every part of life—economic, political, social, ideological, psychological, environmental, gendered, and spiritual—can be addressed.[47]

Second, a greater connection between *rasa* and everyday life has implications for the elements of aesthetic creations deemed appropriate (*aucitya*) for evoking and producing those emotions. Notions of what is "fitting" or "appropriate" for aesthetic treatments of religion are as prominent in Indian Christian worship as they are in Vaiṣṇava and medieval Christian treatments of scripture's eroticism. Sherinian's research reveals that classical karnatak music has historically been favored in the South Indian church. In part, this choice reflected an attempt to raise the status of the low caste Christians who took up this art form. The reasoning behind these choices has to do with propriety. "As judgments are made regarding which music is appropriate for formal church services inside a church building, the qualities of karnatak and folk music are evaluated aesthetically. Generally folk music, the music of the lower castes, is determined to be inappropriate."[48] The term used for folk music is the same as that applied to colloquial Tamil: It is *koccai*, vulgar or degraded. This assessment of folk music is highly invested with caste values.

From the perspective of liberation theology, the notion of appropriateness must be reversed. Appavoo declares "karnatak music's inappropriateness as a vehicle of protest"; for him, "the purpose of art is communication, not performance," and folk music is properly suited to conveying a message of protest and liberation.[49] Although Western and "light" (hybrid Western/film music styles) music have emerged as popular models for church music, Christians have been reluctant to embrace folk forms. Sherinian predicts that only the adoption of folk music as the idiom of the church's acculturation efforts will "strike at the core of the caste/class value system that has plagued and continues to plague the South Indian Church."[50]

Finally, subaltern arts urge *rasa* theory to shift its focus from the interior experience of the individual to the life of the community.[51] Dalit arts bear the stamp of the community. Larbeer and Alexander claim that in the past, "all our [Dalit] cultural expressions were collective."[52] Unlike *bharatanatyam*, a dance form that is performed by highly trained individuals, the entire Dalit community participates in drumming and dancing. As Appavoo puts it, "[*Bharatanatyam*] is so much restricted by skills and symbols. Folk formats have no such restrictions. Anyone can sing a labor song."[53] Appavoo further emphasizes the importance of community in his notion of "one pot" (*oru olai*), a practice of inter-caste food preparation and eating together that also functions as a metaphor for producing and tasting the arts. Unlike the highly subjective notion of revelation implicit in the classical *rasa* formulation, he asserts that God speaks to, and through, the entire community in its expressive life.[54]

Rasa, as a culturally coded mode of feeling, has been carried along on several historical waves of aesthetic expression. In the course of our investigation, we have seen it move from its origins in drama manuals and literary theory, to the devotional imagination, to politicized performance contexts. After these permutations, *rasa*'s core makeup—the combination of excitants, indicators, and transitory emotional states—remains intact. The next chapter investigates the expression and production of one key emotion in the struggle for liberation: the *rasa* of fury.

7 Fury as a Religious Sentiment

The REDS dancers drum up a cauldron of emotions: joy in communal celebration, fear and confusion in the face of violence, courage and defiance toward oppressors, and pride in their victory. The beat of the drum communicates the impetus of these emotions, as do the force of the physical actions of pushing, kicking, and stomping. One of the important emotions that fuels their efforts is anger, which, when distilled into its pure form, can be savored as the *rasa* of fury (*raudra*).[1] Fury is integral to the composition, performance, and reception of Dalit arts for liberation. In the REDS street performance, the theme of the drama is the community's ongoing experience of oppression. Amid a welter of emotions—fear, shame, confusion—anger motivates the dancers to move together and to find a voice.

Sentiments rarely appear in their pure form. Carol Tavris likens emotions to clusters of grapes—they bunch together, and it can take some effort to distinguish them.[2] The *parai* drum evokes one such cluster. On the one hand, it symbolizes the pathos and pain of the Dalit people. Because the drum is made from "polluting" cow hide and beaten at inauspicious times of death, caste Hindus have rendered it, along with the persons who make and play it, degraded and polluted. On the other hand, the drum reveals the presence of the divine in the midst of this pathos as an empowering and emancipating force, as when the lead woman in the REDS drama wields her drumstick defiantly and rebukes her oppressor.[3]

The comparative exercises of the first two divisions of this book lead us to a junction. The calming transcendence of peace can come with the price of inattention to present suffering. The raptures of religious love often come at the expense of the body and women. What religious experience of emotion can ransom these facets of existence? This chapter considers the role of fury in the ethical struggle for justice, drawing upon Hindu, Christian, and subaltern perspectives that we have encountered thus far. The theme of fury, rather than a specific textual comparison, leads the way. I argue that anger, a sentiment often discouraged in religions oriented toward peace and love, can push religious communities to act against injustice and oppression. We continue our case study, then, in order to discern an aesthetic that cries for justice wherever the earth and its inhabitants struggle to flourish.

Anger and the Politics of Representation

Anger is not ordinarily considered a primary religious emotion. *Śānta*, the Hindu religious goal of peace examined in part I of this book, marks the absence of such passions. *Śṛṅgāra*, the loving intent of Kṛṣṇa devotion, employs anger only in an ancillary sense, for in Gauḍīya Vaiṣṇava narratives the divine couple's quarrels resolve into a heightened sense of love. In the Christian tradition, anger is often seen as an unholy obstacle to right relation with God and others. Indeed, scholars have observed a longstanding "embarrassment" in Christian exegesis regarding God's wrath and violent tendencies in scripture; and this ambiguity regarding divine anger extends to human anger as well: Above all, human anger must be controlled.[4]

Anger's prohibition serves sociological functions. In some social settings, the display of anger is unacceptable. In others, it serves to express the displeasure of people in power. In the Hebrew Bible, for instance, a hierarchy "is visible in the attributions of nouns and verbs of anger to kings and princes and not to servants or children, to men and not to women, and, most frequently, to YHWH and Elohim in relation to Israel, whereas it is never associated with Israel in relation to the deity."[5] When subordinate persons express anger, it unsettles and challenges the status quo. The powerful have the most to lose. According to Dalit philosopher M. C. Raj, what dominant groups represent as divine anger "is actually human anger of the dominant world" that justifies and perpetuates domination.[6] He condemns the tendency of these groups to ban expressions of anger, as well as their advice for victims to rely on God for retribution.

One mechanism that suppresses the anger of the oppressed is to project it into terrifying stereotypes. Readers in the United States may remember the controversial cover of *The New Yorker* during the 2008 presidential election. After future first lady Michelle Obama publically alluded to the

American legacy of racial inequality, the cover depicted her as the quintessential "angry black woman," adorned with military fatigues, a large afro, and a machine gun, pumping her fist in what Fox News called a "terrorist fist jab." This image satirically epitomizes the feared, unpatriotic, racialized Other.[7] President Barak Obama has carefully cultivated an unruffled persona that deflects such characterizations; even so, a book titled *The Roots of Obama's Rage* was a best seller in 2010.[8] Persons from historically oppressed groups become mirrors of the fears of dominant groups.

The sentiment of fury is similarly associated with the dark-skinned Other of Vedic texts, which, it should be noted, many contemporary Hindus do not interpret as corresponding with contemporary castes (*varṇa*s) and subcastes (*jāti*s). Bharata attributes *raudra* to those prone to fighting—"Rākṣasas, Dānavas, and violent men."[9] Anger arises in noble persons as the occasion warrants, but it is the special prerogative (*adhikāra*) of certain beings to be angry. The Dānavas are a race of antigods (*asura*s) in Vedic mythology. Who are the *rākṣasa*s? The ambiguity in their identity is instructive. In the Hindu epics, they are depicted as ogres or demons who oppose divine heroes such as Rāma. Bharata describes them as

> furious indeed. . . . [T]hey have many arms, many mouths, disheveled reddish-brown hair standing on end, swollen red eyes, and terrible black figures. Whatever they undertake is furious by nature—all their behavior, speech, or movement of their limbs. By them, as a rule, even love-making is done violently.[10]

The assignment of fury to *rākṣasa*s offers a possible lens into certain upper-caste perceptions of Dalits. If myths record a "history of sentiments," and the *rākṣasa*s in the *Rāmāyana* epic and elsewhere are "a metaphor for particular types of human beings," it is hard not to see in this emotional typology a projection of the dark-skinned Other, both subjugated and feared.[11] In considering the anger of Dalits, we must note how this sentiment has been projected upon them by those who would fear it, and how this fury must therefore flow in subversive, subterranean currents.[12]

I take up aesthetic expressions of Dalit anger not to perpetuate a stereotype (in the next chapter, I consider a full range of Dalit Christian emotional expressions) but to challenge dominant modes of religious emotion and to expose potential new audiences to these expressions. Too often, the most vulnerable populations are completely ignored, or they silence themselves for fear that they will be associated with these stereotypes. Judith Butler argues regarding this silencing effect, "Certain faces must be admitted into public view, must be seen and heard for some keener sense of the value of life, all life, to take hold."[13] As Dalits work to overcome their invisibility within the church and in wider Indian society, they also work to overcome negative representations by defining their own identity. These self-representations in art and writing take precedence here, with the hope that attention to Dalit faces, bodies, and voices can hold theology accountable to human diversity and vulnerability everywhere.

Butler's notion of performed precarity frames my analysis of Dalit protest drumming. I draw out both the limiting forces (precarity) and the agency (performance) entailed in Dalit drumming arts. According to Butler's definition,

> "Precarity" designates that politically induced condition in which certain populations suffer from failing social and economic networks of support and become differentially exposed to injury, violence, and death. Such populations are at heightened risk of disease, poverty, starvation, displacement, and of exposure to violence without protection. Precarity also characterizes that politically induced condition of maximized vulnerability and exposure for populations exposed to arbitrary state violence and to other forms of aggression that are not enacted by states and against which states do not offer adequate protection.[14]

Although some Dalits have been upwardly mobile educationally and economically, all of these factors of precarity obtain among sections of India's Dalit population, as they do for many other men, women, and children across India and the globe. Caste and class marginalization intersect when entire villages lack access to health care, wells, transportation to schools, and regular employment. The poor also contend with feudal land ownership, police corruption, and middle-men who offer devastatingly low prices for their handiwork. Even where community organizing has occurred, these are ongoing challenges.[15] Nevertheless, a vigorous performance of self-representation arises out of this vulnerability.

Performances of anger can be liberative; but anger takes on particular dimensions in particular contexts. Anger is discerned through a complex interplay of language and physiology, and this differs across time and place. Ellen van Wolde observes that metaphors for the experience of anger in American English locate anger in the chest and head ("hot under the collar," "hot-headed"); in Japanese thought, it originates in the belly and rises to the head if uncontrolled; and in biblical Hebrew, anger resides in the nose, nostrils, face, mouth, breath, lips, and tongue.[16] Anger carries cultural freight, and a disparate set of cultural contexts are reflected in the contemporary Dalit Christian milieu. I consider several of these contexts: Indian aesthetics, biblical teachings and contemporary liberation theologies, and aesthetic expressions of protest unique to Dalit communities.

Fury in Classical Indian Context

We may look to the classic text of Indian aesthetics, the *Nāṭya Śāstra*, for how fury is represented in Indian drama. Bharata's outline of *raudra* presents an idealized version for the theatre and indicates features of the furious sentiment likely to be recognized by ancient Indian audiences. The furious sentiment, *raudra rasa*, develops from the foundational emotional state (*sthāyibhāva*) of anger (*krodha*). It is induced by excitants (*vibhāvas*) such as insults, slander, abuse, rape, jealousy, and threat. Onstage, it can be represented by indicators (*anubhāvas*) such as "red pupils, resoluteness, knitting the eyebrows, biting the lips, trembling cheeks, and cracking the knuckles." The transitory emotional states (*vyabhicāribhāvas*) that complement *raudra* are "stupefaction, energy, agitation, indignation, unsteadiness . . . perspiration, trembling, gooseflesh, stammering, and the like." Of all the emotions, anger is most likely to incite activity. Bharata therefore interjects a fourth factor, a series of actions that accompany fury: "chastising, destroying, causing pain, cutting, breaking, attacking, seizing, meeting battle, fighting, and drawing blood" (*NŚ* prose after VI.63, p. 259).[17] As already noted, Bharata associates this sentiment with the ogres or demons (*rākṣasas*) of Hindu mythology.

Raudra is an active, passionate state of mind. Later theorists further describe the poetic styles that best depict it with the words *dīpti*, excitement or flaring up (*DhĀ* 2.9), and *ojas*, a "strong style" that uses harsh phonetic combinations that "jar . . ., instill vigor and become very appropriate to or highly suggestive of the wild Rasa of *raudra*."[18] Fury is consonant with the heroic and terrible *rasas* and can supplement the erotic sentiment (as in a lover's quarrel) or the compassionate sentiment (as in pity for the recipient of angry blows). By contrast, *raudra* impedes the sentiment of peace and therefore stands in opposition to *śānta* and its connection to religious liberation (cf. *Loc* 3.24a).

The definition of liberation is at stake in the question of whether to link *raudra* and faith. For inward-directed spiritualities, liberation is a blissful inner knowledge that pacifies conflictual emotions, regardless of one's external circumstances. For ancient Hebrew prophets and for contemporary liberation movements, however, liberation has to do with removing the material and societal impediments to the flourishing of communities.

Anger in the Christian Prophetic Tradition

Christian theology can be a voice for the suppression and pacification of anger. Many passages in the Hebrew Bible condemn the human anger that arises out of pride or frustration or is expressed too quickly.[19] Christians have interpreted Jesus' statement that "if you are angry with a brother or sister, you will be liable to judgment" (Matt. 5:22, NRSV) as prohibiting anger directed at persons, though not at their sins.[20] Anger does, however, have an undeniable place in the prophetic tradition of both Testaments.

The ancient Hebrew prophets excel in proclaiming the righteous divine anger against injustice:

> Thus says the Lord:
> For three transgressions of Israel,
> and for four, I will not revoke the punishment;
> because they sell the righteous for silver,
> and the needy for a pair of sandals—
> they trample the head of the poor into the dust of the earth,
> and push the afflicted out of the way;
> father and son go in to the same girl,
> so that my holy name is profaned;
> they lay themselves down beside every altar
> on garments taken in pledge;
> and in the house of their God they drink
> wine bought with fines they imposed.
>
> Amos 2:6–8 (NRSV)

Amos prophetically denounces the injustices of Israel, the subordinate partner in the covenant, from the superior divine perspective. Denunciation occurs within a hierarchy: Kings and others in positions of authority possess the right to express fury, and if they do this on behalf of the divine law, they participate in God's righteous anger.[21] We do not directly hear the voices of Israel's defrauded, indentured, trampled, afflicted, and exploited. These persons are more likely to be depicted as feeling anguish, distress, or grief; divine wrath blazes up on their behalf.

Contemporary liberation theologies insist that righteous anger at injustice arises from the afflicted as well. Anger is not inherently sinful. It offers clues to what is wrong in the world. It alerts us that things we hold dear, including our very survival, are under threat. We realize that things are not as they ought to be, and this "ought quality" of anger is essential. "The anger that fuels revolts does not arise, therefore, from objective conditions of deprivation or misery. As long as people regard those conditions as natural and inevitable, as God's law or man's [*sic*] way, they do not feel angry about them."[22] The energy to change a situation can motivate people to claim denied power, resources, and opportunities. Indeed, in the face of creeping numbness or depression, "anger can be a lifeline."[23] Audre Lorde observes, "Anger is loaded with information and energy. . . . When we turn from anger, we turn from insight."[24]

What cause do contemporary Dalits have to be angry? Policies of Untouchability are now illegal. Since India's independence, numerous Dalits have attained higher education, government posts, and middle-class status.[25] Nevertheless, deep structural foundations undergird the caste system in India, and caste and class oppression still go hand-in-hand. Dehumanizing ideologies are notoriously difficult to eradicate. For instance, the stigma of pollution still adheres to services, often related to death and evil spirits, that Paraiyars traditionally perform for the higher castes, including drumming, announcing death, burning the dead, guarding the village, and cattle scavenging.[26] Their anger arises from a long history of oppression on many fronts: social, economic, and political oppression, certainly, but also the psychological and spiritual oppression that takes its toll through repeated messages of inferiority.

The simple matter of dress speaks volumes about this history. Joe Arun describes how some of the older village Paraiyars indicate their acceptance of their subordinate role. Men "still do not wear shirts when they meet the higher castes of the village, they remove their towel from the shoulder in respect," while the women "do not wear blouse and sandals." Arun cites one of the older women saying that "we are [Paraiyars] who should be treated that way, it is written [on] our forehead by God (Brahma)."[27] The younger generation of Dalits refuses to observe this dress code.

One positive role of anger is to forge a unified group identity. A simple binary between oppressor and oppressed can be a powerful means to raise consciousness. In a narrative of ancient origins popular among Dalit activists, light-skinned Aryans (ancestors of caste Hindus) arrived long ago in South India to encounter the nomadic, dark-skinned Dravidian inhabitants. Dalits and other oppressed groups originally belonged to this latter community. The Dravidians who settled and remained separate from Aryan society became the Tribal groups (Ādivāsīs). Others were incorporated into the lowest echelons of the caste system as Śūdras, "Other Backwards Castes," and Dalits. The rest lived a nomadic existence as "raiders," called "Criminal Tribes" by the British.[28] Solidarity between these dispersed groups resists both the colonial divide-and-conquer strategy that pits them against one another, and the strategy of contemporary right-wing political parties to coopt them.[29]

Dalit liberation theology has focused on raising consciousness about the exclusionary forces at work within the church. Secular movements such as the Dalit Panthers, which mirrored the Black Panthers in the United States, provided the early Dalit Christian Liberation Movement with the inspiration to "give public expression to Dalit Christian anger."[30] Christianity holds out the promise of equality in Christ, but caste remains a powerful force within the church. Marriages, eating habits, and even congregational membership take shape along caste lines. Dalit clergy are often denied educational and job opportunities. Dalits and Tribal Christian activists also protest the high-caste values in Christian liturgies that draw upon brahmanical Hinduism for religious language and symbols. Both hegemonic Brahmin culture and middle- and upper-caste non-Brahmin Christians contribute to these aspects of Dalit marginalization.

Anger in response to these multiple layers of oppression differs markedly from the anger that inflicts harm upon others. Carroll Saussy theorizes anger on a continuum between "holy" and "sinful" anger: "Whereas holy anger seeks to right a wrong, whether the evil has been perpetrated on oneself or another, sinful anger is the expression of a wrongdoer, who inflicts evil on wronged people." [31] Thus, insofar as Dalit fury signals the need for change, it is healthy, constructive, and even holy. This is a continuum rather than a strict binary, however, for "most often the wrongdoer is a brokenhearted person, herself or himself wronged."[32] Anger and its causes have systemic reach. Wounds of rejection, trivialization, and violence are perpetrated not only at the individual level but are nurtured by systemic issues of prejudice, oppression, and violence;[33] but recognition of the broken heart at the center of the caste system can fuel a vision for systemic change.

In sum, a model of appropriate, holy anger at racism and casteism opens a space for the anger of the oppressed. The expectation in the Hebrew Bible that only people in power express anger might prevent subaltern people from speaking out. In liberation theology, however, not only God and righteous kings or prophets may wield fury on behalf of the oppressed. Instead, the oppressed themselves come to voice.

Aesthetics in Dalit Protest

In a precarious situation, art offers a way forward. Art offers subtlety, room for interpretation, and the subversive power to communicate in ways that escape the dominant class. In the United States, the spirituals sung by enslaved Africans—"Tell ol' Pharaoh/Let my people go," "Swing low, sweet chariot/comin' for to carry me home"—encoded messages of freedom that facilitated the Underground Railroad, while the slavers heard only harmless religious songs. Sathianathan Clarke similarly notes that much of the Dalits' "rich communal religious reflectivity [is] expressed in non-textual/non-scriptive forms, i.e. music, painting, dance, weaving, song, architecture, etc."[34] The unsaid can be a powerful and paradoxical means of coming to voice.

Philosophies and theologies of Dalit liberation have reclaimed the *parai* drum as a positive symbol of identity of the people. The Dalit Resource Centre at the Tamilnadu Theological Seminary focuses on the liberating power of folk art with the slogan "Dalit arts are weapons of liberation." The Centre has organized more than fifteen annual cultural festivals attended by over fifty drumming troupes.[35] In contrast to elite forms of dance which are often perfected and performed individually, this is the people's art. The drum draws Paraiyars together in community. No stage or special costume is necessary, and the performers are equal to one another. Everyone can join in. The art is not mere entertainment but a part of life.

The drum is especially suited to the expression of anger. As one drum maker claims, "[T]he sound of the drum in its final form should be like the roar of an angry lion."[36] The very act of drumming serves as a release for emotion. M. C. Raj believes that the dominant order, which suppresses anger, deems it vulgar, and postpones its resolution to a later divine justice, results in "an unresolved load of anger" that becomes "unmanageable" and leads to extreme violence. By contrast, the "cosmic order" demands that anger be dealt with "here and now."

People need a "comfort zone," in which it is safe to vent anger without fear of punishment.[37]

According to Raj, the Dalit community provides this comfort zone. There is a variety of ways in which this occurs. For example, Dalits use a form of slang when speaking to one another, which is unique to their community and unappreciated by dominant groups. Raj views the drum in a similar light. With it, the Dalit community has

> invented a linguistic pattern that [is] *entertaining and venting out simultaneously*. The entire community comes together to witness the manifestation of such anger. It becomes a community affair and at the end of it all there is laughter, though there is agony and pain that are integrated into this process.[38]

Communication, entertainment, and psychological healing of the community occur through aesthetic means, at the deeply embodied level of rhythm and movement.

Anger's Precarious Expression

In an ideal world, coming to voice would lead to justice. Oppressive structures would be leveled and perpetrators of injustice held accountable. In practice, this level of justice is seldom attained. Retaliatory attacks on Dalits and the burning of their villages are common responses to Dalit protests. The aesthetic expressions of anger I have described exemplify not "the explicitly combative and radically oppositional symbolization of subaltern religious expression" advocated by some activists but a "realistic element of tacitness and subtlety that ensures the survivability of dimensions of subaltern religion within an overall context of dominating forces."[39] If expressions of anger are to be survivable, they must be subtle. This precarity requires attention in our analysis of Dalit activist drumming.

Recall the street drama recounted at the beginning of part III. In the weave of the dance movements, the dancers organize themselves, surround their task master, push him to the center of the circle, kick him until he falls down, and then step repeatedly on his motionless body. The expression of fury seems quite overt: They marshal their anger, voice it through the defiant tones of the group's spokesperson, and take down their oppressor. Violence is apparently condoned. The REDS philosophy and the framing of the dance drama qualify this impression. Raj, the founder of the organization, has written extensively on the importance of nonviolence for Dalits. According to him, the movements of the dancers symbolize the effort necessary for the community to rise up.[40] To frame this intent, the video disc on which the dance drama was produced begins with a spoken narrative:

> From the day human life started on this earth, we have participated in society with love and courage and worked together and created these special arts. We all walked around this world with head held high. We wore red powder (*kumkum*) on our forehead and started our life. And you took away that from us. And all our achievements and arts and courage have been robbed by Brahmins and others. . . . We are not greedy and we don't want somebody else's assets, but we worked hard to make our life on this earth doing agriculture and other manual labor such as pottery. Now you are trying to rob our properties and assets and we are not going to surrender meekly. We are going remove your efforts from the roots. We have woken up with a great roar and we are going to remove all the barriers including caste barriers. We will break open the caste system. Now we have made blue our color, wear blue powder on our forehead as a symbol, and wear black dress to protest.[41]

This narrative gives a reasonable account of Dalit activism. The activists claim human dignity, signified by the kumkum powder applied to the "third eye," which connects the human being to the divine. They do not want to usurp the vocations or property of others but lay claim to their own property and traditional means of making a living. With a "great roar," they vow to "break open" the caste system. The blue powder symbolizes the dignity they claim for themselves in protest.

The narrator designates "courageous drumming" [*veera gharjane*] as the principal means of protest. The words used for this activity evoke both the heroic *rasa* (*vīra*) and the "roar" of anger that fuels it [*gharjane*, roaring]. She explains, "This drumming is our war of words. We bring this drumming with our warriors and we will stand up together and drum until our last breath. We use these musical drums to carry the message of our arts in every street. We call our drumming 'freedom drumming.'"[42] The war is to be fought with words and with art, and its goal is liberation.

In this example, the message is clear and forceful, but the threat to Brahmin hegemony is not a direct threat to the physical or material well-being of any particular person. The line that the REDS organization has chosen to walk follows the nonviolent strategies of the foundation's hero,

Dr. Bhimrao Ambedkar, who converted to Buddhism out of protest and focused on empowerment as the principal strategy for liberation. This subtlety renders the critique survivable.

An even more delicate balance occurs at the popular level. Arul Joseph, who trains dancers at the Rural Theological Institute of Tamilnadu Theological Seminary, describes how Dalit drumming functions in community celebrations. A traditional warrior dance (*silambattam*) employs two sticks: one for hitting and one for protecting. The dance embodies many emotions: anger, sadness, anticipation, and the willpower to succeed. In one village, a cruel landowner is known for beating his workers. When the festival procession passes his house, the men perform with particular vigor. As Joseph interprets this phenomenon, the message is, "You can beat me, but I have strength too, to beat you, so be careful! But now I am calm and non-violent."[43] This message is never uttered explicitly, but its impression is vividly tattooed in rhythm and movement. Joseph thus views folk dancing and drumming as a "medium to transform [their] feelings," to "change the emotion from sadness to anger," and to change the community's actions from "inefficient to efficient."[44]

The *oyilāṭṭam* folk dance plays a similar role for the Paraiyars. Men form a single line and perform complex foot patterns as they twirl handkerchiefs and sing in a call and response format. Sherinian comments that traditionally this dance may have served the "subversive function of developing physical agility for self-defense," with the handkerchief "a substitute for a twirling sword originally used in this war dance." She observes, "Like many other oppressed groups, untouchables have had to hide their attempts to develop skills of self-defense and gain self-empowerment under the symbolic guise of music, dance performance, and practice of religion."[45] The rhythmic, nonverbal nature of these activities makes them survivable spaces for performance of protest.

Though protests can be quite subtle, such performative contexts sometimes break open into overt caste conflict. In one village in Tamilnadu over a fifty-year period, all of the major confrontations occurring between the Paraiyars and the dominant caste in the village occurred during the Pongal festival, in which Paraiyar drumming plays a major role. The festival affords a large audience for theatrical displays of the tensions between the communities. Many of the activities of the Paraiyars emphasize their pollution: "The Paraiyars are especially shown their lowly place by their activities of drumming, cleaning . . ., and staying away from the sacred spaces. In other words, at the time of festivals the Paraiyars are asked . . . to 'perform' their low identity."[46] Many of the arguments during Pongal in this village resulted in the Paraiyars' refusal to participate in the festival out of protest.

Judith Butler has observed similar patterns of "performed precarity" in other protest movements. She observes that when groups gather in protest, they perform (aggregate, sing, drum) in a way that simultaneously draws attention to their vulnerability and lays claim to greater dignity. For example, when Mexican workers in 2006 gathered in protest in Los Angeles, they sang the national anthem of the United States in English and in Spanish, alternating it with the Mexican national anthem. They performed a right of assembly that many of them did not legally have (as noncitizens) as a way to demand that right in public. They claimed Spanish as a language for the public sphere, something often disavowed by native English speakers.[47] When the protesters in the 2011 Occupy Wall Street movement were evicted from Zucotti Park in New York City, some reassembled in a drum circle near Mayor Michael Bloomberg's home. The eviction was an attempt to remove from view the bodies of Americans vulnerable to spiraling debt, sudden unemployment, and home foreclosure. The wordless re-aggregation of the drummers testified to the persistence of these issues and the humanity of persons affected by them.[48]

As in these examples, Dalit protest drumming lends "sudden visibility and audibility [to] those who are supposed to remain invisible and inaudible."[49] Untouchability is banned in the 1947 Indian constitution, and Dalits now technically have the rights of citizens; yet many are treated in such a way that their full personhood is denied. When villagers refuse to drum at festivals, and when the REDS dancers announce the identity and rights of Dalits, they paradoxically claim rights that are not ordinarily recognized. Their drumming exposes the lie of the end of Untouchability.

Both the spontaneous eruption of drumming in communal gatherings and the activist mobilization of the drum perform Dalit precarity. Dalit dancing and drumming are thus not only performative in an aesthetic sense; they also perform or construct an identity that has in many ways remained unspeakable. These performances are exercises of agency in the midst of precarity.

The Art of the Furious

When we bring *rasa* theory to this analysis, it illuminates the central role of fury as an aesthetic and religious sentiment in the arts of Dalit liberation.

Indian aesthetic theories remind us that when emotion is expressed in aesthetic form, it subtly transforms the everyday emotion (*sthāyibhāva*) that we might feel in direct response to events in our lives. It becomes a more universal emotional "taste" (*rasa*) that can be shared by and with others. Anger (*krodha*) becomes fury (*raudra*). A certain transcendence and release comes through this shared feeling. Here, of course, we are a long way from Abhinavagupta's analogy of *rasa* with the pacified bliss of union with *brahman*. There is a "myness" to the emotion that his theory would not allow, but it is not the private "myness" of solitary suffering. Rather, a shared pathos, courage, and fury arise from the collective experience of the community.

The transformation of individual anger into an aesthetic emotion with spiritual force can be illustrated through the work of faculty and staff at the Tamilnadu Theological Seminary. I highlight three components to this transformation: its motivation by atrocities committed against Dalits, an analogy between aesthetic performance and possession, and the creative reception of the arts.

Anger can be a highly motivating emotion. It can inspire the composition and performance of art somewhat indirectly. Sherinian describes this process in TTS professor James Theophilus Appavoo, who "[absorbs] the tunes, rhythms, and moods of Tamil folk music . . . [and] unconsciously filters this music through his creative emotions—particularly anger—and prescriptive purpose" as he composes songs and liturgies.[50] An egregious event can serve as the impetus to "come out" as a Dalit artist. Caste identification often means the forfeiture of commissions, shows, and recognition; and many Dalit visual artists opt for caste anonymity. In 1998 a group of five artists from the Dalit Resource Centre at the Seminary were the first to enter Ramnad, a town near Madurai where a violent caste riot had led to the burning of huts, the harassment of women, and several killings. They published the art they produced with this epigraph:

> In the shamefaced attitude of the oppressed individual to revealing himself as an oppressed being, . . . Dalit Art finds its birth as an urgent and insistent necessity [as] the expression of our independent identity, of our anger at man killing man, of man breaking out of his death-fear, of our protest against popular art forms.[51]

The fury of the editors of the volume is evident in their introductory essay, which invokes apocalyptic imagery from Revelation: The Son of Man, who suffers under the fist of the empire, looks upon the world with fiery eyes of vindication.[52] Here, consciousness of caste oppression inspires the composition of art by Dalits *as Dalits*, despite the risk of personal hardship.

In contrast to the mainstream aesthetic tradition, in which aesthetic rapture is compared to a pacified union with *brahman*, theorists of Dalit drumming invoke the analogy of possession and animation by the deity. In traditional religion, the *parai* drum provides a powerful outlet for emotion by inviting possession. As Sherinian explains,

> In Tamil village religions, empowerment occurs through transphysical rituals of "possession" by the *sāmi* (deity). The village deity possessing or "coming upon" a villager allows even the weakest members of the community to gain power both physically and emotionally. Emotions such as anger or fear are not pacified but rather channeled into action. The key to inducing this possession is the power of *parai* drumming.[53]

Ritual performance with the *parai* drum can evoke expressions of anger buried beneath layers of trauma. Anger becomes something shared, transcendent, and divine through the ritual.

In this context, religious experience does not escape the traumas of life but bears witness to them. Sherinian recounts the story of a young village girl who became mute after witnessing the murder of a woman by a high-caste man. Only several years later, when she became possessed by the Goddess during a drumming ritual, did she obtain the courage to voice what she had seen and to lead others to the burial site. The power of her ability to stand up to the social hierarchy was mirrored by her physical strength. It was reported that ten men could not restrain her when she was entranced. Sherinian interprets this occurrence in terms of the holistic effect of the drum on the entire person: "Spontaneous ritual action and trance states brought on through drumming . . . can free the mind from the fear of oppression, encouraging the expression of feelings and creating a forum for messages of 'truth.'"[54]

The possession analogy runs through several of Appavoo's songs. In a song addressed to girls, he acknowledges the woes of dowry, bride burnings, domestic abuse, and barrenness. He sings,

> O little girl, you are always crying.
> Get up! Rise up! You are the freedom giving *cindu* song.
> Tell who beat you up. Kill that arrogance.
> You have to become like Mother Mary

[bold enough to be unmarried and pregnant]
That male dominance devil, that demon—
Scare and drive it away, oh mother.[55]

As Sherinian interprets this song, "[R]ising up in social protest is analogous to religious trance [for] both actions involve the same emotional movement and both have the effect of social, psychological, and spiritual transformation." Protest serves as a ritual that enables women to become like or "possessed with/by the power of Mother Mary (to bear liberation)."[56] In this Christian context, anger quite directly becomes a taste of the divine. The girls are roused from acceptance of their personal lot in life and inspired by Mary's example.

The transformative power of possession is also read back onto Jesus. One of Appavoo's songs makes reference to one of the few scriptural instances of Jesus' anger, when he uses a whip to drive the moneychangers out of the temple. Sherinian takes the whip as a reference to folk exorcism rituals that use whips upon the demon-possessed. The song teaches that the divisive god of money must be exorcised so that Jesus might occupy this space: "Those devils created quarrels between us. / Oh, child Jesus, take the whip, come, come quickly to chase away these devils."[57] The song serves as an aesthetic means of invoking the liberating divine presence.

The reception of Dalit arts is essential to their potential to liberate through the *rasa* of fury. Appavoo's choice of folk music as his medium is strategic: It is a means of communication available to everyone, both to hear and to reproduce.[58] His folk songs have taken on a life of their own. For example, poor Dalits modified one song about community organizing to reflect their frustration with its "middle-class" strategies. Appavoo's original lyrics read,

Let us put out petitions, meet the ministers, organize people
And demonstrate our protest.
But do not throw stones at the buses.

The song was recreated by Dalit activists to say,

Let us put petitions and meet the ministers.
But they will not be helpful even to pluck the hair.
Let us fight, only that will change our fate.[59]

In response to their experience of the futility of textbook methods of community organizing, the activists adapted the lyrics to express their anger and resolve. Because folk arts are available to ordinary people, they can be received and recycled in the production of the *rasa* of protest.

Anger plays an important role in the creation, performance, and reception of such liberative art, but anger is not an end in itself. A prophetic vision of flourishing drives these expressions.

Fury and Theology

Christian theology can learn much from this furious art of liberation. We have seen that fury functions as a religious sentiment when it plays a prophetic role. Dalit folk drumming and folk music have been our key exemplars of this liberating *rasa* of fury; but these arts point to important features shared with other prophetic theologies. Fury best serves a theology of liberation when it is embedded in a narrative and when it reflects a holistic understanding of the human person in community.

The repertoire of classical *bharatanatyam* contains a piece that sequentially references all nine of the traditional *rasa*s. This number, "Navarasa," showcases the performer's skill in communicating emotion through stylized gestures and facial expressions.[60] The logic is that if the right kinds of sounds, rhythms, images, and subject matter are combined, and if there are no faults in their application, then the artist can produce any of these nine emotions in the audience. The flaw in this approach is that it reduces *rasa* to technical proficiency and neglects the importance of narrative in evoking emotion. Without a compelling story, the audience may understand the emotion conveyed, but the performance is unlikely to move the audience in a transformative way.

For *rasa* to be an aesthetic sense and not just the name of an emotion, the audience must get caught up in a story. To taste, really and truly, the depths of compassion, one must forget oneself and follow Rāma and Sītā into the forest. To savor love in its purest form, the exploits of Kṛṣṇa and the milkmaids must be narrated compellingly enough so that one inhabits their experience. Without inspired performance, emotion can be reduced to the mere decoration of a text; and without the context of a compelling story, feeling falls flat.[61] The same goes for fury. Paraiyar dancers drum a narrative of their history of oppression. In the REDS drama, the drum evokes the joy of a cultural memory of a life unfettered by violence, the deadening shame of having been beaten down, and the fury that demands restitution. The drum itself embodies this narrative as a polluting, death-related object reclaimed as a positive symbol of the community. There is no decontextualizing this fury. When the drum stirs up the emotions of the dancers, it connects with the emotive force of this history.

Jyoti Sahi captures the narrative element of the drum when he paints drummers and dancers as prophetic figures in relation to biblical and historical themes. The dynamic images are moments in a story.[62] For him, the drum beats the primordial rhythm of Ādivāsī and biblical creation myths. It is the audible image of divine incarnation: "The drum which is made out of natural elements, and represents an embodiment of the Spirit into material forms of Creation, has a 'voice' which . . . stirs primal memories of being one with the Mother who is also the earth."[63] The drum is also related to rituals of sacrifice, for "it has been created out of the body of a sacrificed creature"; yet "it is also a witness to a Spirit world which lies beyond death," which, like the body of Mary, is "a kind of tabernacle, or place in which the Divine word is present."[64] The drum thus calls up stories resonant with liberation.

A Christian theology of fury will be embedded in the liberating story of scripture, where we hear the drum beat of creation that pulses through salvation history, through the liberation of Israel from slavery in Egypt, their return from exile, the eruption of divinity in the incarnation, and the irrepressible advent of the Spirit. The rhythm of this holy fury unsettles the powerful, stirs up deep subterranean impulses toward justice, and coaxes the downtrodden to dance. The frustrations of the oppressed uncover and redeem a deeper history.

The emotional impetus toward freedom is rooted in a holistic understanding of human flourishing, a view of religious emotion that belongs to the entire being—body-mind and spirit-breath. This holism grounds religious experience squarely in this world; it does not aim to transcend the current situation, nor does it place its hope in an otherworldly future. It includes all sectors of society. Drumming is a holistic experience that resists the spiritualization that shadows other aesthetic media of religious emotion. This art rejects the wisdom of the privileged that feeling anger creates negative spiritual effects, that anger should be expressed only if it has first been controlled, and that calmness must reign in order to ensure nonviolence.[65] A holistic approach does not selectively shut down parts of the human emotional spectrum.

One sees the importance of mind, body, and spirit in a holistic approach to religious emotion in Jyoti Sahi's religious art. The reader will recall that Sahi is the artist who designed the Saccidananda Chapel for the National Biblical, Catechetical, and Liturgical Centre, discussed in part I of this work. The religious emotion intended by Catholic inculturation efforts of that period was one of the interior peace of meditation (*śānta*) characteristic of brahmanical wisdom traditions, and I have, by and large, been sympathetic with critiques of this approach. Too often, the spiritualization of emotion has been complicit in the neglect of bodies, women, and material injustice.

By contrast, Sahi's corpus as a whole pushes against the aestheticizing and spiritualizing tendencies of his Indian and Christian contexts. For example, when he focuses on love (which I have argued is significantly spiritualized in Gauḍīya Vaiṣṇava and medieval Christian scriptural exegesis), he has not shied away from the physical, erotic, or feminine. For example, the threshold of the chapel at his art ashram outside Bangalore is marked with the evocative feminine *yoni* shape; and even in the NBCLC chapel, the ascending column recalls the bodies of the meditator and the cosmos. Much of Sahi's work also compellingly paints and theorizes Dalit and Tribal themes. In another of his chapels, built for the Regional Seminary in Orissa, the tabernacle takes the shape of a drum. The prophetic sentiment ensconced in that altar is impossible to spiritualize.[66]

The holistic Dalit arts observed in this chapter address their message not to an otherworldly salvation but to the rectification of injustices in this world. Appavoo theorizes the holistic scope of liberation as encompassing the economic, political, ideological, psychological, environmental, gender-related, as well as spiritual planes. For him, the "'kingdom values' of love, equality, and justice between all in this world" come to fruition "today, not exclusively in heaven or at some indefinite time in the future."[67] Liberating fury refuses a binary of this world and the next.

A holistic vision must ultimately overcome fury's binary structure. While anger can build solidarity among the oppressed, the simple binaries that fuel work for justice must eventually be complexified. To avoid constructing a new fundamentalism on the basis of this anger, liberation movements must attend to spiritual wholeness and eventually to reconciliation. All are caught up together in a web of injury; Appavoo's music therefore "works toward socially empowering the oppressed regardless of religion and changing the values of those who oppress, especially those Christians who continue to practice casteism."[68] Justice and well-being are not only for Christians or only for Dalits. All emotions, all experiences, and all people are caught up in a holistic prophetic vision.

The dissolution of binary logic can aid in healing the values of the dominant group as well as the wounded souls and bodies of those in subjection.

For instance, strategies of stereotype reversal like that of the drum create the space to destroy discriminatory notions of pollution altogether.[69] The diversity of Dalit subgroups may also fruitfully be brought to bear upon the healing process. The cultural and conceptual resources of Tribal, Śūdra, Backward Caste, and Dalit communities illuminate the many facets of oppression and a spectrum of visions of liberation. The complicity of persons in marginalized communities—their internalized inferiority as well as the assimilation to dominant values by the upwardly mobile—may also come into view. And even as the church provides helpful social services, it may also confront its role in perpetuating caste structures.

Anger is by no means the only sentiment expressed or evoked in Dalit folk music. I have focused on *raudra* in this chapter in order to draw out the prophetic critique of the otherworldly aesthetic tendencies that emerged in the previous chapters. In the life of the church, aesthetic forms express a full range of emotions related to the circumstances of the lives and worship of the people. For this reason, the next chapter reconsiders all nine of the *rasa*s.

PART IV

Tastes of the Divine

The wider the mouth is open in astonishment, the more air the animal can take into its body. Wonder, in other words, makes a living being breathe better. . . . The wonderer wonders: jaw dropped in astonishment, incomprehension, anticipation, rage; ears trained on what calls for help, for justice, for thought; eyes wide open to the absence of sense, the limits of knowledge, the touch of all things that opens out possibility. Perhaps that is it, then: [P]erhaps dwelling in wonder is merely a matter of learning to breathe.[1]

8 Toward a Holistic Theology of the Emotions

There is no inherent reason that European philosophical traditions must govern Christian theology across the globe. The cultures of Asia, Africa, and South America, where the majority of Christians now live, offer categories for imagining the life of faith, not only for local or indigenous theologies but for the theological "mainstream" as well. As an aesthetic perspective that relates contextual and bodily aspects of emotion to religious experience, *rasa* sheds light on human flourishing and has much to offer a holistic theology of the emotions.

This venture into the realm of emotion and the arts has opened a discursive space amid the polarities often attributed to aesthetic experience in religion—polarities of mind and body, transcendence and immanence, and interior and exterior. Art can overwhelm the spectator with a sense of divine presence, "but it can too easily be subsumed in the peace of a self-indulgent interiority unless the ethics of engagement . . . are imprinted on the heart of the experiencer."[2] *Rasa* theory helps us see emotion as simultaneously transcendent *and* immanent. The sentiments are rooted in contextual factors and physical cues that evoke embodied responses; yet when we savor them as such, we become aware of partaking of something holy.

The grounded transcendence of art can inspire action. As Don Saliers puts it, "Singing for justice in the face of oppression becomes a political act of resistance to idols, and a prophetic call for the transformation of the order of things."[3] Critical ethical engagement with *rasa* theory has encouraged us to anchor a sense of peace firmly in reality, to tether the rapture of divine love to concerns for justice, and to pray with the Franciscan benediction, "May God bless you with anger at injustice, oppression and exploitation of people, so that you may work for justice, freedom and peace."[4] Despite the temptations of transcendence, the absorption of the spectator in a work of sculpture or drama can attune her to the concerns of this world.

By designating emotions as *rasa*s, a word that connotes juice, sap, flavor, or the essence of a thing, Indian aesthetic theory conceptualizes emotional states as something to be savored. The intense poignancy of aesthetic experience has impelled theorists to view it as theologically significant. Emotions can be tastes of the divine. For Abhinavagupta, all aesthetic experience is analogous with union with *brahman*, but the *rasa* of peace best approximates the serenity of pure meditation. For Gauḍīya Vaiṣṇavas, love communicates most powerfully with divinity. And for Dalit Christians, anger at caste oppression participates in the righteous anger of a just God. The implications for Christian liturgy, pastoral care, and activism are manifold. This chapter, which unfolds only some of the possibilities, is an initial thought experiment in the significance of the nine core emotions (*navarasa*) for Christian theology and practice. Hindu, Dalit, and Indian Christian expressions of these emotions remain my point of departure for constructive reflection.

This constructive task plunges directly into the sticky question of the universality and particularity of emotion. It is an axiom of *rasa* theory that the nine basic emotional states are universal and generalizable. The commonalities in human emotion partially account for how we can understand one another across barriers of language and culture. Even so, there is no pure realm of human nature that transcends culture. We experience emotion in culture-specific ways. As noted in the previous chapter, for example, though anger seems to be a common response to threat or frustration, different cultures conceptualize these feelings differently. Anger is associated with different parts of the body, and the ordinary progression of the feeling to its expression differs across cultures. Power and social status also have much to do with who is allowed to feel and express anger and with how they express it.

As I attend to such factors, my constructive reflections on the nine *rasa*s are just that—constructions. They arise out of the contexts I have compared in this study and out of the feminist and liberation theologies that have framed my critique of them. I therefore bring a distinct ethical focus to bear as my contribution to the comparison. This focus draws out certain tensions internal to the Hindu and Christian traditions. Others, who write from different contexts and concerns, will emphasize other facets of emotional life in relation to theology. I first pick up the prophetic thread from previous chapters to consider a positive role for fury and the other "negative" emotions of terror, disgust, and pathos; and I then weave this liberative strand through the "positive" *rasas* of humor, courage, peace, love, and, finally, wonder.

A holistic theology of the emotions will do more than prescribe emotion's regulation. There are Indian teachers who have developed entire systems of yoga to master the "less agreeable emotions" of anger, disgust, and sadness and foster love, calmness, and devotion in their place.[5] These may be admirable disciplines, but our present concern is to savor each of these emotions from an aesthetic point of view as *rasas*. We will aim to understand emotions as discerning spectators, to critically evaluate their religious usefulness, and to pursue them as potential tastes of the divine.

Fury (*Raudra*)

The collective expression of anger wields great mobilizing force. The surge in Dalit consciousness in the Indian church, fueled by the drumming and dancing examined in part III, is only one example of the liberating power of fury.

The liturgies developed by the Dalit Resource Centre in Madurai integrate fury at the oppressor, at oneself, and at God into a holistic theology of emotion for the communal life of the church. Ceremonies within these collections provide space to express rage that has been built up and tamped down over time. On Worker's Day, the congregation utters curses upon those who exploit laborers and perpetuate injustice.[6] On Martyr's Sunday, they express outrage and lament: After a procession led by the *parai* drums, the congregation narrates recent and historical atrocities committed against them.[7]

Some of the Dalit liturgies also rail against God as the sovereign personal being who bears ultimate responsibility for history. They lift up the injustice of their situation before God on Martyr's Day: "O Lord who created us, why did you create us? . . . Is it to die as silent witnesses to these cruelties? . . . Why did you allow it? Can you remain indifferent?"[8] This is an unusual prayer in the context of communal worship, which ordinarily invokes praise, gratitude, and supplication but not lament. Following examples in scripture, particularly Job and the Psalms, it challenges predominant assumptions that it is a sin, even blasphemy, to express anger at God.[9]

A binary between oppressor and oppressed governs many of the liturgies. One collection explicitly contrasts "the two continuing stories of humankind."[10] The story of the dominant class presents itself as the universal story of divine anger against human sin, the appeasement of this anger, and human escape from punishment. By contrast, the story of the oppressed insists that God's "anger, which is directed only against the dominant, will only subside when the dominant repent" and when Dalits accept this repentance.[11]

This binary is not absolute, however. Jeorg Rieger notes that although "the preferential option for the poor has at times been misunderstood . . . [as] a rigid dualism . . . the term *preferential option* implies and leaves room for other options."[12] Divine and human anger is primarily directed at the oppressors, but the oppressed are sometimes complicit in their own division and destruction. Appavoo's Eucharistic liturgy therefore redirects some of the anger of oppression toward the sins of the Dalit community that perpetuate their fate. In order to avoid God's anger, the litany insists, the community must refrain from the drunkenness and bickering that block the divine liberating presence.[13]

Furthermore, some of the Dalit Resource Centre liturgies create room for the oppressor as well as the oppressed in a vision of "a new united humankind."[14] The Liturgy for Common Worship, for example, enacts a healing process of anger, confession, and forgiveness. The pastor announces, "This is the day that the Lord hath made. We will rejoice and be glad in it." The community pushes back: "How can we rejoice in the Lord when the Dalits suffer atrocities by the dominant caste forces, police officials, and male chauvinists?" After the congregation extemporaneously narrates its experiences of cruelty, individuals stand to ask and receive pardon. The pastor then confesses the temptation to treat his/her vocation "as an opportunity to dominate over others." Non-Dalits confess to using the Dalits as slaves and propping up the unjust caste structure. Men confess to the failure to treat women respectfully as equals. The rich acknowledge their responsibility for the condition of the poor. After each confession, the wronged group expresses forgiveness, even if (as the women respond to the men), "we find it difficult to believe that you sincerely feel sorry for all that you have done to us all these years." After each confession, the two parties share objects symbolic of reconciliation. The ceremony concludes with the Eucharist.[15]

The shared meal of the Eucharist radically contradicts the rationale of Untouchability, which dictates complex rules for avoiding pollution transferred through food. Appavoo's Eucharistic liturgy emphasizes this shared element. In contrast to the use of the sacrament "as a tool of power by all levels of the Christian 'priestly class' to pacify and create obedience and submission," his liturgy aims to empower the people.[16] The form is participatory: The sacrament incorporates the community in several places usually reserved for the priest alone, and it uses the "unrefined" language of ordinary Dalits.[17] Appavoo's myth of *oru olai* (one pot), a story that articulates the power of the shared meal in the South Indian context, narrates the anger, frustration, and humiliation Dalits have experienced in the quest to find enough food. With the shared pot, the burden is distributed across the community, and the resulting meal is a sacrament.[18]

Anger expressed liturgically can speak the truth of a long and ongoing abuse. It can rally oppressed groups to action. It can hold perpetrators accountable for injustice. It can, though by no means always will, lead to reconciliation within the body of Christ. If this is so, Christians might do well to recover what David Blumenthal calls the "lost art of imprecation," the practice of the "well-placed curse" manifest in the Psalms of personal and national anger. Whether direct action is possible, such speech performs the act of invoking justice. [19]

Terror (*Bhayānaka*)

Just as the English word "terror" is rooted in the Latin word *terrere*, to shake or tremble, the *Nāṭya Śāstra* prescribes that the terrible sentiment (*bhayānaka rasa*) "should always be enacted with trembling hands and feet, paralysis, body tremors, heart palpitations, dry palate, and parched throat" (*NŚ* VI.72, p. 265).[20] Threats to our well-being, and aesthetic encounters that recall them, shake us to our core.

Some Christian preachers actively exploit fear in their audiences. The fear of the eternal fires of hell has fueled many Christian sermons. To "sinners in the hands of an angry God," divine wrath is a powerful motivator. Religious terrorism manipulates this emotion. According to some organizations, the terror they inflict is a taste of divine wrath. Violence on earth vindicates God's eternal plan. Theologies of cosmic warfare appear across the spectrum of religions. We see it in Timothy McVeigh's Christian militancy, Christian reconstruction attacks against abortion clinics, Jewish violence against Arabs, the violence of Hamas supporters against Jewish and American targets, Osama bin Laden's concept of *jihad*, the Buddhist offshoot Aum Shinrikyo, and Sikh and Hindu nationalism, to name a handful of examples.[21] As the cosmic battle is enacted, the terrorizing violence of such groups takes on the character of religious ritual.[22]

A person who has been terrorized—either by a wrathful theology or a world permeated by violence and humiliation—can become so habituated to fear that it shapes everything she sees. As Wendy Farley describes it, such a person becomes like a small animal for whom stillness is the best defense. The fear that would otherwise serve as an appropriate mechanism of protection begins to stunt a person's vitality, leading to numbness and paralysis. No defensive or proactive steps are possible. The self-diminishment of the terrorized can be mistaken for religious virtues such as patience, humility, or self-sacrificial love. Farley writes, "Because the religions generally offer humility and patience as crucial antidotes for egocentrism and because they confuse the symptoms of terror with these very virtues, the toxicity of terror is often not only undiagnosed but valorized."[23] In such guises, terror presents itself as a taste of the divine but in actuality has lost its potential to motivate in the face of harm.

In light of these distortions, both heinous and mundane, can terror become a true taste of the divine? I maintain that there is indeed some virtue in allowing ourselves to feel fear, to embrace it and look it in the eye. A. P. Nirmal writes that the emotional response to Dalit anger should be "a certain measure of 'terror'. . . . Our protest should be so loud that the walls of Brahmanism should come tumbling down."[24] The arts of protest awaken anger and activity in the oppressed, but for those who stand to lose even a small amount of their privilege, fear is a common and appropriate response. Like the anger of the oppressed, the terror of the oppressor can bring injustice into view.

Art also taps into the terror of existence more generally. Don Saliers writes of the thin line between beauty and terror, explored to astonishing effect in Britten's "War Requiem" and epitomized in Rilke's observation, "beauty is but the beginning of terror."[25] Our sense of mortality is heightened in the face of violence. We grieve the loss of life. We fear for our loved ones. We quake before the unknown future. And yet, "how often," Saliers observes, "the terrifying and its aftermath of grieving may lead to surprising but near unbearable beauty."[26] The aesthetic realm holds this chaos, distress, and grief and speaks with emotion that transcends words. Art can serve as a ritual that "marks a difference between remaining overwhelmed and inarticulate, and striving to make sense (the *poiesis*) of the experience."[27]

Art can assist in this process, yet much that passes as Christian art today evinces a "reluctance . . . to confront the more difficult aspects of a broken and fractured existence." Terror management theorists tell us that existential fears of death and persistent challenges to one's worldview can lead to an aesthetic preference for art that comforts, in other words, that attempts "to help us *cope* with or *avoid* reality" rather than depict reality as it is.[28] Sentimental religious art might comfort us, but openness to the world requires attentiveness to affliction as well as beauty. Aided by the powerful words and images of ritual, we may discern, evaluate, and respond to the tragic and terrifying aspects of existence.[29]

Disgust (*Bībhatsa*)

Some Tantric, Hindu, and Buddhist meditation practices actively cultivate revulsion toward the world and the body to encourage detachment, renunciation, and compassion. A Christian might be hard pressed to find a constructive theological role for disgust (*bībhatsa*), but the *navarasa* framework invites us to consider it.

When the National Biblical, Catechetical, and Liturgical Centre in South India produced a short *bharatanatyam* piece titled "The Navarasa of Jesus," the choreographers searched for disgust in the life of Jesus. They unearthed one of his hard sayings: "Woe to you, scribes and Pharisees, hypocrites! For you are like whitewashed tombs, which on the outside look beautiful, but inside they are full of the bones of the dead and all kinds of filth" (Matt. 23:27, NRSV). Jesus feels disgust at the attitude of the Pharisees who remind him of whitewashed tombs, outwardly clean but putrefying on the inside. In the dance, the performer depicts the emotion using stock facial expressions and traditional *mudrā*s or hand signals. She first mimics Jesus accusing the Pharisees and then crouches to mime opening a tomb. Her revulsion is obvious: She narrows her mouth and eyes, covers her mouth, turns away with one hand keeping the offending sight at bay, and makes a vomiting motion with the other hand (cf. *NŚ* VI, p. 266).[30]

The analogy between an ethical response to evil and the physical revulsion one feels toward rotting flesh is worth unpacking. Dalit philosopher M. C. Raj writes that violence should generate disgust at a visceral level, but our theological and political language short-circuits the appropriate response. "Sugar-coated discourses" such as invocations of democracy and peace that legitimize war "flagrantly blunt the disgusting ripple impact in the cell systems of organic beings at the sight of violence."[31]

According to Raj, human beings need to listen at the cellular level to the messages that violence sends us because these messages are too often short-circuited by self-justifying rationales.

An example of the visceral ethical reaction of disgust spontaneously emerged on a social networking site after the appearance of a report of the beating death of seventeen-month-old Roy Jones. The boy suffered cardiac arrest after being "repeatedly punched with closed fists and grabbed by the neck." The man charged with first-degree manslaughter in this case, the boyfriend of the toddler's mother, said that "the little boy had been *too feminine* and that he'd been trying to toughen Roy up."[32] Responses to the post came immediately: "Ugh, horrifying"; "That story makes me ill"; and "I just can't bear this." The horror of the crime makes us want to look away, yet the nausea it induces offers the opportunity to evaluate the underlying conditions that make it possible. How "masculine" or "feminine" can a baby be? How do our gendered expectations harm children? What is this supposed connection between violence and masculinity? Between violence and love?

This interrogation is crucial to disgust's ethical function. Martha Nussbaum calls disgust "an unreliable emotion" because revulsion alone cannot dictate ethical evaluations.[33] Though disgust seems to arise unconditioned at the sight or smell of something distasteful and dangerous to our well-being, there is a strong cognitive dimension to disgust. Young children are not squeamish about urine, feces, blood, or other oozing or slimy substances. They learn this response over time. Social norms further condition us when they extend the fear of contamination by these substances (which, it must be noted, are part of every human body) onto persons society deems undesirable. Sometimes the projective logic is one of association: "[U]ntouchables in the Indian caste system were those who cleaned latrines and disposed of corpses; women seem to many men to be particularly closely [*sic*] linked with blood and other bodily fluids through their receptive sexuality, their role in birth, and menstruation." Other projections are more "fantasy-laden": German anti-Semites characterized Jews as "disgusting insects or other vile animals, and also as germs, cancer cells, and 'fungoid growths.'"[34] A similar mechanism toward homosexuals is at work in contemporary American politics, Nussbaum notes, when disgust (as in the refrain that the very thought of gay sex makes straight people want to vomit) serves as rationale for anti-sodomy legislation and new laws banning gay marriage.[35]

All emotional responses require discernment. Disgust in particular can impel human beings to deny the full humanity of others, just as dissatisfaction with oneself can lead to self-destructive behavior. We therefore need a deep commitment to avoid actual causes of harm, as opposed to that which is irrationally projected as harmful. Raj theorizes disgust as a natural impulse of organic beings to *recoil* from violence; but too often, it functions in the opposite way: Disgusting feelings lead to disgusting behavior.[36] Like fury and terror, then, disgust alerts us that things are not as they should be. People of faith are invited not to look away but to interrogate the feeling and its causes and to convert aversion into action for change.[37]

Compassion (*Karuna*)

The basic emotional state of sorrow, relished aesthetically, gives rise to the pathetic sentiment: the *rasa* of compassion. This *rasa* is the mechanism by which one apprehends the sorrow of another—their "affliction with a curse, calamity, separation from loved ones, loss of money, death, captivity, being put to flight, and meeting other disasters" (*NŚ* prose after VI.61, p. 258).[38] The sight of tears, dejected posture, and distressed behavior can awaken compassion in us, if we are properly attuned to the situation.

The sense of sight, both literal and metaphorical in the sense of imagination or apprehension, seems to have particular importance for the pathetic sentiment. The Buddha's enlightenment, which is a visual metaphor (he is *buddha*, awakened, with eyes open), generates a powerful vision of compassion. Indeed, his insight into suffering, its causes, and the connectedness of all things elevates compassionate loving-kindness to the pinnacle of religious emotion. Jyoti Sahi associates this connection between compassion and the visual with the ethical function of art. In 1980, following a shocking event in Bihar in which Dalits were cruelly blinded, he created a painting of humanity being born in the tear of God. He writes,

> [T]his cruel act revealed a blindness in the whole social system that allowed such a thing to happen. The Compassionate Teacher is concerned about blindness, and the human need to be awakened, and see the reality. This theme of vision as opposed to blindness is . . . the basis for an art which emerges out of compassion.[39]

For Sahi, art should awaken compassion for humanity, a life-affirming, hopeful sentiment that "looks for the beautiful" in other people and in creation.[40] Compassion should in turn rouse people out of lethargy and fear. Nirmal exhorts his fellow Dalit Christians not to lapse into weak or ineffectual compassion: "A Christian Dalit theology will be full of *pathos*, but not a passive theology."[41]

The generation of compassion in response to the suffering of others would seem to be the basic pattern of human empathy, rather than a feature peculiar to theatre or the arts. Although the wall separating *rasa* and ordinary emotion (*bhāva*) proves rather thin, this, too, is a culturally variable emotion. Whereas ancient Greek notions of compassion (*eleos* or *oiktos*) are not associated with one gender or another, medieval European constructions of the sentiment are highly feminized. Compassion varies as to whether it is considered a positive or negative emotional experience. The Ifaluk emotion of *fago* encompasses sadness and loss, but the Tibetan Buddhist state of *tsewa* associates compassion with feelings of well-being.[42] There is also little uniformity as to what one should be inspired to do as a result of the apprehension of another's suffering. For instance, in contrast to Sahi's vision of compassion as a force to overcome divisions, "medieval [European] compassion . . . is not easily described as 'altruistic,' for it can be intensely self-interested; it does not often assume that the other's suffering ought to be prevented."[43]

The late medieval European piety of compassion was stimulated in part by paintings of the naked, bleeding, crucified Christ. This art evoked an inner feeling of sorrow thought to be conducive to repentance. The feeling centered on the passion of Christ, an event assumed to be willed by God as reparation for human sin: The suffering deserved by human beings is redemptive when undertaken by Jesus out of compassion on their behalf. Contemporary critics dismiss this Christian aesthetic as an individualistic or world-denying spirituality. They push back at the notion that God wills suffering for spiritual good and instead call Christians to work to end the suffering of others.

Nevertheless, the assumption that the suffering of Jesus or anyone else cannot or should not be prevented should give us pause. It is worth considering the extent to which suffering *can* be alleviated. The ethics of compassion does not always entail the ability to do something about suffering—to put an end to it, to vindicate its victims. Farley notes that suffering arises "through the tragic structures of finitude and freedom": Finite creatures inevitably suffer loss, and their freedom makes it possible to turn against God and against one another.[44] In relation to these structures, divinity responds with the power of compassion. This power does not eliminate conflict but is present within it. "Compassion condemns what causes suffering by inspiring and enabling effective resistance to it," Farley writes; yet when no resistance seems possible, "it is the work of compassion to empower sufferers; this time not for the work of change but to break the dominion of suffering over the spirit."[45] The tear of God in Sahi's painting encapsulates this intense "feeling-with," which makes compassion an enduring religious sentiment.

On the "Negative" Emotions

Are these "negative" feelings—fury, terror, disgust, and compassion—sustainable as religious emotions, or do they consume and kill the soul? Can righteous anger, for example, be sustained without alternating with other, more sanguine, moods of the heart? Christian critics of activist movements often voice such anxieties about the revolutionary fury of oppressed groups. Dalit activist Mohan Larbeer associates this critique with the perspective of privileged persons who understand spirituality as solitude, meditation, and separation from society. Their anxiety belongs to the impulse to control rather than express anger, fear, and disgust. "Be satisfied with what you have," they say. "Your kingdom is not here. Be patient." In contrast, Larbeer declares that in Dalit activism, "the struggle itself gives the power to sustain."[46]

The conditions of hope lie within the terrain of each of the negative emotions. Fury, terror, disgust, and compassion invite appraisal of injuries received, their causes, and appropriate responses. The very ability to become angry seems to "carry the conviction that something *can* be done."[47] Even when tragedy is overwhelming, a compassionate person may transform the situation simply by being present with the sufferer as a witness to their pain.

What, then, of the "positive" emotions, including peace (*śānta*) and love (*śṛṅgāra*) examined in earlier parts of this book? Do they only pacify the oppressed? Not at all, I argue: They are essential to a holistic theological anthropology. Appavoo's Eucharistic liturgy evokes a wide range of emotion: pleading for God's presence in the invocation, joy in the greeting, lament in the confession of sins, humor and irony in the sermon, a lively sense of courage in the rallying Creed, solidarity and joy in the Eucharist, confidence in the Lord's prayer, contemplation in the meal sharing song, and auspicious joy in the parting.[48] The Indian artists engaged in the Kabir Project at the Srishti School of Art and Design retrieve the religious sentiments of peace and love in a liberative direction as they explore the spirituality of Kabir, a low-caste, North Indian saint who combined caste-based critique of religious institutions with iconoclastic meditation and devotional songs.[49] The contemporary revival of the ashram arguably embodies similar objectives. In order to round out a holistic treatment of the emotions, we must revisit peace, love, heroism, and a sense of humor in light of the liberation theologies that have fueled their critique.

The Comic Sentiment (*Hāsya*)

Comparative studies often contrast the seriousness of Christianity with the playfulness of Hindu traditions. Whereas the apostle Paul exhorts Christians to "put away childish things" (1 Cor. 13:11), Hindu traditions are full of revelry, scatology, dance, and pranks. This perceived difference between Hinduism and Christianity has been attributed to several factors: the diminished majesty of deities in a polytheistic context, a nondual philosophy that "inevitably leads to paradoxes and absurdities" in daily life, intimate devotion (*bhakti*) that abolishes divine-human hierarchy, and a notion of play (*līlā*) as constitutive of the life of the gods.[50] Since the publication of Johan Huizinga's *Homo Ludens*, however, humor has gained recognition as a religious sentiment in the West. Twentieth-century theologies of play retrieved the importance of medieval celebrations of carnival and the feast of fools as correctives to an overly serious Christianity. Such moments of levity relax ordinary social constraints and afford a taste of freedom and transcendence.[51]

The humorous sentiment is a chink in *rasa*'s transcendent armor. Because humor remains closer to real life than an aesthetic sentiment ought properly to be, the transcendence of aesthetic enjoyment cannot be complete. "The comic sentiment is anomalous," Lee Siegel writes, "in that we react and laugh in the same way, according to the theorists, both in the theater and in the streets. Though we do not fall in love with the beautiful heroine of a play or recoil in fear from the cruel villain, we do laugh at the ridiculous fool, the clever trickster, or the wild joker. Laughter dissolves distinctions between art and life."[52] Even when humor does act like the other *rasas* and transports an audience through laughter, it retains its incongruity through "its own perverse resistance to the sublime."[53]

Incongruities and improprieties are common causes of laughter. This, too, sets *hāsya* apart from the other *rasas*, in which impropriety (*anaucitya*) is the principal obstructer of aesthetic experience. When the erotic mood is destroyed by the improper placement of ornaments on the body, laughter ensues. The reader will recall that the *rasa* of devotional love must appear within an *appropriate* devotional imagination and that in Kṛṣṇa devotion, anything bordering on physical or sexual love is seen as a distortion of *bhakti rasa*. In humor, however, this impropriety finds a place.

Some theorists view humor, an important component of play, as an effective means of social resistance: "[A]lthough humor is a non-confrontational style of critiquing an oppressive situation, . . . it is often able to portray fraud, hypocrisy, and injustice far more powerfully and emotively than the written word."[54] In this view, making fun of those in power, jokingly exposing the hypocrisy of religious leaders, and venting frustration through humorous inversions of status empower the marginalized. By transcending oppression, subaltern persons claim an alternative identity through a higher, even divine, point of view.

The tension within such occasions for laughter is that although they provide a temporary outlet for frustration, ultimately they ensure business as usual for religious and social institutions. In a survey of ethnographic studies in the Indian context, Selva Raj and Corinne Dempsey conclude that "this restorative quality implicit in ritual play . . . ensures not only its repeated occurrence in institutionally sanctioned arenas but also elicits institutional endorsement for such play."[55] The Holi festival is a good example. Despite its reversals—wild, unconstrained behavior in wars of colored powder, women beating men with sticks—Whitney Sanford finds that Holi actually resolves tensions and strengthens social bonds: "[T]he satire and frivolity that enliven these narratives and practices may appear to further subvert hierarchies and stability, while in fact they work to strengthen them."[56] In short, institutions rely upon humorous release mechanisms for their continued functioning. Holi and the medieval feast of fools occur in ritual contexts that safely demarcate them from normal life.

In light of such insights, theologian Kathleen Sands charges that humor in the religious context too often "exposes only to cover up more effectively."[57] Ordinarily, when comedy exposes the folly of the wise and the vice of the virtuous, social and ritual mechanisms kick in to neutralize the critique.

> The comic view is made to seem self-evidently superior and closer to if not identical with the perspective of faith. The comic, then, has been used as a form of theodicy, the justification of God—in other words, the justification

> of power as ultimately coherent and good. In sum the theoretical gesture of theologies of humor . . . is thus to re-cover what humor threatens to expose—the "ifs, ands, and butts" that undermine all claims to unconditional, universal, and self-consistent knowledge.[58]

Indeed, it is just such a cover-up that I have resisted throughout this study. With Sands, I am interested in humor's prophetic ability to expose power and to condition ethics in light of this exposure. She advocates a queer theology of humor that exposes more than it covers. Rather than covering the butts of the joke, "beginning with the butts . . . turns theology from the defense of the divine to the interrogation of power."[59] This unrelenting exposure challenges (hetero-) normativity and sets the pace for a non-absolutizing ethics.

The queer knowledge that results from the humor of inappropriate exposure has the potential to transform ethics. It implicates everyone—those who are the target of the joke and those who "get" it. Humor can be socially transformative, Sands insists, but this will be "a function of which norms it exposes, not of the transgression or transcendence of norms as such. . . . The most transgressive humor is that which sees from the perspective of the marginalized and makes critically visible the most ubiquitous forms of power."[60] Humor can engender liberation for the oppressed if what it uncovers convicts the oppressor. Conversely, humor can engender humility in the oppressor: To laugh at oneself is to open oneself to critique and reform.

Heroism (*Vīra*)

In Sanskrit literature, the heroic sentiment is embodied in the warrior, whose sacred duty (*dharma*) is to fight bravely. Kṛṣṇa exhorts Arjuna to such action in the Bhagavad Gītā. Arjuna must overcome his qualms about killing friends and relatives on the battlefield and do his duty as a warrior. Kṛṣṇa urges him to fight like a man: "Don't yield to impotence! . . . Rise to the fight, Arjuna!"[61] Indeed, the Vedic word *vīrá* (cognate with the Latin *vir* and English "virile") designates an essential manliness, typically proven in battle.[62] Hindu traditions draw out the moral implications of courage beyond the sphere of epic military or ascetic struggles. The *Mahābhārata* epic is commonly read today as a treatise about sacred duty in general. In its long process of composition and redaction, concerns of the brahmin caste came to supplement and overlay the "originally kṣatriya" values of the text, so that heroism extends beyond the efforts of the brave warrior to the question of right action for everyone.[63]

Four kinds of heroes appear in the Indian dramatic tradition: the hero in battle (*yuddha vīra*), the generous hero (*dāna vīra*), the compassionate hero (*dayā vīra*), and the righteous hero (*dharma vīra*).[64] The four share important qualities, which are outlined in the *Nāṭya Śāstra*. The root emotion of each type of heroism is effort or energy (*utsāha*). This *rasa* is determined by "composure, mental effort, prudent discipline, boldness in attack, power, and majestic glory." All heroes represent themselves with "firmness, fortitude, liberality, and clarity of intellect" (*NŚ* prose after VI.66, p. 262).[65] Moral qualities of generosity, compassion, and piety can be markers of the heroic. Abhinavagupta goes as far as to locate these forms of heroism (in ascetics and others) within the transcendent *rasa* of peace (*śānta*) if they are performed without egoism.[66] As a taste of the divine, *vīra* is a courageous orientation to life.

Martial heroism has, at times, been defended as a Christian virtue, but its crusading spirit rests uneasily in the postcolonial moment. "Onward Christian Soldiers" now echoes as the shameful anthem of everything in Christianity that dominates and destroys. We also know that today we are simultaneously weary of violence and deadened to it.[67] The bravery of the early Christian martyrs, who succumbed to violence rather than inflicting it, might offer a nonviolent variant of heroism; yet this valorization of martyrs also gives us pause in light of feminist critiques of redemptive suffering and of the masculine construction of the virtue of courage.[68] Notwithstanding exceptional "virile woman" like the female martyrs, the gendered coding of this language has historically ensured female subordination in the Church.[69]

If, in India as in the Christian West, an aristocratic ideal of the warrior or knight no longer governs prevailing religious ideals, and if the battlefield no longer signifies the epitome of virtue, in what sense does heroism belong to a theology of aesthetic sentiments? What can *vīra* signify in a contemporary religious context?

Twentieth- and twenty-first-century Christian theologians have revived heroic qualities in a variety of ways. Some offer what we might see as a parallel to the righteous hero (*dharma vīra*) by calling for a renewal of heroic individual excellence in the face of diluted Christian standards. In contrast with the classical Greek and Roman epic heroes, who take control of their own destinies, Brian Hook and R. R. Reno ground a case for "self-denial as a form of human excellence" in the radical obedience of Abraham,

Jesus, and the early Christian martyrs and ascetics.[70] In both models, excellence is reserved for exceptional persons, and the elevation of the exceptional heroic man has the effect of putting ideals out of the reach of ordinary persons. Indeed, these authors scoff at the idea that a person "can be a heroic mom" by being committed to her individual sense of calling.[71]

Other models emphasize opportunities for courage in everyday life. The challenges of the modern existential situation have fueled reflections on courage by prominent theologians including Reinhold Niebuhr, Karl Rahner, and Paul Tillich. In the face of anxiety produced by the specters of mortality, guilt, meaninglessness, and despair, Tillich writes of the "courage to be." More than facing the object of one's fears, this courage is the affirmation of the self despite the awareness that one is hedged about with nonbeing. Here, the individual takes the risk of faith and "strives for a participation in the ground of being."[72] Courage becomes a taste of the divine. In Tillich, as in fellow thinkers who emphasize creaturely vulnerability, the heroic is transposed into an existential key.

Still others move to redefine heroism in a collective sense. In the face of corporate control and a sense of powerlessness among middle-class Americans, heroism means "reclaiming the sense of empowerment to create new social worlds . . . [and] putting our apparent individual and social interests at risk before the promises of a better order for all."[73] A collective and constrained version of the generous hero (*dāna vīra*) takes shape as a liberation theology for the middle sectors of American society, which would join in solidarity with the poor and working classes to rethink economic and social structures.

Across these varied contexts and meanings of the heroic sentiment, the arts have a hortatory role. Art can evoke fear and existential anxiety, but it can also enfold such fears in a spirit of transcendence. Tillich writes of being arrested by "the power of being itself" as he encountered it in a Botticelli painting. He testifies that this revelatory experience "created a union of [the artistic and the philosophical] in my mind which thereafter was never disrupted."[74] Not only art but also everyday encounters with the beautiful, the terrifying, and the awe-inspiring can awaken a sense of courage to participate in a greater reality and to live out a destiny called forth by that reality.

Peace (*Śānta*)

This book began with the worry that as a primary religious emotion, peace (*śānta*) glosses over and transcends the conflicts that generate socially liberating knowledge. It tames the fury, disgust, and terror that alert us to deep disorder around us. It soothes upheavals of the heart, including the compassion and love that impel us to help others. It leans strongly toward social conservativism with its emphasis on order and harmony.

As we have discussed, one of India's most prominent theorists of the peaceful sentiment, Ananda Coomaraswamy, exemplifies these tendencies. He lauds the Indian philosophical and aesthetic search for the eternal order and purpose, which ideally culminates in a harmonious society organized according to that order so that individuals can realize that purpose. The social ideal of *svadharma*, the idea that all persons must follow a path dictated by their "social and spiritual status," expresses this harmony. For Coomaraswamy, the caste system and conventional gender relations "constitute the natural hierarchy of human society."[75] Society should be ruled by the "true Brahmans," who have perfected the ideal of *śānta* and "attained peace, or at least have attained to occasional and unmistakable vision of life as a whole."[76] Peace is the inner feeling of unity with the cosmic order.

In contrast to the peace that passeth all social critique, some today give voice to the transformative social implications of mystical insight. The creation spirituality of Matthew Fox, the Engaged Buddhism of Thich Nhat Hanh, and the *via transformativa* proposed by Dorothy Sölle illustrate how experience of a transcendent reality calls our everyday assumptions into question.[77] "By providing the direct experience of a reality that transcends and overwhelms the meaning, density, finality, and obviousness of the reality of everydayness, the mystical experience relativizes conventional judgments about plausibility and frees the person having the experience from conventional definitions of reality," writes Robert Egan. "Things do not have to be the way they seem to be."[78] Hierarchies of gender, race, and caste are not final. Corporations and military regimes are not invincible. The natural world holds unseen possibility.

The NBCLC's treatment of *śānta* in the dance piece "The Navarasa of Jesus" also resists the spiritualizing strain of mysticism and the hegemonic social norms it implies. The final vignette is introduced by the voice of the resurrected Jesus saying to his frightened disciples, "I give you peace; go give peace to the people." The narrator clarifies the significance of this peace: "Jesus came to bring about peace between various groups through prayer, dialogue, and nonviolence." The dancers then enact a conflict involving theft and physical violence. Jesus intervenes, and the two parties embrace. With a serene countenance, Jesus then moves into a yogic pose (*vṛkṣāsana*): He embodies true peace, a social state as well as a state of mind.[79] This production marks an aesthetic shift at the Centre since its erection of the Saccidananda Chapel: The meditative bliss evoked by the building has transmuted into an emphasis on social reconciliation.

Coomaraswamy and the NBCLC share the assumption that peace means the subjection of differences to the one true order. If this is so, then the hierarchies of gender and caste in Coomaraswamy's case, and Jesus' ethical imperatives in the case of "The Navarasa of Jesus," become competing bases for social harmony. The undifferentiated bliss of union with *brahman* and subjection to the will of the Triune God become rival alternatives for ultimate inner peace. These orthodoxies find themselves at war rather than peace, for each religious tradition competes to subordinate persons to their vision of reality. The enjoyment of spiritual peace arrives through the silencing of differences.

In light of this paradox of peace, which suspiciously resembles the rationale for never-ending military conflicts, Roland Faber ventures a hope for "a new sense of (religious) peace" that does not overcome complexity in the name of unity—with one another or with the divine. As he describes it, this is "not a peace that lives from pacification in the name of the legitimized violence of hierarchical orthodoxies, but a peace that will only make sense with a life *from* and *within* the multiplicity of uncertain, vague, complex, differentiated, and ever-new differently differentiating voices that speak with the voice of mutual immanence."[80] Dalit Christians, bound with caste Christians in the body of Christ, have contributed mightily toward an internally differentiated voice for the Indian church. Their struggle for liberation is a struggle against the temptations of violence, especially in a milieu in which so much violence has been perpetrated upon them. Against the violence of the One, the many faces of difference—too ambiguous and numerous to enlist—hold the possibility of peace.

Love (*Śrngāra*)

> But the greatest of these is love.
>
> (1 Cor. 13:13)

True peace, a peace that envelops the heart and draws differing communities into an embrace, cannot arrive without love. Love is essential to the religious function of each of the *rasas*. Love checks the cruelty of disgust, anger, humor, and courage. It is a thin strand of hope amid terror. It fuels compassion, and it fires the contemplative to action.

Bhoja, an early theorist of *rasa*, claimed that love is at the heart of aesthetic experience. For him, all emotion boils down to a variety of self-love (*preman* or *ahaṃkāra śṛṅgāra*). Every emotion is rooted in the subject's experience of, and enjoyment of, the self. Self-love impels activity: "If a person laughs, it is because he *loves* to laugh; if he fights, he *loves* to do so."[81] This thesis resembles Abhinivagupta's unification of *rasa* in *śānta* insofar as both involve an essential experience of the self (or Self). I submit that there is an inherent other-love in *rasa* as well. The encounter with the other, whether it is the author's aesthetic vision or the divine other who meets us in the moment of transcendence, is a movement of fascination, of love.

One of the great benefits of a comparative approach to love is its capacity to illuminate the beautiful diversity of this sentiment. Rooted in the Greek of the New Testament, Christians are familiar with three faces of love: friendship (*philia*), erotic love (*eros*), and charity (*agape*). Christian theology has a history of overemphasis on self-giving *agape*, which can perpetuate unhealthy self-negation in people who are vulnerable to abuse. In response to such criticisms, Christian theology has begun to embrace another face of love, the divine *eros* that, rather than being reduced to (and feared as) the sexual urge, overflows as a powerful force of creation, redemption, and embodied flourishing.[82] Diverse Christian concepts of love mutually correct one another.

Christian theology offers the comparative reader the other-directedness of *philia, eros*, and *agape*. To be sure, loving the community of devotees is essential to Kṛṣṇa *bhakti*, but the overwhelming focus is perfection of one's chosen love relationship to the Lord. God is love in both traditions, but the mystical traditions of Christianity view God's love for the world, rather than divine play, as the impetus for all creation. It is the force that sustains existence. It reconciles the world back to God and human beings back to God and one another. God is Mother, Lover, and Friend; and the movement of the heart to the other in all these capacities is the model for human relationships.[83] As we raise children, make love, befriend others, and give generously, we return love to God.

The genius of Kṛṣṇa devotion is that it explores these powerful human loves in relation to the divine. Rūpa's *bhakti rasa* outlines five primary faces of love, all of which can be directed toward the deity. Kṛṣṇa devotees are not only, or even primarily, children of the Heavenly Father. Rather, they love God as tenderly as God's own parents. They joke and frolic with him as childhood friends. They respect him as a wise and beloved elder brother or king. They stand in awe. But most importantly, they dwell imaginatively within the forest bowers where he and Rādhā share the heights of intimacy. Christians taste something of these five forms of love of God as they contemplate Kṛṣṇa and his devotees.

A comparative approach thus uncovers the rich texture of emotion. Reverence and quiet reflection are revealed as shades of love. Christian and Hindu conceptions of friendship rest side-by-side, affirming the delight of the mutuality of equals. The parental modes reverse one another: one tradition adores God as Parent, the other as Child. The erotic register extends beyond sex as a metaphor for divine-human intimacy, pushing toward an irrepressible flow of abundant good will for all. We also recognize semblances (*ābhasas*) of this sentiment. Concupiscence warps the love that connects us with God and others. Addiction obsesses over good things that might ease our boredom, pain, and anxiety. *Kāma* is concerned solely with pleasure. Love can be distorted just as grotesquely as the other basic emotions.

Are these faces of love enough? The social conservatism of Christian and Gauḍīya Vaiṣṇava love mysticism kindle in me a desire for still other forms of love. If we claim love as our goal, yet we treat people as objects, the female form as the embodiment of temptation, and homoerotic love as demonic, the fullness of love cannot be realized. A promiscuous *eros* chases us onward, beyond what these conventions deem orderly or appropriate. It may take the form of a prophetic fire that draws the line between oppressor and oppressed clearly and forcefully; but this is not the only way. Anne Joh offers the Korean notion of *jeong*, a love that emerges, sometimes paradoxically, out of painful or unequal relationships. Its "call for vulnerability challenges us to identify ourselves with those whom we perceive to be the Other." *Jeong* blurs boundaries even between oppressed and oppressor. When this love overcomes the binarism embedded in liberatory anger, relational transformation can take place.[84] Intercultural conversations on the emotions refract the shades of love into a dazzling spectrum of possibility beyond the limited comparisons I offer here.

Through a comparative lens, we see *rasa* itself as transformative eros. In the theology that undergirds Hindu notions of *rasa*, a human sensitivity to the other is rooted in a relation to the divine.[85] Similarly, in Trinitarian Christian theology, the creativity, self-differentiation, and involvement of

God in the world undergirds the human capacity to connect with others. The implicit ethics is emotional and engaged. Rita Sherma argues that

> *rasa* cannot be attained through either a quietist disengagement (*nivritti*) [or] an active but desireless involvement with the world (*niskama-karma*). It seems self-evident that *rasa* requires vulnerability, openness, sensitivity, passion, and emotion. For, *rasa* is not hedonism; it is not *rasa* unless it provokes a sudden, poignant recollection of the presence of the Divine. And *rasa* is not always evocative of delight. A moving and tragic story is capable of bringing about *rasa*; here it would be the *rasa* of deep compassion.[86]

These aspects of *rasa* theory challenge the tenet of aesthetic generalization (*sādhāraṇīkaraṇa*), which postulates that emotions are experienced in universal ways and that preoccupation with the feelings and circumstances of particular persons detracts from the aesthetic experience. Such a stance short circuits the love at the heart of *rasa* and the work of the emotions for justice. Our inevitable situatedness in terms of gender, caste, class, religion, and other markers of difference calls for empathy, a shared heart (*sahṛdaya*) that attends to the other. A critical corrective to aesthetic theories of religion will resist the sentimental, aestheticizing tendencies of inner-worldly approaches to religious experience. The universal in art and in each of the nine basic emotions calls us back to our common but fragile connections to one another as particular, embodied beings.

Nava rasa

Nava in Sanskrit means both "nine" and "new." This brief assessment of the nine core emotions in *rasa* theory offers them as new material for Christian theological reflection. Some of the feeling states emblematic of Christian experience, such as contrition and gratitude, have been set aside to make room for consideration of the nine emotions considered most basic in Indian aesthetic theory. This new starting point encourages us to attend to sentiments often treated as peripheral and to reframe those seen as central. Contrition, for example, can be a variation of the pathetic/compassionate sentiment (*karuṇa*). Gratitude might be a complementary transient emotion for any number of the nine *rasas*.[87]

This exploration sheds new light on the relation of the mind and body in emotion, and of the universal and particular across cultures. *Rasa* theory combines sensation (in the excitants or *vibhāvas*), resulting behaviors that indicate the presence of emotion (in the indicators or *anubhāvas*), other feelings that give texture and contour to emotions in particular persons and situations (in the transitory emotions or *vyabhicāribhāvas*), and, of course, the emotion (*bhāva*) of the character experiencing all of these things. The spectator experiences *rasa* when she appreciates each of these in an aesthetic context. She attends closely to the particular situation at the same time as she savors the bliss offered by aesthetic experience. She oscillates between the particular and the universal. In contemporary theorizing on the emotions, a desire to articulate a common ground, perhaps with rules that allow us to live a common life together, resides alongside a desire to recognize and respect the particularities that set us apart. *Rasa* theory nestles squarely in the midst of these tensions. A good deal of idealization (*sādhāraṇīkaraṇa*) occurs in this theory, but its concern with how aesthetic emotion is produced demands attention to particular, embodied means of eliciting emotional response.

Bringing *rasa* into conversation with Western discourse on the emotions amplifies the general/particular dialectic. The cultural particularity of some means of evoking emotion (stylized *mudrās* and gestures, for example) remains in tension with the recognizability of emotions more broadly. An Anglo-American cannot be expected to understand that a certain shape and vibration of a dancer's hand depicts a bee seeking honey and that this movement combined with suggestive glances denotes sexual intercourse; but this spectator certainly can recognize tears of sadness. The great abstraction of *rasa* as aesthetic emotion never leaves behind the sensory and affective components that produce it. The theory thus also illuminates the tension between the commonalities and the social construction of experience inherent in any comparative project.

To bring this cross-cultural exploration to a close, we turn finally to the last remaining *rasa*, the aesthetic experience of wonder.

9 Wonder

The sight of celestial beings evokes wonder. So does the expression of religious devotion in monuments of paint and stone. Mary trembles before the appearance of the angel. Arjuna gasps in astonishment when Kṛṣṇa, his charioteer, is revealed in his true divine form. The tourist pauses, awestruck, as she enters the halls of the Meenakshi Temple, just as she does when she sets foot in a great cathedral. She cannot take it all in.

Faced with eruptions of the wondrous across the world's religious traditions, we seek manageable strategies for making them comprehensible. Interreligious dialogue often takes its point of departure from the attempt to identify shared beliefs, shared approaches to scripture, or shared projects for collaboration. While the search for theological and ethical common ground is an admirable goal, it runs the risk of diminishing the irreducibility of religious traditions. Such strategies fail to satisfy the affective dimension of wonder that arises in encounters with religious others. In defense of the authority such encounters might hold for Christian life, this final chapter gestures toward a Christian theology of religious pluralism that appreciates both the incomprehensibility of otherness and the affect it awakens.

Three categories from the classical Indian aesthetic theory will guide this aesthetics of religious pluralism: the aesthetic emotion of wonder (*adbhuta rasa*), the sympathetic spectator (*sahṛdaya*), and transitory or nurturing emotional states (*vyabhicāribhāva*s or *sañcāribhāva*s).

The Aesthetic Experience of Wonder (*Adbhuta*)

This book has touched upon eight of the nine primary human emotions identified in Indian aesthetic theory: the peaceful, erotic, furious, fearful, disgusting, compassionate, comic, and heroic sentiments. As *rasa*s, each aesthetic emotion has the potential to transport the attuned spectator to an experience of the divine. In their particular flavors, they offer unique tastes of divinity: love of God, compassion for others, disgust and fury at injustice, courage in the face of despair, and so forth. Each also carries potential pitfalls or distractions: love and peace have their interior and world-denying aspects, disgust and anger tempt us to forget the humanity of others. Although it harbors its own temptations, I have saved the *rasa* of wonder (*adbhuta*) for the conclusion of this study because it resembles the sublime appreciation that happens when we come to understand the distinctive features of another religious tradition.

Bharata's *Nāṭya Śāstra* notes that wonder, "the marvelous sentiment," arises from celestial encounters and joyous events. This *rasa* is the aesthetic development of the ordinary emotion of astonishment. In art, it is evoked by excitants (*vibhāva*s) such as magical illusions, magnificent architecture, and the appearance of divine beings. Characters respond with the appropriate physical indicators (*anubhāva*s): wide eyes, fixed gaze, goose bumps, tears of joy, and spontaneous utterances of amazement. Transitory states (*vyabhicāribhāva*s) in characters experiencing wonder—paralysis, choked voice, agitation, and so forth—may accompany and further foster this sentiment in the viewer (*NŚ* prose after VI.74, p. 267).

Robert Fuller observes that wonder in the Indian tradition is more than simple interest or curiosity. Wonder "is a reaction to the opportunity to witness divine, heavenly, or exalted phenomena" and is, therefore, related to the central moment of devotional worship, the moment of seeing and being seen by divinity (*darśana*).[1] A parallel tradition in Western thought also links wonder at the unseen to spiritual and ethical inclinations.

> Wonder entices us to consider the reality of the unseen, the existence of a more general order of existence from which this world derives its meaning and purpose. It is thus only to be expected that wonder also entices us to believe that our supreme good lies in harmoniously adjusting ourselves thereto. Wonder, it would seem, is one of the principal sources of humanity's spiritual impulse.[2]

Fuller argues that this stance of openness and receptivity has important adaptive and cognitive functions. Wonder shapes our fundamental orientation to the world. In human psychological development, wonder enables us to put aside exclusive self-interest and develop higher moral functions of empathy, compassion, and care. The lasting motivations born of wonder in the natural world are adaptive for our species' long-term relationship with our environment.

The non-utilitarian and other-centered aspects of wonder epitomize *rasa*'s transcendence. If part of what distinguishes *rasa* from ordinary emotion (*bhāva*) is that it transports the viewer away from self-reference, then even in its ordinary manifestation, wonder has an innately rasic function. As Martha Nussbaum describes it, "This emotion responds to the pull of the object, and one might say that in it the subject is maximally aware of the value of the object, and only minimally aware, if at all, of its relationship to her own plans."[3] Self-reference is momentarily suspended. We should note, however, that wonder differs from the theory that *rasa* is the viewer's absorption into emotion in its most *general* form (the principle of *sādhāraṇīkaraṇa*). Here, the viewer is entranced by the astounding features of a *particular* marvelous object. Rather than transcend difference, wonder attends to it acutely.

Wonder as Religious Orientation

Wonder attends to that which is other: the transcendent, the marvelous, the fascinating. Invoking Clifford Geertz, Fuller argues that rituals encapsulate the experience of wonder through repetition and so "establish powerful, pervasive, and long-lasting moods and motivations" for participants. "Moreover, wonder continually revitalizes such paradigms by connecting them with belief in a general order of existence, a cosmic frame of reference."[4] The fascination and awe inherent in experiences of nature, ritual, and sacred text fuel a range of religious expressions.

Religious traditions not only ritualize the experience of wonder but are also objects of wonder in themselves. We can see how this is the case in comparison with three realms of experience that Fuller theorizes as leading to personal transformation: the practice of meditation, deep encounters with others, and the aesthetic response to art.

Spiritual disciplines such as meditation offer one path to the wondrous experience of the greater order of things. Though techniques and aims differ, these disciplines often close down ordinary ways of experiencing the world through silence or dimmed lights and replace them with different stimuli such as drumming, icons, mandalas, or koans. Neural imaging studies show brain functions conducive to peace, oneness, and "belief in a higher power" in practitioners of diverse prayer and meditation techniques.[5] When customary perceptions are muted, practitioners report experiencing a "deeper or more profound" awareness or even the "ground or core" of ordinary consciousness, which can foster openness to the truth or unity of religions.[6] Regular practices of prayer and previous mystical experiences seem to predispose persons cognitively to appreciate the religious experiences of others. Participation in shared practices such as meditation, yoga, or service activities offers explicit points of contact between persons of different faiths.

The interpersonal dimension of spiritual disciplines also contains the transformative seeds of wonder. When we experience deep interpersonal connection, we awaken to a larger reality; and when we connect with a participant in another religious tradition, we obtain a taste of *their* larger reality. The wonder of the I-Thou relationship allows the religious other to stand forth in her unique form, unsubsumed by familiar categories.

Interreligious encounters can also provoke the physiological and cognitive responses that typically take place in aesthetic experience. For example, both offer new data that we must accommodate or assimilate.

> Our natural tendency when viewing visual art is to assimilate its patterns and forms to our existing cognitive schemata. This perceptual activity inherently produces arousal and pleasure. Some works of art, however, are not easily assimilated to existing schemata. They prompt us to learn, to accommodate to new perceptual and cognitive schemata. This experience of accommodation . . . is itself often pleasurable.[7]

Human beings are drawn to the creative tension between that which we understand and that which escapes our understanding. Music plays upon human emotions by creating expectations in the listener, deviating from them, and fulfilling them. Music surprises us with beauty and evokes wonder at the order underlying complex patterns: "Catching a glimpse of this 'deeper order' is in itself an experience of ecstasy; that is, it allows us to feel that, however briefly, we have attained a greater grasp of the world and its possibilities."[8] Like works of art, religious traditions amaze us with their complexity. We search for familiar patterns of belief and practice. Our expectations are often thwarted, only to be resolved in a deeper understanding of a community's unique grammar and logic. An aesthetic stance does not move immediately to the assessment of the truth of what is encountered but instead pauses in amazement. A deep encounter with other religious traditions offers a glimpse of God, world, and self through another set of lenses. It suggests an inexhaustibly rich divine depth that underlies religious diversity.[9] Insofar as it allows us to step momentarily outside ourselves, it is ecstasy.

Wonder and Religious Difference

We ecstatically step outside ourselves in the encounter with divine and human others, but then we come back to ourselves once more. The journey affects us at many levels. When we read the texts of others, observe their religious practices, or simply attempt to understand our neighbors, we are engaged as whole and complex persons. Intellectually, we may try to reconcile what we already believe with what we have encountered. Spiritually, we may consider how the encounter affects our commitment to our own religious tradition. But perhaps the most fundamental response occurs on an emotional or affective level. Stressing the affective aspect of encounter, comparative theologian Francis X. Clooney recommends a process of comparative reading that renders the reader "vulnerable to intellectual, imaginative, and affective transformation" by the texts of other traditions.[10] By intensifying emotion within the reader, religious texts inspire the determination to live according to their reality. They can exert these effects not only on the intended audience but on outsiders as well. The interreligious reader might be inspired to revisit and intensify parallel emotional dynamics in her own tradition.

The texts and performances surveyed in this study exert rhetorical force. They offer visions of reality, inspire emotional responses, and model behavioral transformations appropriate to those realities. As in the Hindu texts Clooney presents, which invite the reader to a posture of loving surrender to Viṣṇu and his consort Śrī, the Hindu and Christian subtraditions we have studied here invite affective postures of peace, love, and fury. Insiders and outsiders to these traditions can be edified by tasting these *rasa*s as religious emotions. Christian contemplation can be enhanced by the peace of Hindu wisdom traditions, Hindu devotion can be inspired by the love of Christ, dominant traditions can be urged to justice by subaltern fury, and so on.

Beyond the intended impact of texts and practices that foster love, peace, and fury, however, these primary emotions exert an aesthetic force of their own. They act as *rasa*s: The affects that arise in us as the audience are transmuted into a sense of aesthetic wonder. The religious reader may experience peace, love, or fury as evoked in a text or performance; but when this experience rises to the level of aesthetic rapture (*rasa*), it takes on additional significance. We may follow Abhinavagupta in his insight about the theological significance of this moment. His analogy between aesthetic appreciation and theological wonder highlights how both pull the individual away from ordinary egoic concerns. Immersed in *rasa*, we suspend habitual attachments to identity. In his Kashmir Śaiva theological framework, the same suspension happens in the instant one tastes nondual union with the divine reality.[11]

Christian theologian Jeannine Hill Fletcher makes a similar appeal to the wonder of religious pluralism. She observes that the distinctiveness of religious traditions, affirmed by postliberal theologians such as George Lindbeck, can be an obstacle to dialogue. If we do not share a common story or language, how can we engage in conversation? Is true understanding possible with anything less than full participation in the other religious community? Most people do not have this opportunity, but everyday points of contact, collaboration, and fruitful conversations do, in fact, ensue across religious differences. Hill Fletcher argues that the initial moment of incomprehension is the key to their success.

> The experience of unknowing in the encounter with otherness offers an immediate theological wellspring because, prior to the endeavor to learn from other faiths, there can be a moment of profound wonder, a moment that comes *before* understanding. It is a moment more immediate to the encounter. The moment in which I "don't get it" is the moment of encounter when all one's orientations and understandings are no longer useful for making sense of the reality encountered. . . . The moment of wonder in the presence of a tradition one does not understand can be a moment that brings one to the awareness of the incomprehensible mystery of God.[12]

The face of the other brings us face to face with divine mystery. The affirmation of divine mystery is foundational to the endeavor of Christian theology. In interreligious encounter, as in the encounter with holy mystery, a person never expects complete understanding. Without becoming an insider to a religious tradition, we cannot experience it in full. Even then, the mystery of the divine remains; and yet, we seek to know more. These musings point the way to a theologically instructive form of wonder. In the encounter with the other, the mind desires understanding even as it knows this is beyond reach. The goal is not "exhaustive comprehension" or vindication of one's own beliefs but "wonder itself."[13]

Wonder, as a *rasa* and as the experiential core of *rasa* itself, opens us to the divine. We need not follow Abhinavagupta to the point of claiming a universal content to religious experience to make this claim. The apophatic moment, which cannot comprehend *what it is* that is not comprehended, is the paradoxically *contentless core* that aesthetic, interreligious, and mystical encounters share. In the wondrous encounter, the disorientation of coming face-to-face with the irreducible distinctiveness of another religious worldview participates in the astonishment aroused by divine mystery.

Rasa theory offers a theoretical framework for understanding why and how this affective response of wonderment is possible and why it is both theologically significant and beneficial in the context of religious pluralism. In comparative theological work lies an aesthetic appeal: The very encounter with religious others awakens interest. While this initial interest may be positive or negative, wonder deepens with understanding. As we develop this orientation of wonder and consciously bring it to such encounters, we become *sahṛdaya*s, persons whose hearts are attuned to the situation of the other.

The Sympathetic Spectator

According to classical Indian aesthetic theory, the discerning viewer (*sahṛdaya*) is one whose heart (*hṛd*) unites with (*sa*) art experience.[14] Within such a sympathetic spectator, the emotions expressed in a drama or other works of art are elevated to their refined state. The ideal viewer suspends self-interest and relishes the emotion in itself.

How does this happen? We have learned that aesthetic emotion (*rasa*) is produced through the combination of the excitants that would arouse a particular emotion (*vibhāvas*), physical indicators of that emotion in the characters (*anubhāvas*), and other transitory emotional states compatible with it (*vyabhicāribhāvas*) (*NŚ* prose after VI.31, p. 227). Immersion in a work of art brings the spectator beyond feeling the emotions of the characters (which, in the case of tragedy, would be painful) to a state of blissful contemplation. The sympathetic viewer has the transcendent experience of savoring the very essence (*rasa*) of emotion.

The *Nāṭya Śāstra* is confident that art brings out the best in those who are attentive to it. Drama teaches "duty to the unscrupulous, love to lovers, restraint to the undisciplined, self-control to the disciplined, boldness to cowards, energy to heroes, intelligence to those who lack it, and wisdom to the learned" (*NŚ* I.108–109, p. 31).[15] In his commentary, Abhinavagupta elaborates that drama interrupts the pain of those who are ill, brings delight to the tired and sorrowful, and instructs happy persons in the four ends of life.[16] Art burnishes the virtues we already display, and it unearths those we have allowed to lie dormant.

The spectator is not passive in this experience. The drama does not work upon audience members apart from their attentiveness and their effort to appreciate the unique combination of elements that, in the right conditions, allows *rasa* to arise. The quality of the audience's presence can affect the performance itself. Even if all the appropriate excitants, responses, and accompanying emotions are present in the plot and characters, *rasa* will not appear if the audience is insensate to their magic. Cultural refinement and education in the subtleties of the artist's craft are important, but they are not the sole criterion for the evocation of *rasa*. One performer describes a village festival in which she performed a dance depicting Kṛṣṇa's mother holding the baby on her lap: "I looked at Krishna—isn't he beautiful? Then I looked towards the audience. They were nodding! Yes, nodding! We were seeing Krishna together! It was as we say *anukirtanam* (a recreation, making anew.) The moment with Krishna, it is a presence at *that point* of time."[17] Such heartfelt absorption is the most important qualification of the sympathetic spectator.

The devotional use of drama in Gauḍīya Vaiṣṇava *rāsa līlā*s nicely exemplifies the necessity of audience preparation and attention. *Rāsa līla*s in Vrindavan are performed with young boys playing the majority of the parts. They are not skilled actors. By the standards of the classical dramatic tradition, their technical shortcomings should severely inhibit the production of *rasa*. Yet, for devotees, such performances raise the experience of devotional love to a fever pitch. This depends to a large extent on the expectations the audience brings to the performance. This phenomenon is not unfamiliar to Western audiences: "Even in the darkened, silent theatres of Western traditions, the experiences that audiences have arise more from their own active acting than from the talent and skill of the performers," writes David Mason. He describes "audience members themselves as performers" as they watch the *rāsa līlā*.[18] So, too, initiates in this tradition mentally develop their own characters in the Lord's drama.

Rasa arises in the audience when the performance has been successful. The success of a performance is measured in the *Nāṭya Śāstra* on human (*mānuṣī*) and divine (*daivikī*) levels, depending on the reactions of the spectators (*NŚ* VI.26, pp. 225–226). Ordinary spectators might respond to the superficial aspects of the artwork with applause or murmurs of appreciation. "Divine" success, however, occurs when people who are especially cultured, educated, or prepared encounter a phenomenal performance. As such a person listens to a live concert, his chest expands, tears well in his eyes, and his skin ripples with delight. In the fading final bars, he is loath to break the spell. Applause seems a sacrilege. This is the height of *rasa*: "When the response is not a tumultuous commotion, when there is in fact not the slightest sound or disturbance among the audience . . . that success is regarded as divine."[19]

"Divine" is not only a metaphor for an exceptionally moving performance. In the devotional realm, the heights of *rasa* are achieved not only through human effort and preparation but also through divine grace. As Margaret Case observes of the *rāsa līlā*s in Vrindavan, "What is seen, though profoundly personal, is . . . understood by a community to be a manifestation of divinity."[20] The audience's mental immersion in the narratives, characters, and physical setting of Kṛṣṇa's realm grants them special access to his divine play.

Some Christian theologians have considered acting, theatre, and mimesis as models of the Christian life,[21] and David Haberman reads the Gauḍīya Vaiṣṇava tradition in terms of acting.[22] Although the participation is active, however, it is audiences, not actors, who experience *rasa*. If devotees became the principal actors, the emotions would be their own ordinary feelings (*bhāva*) and not sentiment savored in its pure form (*rasa*). I would like to focus on the role of the audience in tasting *rasa* as an analogue to what persons of faith experience when they observe other faith traditions.

The enticing, disorienting experience of religious otherness encourages us to become *sahṛdaya*s, appreciative viewers who care enough about others to learn to savor their distinctive qualities. The combination of preparation and grace that is the mark of the *sahṛdaya*'s aesthetic experience also occurs as persons of faith encounter one another. As we come to appreciate the distinct contours of our neighbor's faith, caring enough to learn the idioms, images, and narratives that evoke devotional sentiment for them, we prepare for a taste of the divine that enhances our own devotion.

The Complementary Emotional State

The ecstasy of wonder is not a place that the *sahṛdaya* can permanently dwell. The rapture slips away and everyday life ensues. Nevertheless, she may emerge transformed. She may test perceptions awakened in a wondrous glimpse of possibility. In the natural world, this is how scientific discovery is born: "Wonder . . . encourages the construction of hypothetical or possible orders of existence that might causally account for unexpected perceptions. Wonder is thus one of the major sources of our capacity to entertain the possible."[23] So, too, with theological discovery. Although assessment might not be our immediate response to an encounter with religious others, we do eventually make decisions about what to do with their alternative ways of ordering the world. We enact a theology of religious pluralism that orders these perspectives within the context of a life of faith.

The final category of "transitory" or "nurturing" emotions (*vyabhicāribhāva*s, *sañcāribhāva*s) allows the Christian *sahṛdaya* to return from wonder and reflect upon how the interfaith encounter affects her own faith. As a whole, an excellent work of art will evoke one primary *rasa*: A tragedy will raise feelings of compassion (*karuṇa*), whereas a romance will develop the sentiment of love (*śṛṅgāra*). But according to the *rasa sūtra*, this primary *rasa* arises not only through the combination of excitants (*vibhāva*s) and appropriate indicators (*anubhāva*s) but through transitory emotions (*vyabhicāribhāva*s, also called nurturing emotions, *sañcāribhāva*s) that foster the main sentiment. These emotions arise temporarily throughout a drama to give fresh perspectives on the main emotional theme. For example, a love story can be enhanced by feelings of jealousy, bashfulness, anxiety, anger in the form of lover's quarrels, despondency in the absence of the beloved, the humor of flirtatious pranks, and so on. Traditions of Kṛṣṇa devotion modify the theme of the *vyabhicāribhāva* to suggest that every human emotion has a place in developing the ultimate affective goal of devotion (*bhakti*) (*BhRS* 2.5.45). All *rasa*s become *vyabhicāribhāva*s in relation to *bhakti rasa*. Every emotion, when related to the primary religious narrative, enhances devotion.

Christian devotion is similarly enhanced through appreciation of other religious expressions. In other words, just as the overall mood of love can incorporate aspects of bashfulness, anxiety, and jealousy, the appreciation of other religious modalities can enrich one's primary mode of piety. Christian devotion, contemplation, or action may remain one's central or stable emotion (*sthāyibhāva*), yet these will be enriched or expanded on account of a deep diversity of experience.

Rasa and Interfaith Complementarity

For the person who pursues the wonder of encounter toward greater understanding, this enrichment is a process of religious formation. Clooney recommends a "necessary interim stage of detached objectivity."[24]

At first, the reader should discipline herself to set aside normative and evaluative questions. Over time, however, the texts, practices, and performances of the other tradition exercise a rhetorical appeal. Engaged readers cross the distance between themselves and the text. "Engaged in the reading to fill in the gaps, she or he becomes increasingly affected by it," Clooney writes. "Attentive readers revise and improvise their own ongoing projects of self-formation."[25] Readers may not ultimately be persuaded to accept the texts' view of reality, but in the traverse between their own view of reality and another, they may be transformed in subtle ways.

Although there is nothing predictable about this interplay, I have suggested that Christian readers might enhance their peaceful contemplation, reinforce their heartfelt love of God, or find fuel for prophetic zeal as they immerse themselves in Hindu texts. These affects might also be modified through the encounter. Activism might become grounded in a practice of meditation. Love of Christ might find new dimensions of friendship, parental affection, or eros. Prayer might develop the shades of disgust, fury, or courage that would otherwise go unnoticed. The point here is not to prescribe or discipline the emotions but to "stay with the particularities of the reading process across religious boundaries and the affective states generated in this process."[26] Ongoing encounter nurtures our primary religious orientation, and wonder unfolds into manifold affective tastes of the divine.

The ability to contemplate two visions of reality at the same time may be an essentially aesthetic skill. Jon Paul Sydnor illustrates how viewing religious works of art together deepens understanding, even as this understanding eludes words. Here, "vision and speech are not hegemonized or prioritized one over the other but instead exist in complementary relation, each reliant on the other for its own fullness of being."[27] When we discuss a work of art, he notes, the work and not our language about it takes priority: Our language refers back to the work itself.

> The same relationship to language can safely be assumed for the other non-discursive manifestations of religion: ritual, ethics, statuary, music, dance, painting and architecture. In each, language must maintain an other-referential discipline in order to prevent self-inflation into a mistaken autonomy. In each, language must point away from itself and toward its subject in order to avoid accidental and distorting dominance.[28]

This "other-referential discipline" is the stance of the connoisseur as *sahṛdaya*. This stance is apropos to the wonder we experience toward discursive forms of religions as well. The inner complexity and coherence of a theological system are beautiful to behold.

Because religious traditions seem to demand total commitment, logic and language often fail the appreciative spectator who dwells in the space between commitment to her own faith tradition and commitment to understanding of another tradition.[29] The Indian notion of complementary emotional states gives words to the experience of this space. Its logic can be elaborated through the epistemology of complementarity thinking. Born in the realm of quantum physics, complementary reasoning allows the simultaneous existence of two apparently contradictory ideas: light as wave and light as particle. Rather than excluding one another, "'wave' and 'particle' become co-referential and take on new significance."[30] Sydnor applies this reasoning to the differing accounts of reality offered by Buddhists and Christians. The accounts of Buddhism and Christianity may both be true; likewise, neither may be absolutely true. The subject matter of theology necessitates that our knowledge of ultimate reality will always be partial and incomplete.

Paradox is not the enemy. Theologians need not explain away the fascination that seemingly incompatible points of view hold for us. To be sure, strategies to reconcile differing theologies do exist. Theologies of religious pluralism offer theories to help us understand the saving power of Kṛṣṇa alongside that of Christ. They might suggest that all saviors are faces of the cosmic Christ, that both Kṛṣṇa and Christ manifest a transcendent Real, that they offer genuinely different paths to divinity, or that they represent distinct religious ends. Such doctrines may be adopted in advance of interreligious encounters or used to explain them after the fact; but in the end, there is no accounting for taste. The old adage carries a nugget of wisdom: Although we can train our aesthetic lenses to understand form and style, we are often at a loss to explain what moves us. And, indeed, once we can explain *why* something is beautiful, it can lose some of its charm. The absorbed Christian spectator relishes the interfaith encounter, and a bit of this wonderment remains with her as she continues to live out her commitment to Christ.

In Conclusion: Opening

Wonder has been seen by some theorists as the synthesis of all *rasas*. It is said that wonder assists the emotions of love and heroism, reverses itself in comedy, and appears at the climax of any aesthetic experience. An aspect of surprise is also essential to art's success, as when the skillful storyteller strategically conceals and reveals details until the plot comes to a thrilling conclusion.[31]

Every aesthetic emotion has the potential to transport the attuned spectator to an experience of the divine. Although wonder opens us up to otherness and embodied particularity, it also partakes of the ethical ambivalence that attends aesthetic emotion. The predominant critique of an aesthetic focus in religion is that truth gets swallowed up in awe, that thinking gets overwhelmed by feeling. Wonder's special temptation is that, even as it opens us to that which is beyond ourselves, it threatens to close off critical inquiry.

The strategic employment of music and film in the Third Reich capitalized on this phenomenon. Recognizing, as Joseph Goebbels did, that "the moment that propaganda becomes conscious, it is ineffective," the highest officials exercised tight control over the production, funding, marketing, and censorship of the arts. The arts sanctioned by the regime created a comforting and inspiring vision of the common good that numbed the populace to the insidious realities around them.[32] The opening scene of the film *Schindler's List* stuns the viewer with the paradox of beauty alongside evil: Over the horrors of a pogrom in a Jewish ghetto in Poland waft the strands of a Bach piano sonata perfectly executed by an SS trooper who has found a piano in someone's living room.[33] It is perhaps no accident that Martin Heidegger, the Western philosopher who tried ardently to reopen wonder, fell headlong into the ideology of National Socialism. Hannah Arendt finds four risks of wonder encapsulated in Heidegger's error: Wonder can tempt us to escape from the messy obligations of reality, it allows us to become starstruck by dictators and tyrants, it can alienate us from the world to the extent that we can hardly relate to it in language, and it can obstruct our ability to form beliefs or make decisions.[34]

In Mary-Jane Rubenstein's assessment of the history of wonder, however, she observes that proper attention to the object of emotion is what resists the temptations of the aesthetic: "[A]ny unquestioning capitulation to ideology, Heidegger's included, is a matter not of too much wonder, but rather of too little." She advises that we delay resolution and certainty to remain within the unsettling "wound" of wonder: "[J]ust as a wound ceases to be itself when it heals, wonder is only wonder when it remains open."[35] The bandages of certainty and the sutures of belief offer the comforting but dangerous illusion that we are self-contained and whole.

Wonder in the face of religious difference faces the same temptation. We might enter into rational discourse with religious others, and we might attempt to articulate a coherent theology after this encounter, but we are lost if we cease to be amazed by difference. The razor's edge lies somewhere between the willingness to be uncritically swept away and the struggle to find language for what fascinates us. The ethics of this *rasa* demands a "wondrous openness to alterity [that] can be sustained only by . . . a tireless refusal to ground once and for all the identity of the self, the other, our god, this nation, or that people."[36] To cultivate the wonder of this edge is to remain open to the mystery of the other and of the divine.

The aesthetic framework I have developed here prevents the theologian from reducing religious differences to aspects of the same. The sympathetic observer's appreciation of Kṛṣṇa *bhakti* does not mean that she must understand it as another form of worship of the Holy Trinity. It is a unique religious flavor. If she is willing to learn from her religious neighbors, she learns to savor their faith in its distinctive idioms. The sympathetic spectator takes in these tastes of the divine so that they nurture the faith formed within her primary community—in part, precisely because it opens this faith up to wonder. The stance of wondrous appreciation heightens the apprehension of the depth and riches of the divine.

The tensions in which aesthetic appreciation entangle us are not meant to be unraveled. Not completely. *Rasa* is not an escapist transcendence, but it transports us nonetheless. Its raptures are firmly planted in bodies: those that evoke it and those that resonate with its frequency. It opens us simultaneously to what is common in the human emotional vocabulary and to the marvel of our irreducible differences. We savor the space between self and other. In these embodied tastes of the divine, we taste something of the peace, love, and furious justice that may even delight divinity itself.

NOTES

Frontmatter

1. Robert P. Goldman and Sally J. Sutherland Goldman, *Devavāṇīpraveśikā: An Introduction to the Sanskrit Language*, 3rd ed. (Berkeley: University of California Center for South Asia Studies, 1999), 5–8.
2. The work was likely composed between the second century B.C.E. and the fourth century C.E. Susan L. Schwartz, *Rasa: Performing the Divine in India* (New York: Columbia University Press, 2004), 4.
3. Francis X. Clooney, "Passionate Comparison: The Intensification of Affect in Interreligious Reading of Hindu and Christian Texts," *Harvard Theological Review* 98.4 (2005): 367–368.
4. Nandini Bhattacharyya-Panda, *Appropriation and Invention of Tradition: The East India Company and Hindu Law in Early Colonial Bengal* (Oxford: Oxford University Press, 2008), 3. Cf. Edward W. Said, *Orientalism* (New York: Vintage Books, 1978); and Ronald Inden, *Imagining India* (Oxford: Basil Blackwell, 1990).
5. Hugh Nicholson, *Comparative Theology and the Problem of Religious Rivalry* (Oxford: Oxford University Press, 2011), chapter 1.
6. Hugh Nicholson, "The Reunification of Theology and Comparison in the New Comparative Theology," *Journal of the American Academy of Religion* 77.3 (2009): 613–614.
7. For an overview of this "particularist" approach to religion, see Paul Hedges, *Controversies in Interreligious Dialogue and Theology of Religions* (London: SCM Press, 2010), chapter 4.
8. Arvind Sharma, *Religious Studies and Comparative Methodology: The Case for Reciprocal Illumination* (Albany: State University of New York Press, 2005), 45, 52.
9. Nicholson, "The Reunification of Theology and Comparison in the New Comparative Theology," 616.
10. Ibid., 628–629.
11. Nicholson, *Comparative Theology and the Problem of Religious Rivalry*, 8.
12. Sharma, *Religious Studies and Comparative Methodology*, 19.
13. John S. Dunne, C.S.C., *A Search for God in Time and Memory* (London: MacMillan, 1967, 1969), viii–ix.
14. See Reid B. Locklin and Hugh Nicholson, "The Return of Comparative Theology," *Journal of the American Academy of Religion* 78.2 (2010).

15. Sharma, *Religious Studies and Comparative Methodology*, 25.
16. Christian pronouncements on the possibility of salvation in other traditions are especially subject to scrutiny, and comparative theologians tend to avoid them. See James L. Fredericks, *Faith among Faiths: Christian Theology and Non-Christian Religions* (Mahwah, N.J.: Paulist Press, 1999).
17. An accessible introduction to these practices can be found in Francis X. Clooney, *Comparative Theology: Deep Learning Across Religious Borders* (West Sussex: Wiley-Blackwell, 2010). The issue of Christian hegemony in the discipline of comparative theology is fruitfully explored by an emerging group of scholars in Francis X. Clooney, ed., *The New Comparative Theology: Interreligious Insights from the Next Generation* (London: T&T Clark, 2010).
18. Linda Tuhiwai Smith, *Decolonizing Methodologies: Research and Indigenous Peoples* (New York: Zed Books, 1999), 56.
19. José Ignacio Cabezón, "The Discipline and Its Other: The Dialectic of Alterity in the Study of Religion," *Journal of the Academy of Religion* 74:1 (March 2006): 30–31.
20. Bill Ashcroft, Gareth Griffiths, and Helen Tiffin, *The Empire Writes Back: Theory and Practice in Post-Colonial Literatures* (London: Routledge, 1991), 38.
21. Kathryn Tanner, *Theories of Culture: A New Agenda for Theology* (Minneapolis: Fortress Press, 1997), 58.
22. Francis X. Clooney, *Theology after Vedanta: An Experiment in Comparative Theology* (Albany: State University of New York Press, 1993), 187.
23. Paul F. Knitter, *Introducing Theologies of Religions* (Maryknoll, N.Y.: Orbis, 2002), 141.
24. Cf. Jonathan Z. Smith, "The 'End' of Comparison," in *A Magic Still Dwells: Comparative Religion in the Postmodern Age*, ed. Kimberley C. Patton and Benjamin C. Ray (Berkeley: University of California Press, 2000), 237–241.
25. I am spurred by Audre Lorde's pointed charge that the guilt of the privileged is "all too often . . . just another name for impotence, for defensiveness destructive of communication; it becomes a device to protect ignorance and the continuation of things the way they are, the ultimate protection for changelessness. . . . If it leads to change then it can be useful, since it is then no longer guilt but the beginning of knowledge." Audre Lorde, *Sister Outsider: Essays and Speeches* (Berkeley, Calif.: Crossing Press, 1984), 130.
26. Catherine Keller, Michael Nausner, and Mayra Rivera, Introduction to *Postcolonial Theologies: Divinity and Empire*, ed. Catherine Keller, Michael Nausner, and Mayra Rivera (St. Louis, Mo.: Chalice Press, 2004), 14.
27. I am especially indebted to works of theological anthropology that locate emotion in a holistic unity of body and soul. Augustine's musings on the relation between feeling and knowing laid the foundation for much of this work. Christian authorities including Bernard of Clairvaux, Bonaventure, Ignatius of Loyola, Jonathan Edwards, John Wesley, and Friedrich Schleiermacher affirmed the value of affectivity; and Jürgen Moltmann and many feminist and womanist figures have culled their insights for a holistic anthropology.
28. John Corrigan, "Introduction: A Critical Assessment of Scholarly Literature in Religion and Emotion," in *Emotion and Religion: A Critical Assessment and Annotated Bibliography*, ed. John Corrigan, Eric Crump, and John Kloos (Westport, Conn.: Greenwood Press, 2000), 10–11.
29. John Corrigan, "Introduction: Emotions Research and the Academic Study of Religion," in *Religion and Emotion: Approaches and Interpretations*, ed. John Corrigan (Oxford:

Oxford University Press, 2004), 7–13. Helpful overviews of central figures and issues can be found in John Corrigan, ed., *The Oxford Handbook of Religion and Emotion* (Oxford: Oxford University Press, 2008).

30. John Corrigan, "Introduction: The Study of Religion and Emotion," in *The Oxford Handbook of Religion and Emotion*, ed. John Corrigan (Oxford: Oxford University Press, 2008), 7.
31. Charles Altieri, *The Particulars of Rapture: An Aesthetics of the Affects* (Ithaca, N.Y.: Cornell University Press, 2003), 155.
32. Martha C. Nussbaum, *Upheavals of Thought: The Intelligence of the Emotions* (Cambridge: Cambridge University Press, 2001), 681, 713.
33. Altieri, *The Particulars of Rapture*, 182.
34. Jonathan Edwards, *Treatise Concerning Religious Affections*, ed. John E. Smith (New Haven, Conn.: Yale University Press, 1959), 101.
35. Rabindranath Tagore, *Gitanjali*, trans. Rabindranath Tagore. http://www.sacred-texts.com/hin/tagore/gitnjali.htm.

Introduction: Rasa

1. Schwartz, *Rasa*, 7. Cf. J. L. Masson and M. V. Patwardhan, *Aesthetic Rapture: The Rasādhyāya of the Nāṭyaśāstra*, vol. II (Poona: Deccan College Postgraduate and Research Institute, 1970), 67n379.
2. Bharata's reliance on previous authors indicates that the aesthetic sense of *rasa* precedes the *Nāṭya Śāstra*. Masson and Patwardhan, *Aesthetic Rapture*, 69n386.
3. Schwartz, *Rasa*, ix.
4. Ibid., 3.
5. Ibid., 14.
6. Manomohan Ghosh, Introduction to *The Nāṭyaśāstra: A Treatise on Ancient Indian Dramaturgy and Histrionics Ascribed to Bharata-Muni*, Vol. 1, 2nd ed. (Calcutta: Manisha, 1967), xlix.
7. Masson and Patwardhan, *Aesthetic Rapture*, vol. 1, 36. Cf. Schwartz, *Rasa*, 23.
8. Schwartz, *Rasa*, 14, 25. Cf. Kapila Vatsyayan, *Bharata: The Nāṭyaśāstra* (New Delhi: Sahitya Akademi, 1996), chapter 4.
9. *Taittiriya Upanishad*, trans. Max Müller (1884), http://en.wikisource.org/wiki/Taittiriya_Upanishad.
10. Donna M. Wulff, "Religion in a New Mode: The Convergence of the Aesthetic and the Religious in Medieval India," *Journal of the American Academy of Religion* 54.4 (1986): 683.
11. The language of the "heart strangely warmed" comes from John Wesley, to whom the four-source paradigm referenced here, the "Wesleyan Quadrilateral," is sometimes attributed.
12. Ann Taves, *Religious Experience Reconsidered: A Building-Block Approach to the Study of Religion and Other Special Things* (Princeton, N.J.: Princeton University Press, 2009), 91.
13. Robert C. Roberts, "Emotions Research and Religious Experience," in *The Oxford Handbook of Religion and Emotion*, ed. John Corrigan (Oxford: Oxford University Press, 2008), 493.
14. Ibid., 493.
15. Altieri, *The Particulars of Rapture*, 154–156.

16. Ibid., 31. In his "expressivist model," "many of the values the emotions constitute have to be appreciated simply in terms of what they make manifest as manners of being that individuals pursue" (159).
17. June McDaniel, "Emotion in Bengali Religious Thought: Substance and Metaphor," in *Religion and Emotion: Approaches and Interpretations*, ed. John Corrigan (Oxford: Oxford University Press, 2004), 255.
18. Ibid., 253.
19. My translation of the *rasa sūtra*: *tatra vibhāvānubhāvavyabhicārisaṃyogādrasaniṣpattiḥ* (*NŚ* prose after VI.31, p. 227). Unless otherwise noted, all translations from the *NŚ* are my own. I have consulted *Nāṭyaśāstra of Bharatamuni: Text, Commentary of Abhinava Bhāratī by Abhinavaguptācārya and English Translation*, vol. 1, trans. M. M. Ghosh, ed. Pushpendra Kumar (Delhi: New Bharatiya Book Company, 2006). Page references follow the Kumar edition.
20. Cf. *NŚ* prose after VI.45, pp. 247–252.
21. See *NŚ* prose after VI.23, pp. 224–225 and *NŚ* prose after VII.93, pp. 307–308.
22. Masson and Patwardhan, *Aesthetic Rapture*, vol. 2, 63n362.
23. Cf. *NŚ* VI; but see V. Raghavan, *The Number of Rasa-s*, 3rd ed. (Madras: The Adyar Library and Research Centre, 1975), 69–103, for a summary of the debate over the *sthāyin* of peace.
24. K. S. Ramaswami Sastri, "Preface to the Second Edition," in *Nāṭyaśāstra of Bharatamuni*, ed. M. Ramakrishna Kavi (Baroda: Oriental Institute, 1980 [1956]), 25.
25. Still others correlate the *rasas* with the three cosmic principles (the *guṇas*) that combine to give material reality its distinct characteristics: peace and compassion with the pure or sattvic principle; love, heroism, and humor with the passionate or rajasic principle; and wonder, fury, disgust, and fear with the dark, heavy, tamasic principle. Radhakamal Mukerjee, *The Cosmic Art of India: Symbol* (Mūrti), *Sentiment* (Rasa) *and Silence* (Yoga) (Bombay: Allied Publishers Private Limited, 1965), 108–109.
26. Compatible and incompatible emotional states are listed in *NŚ* VII.108–117, pp. 310–312.
27. Cf. Altieri, *The Particulars of Rapture*, 158–166.
28. Haberman, *Acting as a Way of Salvation: A Study of Rāgānugā Bhakti Sādhana* (Delhi: Motilal Banarsidass, 1988), 26.
29. Although these points are debated, the general rule holds until the introduction of *bhakti* perspectives. See J. L. Masson and M. V. Patwardhan, *Śāntarasa and Abhinavagupta's Philosophy of Aesthetics* (Pune: Bhandarkar Oriental Research Institute, 1969), 85; Masson and Patwardhan, *Aesthetic Rapture*, vol. 2, 59n351 and 72n390; and Haberman, *Acting as a Way of Salvation*, 36–37.
30. According to legend, the first poet Valmiki was aesthetically moved to write the *Rāmāyana* when he witnessed the grief of a bird after a hunter killed its mate. This moment might be described as *rasa* if he was a spectator somewhat removed from the event, but not if he was directly saddened by the grief of the creature.
31. Cited in Ananda Coomaraswamy, *The Dance of Śiva: Essays on Indian Art and Culture* (New York: Dover Publications, 1985), 54.
32. For the theoretical precedents for this interpretation, see David L. Haberman, Introduction to *The Bhaktirasāmṛtasindhu of Rūpa Gosvāmin*, trans. David L. Haberman (Delhi: IGNCA and Motilal Banarsidass, 2003), xlvi, lii.
33. *ebhyaśca sāmānyaguṇayogena rasā niṣpadyante* (*NŚ* prose after VII.6, p. 279).

34. This is the analogy of Jagannātha, cited in Masson and Patwardhan, *Śāntarasa and Abhinavagupta's Philosophy of Aesthetics*, 174.
35. Ibid., 49.
36. Sastri, "Preface to the Second Edition," 52.
37. Masson and Patwardhan, *Śāntarasa and Abhinavagupta's Philosophy of Aesthetics*, 4.
38. Sushil Kumar De, *Some Problems of Sanskrit Poetics* (Calcutta: Firma K. L. Mukhopadhyay, 1959), 14.
39. K. S. Ramaswami Sastri, *Indian Aesthetics* (Srirangam: Sri Vani Vilas Press, 1928), 201–202, cf. 108.
40. De, *Some Problems of Sanskrit Poetics*, 15.
41. Anand Amaladass, S.J., "'Dhvani' Theory in Sanskrit Poetics," *Biblebhashyam* 5.4 (1979): 266–267.
42. For elaborations upon the role of *dhvani* in Indian literary theory, see Anand Amaladass, S.J., *Philosophical Implications of Dhvani: Experience of Symbol Language in Indian Aesthetics* (Vienna: De Nobili Research Library, 1984); P. K. Panda, *Concept of Dhvani in Sanskrit Poetics: Indian Theory of Suggestion and Principles of Literary Criticism in the Light of Ānandavardhana's Dhvanyāloka and Its Commentator Madhusudan Miśra's Avadhāna Commentary* (Delhi: Penman Publishers, 1988); and V. M. Kulkarni, *Outline of Abhinavagupta's Aesthetics* (Ahmedabad: Saraswati Pustak Bhandar, 1998).
43. Francis X. D'Sa, S.J., "'Dhvani' as a Method of Interpretation," *Biblebhashyam* 5.4 (1979): 280.
44. Ibid., 288; George M. Soares Prabhu, "And There Was a Great Calm: A 'Dhvani' Reading of the Stilling of the Storm (Mk. 4, 35–41)," *Biblebhashyam* 5.4 (1979): 307; Matthew Vellanickal, "Drink from the Source of the Living Water," *Biblebhashyam* 5.4 (1979): 313.
45. Amaladass, *Philosophical Implications of Dhvani*, 79, 9.
46. Jyoti Sahi, "Cultural Patchworks: A *Dhvani* Understanding of Art and Secularism. Part I: Outline of the Position of Art within the Secular Space of the Modern State." April 20, 2010. http://jyotiartashram.blogspot.com/2010/04/cultural-patchwork-part-1.html.
47. Jyoti Sahi, "Cultural Patchworks: A *Dhvani* Understanding of Art and Secularism. Part II: Towards a Spirituality of Art within Secular Society." April 20, 2010. http://jyotiartashram.blogspot.com/2010/04/cultural-patchwork-part-ii.html.
48. Sahi and his colleagues in the Kabir Project at the Srishti School of Art and Design explore this model's implications for interfaith spirituality. Jyoti Sahi, "Cultural Patchworks: A *Dhvani* Understanding of Art and Secularism. Part III: Indian Art and the Representation of a Secular Christ." April 20, 2010. http://jyotiartashram.blogspot.com/2010/04/cultural-patchwork-part-iii.html.
49. Caroline MacKenzie, "Liberation and Imagination: Art, Theology and Women's Experience," *Feminist Theology* 8 (1995): 14. See also Caroline MacKenzie, "Art and Architecture as Locus for Dialogue: Inter-Religious Dialogue through Art," *Hindu-Christian Studies Bulletin* 4 (1991): 31.
50. MacKenzie, "Liberation and Imagination," 15.
51. Martin Kämpchen and Jyoti Sahi, *The Holy Waters: Indian Psalm-Meditations* (Bangalore: Asian Trading Corporation, 1984).
52. Jonathan Edwards, *Religious Affections*, ed. John E. Smith, Works of Jonathan Edwards 2 (New Haven, Conn.: Yale University Press, 1959), 95.
53. Cf. Catherine A. Lutz and Lila Abu-Lughod, eds., *Language and the Politics of Emotion* (Cambridge: Cambridge University Press, 1990).

54. Rita Dasgupta Sherma, "Eros, Ethics, and Enlightenment: Towards a Reconstructive Approach to Ultimate and Penultimate Goals in Hindu Theology," accessed April 25, 2012, http://www.infinityfoundation.com/mandala/s_es/s_es_sherm_eros_frameset.htm.

Part I / 1. The Bliss of Peace

1. For the artist's description of this space, see Sahi, *Stepping Stones: Reflections on the Theology of Indian Christian Culture* (Bangalore: Asian Trading Corporation, 1986), 55–56, 163–165, 180–183. The NBCLC has also published a guide to its buildings: *NBCLC Campus: Milieu of God-Experience, An Artistic Synthesis of Spirituality* (Bangalore: NBCLC, 2005).
2. Unless otherwise noted, translations of *DhĀ* and *Loc* are my own. I have indicated the corresponding pages in Daniel H. H. Ingalls, Jeffrey Moussaieff Masson, and M. V. Patwardhan, *The* Dhvanyāloka *of Ānandavardhana with the* Locana *of Abhinavagupta* (Cambridge, Mass.: Harvard University Press, 1990); and Masson and Patwardhan, *Śāntarasa and Abhinavagupta's Philosophy of Aesthetics.* Transliterations of the Sanskrit text follow Acharya Jagannath Pathak, *Dhvanyaloka of Sri Anandavardhanacharya with the Lochana Sanskrit Commentary of Sri Abhinavagupta* (Varanasi: Chowkhamba Vidyabhawan, 2003). The numbering of the verses follows the translation of Ingalls et al., *The* Dhvanyāloka *of Ānandavardhana with the* Locana *of Abhinavagupta.*
3. The fragmentary and corrupt text of the *Abhinavabhāratī (ABh)* has not been translated fully into English. The Sanskrit text of the commentary on chapter VI can be found in *Nāṭyaśāstra of Bharatamuṇi, Vol. I, Bare Text of Chs. I–VII (with Commentary Abhinavabhāratī on Adhyāya VI only)*, ed. M. Ramakrishna Kavi and K. S. Ramaswami Sastri (Baroda: Oriental Institute, 1980), 95–176. The section of the text relevant for this chapter, Abhinavagupta's commentary on the interpolated *śānta rasa* section of chapter VI, has been translated in Masson and Patwardhan, *Śāntarasa and Abhinavagupta's Philosophy of Aesthetics*, 120–143 and also in Edwin Gerow, "Abhinavagupta's Aesthetics as a Speculative Paradigm," *Journal of the American Oriental Society* 114.2 (1994): 193–208. My notes on the *ABh* refer the reader to the latter texts.
4. Abhinavagupta was not the first to do this, but the texts of the previous theorists whose ideas he incorporates are lost to us today. See Edwin Gerow and Ashok Aklujkar, "On *Śānta Rasa* in Sanskrit Poetics," *Journal of the American Oriental Society* 92.1 (1972): 81.
5. Gerow and Aklujkar, "On *Śānta Rasa* in Sanskrit Poetics," 83.
6. *tṛṣṇānāṃ viṣayābhilāṣāṇāṃ yaḥ kṣayaḥ sarvato nivṛttirūpo nirvedaḥ tadeva sukhaṃ tasya sthāyibhūtasya yaḥ paripoṣo rasyamānatākṛtastadeva lakṣaṇaṃ yasya sa śānto rasaḥ. Loc* 3.26a, translated by Ingalls, Masson, and Patwardhan: *The* Dhvanyāloka *of Ānandavardhana with the* Locana *of Abhinavagupta*, 521.
7. Paul Tillich, *On Art and Architecture*, ed. John Dillenberger and Jane Dillenberger, trans. Robert P. Scharlemann (New York: Crossroad, 1989), 12.
8. Karl Rahner, "The Religious Meaning of Images," in *Theological Investigations,* vol. XXIII, trans. Joseph Donceel, S.J., and Hugh M. Riley (New York: Crossroad, 1992), 159.
9. Hans Urs von Balthasar, *The Glory of the Lord: A Theological Aesthetics, Volume I: Seeing the Form*, ed. Joseph Fessio, S.J., and John Riches, trans. Erasmo Leiva-Merikakis (San Francisco: Ignatius Press, 1982), 38.
10. Elsewhere, von Balthasar attempts to express a beauty that encompasses the woundedness of Christ's incarnation and death in lyrical rather than systematic theological form.

See Hans Urs von Balthasar, *Heart of the World*, trans. Erasmo S. Leiva (San Francisco: Ignatius Press, 1979).

11. *yastvalaukikacamatkārātmā rasāsvādaḥ kāvyagatavibhāvādicarvaṇāprāṇo nāsau smaraṇānumānādisāmyena khilīkārapātrīkartavyaḥ. Loc* 1.18. Cf. Ingalls et al., *The* Dhvanyāloka *of Ānandavardhana with the* Locana *of Abhinavagupta*, 191.
12. This makes the suggestion of *rasa* unique, because the other two things that can be suggested, facts (*vastu*) and figures of speech (*alaṃkāra*), can be denoted directly. Cf. *DhĀ* and *Loc* 1.4a and Kulkarni, *Outline of Abhinavagupta's Aesthetics*, 53–57.
13. *na cāsau carvaṇā . . . kutaścitpramāṇāntarādutpannā alaukike pratyakṣādyavyāpārāt. Loc* 1.18. Cf. Ingalls et al., *The* Dhvanyāloka *of Ānandavardhana with the* Locana *of Abhinavagupta*, 191–192.
14. *Loc* 1.18. Cf. Ingalls et al., *The* Dhvanyāloka *of Ānandavardhana with the* Locana *of Abhinavagupta*, 192. This is a similar argument (as in *DhĀ* 1.1d) as that against those who claim that suggestion (*dhvani*) can be reduced to one of the powers of language, such as secondary usage, inference, or direct denotation.
15. This last point is extrapolated in the readings of the *ABh* in Kulkarni, *Outline of Abhinavagupta's Aesthetics*, 58–59; and Masson and Patwardhan, *Aesthetic Rapture*, 69n388.
16. *DhĀ* and *Loc* 1.5. Other theorists disagree with Abhinavagupta on the blissful nature of all *rasa*. See Kulkarni, *Outline of Abhinavagupta's Aesthetics*, 46–52, 69–80.
17. R. Gnoli, *The Aesthetic Experience According to Abhinavagupta* (Varanasi: Chowkhamba Sanskrit Series, 1985), xxiin1; xli.
18. *parabrahmāsvādasabrahmacāritvaṃ cāstvasya rasāsvādasya. Loc* 2.4, translated by Ingalls et al., *The* Dhvanyāloka *of Ānandavardhana with the* Locana *of Abhinavagupta*, 226. Cf. *ABh* on the *rasa sūtra*, translated in Gnoli, *The Aesthetic Experience According to* Abhinavagupta, 46–49.
19. Cf. *ABh* VI.33, translated in Masson and Patwardhan, *Aesthetic Rapture*, vol. II, 69n388: "With a mind that lacks any possibility of obstruction from another sense-organ (i.e. that is completely concentrated), they enjoy (literature) because they are completely absorbed in the thrill of imaginative delight that is devoid of any thought of 'I' or 'You.' This imaginative delight is really not different from the inner experience (*carvaṇā*) of one's own consciousness which is extremely beautiful because it is pervaded (*anuvedha*) by a great variety of latent impressions (propensities) of experienced happiness, sorrow, etc."
20. *ABh* on the *rasa sūtra*, translated in Gnoli, *The Aesthetic Experience According to Abhinavagupta*, 64–67.
21. Kulkarni, *Outline of Abhinavagupta's Aesthetics*, 64–65.
22. For a summary of Abhinavagupta's synthesis, see Raghavan, *The Number of Rasa-s*, 197–199.
23. Masson and Patwardhan, *Śāntarasa and Abhinavagupta's Philosophy of Aesthetics*, 34. Masson and Patwardhan assess various theories for the date of the interpolated passage and believe that it was most likely "added to the text sometime before the time of Udbhaṭa [who made the first extant reference to it], i.e. eighth century [C.E.]" (35). Schwartz concurs with this dating: Schwartz, *Rasa*, 15.
24. Raghavan lays out this debate in detail. Other contenders for the primary rasa include *karuṇa*, variations on *śṛṅgāra* (*ahaṃkāra-śṛṅgāra*, *preman*, and *rati-śṛṅgāra*), and *adbhuta*. Raghavan, *The Number of Rasa-s*, 199–212.

25. Translators differ on whether Abhinavagupta viewed the *Nāgānanda*, a drama in which the hero is a renouncer, in terms of *śānta* or of *vīra*, the heroic sentiment. Compare *ABh* in Masson and Patwardhan, *Śāntarasa and Abhinavagupta's Philosophy of Aesthetics*, 135–137, with *ABh* in Gerow, "Abhinavagupta's Aesthetics as a Speculative Paradigm," 203–205.
26. *DhĀ* and *Loc* 4.5 in Ingalls et al., *The* Dhvanyāloka *of Ānandavardhana with the* Locana *of Abhinavagupta*, 690–700.
27. *DhĀ* and *Loc* 3.26b in Ingalls et al., *The* Dhvanyāloka *of Ānandavardhana with the* Locana *of Abhinavagupta*, 324–325. For his part, Abhinavagupta equates *dayāvīra*, compassionate heroism, with *śāntarasa* because it is devoid of egoism. *ABh* in Masson and Patwardhan, *Śāntarasa and Abhinavagupta's Philosophy of Aesthetics*, 133 (cf. *Śāntarasa* 96, 101, 102n3).
28. *Loc* 3.26a in Ingalls et al., *The* Dhvanyāloka *of Ānandavardhana with the* Locana *of Abhinavagupta*, 521; cf. Masson and Patwardhan, *Śāntarasa and Abhinavagupta's Philosophy of Aesthetics*, 99n1.
29. *ABh* in Masson and Patwardhan, *Śāntarasa and Abhinavagupta's Philosophy of Aesthetics*, 121.
30. *Loc* 3.26a in Ingalls et al., *The* Dhvanyāloka *of Ānandavardhana with the* Locana *of Abhinavagupta*, 521; cf. *ABh* in Masson and Patwardhan, *Śāntarasa and Abhinavagupta's Philosophy of Aesthetics*, 137. The reasons for not representing the "culminating state" of certain *rasa*s has much to do with the principle of *aucitya* (propriety) discussed in the next chapter; cf. Gerow, Abhinavagupta's Aesthetics as a Speculative Paradigm," 205n193.
31. *tasya yamaniyamādhātmadhyānadhāraṇopāsanasarvabhūtadayāliṅgagrahaṇādibhir-anubhāvairabhinayaḥ prayoktavyaḥ*. Kavi and Sastri, eds., *Nāṭyaśāstra of Bharatamuṇi, Vol. I*, 167–168; cf. Masson and Patwardhan, *Śāntarasa and Abhinavagupta's Philosophy of Aesthetics*, 91.
32. Abhinavagupta may not have had access to a manuscript with the *rasa sūtra*, but his exposition deals with its various elements. Masson and Patwardhan, *Śāntarasa and Abhinavagupta's Philosophy of Aesthetics*, 92n1.
33. *ABh* in Masson and Patwardhan, *Śāntarasa and Abhinavagupta's Philosophy of Aesthetics*, 139. Because the other *rasa*s have a presiding deity, other theorists assign either the Buddha or the Śiva of Tantric traditions to *śānta*. Abhinavagupta disagrees with this move, since *śānta* properly underlies all the *rasas*, each of which has its own deity. Masson and Patwardhan, *Śāntarasa and Abhinavagupta's Philosophy of Aesthetics*, 139n2; 141n5.
34. *tasya ca bhavitavyameva prāktanakuśalaparipākaparameśvarānugrahādhyātmara-hasyaśāstravītarāgapariśīlanādibhirvibhāvairitīyataiva. Loc* 3.26a. Cf. Ingalls et al., *The* Dhvanyāloka *of Ānandavardhana with the* Locana *of Abhinavagupta*, 522.
35. *ABh* in Masson and Patwardhan, *Śāntarasa and Abhinavagupta's Philosophy of Aesthetics*, 120–121.
36. Ibid., 124–128.
37. Ibid., 128–130.
38. *svaṃ svaṃ nimittamāsādya śāntādbhāvaḥ pravartate | punarnimittāpāyo tu śānta eva pralīyate* || Cited in *Loc* 3.26a, cf. Ingalls et al., *The* Dhvanyāloka *of Ānandavardhana with the* Locana *of Abhinavagupta*, 521; and variant reading in Kavi and Sastri, eds., *Nāṭyaśāstra of Bharatamuṇi, Vol. I*, 170.
39. *ABh* in Masson and Patwardhan, *Śāntarasa and Abhinavagupta's Philosophy of Aesthetics*, 130–131. In Gerow's translation of the *ABh*, "the Self [*ātman*] . . . is the stable (basis of

śānta rasa)." *Abhinavagupta's Aesthetics as a Speculative Paradigm*, 199–200. This translation supports Gerow's argument that *śānta* is unique in its relation to the very condition of *rasa* (see Gerow and Aklujkar, "On *Śānta Rasa* in Sanskrit Poetics," 82), but it is not clear how the *ātman* is an emotional state (*bhāva*).

40. *ABh* in Masson and Patwardhan, *Śāntarasa and Abhinavagupta's Philosophy of Aesthetics*, 142.
41. *mokṣaphalatvena cāyam paramapuruṣārthaniṣṭatvātsarvarasebhyaḥ pradhānatamaḥ.* *Loc* 3.26b. Cf. Ingalls et al., *The* Dhvanyāloka *of Ānandavardhana with the* Locana *of Abhinavagupta*, 525.
42. *Loc* 3.26a, Ingalls et al., *The* Dhvanyāloka *of Ānandavardhana with the* Locana *of Abhinavagupta*, 521.
43. Masson and Patwardhan, *Śāntarasa and Abhinavagupta's Philosophy of Aesthetics*, 123n1.
44. Cf. *Loc* 1.18, 2.4.
45. Masson and Patwardhan, *Śāntarasa and Abhinavagupta's Philosophy of Aesthetics*, 161–162.
46. Ibid., xvii. Cf. Masson and Patwardhan, *Aesthetic Rapture*, vol. II, 35n221 and 70n388.
47. *parameśvaraviśrāntyānanda . . . tadānandavipruṣmātrāvābhāso hi rasāsvāda.* *Loc* 3.43b, cf. Ingalls et al., *The* Dhvanyāloka *of Ānandavardhana with the* Locana *of Abhinavagupta*, 655.
48. This is Madhusūdanasarasvatī's point in his *Śrībhagavadbhaktirasāyanam* I.12, cited in Masson and Patwardhan, *Śāntarasa and Abhinavagupta's Philosophy of Aesthetics*, 159–160.
49. Kulkarni, *Outline of Abhinavagupta's Aesthetics*, 65.
50. For a survey of his life and work, see Vishwanath S. Naravane, *Ananda K. Coomaraswamy* (Boston: Twayne Publishers, 1977).
51. He also translates an important manual of dance: Ananda Coomaraswamy, *The Mirror of Gesture: Abhinaya Darpana of Nandikeśvara*, 4th ed. (New Delhi: Munshiram Manoharlal Publishers, 1987).
52. Ananda K. Coomaraswamy, *The Dance of Śiva: Essays on Indian Art and Culture* (New York: Dover Publications, 1985), 35–36.
53. See, especially, the essay, "The Christian and Oriental, or True, Philosophy of Art," in Ananda K. Coomaraswamy, *Christian and Oriental Philosophy of Art* (New York: Dover Publications, 1956), 23–60.
54. Coomaraswamy, *The Dance of Śiva*, 36.
55. Coomaraswamy, *Christian and Oriental Philosophy of Art*, 32.
56. Coomaraswamy, *The Dance of Śiva*, 37.
57. Coomaraswamy, *Christian and Oriental Philosophy of Art*, 41, 53. He sees the same teaching in Christian notions of doing God's work and in Kṛṣṇa's statement in the Bhagavad Gītā, "I am the Doer" (41).
58. Coomaraswamy, *The Dance of Śiva*, 32
59. Coomaraswamy, *Christian and Oriental Philosophy of Art*, 35.
60. K. Krishnamoorthy, "The Relevance of RASA Theory to Modern Literature," in *Some Aspects of the Rasa Theory*, ed. V. M. Kulkarni (Delhi: B. L. Institute of Indology, 1986), 89; R. B. Patankar, "Does the Rasa Theory Have Any Modern Relevance?" in *Some Aspects of the Rasa Theory*, ed. V. M. Kulkarni (Delhi: B. L. Institute of Indology, 1986), 115.
61. Krishnamoorthy, "The Relevance of RASA Theory to Modern Literature," 89.
62. Patankar, "Does the Rasa Theory have any Modern Relevance?," 110–120.

63. T. S. Nandi, "Worldly Nature of Rasa," in *Some Aspects of the Rasa Theory*, ed. V. M. Kulkarni (Delhi: B. L. Institute of Indology, 1986), 43. Nandi points to a number of authorities, including Bharata's metaphor of *rasa* as taste, which grounds *rasa* in worldly experience (48); Lollaṭa's location of *rasa* not only in the spectator but in the poet, the actor, and the original character as well (46); and Śankuka's description of *rasa* as imitation (46).
64. Rekha Jhanji, *The Sensuous in Art: Reflections on Indian Aesthetics* (Shimla: Indian Institute of Advanced Study, 1989), 66.
65. Ibid., 66.
66. Ibid., 69.
67. Coomaraswamy, *The Dance of Śiva*, 36.
68. From Coomaraswamy's essay, "Why Exhibit Works of Art?" in *Christian and Oriental Philosophy of Art*, 16–17.
69. Compare Coomaraswamy's position mentioned previously with that of Masson and Patwardhan in *Śāntarasa and Abhinavagupta's Philosophy of Aesthetics*, 161–163.
70. Kapila Vatsyayan, *Bharata*, 146.
71. See, for example, B. N. Pandit, *Aspects of Kashmir Śaivism* (Srinagar: Utpal Publications, 1977), 45.
72. Masson and Patwardhan's essential English-language studies of the *Abhinavabhāratī* and the *Locana* were published in 1969 and 1970, respectively.
73. Abhinavagupta, *The Doctrine of Divine Recognition (Īśvara Pratyabhijñā Vimarśinī of Abhinavagupta)*, 3 vols., ed. R. C. Dwivedi, K. A. Subramania Iyer, and K. C. Pandey (Delhi: Motilal Banarsidass, 1986).
74. See Jaideva Singh, Introduction to *Vijñānabhairava or Divine Consciousness: A Treasury of 112 Types of Yoga*, trans. Jaideva Singh (Delhi: Motilal Banarsidass, 1979), xxiv–xxvi.
75. Mark S. G. Dyczkowski, *The Doctrine of Vibration: An Analysis of the Doctrines and Practices of Kashmir Shaivism* (Delhi: Motilal Banarsidass, 1989), 172–173. For examples of meditations on such moments of transition, see *The Stanzas on Vibration: The Spandakārikā with Four Commentaries*, trans. Mark S. G. Dyczkowski (Varanasi: Dilip Kumar Publishers, 1994), 100–102, 219–220, 275.
76. *gītāviṣayāsvādāsamasaukhyaikatātmanaḥ* | *yoginastanmayatvena manorūḍestadātmatā* || My translation of verse 73, cf. Singh, *Vijñānabhairava or Divine Consciousness*, 69.
77. Singh, *Vijñānabhairava or Divine Consciousness*, 63.
78. Jaideva Singh, "Exposition," in Abhinavagupta, *Parā-trīśikā-Vivaraṇa: The Secret of Tantric Mysticism*, ed. Bettina Bäumer, trans. with notes by Jaideva Singh, corrected by Swami Lakshmanjee (Delhi: Motilal Banarsidass, 1988), 52.
79. Abhinavagupta, *Parā-trīśikā-Vivaraṇa*, 38–46.
80. Cf. Gerow and Aklujkar, "On *Śānta Rasa* in Sanskrit Poetics," 82.
81. Vatsyayan, *Bharata*, 145. Susan Schwartz comments, "Like the elaborate rituals described in the Vedic texts, the theater offers in microcosm a representation of the greater, macrocosmic realities, and in so doing, allows those prepared to understand a path to transcendence." Schwartz, *Rasa*, 14.
82. Cf. Vatsyayan, *Bharata*, 154; and Sastri, "Preface to the Second Edition," 16.
83. Bettina Bäumer, "Aesthetics of Mysticism or Mysticism of Aesthetics? The Approach of Kashmir Śaivism," in *Mysticism in Shaivism and Christianity*, ed. Bettina Bäumer (New Delhi: D. K. Printworld, 1997), 341.
84. Masson and Patwardhan, *Aesthetic Rapture*, vol. I, 25.

2. *Suffering and Peace*

1. Jyoti Sahi, *The Child and the Serpent: Reflections on Popular Indian Symbols* (Bangalore: Asian Trading Corporation, 1994).
2. Jyoti Sahi, "School for Storytelling and Seeing," *Jyoti Art Ashram* (blog), February 25, 2007, http://jyotiartashram.blogspot.com/2007_02_01_archive.html. The attentive reader will note that Sahi's list of *rasas* equates *hāsya* (the humorous sentiment) with joy and replaces wonder (*adbhuta*) with sorrow (*śoka*).
3. M. Thomas Thangaraj, "Indian Christian Tradition," in *Religions of South Asia: An Introduction*, ed. Sushil Mittal and Gene Thursby (London: Routledge, 2006), 190.
4. For one transitional document, see Michael Amaladoss, S.J., *Beyond Inculturation: Can the Many Be One?* (Delhi: Vidyajyoti Education and Welfare Society/ISPCK, 1998).
5. M. Thomas Thangaraj, "Indian Christian Tradition," 197. These themes arose repeatedly as I discussed my research with Hindus and Christians in India.
6. Trinh T. Minh-ha, *When the Moon Waxes Red: Representation, Gender, and Cultural Politics* (London: Routledge, 1991), 3.
7. Swami Amalorananda (D. S. Amalorpavadass), *Integration and Interiorization* (Mysore: Anjali Ashram, 1990).
8. "Om Dyaun Santi, Antharikshan Santi, Prithvi Santi, Apah Santi, Vishve deva Santi, Vishve nara Santi, Brahma Santi, Sarvan Santi, Santireva Santi, Sama Santiredhi. Om Santi, Santi, Santi! [*sic*]." Amalorpavadass, *Integration and Interiorization*, 32.
9. I attended the Wednesday-evening "Indian Mass" several times in May 2010. A critical description of this service and a portion of its text can be found in Collins, *Christian Inculturation in India* (Burlington, Vt.: Ashgate, 2007), 149–153 and 201–210.
10. Amalorpavadass, *Integration and Interiorization*, 31.
11. D. S. Amalorpavadass, *Inculturation Realizes the Church's Universality, Fulness [*sic*] and Unity*. Inculturation Pamphlet Series, no. 7 (Bangalore: NBCLC, n.d.).
12. Amalorpavadass, *Integration and Interiorization*, 23.
13. Ibid., 14–15.
14. Sahi, *Stepping Stones*, 169.
15. Ibid., 65.
16. Ibid., 134.
17. Ibid., 129.
18. Sahi, *Holy Ground: A New Approach to the Mission of the Church in India* (Auckland: Pace Publishing, 1998), 44. A brief biography can be found in Eric Lott and Jyoti Sahi, *Faces of Vision: Images of Life and Faith* (Leicester, UK: Christians Aware, 2008), 1–7.
19. Sahi, *Holy Ground*, 92.
20. Ibid., 93–94.
21. Jyoti Sahi, "The Yoga of Art," *Jyoti Art Ashram* (blog), July 22, 2007, http://jyotiartashram.blogspot.com/2007/07/yoga-of-art-relation-of-art-to-yoga-has.html.
22. "The Yoga of the Heart in Relation to a Vision of Reality," *Jyoti Art Ashram* (blog), July 20, 2007, http://jyotiartashram.blogspot.com/2007/07/yoga-of-heart-in-relation-to-vision-of.html.
23. Jyoti Sahi, "The Yoga of the Heart in Relation to Eastern Practices of Meditation," *Jyoti Art Ashram* (blog), July 20, 2007, http://jyotiartashram.blogspot.com/2007/07/yoga-of-heart-in-relation-to-eastern.html; cf. Jyoti Sahi, "Some Reflections on Yoga and

Jesus," *Jyoti Art Ashram* (blog), June 29, 2007, http://jyotiartashram.blogspot.com/2007_06_01_archive.html.

24. Cf. Gottfried Rothermindt, "Umstrittene Indische Christliche Kunst," *Zeitschrift für missionswissenschaft und Religionswissenschaft* (Jan. 1982), 1.
25. Sahi, *Stepping Stones*, 57. Several of his Christian mandalas can be found at Jyoti Sahi, "Mandala of the Kingdom of Heaven." *Jyoti Art Ashram* (blog). October 2, 2007, http://jyotiartashram.blogspot.com/2007/10/mandala-of-kingdom-of-heaven.html.
26. Sahi, *Stepping Stones*, 59.
27. NBCLC, *NBCLC Campus*, 76–79. Sahi has written extensively on his engagement with tribal forms: Jyoti Sahi, "Wayanad: A Land of Ancient Forests," *Jyoti Art Ashram* (blog), February 5, 2010, http://jyotiartashram.blogspot.com/2010_02_01_archive.html.
28. Sahi, *Stepping Stones*, 166. Tribal and Dalit theologies provide the basis for much of his thought on ecology. See, for example, Jyoti Sahi, "Dalit and Tribal Theologies," *Jyoti Art Ashram* (blog), September 29, 2009, http://jyotiartashram.blogspot.com/2009_09_01_archive.html.
29. "Water symbolism extends beyond any religion as such, because it arises out of . . . everyday experience." Sahi, *Stepping Stones,* 168.
30. See Sahi, *Stepping Stones*, 59–60, and *Holy Ground*, chapter 7.
31. Kämpchen and Sahi, *The Holy Waters*, 117.
32. Sahi, *Stepping Stones,* 60.
33. Ibid., 167–168.
34. Ibid., 165. Sahi calls the grilles a "distraction" from this elemental theme (164).
35. "Hindu canons of art have explicitly laid it down that the artist must only depict the eternal and perfect, not the ephemeral and accidental. Thus suffering never found a place in the great tradition of Indian art—suffering in the sense of the depiction of human misery, and the plight of modern historical man [*sic*]." Sahi, *Stepping Stones,* 141; cf. 60.
36. Sahi, *Holy Ground*, 22, 25–26, 28–29.
37. Sahi, *Stepping Stones*, 75, 121; cf. 153. Sahi views art as sacramental, a "channel of grace" that "celebrates the incarnation, because it not only depicts what has happened in the past but also through the images it helps us feel that Christ is present and among us today" (73).
38. Sahi, *Stepping Stones*, 122, 121.
39. Ibid., 113, 115.
40. Ibid., 144.
41. Ibid., 145, 148–149. An example of the cross of light in his work can be found at Jyoti Sahi, "The Cross of Light," *Jyoti Art Ashram* (blog), October 23, 2010, http://jyotiartashram.blogspot.com/2010/10/cross-of-light.html.
42. Sahi fleshes out his insights on the cross in Jyoti Sahi, "The Way of the Cross as Dreaming the Mandala," *Jyoti Art Ashram* (blog), April 20, 2009, http://jyotiartashram.blogspot.com/2009_04_01_archive.html. The cosmic cross can be seen at Jyoti Sahi, "The Cosmic Cross," *Jyoti Art Ashram* (blog), October 23, 2010, http://jyotiartashram.blogspot.com/2010/10/cosmic-cross.html.
43. For one of many examples of the cross as a tree, see Jyoti Sahi, "Jesus Dies on the Tree," *Jyoti Art Ashram* (blog), October 8, 2007, http://jyotiartashram.blogspot.com/2007/10/jesus-dies-on-tree.html.

44. Sahi, *Stepping Stones*, 144–145. For one such image of the dancer on the cross, see Jyoti Sahi, "Dancer on the Cross," *Jyoti Art Ashram* (blog), October 7, 2007, http://jyotiartashram.blogspot.com/2007/10/dancer-on-cross.html.
45. Sahi, *Stepping Stones*, 76–77.
46. Ibid., 146.
47. Ibid., 147.
48. Ibid., 147.
49. Ibid., 123
50. Sahi, *Holy Ground*, 79.
51. Sahi, *Stepping Stones*, 16.
52. Ibid., 15.
53. Jyoti Sahi, personal conversation with the author, Bangalore, April 28, 2010. As noted in the introduction, *dhvani* was an important theological emphasis during the heyday of the inculturation movement in India.
54. The Psalms and the Christian patristic writers explore the depth and range of such emotion, as do Sahi and Martin Kämpchen in *The Holy Waters*.
55. Sugiharto notes exceptions to this generalization: Michael Polanyi has begun to recuperate emotion as a mode of knowing, in contrast to a strong empiricist tradition; and there is a "sensibility towards virtues" in the work of Blaise Pascal, Max Scheller, and Hans-Georg Gadamer. Bambang Sugiharto, "Javanese Epistemology Revisited," unpublished paper presented to the Institute for Advanced Study in Asian Cultures and Theologies, Hong Kong, 2007, 11.
56. This lovely term is Mayra Rivera's: Mayra Rivera, *The Touch of Transcendence: A Postcolonial Theology of God* (Louisville: Westminster John Knox Press, 2007).

Part II/3. The Rasa *of Love Incarnate*

1. This performance is recounted in David V. Mason, *Theatre and Religion on Krishna's Stage: Performing in Vrindavan* (New York: Palgrave MacMillan, 2009), 4–10. For a vivid description of an eight-day festival production of Kṛṣṇa's activities (the *aṣṭayāma līlā*), see chapters seven and eight of Margaret H. Case, *Seeing Krishna: The Religious World of a Brahman Family in Vrindaban* (Oxford: Oxford University Press, 2000). Descriptions of such performances can also be found in David R. Kinsley, *The Divine Player: A Study of Kṛṣṇa Līlā* (Delhi: Motilal Banarsidass, 1979); and John Stratton Hawley, *At Play with Krishna: Pilgrimage Dramas from Brindavan* (Princeton, N.J.: Princeton University Press, 1981).
2. Donna M. Wulff, *Drama as a Mode of Religious Realization: The Vidagdhamādhava of Rūpa Gosvāmī* (Chico, Calif.: Scholars Press, 1984), 20.
3. The concept of divine play (*līlā*) spans a number of religious traditions. See William S. Sax, ed., *The Gods at Play:* Līlā *in South Asia* (New York: Oxford University Press, 1995).
4. David L. Haberman, *Acting as a Way of Salvation: A Study of Rāgānugā Bhakti Sādhana* (Delhi: Motilal Banarsidass, 1988), 66.
5. Stephen D. Moore, "The Song of Songs in the History of Sexuality," *Church History* 69.2 (2000): 329.
6. June McDaniel, "Blue Lotuses Everywhere: Divine Love in Gauḍīya Vaiṣṇava and Catholic Mysticism," *Journal of Vaishnava Studies* 5 (1996–1997): 95.

7. Sushil Kumar De, "The Bhakti-Rasa-Sastra of Bengal Vaisnavism," *The Indian Historical Quarterly* 8 (1932): 688.
8. Moore, "The Song of Songs in the History of Sexuality," 339.
9. Mark S. Burrows, "Foundations for an Erotic Christology: Bernard of Clairvaux on Jesus as 'Tender Lover,'" *Anglican Theological Review* 80.4 (1998): 479–480.
10. References to the *BhP* follow Edwin F. Bryant, trans., *Krishna: The Beautiful Legend of God: Śrīmad Bhāgavata Purāṇa, Book X, With Chapters I, 6, and 9–31 from Book XI* (New York: Penguin, 2003).
11. Kṛṣṇadāsa Kavirāja, Caitanya Caritāmṛta *of Kṛṣṇadāsa Kavirāja*, ed. Tony K. Stewart (Cambridge, Mass.: Harvard University Press, 1999) 2.8.233, p. 459, cf. 206.
12. For a critical biography of Caitanya and a history of the early movement in Bengal, see Edward C. Dimock Jr. and Tony K. Stewart, Introduction to *Caitanya Caritāmṛta of Kṛṣṇadāsa Kavirāja*, ed. Tony K. Stewart (Cambridge, Mass.: Harvard University Press, 1999), 10–25.
13. Dimock and Stewart, Introduction to *Caitanya Caritāmṛta of Kṛṣṇadāsa Kavirāja*, 118.
14. *anyābhilāṣitāśūnyaṃ jñānakarmādyanāvṛtam | ānukūlyena kṛṣṇānuśīlanaṃ bhaktiruttamā* || *BhRS* 1.1.11. Unless otherwise noted, translations of the *BhRS* are my own. I have consulted Rūpa Gosvāmin, *The Bhaktirasāmṛtasindhu of Rūpa Gosvāmin*, trans. David L. Haberman (Delhi: IGNCA and Motilal Banarsidass, 2003); and Rūpa Gosvāmin, *Bhaktirasāmṛtasindhu*, trans. Swami B. H. Bon Maharaj (Vrindavan: Institute of Oriental Philosophy, 1965).
15. Schwartz, *Rasa*, 20.
16. Cf. Haberman, *BhRS*, 112n2.
17. Schwartz, *Rasa*, 9. Cf. Vatsyayan, *Bharata*, 25.
18. *hṛṣīkeṇa hṛṣīkeśasevanaṃ bhakti rucyate. BhRS* 1.1.12, citing the *Śrī Nārada Pañcarātra*.
19. For Rūpa, Kṛṣṇa is the very essence of *rasa* (*BhRS* 1.1.2, cf. 4.8.83–85).
20. Haberman, Introduction to *The Bhaktirasāmṛtasindhu of Rūpa Gosvāmin*, xlvi, lii. Neal Delmonico argues that Rūpa's notion of *rasa* is, in fact, much closer to that of Bhoja, an eleventh-century king and aesthetic theorist, than to Abhinavagupta. Neal G. Delmonico, *Sacred Rapture: A Study of the Religious Aesthetic of Rupa Gosvamin*, Ph.D. diss., The University of Chicago, 1990, 236.
21. A. Whitney Sanford, "Painting Words, Tasting Sound: Visions of Krishna in Paramānand's Sixteenth-Century Devotional Poetry," *Journal of the American Academy of Religion* 70.1 (2002): 66.
22. In the subsequent explanation, I follow Haberman's translation of the names of the five *bhakti rasa*s from his edition of the *BhRS*.
23. Cf. Haberman, *BhRS*, 348n3. Although the terminology is somewhat fluid, the foundational emotions of the five *bhakti rasa*s can be listed as follows: *śānta rati* for *śānta*, *prīta* for *dāsya*, *preyas* for *sakhya*, *vātsalya* for *vatsalya*, and *madhurā rati* for *madhura.* Wulff, *Drama as a Mode of Religious Realization*, 27–28.
24. Haberman, Introduction to *The Bhaktirasāmṛtasindhu of Rūpa Gosvāmin*, lxi.
25. Paul Toomey notes that "everyday behavior in Indian families recognizes the fact that the process of mothering, unlike the process of childbearing, can involve any number of surrogates in addition to, or instead of, the real mother." Paul M. Toomey, "Krishna's Consuming Passions: Food as Metaphor and Metonym for Emotion at Mount Govardhan,"

in *Divine Passions: The Social Construction of Emotion in India*, ed. Owen M. Lynch (Berkeley: University of California Press, 1990), 167.

26. Donna Wulff, *Drama as a Mode of Religious Realization*, 147.
27. Haberman summarizes the excitants, indicators, and responses (*vibhāvas*, etc.) for each of the five. Haberman, Introduction to *The Bhaktirasāmṛtasindhu of Rūpa Gosvāmin*, lx–lxiv.
28. Haberman, Introduction to *The Bhaktirasāmṛtasindhu of Rūpa Gosvāmin*, xxxvii. This twofold distinction appears in Abhinavagupta, but not in Bharata. Masson and Patwardhan, *Aesthetic Rapture*, vol. II, 78n414.
29. *nṛtyaṃ viluṭhitaṃ gītaṃ krośanaṃ tanumoṭanam | huṅkāro jṛmbhaṇaṃ śvāsabhūmā lokānapekṣitā | lālāsravoṭṭahāsaśca ghūrṇā hikkādayopi ca || BhRS* 2.2.2.
30. Haberman, Introduction to *The Bhaktirasāmṛtasindhu of Rūpa Gosvāmin*, lvii. In the *Nāṭya Śāstra*, the actor must, of course, feign these states, but this requires a special degree of mental concentration (*NŚ* VI.23, pp. 224–225).
31. See Edward C. Dimock Jr.'s study of this group: *The Place of the Hidden Moon: Erotic Mysticism in the Vaiṣṇava-Sahajiyā Cult of Bengal* (Chicago: The University of Chicago Press, 1966).
32. *syāddṛḍheyaṃ ratiḥ premā prodyansnehaḥ kramādayam | syānmānah praṇayo rāgo 'nurāgo bhāva ityapi ||bījamikṣuḥ sa ca rasaḥ sa guḍaḥ khaṇḍa eva saḥ| sa śarkarā sitā sā ca sā yathā syātsitopalā || UN* 14.59–60. Translations from the *UN* are my own. I follow the Sanskrit text of Rūpa Gosvāmin, *Ujjvalanīlamaṇiḥ* (Vrindavan: Gauḍīya Vedānta, 2003), in consultation with the paraphrase in Rūpa Gosvāmin, *Śrī Ujjvala-nīlamaṇi*, ed. Pūrṇaprajña Dāsa, trans. Kuśakratha Dāsa (Vrindavan: Rasbihari Lal and Sons, 2006).
33. Wulff elaborates the differences between the two *gopīs* in *Drama as a Mode of Religious Realization*, 140–143.
34. I am indebted to Urmila Śarma for these interpretations of *UN* chapter 14. Personal conversation with the author, Varanasi, April 11, 2010.
35. *kandarpotsavapaṇḍitasya maṇitairākrāntakuñjāntayā | sārddhaṃ rādhikayā harernidhuvanakrīḍāvidhirvarddhate || UN* 15.252. Cf. Dāsa, *Śrī Ujjvala-nīlamaṇi*, 253.
36. See *Love Song of the Dark Lord: Jayadeva's* Gītagovinda, ed. and trans. Barbara Stoler Miller (New York: Columbia University Press, 1977). Also see the Bengali hymns translated in Edward C. Dimock Jr. and Denise Levertov, *In Praise of Krishna: Songs from the Bengali* (New York: Anchor Books, 1967).
37. A conversation with Srivatsa Goswami, head of the historic Jai Singh Ghera ashram in Vrindavan, pointed me to the importance of this teaching for many lay Vaiṣṇavas. Srivatsa Goswami, personal conversation with the author, Vrindavan, March 30, 2010.
38. *anaucityādyate nānyadrasabhaṅgasya kāraṇam | prasiddhaucityabandhastu rasasyopaniṣatparā || DhĀ* 3.10–14a.
39. De, *Some Problems of Sanskrit Poetics*, 41.
40. V. Raghavan, *Studies on Some Concepts of the Alaṃkāra Śāstra*, 2nd ed. (Madras: Adyar Library and Research Center, 1973 [1942]), 217–218.
41. For examples, see *DhĀ* 3.9–14, 17–19, 24–26.
42. *strīnīcaprakṛtiḥ hyeṣa śoko vyasanasaṃbhavaḥ | dhairyaṇottamamadhyānāṃ nīcānāṃ ruditena ca || NŚ* VII.14, p. 282.

43. Raghavan, summarizing contributions of Bhāmaha and Daṇḍin, *Studies on Some Concepts of the Alaṃkāra Śāstra*, 221.
44. Raghavan, *Studies on Some Concepts of the Alaṃkāra Śāstra*, 277–278. For additional obstacles (*vighnas*) that stand in the way of the flowering of *rasa*, see Abhinavagupta's *ABh* on the *rasa sūtra* in Gnoli, *The Aesthetic Experience According to Abhinavagupta*, 62–78.
45. *na kāryaṃ śayanaṃ raṅge nāṭyadharmaṃ vijānatā | kenacid vacanārthena aṅkacchedo vidhīyate || yad vā śayītārthavaśād ekākī sahito 'pi vā | cumbanāliṅganaṃ caiva tathā guhyaṃ ca yad bhavet || dantaccedyaṃ nakhacchedyaṃ nīvīsraṃsanam eva ca | stanāntaravimardaṃ ca raṅgamadhye na kārayet || bhojanaṃ salilakrīḍā tathā lajjākaraṃ ca yat | evaṃ vidhaṃ bhaved yad yat tat tad raṅge na kārayet || pitāputrasnuṣāśvaśrūdṛśyaṃ yasmāt tu nāṭakam | tasmād etāni sarvāṇī varjanīyāni yatnataḥ* || These verses are attributed to Bharata as *NŚ* XX.295–299 in Masson and Patwardhan, *Aesthetic Rapture*, vol. 1, 37; and vol. 2, 51n302. I have been unable to locate this passage in the Kumar edition of the *NŚ*.
46. De, *Some Problems of Sanskrit Poetics*, 40–41.
47. *DhĀ* 3.6e, III.10–14b, cf. Masson and Patwardhan, *Aesthetic Rapture*, vol. 1, 21.
48. *ABh* cited in Masson and Patwardhan, *Śāntarasa and Abhinavagupta's Philosophy of Aesthetics*, 64n4.
49. Masson and Patwardhan, *Aesthetic Rapture*, vol. 1, 9–10, 21.
50. Wulff, *Drama as a Mode of Religious Realization*, 166.
51. Haberman, *BhRS*, 645n46.
52. Haberman, Introduction to *The Bhaktirasāmṛtasindhu of Rūpa Gosvāmin*, xlix.
53. *evaṃ śaśāṅkāṃśuvirājitā niśāḥ sa satyakāmo 'nuratābalāgaṇaḥ | siṣeva ātmanyavaruddhasaurataḥ sarvāḥ śaratkāvyakathārasāśrayāḥ* || *BhP* 10.33.26. Kṛṣṇa is here called *satya kāmaḥ*, which Schweig translates as "perfectly fulfilled in all desires and pure within himself." Graham M. Schweig, *Dance of Divine Love: The Rāsa Līlā of Krishna from the Bhāgavata Purāṇa, India's Classic Sacred Love Story* (Delhi: Motilal Banarsidass, 2007 [2005]), 73.
54. *tadaṅgopacitāśīṣaḥ*; *BhP* 10.33.1. Cf. Schweig, *Dance of Divine Love*, 65.
55. *sa kathaṃ dharmasetūnāṃ vaktā kartābhirakṣitā | pratīpamācarad brahman paradārābhimarśanam* || *BhP* 10.33.28. Cf. Schweig, *Dance of Divine Love*, 73.
56. Schweig annotates these verses and their alternate meanings in *Dance of Divine Love*, 30–32, 211–216.
57. Kinsley, *The Divine Player*, 91–92.
58. Ibid., 107–108.
59. Urmila Śarma, personal conversation with the author, Varanasi, April 12, 2010.
60. Jīva Gosvāmī, *Śrī Prīti-sandarbha*, 2 vols., ed. Pūrṇaprajña Dāsa, trans. Kuśakratha Dāsa (Vrindaban: Ras Bihari Lal and Sons, 2007), *anuccheda* 103. Schweig summarizes the debate among traditional commentators as to whether the love of Kṛṣṇa and the *gopīs* is *svakīya* ("love for one's own spouse") or *parakīya* ("love for a paramour") in *Dance of Divine Love*, 280–282.
61. Jīva Gosvāmī, *Śrī Kṛṣṇa-sandarbha*, vol. 3, ed. Pūrṇaprajña Dāsa, trans. Kuśakratha Dāsa (Vrindaban: Ras Bihari Lal and Sons, 2006), *anuccheda* 178, pp. 256–299. Schweig treats these arguments in *Dance of Divine Love*, 282–284.
62. *tasmāt tatkāmasya preyasīviṣayakaprītiviśeṣamātraśarīratvam | ato na doṣaś ca. Prīti Sandarbha* 143. Cf. Jīva Gosvāmī, *Śrī Prīti-sandarbha*, 649.

63. Hawley dates the first appearance of this narrative to the sixteenth-century poetry of Nanda Dās. Hawley, *At Play with Kṛṣṇa*, 294n1.
64. Ibid., 157–163, cf. 185.
65. Haberman, *Acting as a Way of Salvation*, 75.
66. *vartitavyaṃ śamicchadbhirbhaktavatna tu kṛṣṇavat | ityevaṃ bhaktiśāstrāṇāṃ tātparyasya vinirṇayaḥ || . . . naitatsamācarejjātu manasāpi hyanīśvaraḥ | vinaśyatyācaranmauḍyādyathā rudro 'bdhijaṃ viṣam || UN* 3.24, 26. Cf. Dāsa, *Śrī Ujjvala-nīlamaṇi*, 27.
67. Haberman defends the use of the term "imitation" as opposed to those who would translate "putting oneself in the service of" or "becoming subordinate to" the characters in Kṛṣṇa's drama. He likes Donna Wulff's term "conforming (oneself) to," but writes, "I think 'imitation' is an equally acceptable translation, if we keep in mind that it is not 'mere imitation,' but an imitation that includes a particular intention: the realization of the world of the one who is being imitated. Those writers who would deny the imitative nature of Rāgānugā are, I think, speaking from a more recent and limited understanding of the *sādhana*, though of course imitation does certainly involve subordination to the one being imitated." Haberman, *Acting as a Way of Salvation*, 78–79. Cf. Wulff, *Drama as a Mode of Religious Realization*, 29–32.
68. Haberman, *Acting as a Way of Salvation*, 96, 137–139.
69. See ibid., 86–87, 91ff.
70. Ibid., 98–104.
71. See Viśvanātha Cakravartī Ṭhakurā, *Rāga Vartma Candrikā: A Moonbeam to Illuminate the Path of Spontaneous Devotion*, trans. Bhaktivedānta Nārāyaṇa Mahārāja (Mathurā: Gauḍīya Vedānta Publications, 2001), 42–51.
72. *tathā ca siddha rūpeṇā mānasī sevā śrī rādhālalitāviśākhāśrīrūpamañjaryyādīnām anusāreṇa karttavyā | sādhaka rūpeṇa kāyikyādi sevātu śrī rūpasanātanādi vrajavāsinām anusāreṇa karttavyety arthaḥ* | My translation, cf. Viśvanātha Cakravartī Ṭhakurā, *Śrī Bhakti-rasāmṛta-sindhu-bindu: A Drop of the Nectarine Ocean of Bhakti-rasa*, trans. with commentary by Bhaktivedānta Nārāyaṇa Mahārāja (Mathurā: Gauḍīya Vedānta Publications, 1996), 121–122. Cf. Haberman, *Acting as a Way of Salvation*, 102.
73. Bhaktivedānta Nārāyaṇa Mahārāja, "Four Classes on *Rāga Vartma Candrikā*," in *Rāga Vartma Candrikā*, ed. Viśvanātha Cakravartī Ṭhākura (New Delhi: Gauḍīya Vedānta Samiti, 2001), 171–172, cf. 85.
74. Wulff, *Drama as a Mode of Religious Realization*, 32.
75. My translations of *sambhogecchāmayī* and *tattadbhāvecchātmikā*. Haberman discusses these options in *Acting as a Way of Salvation*, 81.
76. Viśvanātha calls this detrimental practice *ahaṅgrahopāsana*, which Bhaktivedānta Nārāyaṇa Mahārāja translates as "considering oneself non-different from the object of worship." Text 12 in Viśvanātha Cakravartī Ṭhākura, *Rāga Vartma Candrikā*, 36. Cf. Haberman, *Acting as a Way of Salvation*, 82–83.
77. Dimock, *The Place of the Hidden Moon*, 130, cf. 14–18.
78. Haberman, *Acting as a Way of Salvation*, 81–82.
79. Ibid., 84.
80. Ibid., 91.
81. In Wulff's analysis, Rūpa's own play, the *Vidagdhamādhava*, plants the seeds for the development of *mañjarī bhakti* in its extensive treatment of the supporting characters

in the love affair between Rādhā and Kṛṣṇa. See Wulff, *Drama as a Mode of Religious Realization*, 176–177.

82. Wulff, *Drama as a Mode of Religious Realization*, 175.
83. Ibid., 34.
84. Haberman, *Acting as a Way of Salvation*, 69.
85. *kśāntiravyarthakālatvaṃ viraktirmānaśūnyatā | āśābandhaḥ samutkaṇṭhā nāmagāne sadā ruciḥ || āsaktistadguṇākhyāne prītistadvasatisthale | ityādyo 'nubhāvāḥ. . . ||* *BhRS* 1.3.25–26.
86. Acyut Lal Bhatt, personal conversation with the author, Vrindavan, March 26, 2010.

4. *A Dilemma of Feeling*

1. Citations from the sermons (Serm.) follow the translations of the Cistercian Fathers Series: Bernard of Clairvaux, *On the Song of Songs I*, trans. Kilian Walsh, Cistercian Fathers Series 4 (Kalamazoo, Mich.: Cistercian Publications, 1971); Bernard of Clairvaux, *On the Song of Songs II*, trans. Kilian Walsh, Cistercian Fathers Series 7 (Kalamazoo, Mich.: Cistercian Publications, 1976); Bernard of Clairvaux, *On the Song of Songs III*, trans. Kilian Walsh and Irene M. Edmonds, Cistercian Fathers Series 31 (Kalamazoo, Mich.: Cistercian Publications, 1979); and Bernard of Clairvaux, *On the Song of Songs IV*, trans. Irene Edmonds, Cistercian Fathers Series 40 (Kalamazoo, Mich.: Cistercian Publications, 1980).
2. See Michal Kobialka, *This is My Body: Representational Practices in the Early Middle Ages* (Ann Arbor: The University of Michigan Press, 1999), chapter 3.
3. Denys Turner, *Eros and Allegory: Medieval Exegesis of the Song of Songs* (Kalamazoo, Mich.: Cistercian Publications, 1995), 163.
4. Important early Christian exegetes of the Song include Origen and Gregory of Nyssa. In the twelfth century, however, "Anselm of Laon, Bruno of Segni, Bernard of Clairvaux, Rupert of Deutz, Honorius of Autun, Philip of Harveng, Gilbert de la Porree, William of St. Thierry, Gilbert of Hoyland, John of Ford, Thomas the Cistercian, and Alain de Lille all produced *expositiones* of the Song." Ann W. Astell, *The Song of Songs in the Middle Ages* (Ithaca, N.Y.: Cornell University Press, 1990), 8–9.
5. A fourth sense, the anagogical, refers to the fulfillment of the events of salvation history in the eschaton. For a discussion of this sense of the Song in medieval commentary, see Turner, *Eros and Allegory*, 83–92.
6. Origen, *The Song of Songs: Commentary and Homilies*, trans. R. P. Lawson, Ancient Christian Writers Series 26 (New York: Newman Press, 1956), 21.
7. Ibid., 58.
8. Ibid., 58.
9. Origen, *De Principiis*, trans. Frederick Crombie, rev. and ed. Kevin Knight. Ante-Nicene Fathers 4 (Buffalo, N.Y.: Christian Literature Publishing Co., 1885), IV.15. http://www.newadvent.org/fathers/0412.htm.
10. Origen, *The Song of Songs*, 24.
11. Astell, *The Song of Songs in the Middle Ages*, 178.
12. Scripture references in this chapter follow the Vulgate version of the Song of Songs, which is the translation familiar to Bernard.
13. Astell, *The Song of Songs in the Middle Ages*, 17.

14. Ibid., 39, 19.
15. Astell, *The Song of Songs in the Middle Ages*, 89–90. For more on Bernard's context, see Jean Leclerq, *Monks and Love in Twelfth-Century France* (Oxford: Clarendon Press, 1979), 8–26.
16. Astell, *The Song of Songs in the Middle Ages*, 30.
17. Jean Leclercq, *A Second Look at Bernard of Clairvaux*, trans. Marie-Bernard Saïd (Kalamazoo, Mich.: Cistercian Publications, 1990), 111.
18. For one contemporary effort in this direction, see Christopher Pramuk, "Sexuality, Spirituality and the 'Song of Songs,'" *America* 193.13 (2005): 8–12.
19. Not only the Bride but also the divine Bridegroom and Bernard as abbot possess such maternal breasts. Caroline Walker Bynum explicates the importance of maternal imagery for Cistercians in chapter 4 of *Jesus as Mother: Studies in the Spirituality of the High Middle Ages* (Berkeley: University of California Press, 1982).
20. Schweig, *Dance of Divine Love*, 8. The other contender for this designation is the twelfth-century *Gīta Govinda* of Jayadeva, which is more sexual than the amorous *rāsa līlā* passage, but it has had a narrower band of influence and lacks an immediate scriptural context. Schweig, *Dance of Divine Love*, 8–11, esp. 8n14.
21. Urmila Sharma, personal conversation with the author, Varanasi, April 12, 2010.

5. *Love, Bodies, and Others*

1. See Kobialka, *This Is My Body*, chapter 4.
2. Edwin F. Bryant, Introduction to *Krishna: The Beautiful Legend of God: Śrīmad Bhāgavata Purāṇa, Book X, With Chapters 1, 6, and 29–31 from Book XI*, trans. with introduction and notes by Edwin F. Bryant (New York: Penguin, 2003), lviii.
3. Cf. Alf Hiltebeitel and Kathleen M. Erndl, ed., *Is the Goddess a Feminist? The Politics of South Asian Goddesses* (New York: New York University Press, 2000).
4. Grace Jantzen, *Power, Gender, and Christian Mysticism* (Cambridge: Cambridge University Press, 1995), 123–124.
5. Jantzen, *Power, Gender, and Christian Mysticism*, 128.
6. Maren Lytje, "The Interior and the Abject: Uses and Abuses of the Female in the Middle Ages," *Culture and Religion* 5.3 (2004): 288–289.
7. Cited in Jean Leclercq, *Women and St. Bernard of Clairvaux*. Cistercian Studies Series 104 (Kalamazoo, Mich.: Cistercian Publications, 1989), 122.
8. John Stratton Hawley, *Songs of the Saints of India* (New York: Oxford University Press, 1988), 126.
9. Leclercq, *Women and St. Bernard of Clairvaux*, 122.
10. Michelle Voss Roberts, "Power, Gender, and the Construction of a Kashmir Śaiva Mystic," *Journal of Hindu Studies* 3.3 (2010): 285–286, 296n36.
11. Bynum, *Jesus as Mother*, 135–154. Shawn M. Krahmer extends Bynum's analysis in "The Virile Bride of Bernard of Clairvaux," *Church History* 69.2 (2000): 304–327.
12. See David Damrosch's excellent article, "*Non Alia Sed Aliter*: The Hermeneutics of Gender in Bernard of Clairvaux," in *Images of Sainthood in Medieval Europe*, ed. Renate Blumenfeld-Kosinski and Timea Szell (Ithaca, N.Y.: Cornell University Press, 1991), 181–195.
13. Jantzen, *Power, Gender, and Christian Mysticism*, 146.

14. Ibid., 145. For further discussion of the embodied aspects of medieval Christian women's spirituality, see Bynum, *Jesus as Mother*; Amy Hollywood, *Sensible Ecstasy: Mysticism, Sexual Difference, and the Demands of History* (Chicago: The University of Chicago Press, 2002); and Elizabeth Alvida Petroff, *Body and Soul: Essays on Medieval Women and Mysticism* (Oxford: Oxford University Press, 1994).
15. Leena Taneja, "Tracing the Absence of Faith: Hermeneutics, Deconstruction, and the School of Gauḍīya Vaiṣṇavism," PhD diss., George Washington University, 2005, 201.
16. Taneja, "Tracing the Absence of Faith," 249.
17. Bruce Holsinger, "The Color of Salvation: Desire, Death, and the Second Crusade in Bernard of Clairvaux's *Sermons on the Song of Songs*," in *The Tongue of the Fathers: Gender and Identity in Twelfth-Century Latin*, ed. David Townsend and Andrew Taylor (Philadelphia: University of Pennsylvania Press, 1998), 165.
18. Beverly M. Kienzle, "Tending the Lord's Vineyard: Cistercians, Rhetoric, and Heresy, 1143–1229. Part I: Bernard of Clairvaux, the 1143 Sermons and the 1145 Preaching Mission," *Heresis* 25 (1995): 40.
19. Ibid., 42.
20. André LaCocque and Paul Ricouer, *Thinking Biblically: Exegetical and Hermeneutical Studies* (Chicago: The University of Chicago Press, 1998), 251.
21. Ibid., 253.
22. Ibid., 265, 267. Michael Fishbane has made a similar argument regarding the importance of *Peshat*, the plain meaning of the scripture, in Jewish reading practices: Michael Fishbane, "Biblical Hermeneutics and Philosophical Theology," a paper delivered at "The *Song of Songs*: Translation, Reception, Reconfiguration," Spring Conference, Center for the Study of World Religions, Harvard University, April 14, 2013.
23. Stephanie Paulsell and Harvey Cox, *Lamentations and the Song of Songs* (Louisville: Westminster John Knox Press, 2012), 175.
24. Ibid., 177.
25. LaCocque and Ricoeur, *Thinking Biblically*, 302.
26. Claire F. Brunetti, "Songs of Silence: The Affection for Bride and Body in the Rhetoric of Bernard of Clairvaux, Margery Kempe, and Teresa of Jesus," PhD diss., University of Florida, 1991, 38.
27. The theme of divine absence has been fruitfully explored in comparative perspective. Francis Clooney, for example, reads the Song in comparison with Śrīvaiṣṇava poetry, and Gloria Hernández reads Gauḍīya Vaiṣṇava treatments of Kṛṣṇa's *rāsa līlā* through the lens of St. John of the Cross's dark night of the soul. See Francis X. Clooney, *His Hiding Place is Darkness: A Hindu-Catholic Theopoetics of Divine Absence* (Stanford, Calif.: Stanford University Press, 2013); and Gloria M. Hernández, "'Where Did You Hide?' Locating the Divine in the *Cántico Spiritual* and *Rāsa Līlā*," *Journal of Hindu-Christian Studies* 25 (2012).
28. Barbara A. Holdrege, "Body Connections: Hindu Discourses of the Body and the Study of Religion," *International Journal of Hindu Studies* 2.3 (1998): 341–346. The reading undertaken here is one attempt to discover the place of the erotic in what Holdrege designates the "devotional body" (370). Also see Barbara A. Holdrege, *Bhakti and Embodiment: Fashioning Divine Bodies and Devotional Bodies in Kṛṣṇa Bhakti* (London: Routledge, 2013).
29. Michael Casey, *Athirst for God: Spiritual Desire in Bernard of Clairvaux's Sermons on the Song of Songs* (Kalamazoo, Mich.: Cistercian Publications, 1988), 94, cf. 94–97.

30. Julia Kristeva, *Tales of Love*, trans. Leon S. Roudiez (New York: Columbia University Press, 1987), 159. Kristeva notes that affect is "closely related to desire," though desire emphasizes lack, and affect "gives greater importance to the movement toward the other and to mutual attraction." Kristeva, *Tales of Love*, 155. Cf. Astell, *The Song of Songs in the Middle Ages*, 6.
31. Origen, *The Song of Songs*, 79.
32. For discussions of the spiritual senses in these figures, see Stephen Fields, S. J., "Balthasar and Rahner on the Spiritual Senses," *Theological Studies* 57 (1996): 224–241; and Michelle Voss Roberts, "Neither *Bhukti* nor *Mukti*: The New Sensorium in Devotional Practice," *Practical Matters* (Spring 2009): http://www.practicalmattersjournal.org/issue/1/analyzing-matters/neither-bhukti-nor-mukti.
33. Philip Endean, "The Ignatian Prayer of the Senses," *The Heythrop Journal* 31 (1990): 407.
34. Sanford, "Painting Words, Tasting Sound," 70–72. Also see K. D. Tripathi, "From Sensuous to Supersensuous: An Inquiry into Some Terms of Indian Aesthetics," in *Prakrti III: The Agamic Tradition and the Arts*, ed. Bettina Bäumer (New Delhi: IGNCA and D.K. Printworld, 1994). For a constructive Christian treatment of synaesthesia, see Don S. Saliers, "Sound Spirituality: On the Formative Expressive Power of Music for Christian Spirituality," *Christian Spirituality Bulletin* 8.1 (2000).
35. Schwartz, *Rasa*, 77.
36. Here, I follow Abhinavagupta's discussion in the *ABh* in Raniero Gnoli, trans., *The Aesthetic Experience According to Abhinavagupta*, 62–78.
37. Insiders to religious traditions may attribute "religious experience" to supernatural activity, to natural features of the psyche, or to some combination of the two. See Ann Taves, *Fits, Trances and Visions: Experiencing Religion and Explaining Experience from Wesley to James* (Princeton, N.J.: Princeton University Press, 1999).
38. Gnoli, *The Aesthetic Experience According to Abhinavagupta*, 68.

Part III / 6. Dalit Arts and the Failure of Aesthetics

1. N. D. Rajkumar, "Neeli Suria: A Dalit Dance and Drama Programme," Video CD. (Tumkur: Booshakthi Kendra, n.d.). I am grateful for Manjunath Shammanna's assistance in translating and interpreting the Kannada text (personal e-mail to the author, September 3, 2011).
2. C. Joe Arun, *Constructing Dalit Identity* (Jaipur: Rawat Publications, 2007), 35. Arun's study illuminates activist uses of the drum, but it also draws attention to other important strategies including celebration of eating beef as a cultural practice and refusal to perform other polluting services, such as scavenging dead cattle.
3. Wendy Doniger helpfully distinguishes the various names and groupings in *The Hindus: An Alternative History* (New York: Penguin, 2009), 37–39.
4. M. C. Raj, personal conversation with the author, Bangalore, May 11, 2010.
5. Ibid.
6. M. C. Raj, "Dalit Spirituality." February 5, 2011. http://dalitreds.org/2011/02/05/dalit-spirituality-by-m-c-raj/.
7. Raj, "Dalit Spirituality."
8. Gayatri Chakravorty Spivak, "Strategy, Identity, Writing," in *The Postcolonial Critic*, ed. Sarah Harasym (New York: Routledge, 1990), 42.

9. Arvind P. Nirmal, "Towards a Christian Dalit Theology," in *A Reader in Dalit Theology*, ed. Arvind P. Nirmal (Madras: Gurukul, 1991), 59.
10. Zoe Sherinian, "The Indigenization of Tamil Christian Music: Folk Music as Liberative Transmission System," PhD diss., Wesleyan University, 1998, 176.
11. Some, particularly those run by Protestant organizations, focused on service to the community; but most of the Catholic ashrams were monastic centers for meditation and scriptural study, often with a guru figure. Henri Le Saux (Swami Abhishiktananda) and Bede Griffiths of the Shantivanam ashram in Tamilnadu are perhaps the best-known exemplars of the latter model. Griffiths' theology was deeply influenced by his nondualist experiences of meditation. For a helpful discussion of the ashram movement, see Richard W. Taylor, "From Khadi to Kavi: Toward a Typology of Christian Ashrams," *Religion and Society* 24.4 (1977): 19–37; and Selva Raj, "Adapting Hindu Imagery: A Critical Look at Ritual Experiments in an Indian Catholic Ashram," *Journal of Ecumenical Studies* 37 (2000): 333–353.
12. Nirmal, "Towards a Christian Dalit Theology," 57.
13. Ibid., 56.
14. He cites, in particular, the Dalit Sahitya (literature) movement and the Dalit Panthers. For background on these movements, see Gail Omvedt, *Dalit Visions: The Anti-caste Movement and the Construction of an Indian Identity* (Hyderabad: Orient Longman, 1995).
15. Nirmal, "Towards a Christian Dalit Theology," 61.
16. Ibid., 62.
17. David Mosse, "The Catholic Church and Dalit Christian Activism in Contemporary Tamil Nadu," in *Margins of Faith: Dalit and Tribal Christianity in India*, ed. Rowena Robinson and Joseph Marianus Kujur (New Delhi: Sage Publications, 2010), 250.
18. David Carroll, *Paraesthetics: Foucault, Lyotard, Derrida* (New York: Methuen, 1987), xiii. Toward this political end, Carroll proposes a deconstructive mode of thought he calls a "paraesthetics."
19. Nussbaum, *Upheavals of Thought*, 681.
20. Manmasih Ekka, "Liberation Theme in Tana Bhagat Prayers," in *Doing Theology with the Poetic Traditions of India: Focus on Dalit and Tribal Poems*, ed. Joseph Patmury (Bangalore: PTCA/Sathri, 1996), 184.
21. Nussbaum, *Upheavals of Thought*, 496.
22. Ibid., 497–498.
23. Ibid., 494.
24. Nirmal, "Towards a Christian Dalit Theology," 54.
25. Nrtyavani gives *rasa* special attention in a piece titled "The Navarasa of Jesus," which explores Jesus' experience of the nine basic emotions. National Biblical Catechetical and Liturgical Centre, *The Navarasa of Jesus*, VCD (Bangalore: NBCLC, n.d.). My analysis of this piece can be found in Michelle Voss Roberts, "Tasting the Divine: The Aesthetics of Religious Emotion in Indian Christianity," *Religion* 42.4 (2012).
26. Rajiv Malhotra and Aravindan Neelakandan, *Breaking India: Western Interventions in Dravidian and Dalit Faultlines* (Delhi: Amaryllis Publishers, 2011), 113, 115; cf. 113–120.
27. Sahi, *Stepping Stones*, 56; and personal e-mail to the author, September 1, 2011.
28. Fr. Anthony Kalliath, personal conversation with the author, NBCLC, May 19, 2010. An additional complicating factor includes the history of the *devadāsīs* being outlawed under the British as a purported form of temple prostitution. *Bharatanatyam* has been

revitalized but has not entirely left this legacy behind. See Anne-Marie Gaston, "Dance and the Hindu Woman: Bharatanāṭyam Re-ritualized," in *Roles and Rituals for Hindu Women*, ed. Julie Leslie (Rutherford, N.J.: Fairleigh Dickinson University Press, 1991).

29. Raj's analysis focuses on the Christian ashram movement, which he views as a failure in terms of evangelism because they did not win many converts and tended to appeal to foreigners more than Indians. Raj, "Adapting Hindu Imagery," 350.

30. Jyoti Sahi, personal conversation with the author, Bangalore, April 28, 2010. See also Sahi, *Stepping Stones*, 55–56.

31. The NBCLC website reports, "[B]ecause of certain restraints, we no longer have the dance artists as our resident staff. They now live out independently, working in schools . . . and when their services are needed they perform in the name and on the platform of the NBCLC" (accessed September 1, 2011, http://nbclc.in/nri.html).

32. Fr. Anthony Kalliath, personal conversation with the author, NBCLC, May 19, 2010.

33. M. C. Raj, personal conversation with the author, Bangalore, May 11, 2010.

34. Jyoti Sahi, "Dalit as a Cultural Memory: The Creative Language of the 'Panchama,'" in *The Colours of Liberation*, ed. P. Mohan Larbeer and V. Alexander (Madurai: Dalit Resource Center, 2000), 1.

35. *rakṣodānavoddhatamanuṣyaprabhavaḥ* (*NŚ* prose after VI.63, p. 259); *strīnīcaprakṛtāveṣa bhūyiṣṭhaṃ dṛśyate rasaḥ* (*NŚ* VI.51, p. 255); *uttamaprakṛtiḥ* (*NŚ* prose after VI.66, p. 262).

36. Masson and Patwardhan, *Aesthetic Rapture*, 89n459.

37. Cf. Masson and Patwardhan, *Aesthetic Rapture*, vol. 1, 33–34, and vol. II, 70n388; and Masson and Patwardhan, *Śāntarasa and Abhinavagupta's Philosophy of Aesthetics*, 57–58.

38. Barbara H. Rosenwein, *Emotional Communities in the Early Middle Ages* (Ithaca, N.Y.: Cornell University Press, 2006); cf. Jan Plamper, "The History of Emotions: An Interview with William Reddy, Barbara Rosenwein, and Peter Stearns," *History and Theory* 49 (2010): 252–253.

39. J. T. Appavoo, interview, Madurai, March 10, 1994. Cited in Sherinian, "The Indigenization of Tamil Christian Music," 555.

40. P. Sambamurthy, *A Dictionary of South Indian Music and Musicians* (Madras: Indian Music Publishing House, 1984 [1952]), 141, cited in Sherinian, "The Indigenization of Tamil Christian Music," 16.

41. Sherinian, "The Indigenization of Tamil Christian Music," 211.

42. Cf. Kuruvilla George, *From People's Theatre to People's Eucharist: Recovering the Drama of Christian Worship* (Delhi: ISPCK, 2002), 146–147.

43. Sherinian, "The Indigenization of Tamil Christian Music," 210.

44. Sathianathan Clarke, *Dalits and Christianity: Subaltern Religion and Liberation Theology in India* (Delhi: Oxford University Press, 1998), 113–118.

45. Ibid., 163.

46. Zoe Sherinian, "Dalit Theology in Tamil Christian Folk Music: A Transformed Liturgy by James Theophilus Appavoo," in *Popular Christianity in India: Riting Between the Lines*, ed. Selva J. Raj and Corinne G. Dempsey (Albany: State University of New York Press, 2002), 236.

47. For a discussion of these eight dimensions, see James Theophilus Appavoo (Parattai), "Dalit Way of Theological Expression," in *Frontiers of Dalit Theology*, ed. V. Devasahayam (Gurukul: ISPCK, 1997), 283–289.

48. Sherinian, "The Indigenization of Tamil Christian Music," 211, cf. 287.
49. Ibid., 516.
50. Ibid., 287–288.
51. This communal emphasis was somewhat present in Gauḍīya Vaiṣṇava worship, in which love for Kṛṣṇa is evoked in the fellowship of other devotees through activities such as group singing, viewing *rāsa līlās*, and sharing festival meals; but, as I have argued, the primary purpose is to foster the individual's participation in Kṛṣṇa's transcendent realm.
52. P. Mohan Larbeer and V. Alexander, Introduction to *The Colours of Liberation*, ed. P. Mohan Larbeer and V. Alexander (Madurai: Dalit Resource Centre, 2000), xii.
53. James Theophilus Appavoo (Parattai), *Folklore for Change* (Madurai: TTS Publications, 1986), 98.
54. Sherinian, "The Indigenization of Tamil Christian Music," 585–589.

7. Fury as a Religious Sentiment

1. Technically, anger (*krodha*) is the *sthāyibhāva* or foundational emotion of the *rasa* of fury (*raudra*). I will use the terms "anger" and "fury" interchangeably, as has become common in Indian discussions of this *rasa*.
2. Carol Tavris, *Anger: The Misunderstood Emotion* (New York: Simon and Schuster, 1982), 96.
3. Clarke, *Dalits and Christianity*, 167–168.
4. Michael C. McCarthy, "Divine Wrath and Human Anger: Embarrassment Ancient and New," *Theological Studies* 70 (2009): 845–847. For other treatments of divine and human anger, see Bruce Edward Baloian, *Anger in the Old Testament* (New York: Peter Lang, 1992); Carroll Saussy, *The Gift of Anger: A Call to Faithful Action* (Louisville: Westminster John Knox Press, 1995); and William C. Mattison III, "Jesus' Prohibition of Anger (Mt 5:22): The Person/Sin Distinction from Augustine to Aquinas," *Theological Studies* 68 (2007): 839–864.
5. Ellen van Wolde, "Sentiments as Culturally Constructed Emotions: Anger and Love in the Hebrew Bible," *Biblical Interpretation* 16 (2008): 16.
6. M. C. Raj, *Dalithink: An Adventure into Dalit Philosophy* (Tumkur: Ambedkar Resource Center, 2006), 210–211.
7. D. Soyini Madison, "Crazy Patriotism and Angry (Post)Black Women," *Communication and Critical/Cultural Studies* 6.3 (2009): 321–326; cf. chapter 7 of Melissa V. Harris-Perry, *Sister Citizen: Shame, Stereotypes, and Black Women in America* (New Haven, Conn.: Yale University Press, 2011). It is the *projected* rage that is at issue here. As Ellis Cose elucidates, the Black American middle class has much cause for frustration. See Ellis Cose, *The Rage of a Privileged Class* (New York: HarperPerennial, 1993).
8. Dinesh D'Souza, *The Roots of Obama's Rage* (Washington: Regnery, 2010).
9. *rakṣodānavoddhatamanuṣyaprabhavaḥ* (*NŚ* prose after VI.63, p. 259).
10. *te hi svamāvata eva raudrāḥ | kasmāt – bahubāhavo bahumukhāḥ proddhavikīrṇapiṅgalaśirojāḥ raktodvṛttavilocanā bhīmāsitarūpiṇaścaiva | yacca kiñcitsamārabhante svabhāvaceṣṭitaṃ vāgaṅgādikaṃ vā tatsarvaṃ raudrameveti | śṛṅgāraśca taiḥ prāyaśaḥ prasabhaṃ sevyate* | (*NŚ* prose after VI.63, p. 259).
11. Wendy Doniger, *The Hindus*, 23.
12. For instance, some Dalit retellings of the *Rāmāyana* subversively cast the *rākṣasa* king Rāvaṇa as a Dravidian hero, "treacherously murdered by the forces of the evil Rama coming from the north" (Doniger, *The Hindus*, 667).

13. Judith Butler, *Precarious Life: The Powers of Mourning and Violence* (London: Verso, 2004), xviii.
14. Judith Butler, "Performativity, Precarity and Sexual Politics," *Revista de Antropologia Iberoamericana* 4.3 (2009), ii. www.aibr.org.
15. For a chronicle of these problems as confronted by the Rural Theological Institute of Tamilnadu Theological Seminary, see A. Royapan Isaac and S. Selvaraj, *The Beginning of Our Rural Journey* (Madurai: Tamilnadu Theological Seminary, 2009), especially chapter 5.
16. van Wolde, "Sentiments as Culturally Constructed Emotions," 5–12.
17. *tasya ca tāḍanapāṭanapīḍana chedanabhedanapraharaṇāharaṇaśastrasaṃpātasaṃprahārar udhirākarṣaṇāddāni karmāṇi | punaśca raktanayana bhukuṭīkaraṇāvaṣṭambhadantauṣṭhap īḍanagaṇḍasphuraṇahastāgraniṣpeṣādibhiranubhāvairabhinayaḥ prayoktavyaḥ | bhāvāścāsya sammohotsāhavegāmarṣacapalataugrya -svedavepathuromāñcagadgadādayaḥ |* (*NŚ* prose after VI.63, p. 259).
18. Raghavan, *Studies on Some Concepts of the Alaṃkāra Śāstra*, 237.
19. Baloian, *Anger in the Old Testament*, chapter 2.
20. Mattison, "Jesus' Prohibition of Anger (Mt. 5:22)," 839–864.
21. van Wolde, "Sentiments as Culturally Constructed Emotions," 12, 14.
22. Tavris, *Anger*, 50, 262.
23. Saussy, *The Gift of Anger*, 16.
24. Audre Lorde, *Sister Outsider*, 127, 131.
25. This class of leadership faces frustrations in maintaining their gains, but I am interested in the anger generated by the severe class inequality that persists. Cf. J. V. Deshpande, "Behind Dalit Anger," *Economic and Political Weekly*, August 16–23, 1997: 2090–2091.
26. Arun, *Constructing Dalit Identity*, 184.
27. Ibid., 38. For the religious myth behind this justification, see ibid., 202.
28. Mohan Larbeer cites a theory of Dalit leader Ambedkar to this effect in P. Mohan Larbeer, "Dalit Identity—A Theological Reflection," in *Frontiers of Dalit Theology*, ed. V. Devasahayam (Madras: ISPCK/Gurukul, 1997), 382.
29. For a survey of issues facing Ādivāsī populations, see Lancy Lobo, "Christianization, Hinduization and Indigenous Revivalism among the Tribals of Gujarat," in *Margins of Faith: Dalit and Tribal Christianity in India*, ed. Rowena Robinson and Joseph Marianus Kujur (New Delhi: Sage Publications, 2010).
30. David Mosse, "The Catholic Church and Dalit Christian Activism in Contemporary Tamil Nadu," 241–242.
31. Saussy, *The Gift of Anger*, 115.
32. Ibid.
33. Ibid., 16, cf. 113–114.
34. Clarke, *Dalits and Christianity*, 22.
35. Dalit Resource Centre, accessed December 24, 2011, http://www.drctts.com/DRC_htm/Dalit_Arts.htm.
36. Arun, *Constructing Dalit Identity*, 189.
37. Raj, *Dalithink*, 211, 209.
38. Ibid., 210; emphasis in original.
39. Clarke, *Dalits and Christianity*, 129. Clarke therefore cautions against "avant-garde representations [that] express what the dominant communities think ought to be the case from the distanced and romanticized perception of the subaltern" (129).

40. M. C. Raj, personal conversation with the author, Bangalore, May 11, 2010. Cf. Raj, *Dalithink*, 211–241.
41. Rajkumar, "Neeli Suria," translated by Manjunath Shamanna, e-mail to the author, Sept. 3, 2011.
42. Ibid.
43. Arul Joseph, personal conversation with the author, Tamilnadu Theological Seminary, Madurai, May 22, 2010.
44. Ibid.
45. Zoe Sherinian, "Musical Style and the Changing Social Identity of Tamil Christians," *Journal of Ethnomusicology* 51.2 (2007): 267.
46. Arun, *Constructing Dalit Identity*, 173; cf. Appendix (292–298) for a chronological account of the Pongal incidents.
47. Butler, "Performativity, Precarity and Sexual Politics," iv–vi.
48. Judith Butler, "New Thoughts on Solidarity," unpublished speech at the annual meeting of the American Academy of Religion, San Francisco, Calif., November 19, 2011.
49. Butler, "Performativity, Precarity and Sexual Politics," v.
50. Sherinian, "The Indigenization of Tamil Christian Music," 576.
51. Chandru, cited in the epigraph of Larbeer and Alexander, *The Colours of Liberation*, v.
52. Larbeer and Alexander, Introduction to *The Colours of Liberation*, viii–ix.
53. Sherinian, "Dalit Theology in Tamil Christian Folk Music," 236.
54. Sherinian, "The Indigenization of Tamil Christian Music," 566.
55. Appavoo's song, "*Ammādi kuṭṭi poṇṇē*," trans. Neena and Audry Appavoo, cited in Sherinian, "The Indigenization of Tamil Christian Music," 269–270.
56. Sherinian, "The Indigenization of Tamil Christian Music," 269n108.
57. Appavoo's song, "*maṉasamāttuyappā*," cited in Sherinian, "The Indigenization of Tamil Christian Music," 385–386.
58. Appavoo theorizes this preference for "humanly produced and transmitted media" in James Theophilus Appavoo (Parattai), "Communication for Dalit Liberation," in *Frontiers of Dalit Theology*, ed. V. Devasahayam (Gurukul: ISPCK, 1997), 369–371.
59. Sherinian, "The Indigenization of Tamil Christian Music," 550.
60. For an example from the Christian context, see NBCLC, "The Navarasa of Jesus."
61. Sahi sees the severance of these two elements as the reason for the aesthetic failure of much Indian Christian art, which "has unfortunately too often just become a way of 'proclaiming the gospel' in a very literal, and even sentimental sense. It is strictly Alamkara, or decoration, lacking Rasa, or aesthetic experience." As he explains, "When the dance shifts from *Nritya* to *Natya*, from movement to [mere] narration [or illustration], there is a danger that the primordial energy of the dance becomes neutralized, or merely subservient to the word." Jyoti Sahi, "Towards a Spiritual Understanding of Dance," unpublished manuscript, e-mail to the author, June 20, 2011.
62. See Eric Lott and Jyoti Sahi, *Faces of Vision*, 42–44, 61–64.
63. Jyoti Sahi, "The Drum and the Dancer in Adivasi Culture," unpublished manuscript, e-mail to the author, November 20, 2011.
64. Jyoti Sahi, "The Drum and the Dancer in Adivasi Culture."
65. Cf. Peter Marchand, *The Yoga of the Nine Emotions: The Tantric Practice of Rasa Sadhana, Based on the Teachings of Harish Johari* (Rochester, Vt.: Destiny Books, 2006), 72–73.
66. Jyoti Sahi, *Kristo Jyoti Chapel: Notes and Sketches by Jyoti Sahi* (Sambalpur, Orisa: Kristo Jyoti Mohavidyaloyo, 1993), 25; and Jyoti Sahi, "The Drum and the Dance in Adivasi

Culture," in *Silver Jubilee Souvenir (1987–2012) of the Interdiocesan Regional Theologat of Odisha* (Sambalpur, Orisa: Khristo Jyoti Mohavidyaloyo, 2012), 54–57.

67. Sherinian, "Dalit Theology in Tamil Christian Folk Music," 235–236. Cf. Appavoo, "Dalit Way of Theological Expression."
68. Sherinian, "Dalit Theology in Tamil Christian Folk Music," 235–236.
69. Namsoon Kang notes the "ironic yet understandable" strategy of adopting monolithic notions of culture: "When the discriminatory stereotype is deeply held, the groups who are discriminated against are induced to convert it into a basis for self-esteem. This occurs not so much because, given the persistence of such a stereotype, it is strategically easier to turn it to their own advantage rather than destroy it, as because the conversion strategy promises to heal a people's wounded self-respect more powerfully than does the strategy of destroying the stereotype." Namsoon Kang, "Who/What Is Asian?" in *Postcolonial Theologies: Divinity and Empire*, ed. Catherine Keller, Michel Nausner, and Mayra Rivera (St. Louis, Mo.: Chalice Press, 204), 104.

Part IV / 8. Toward a Holistic Theology of the Emotions

1. Mary-Jane Rubenstein, *Strange Wonder: The Closure of Metaphysics and the Opening of Awe* (New York: Columbia University Press, 2008), 194, 195–196.
2. Sherma, "Eros, Ethics, and Enlightenment."
3. Don S. Saliers, *Music and Theology* (Nashville: Abingdon Press, 2007), 44.
4. "Franciscan Benediction," quoted in Phillip Yancey, *Prayer: Does It Make Any Difference?* (Grand Rapids, Mich.: Zondervan, 2010), 105.
5. For example, Marchand, *The Yoga of the Nine Emotions*, 113. What Marchand and Johari treat as *rasas* are more properly seen as *bhāvas* in the aesthetic context (176).
6. Dalit Resource Centre, *Vazhipaduvom (Dalit Liturgies)* (Madurai: Dalit Resource Centre, 2000), 15.
7. Ibid., 21–22.
8. Ibid., 22.
9. Cf. Andrew D. Lester, "Why Hast Thou Forsaken Me! Anger at God," *The Journal of Pastoral Theology* 16:1 (2006): 53–70.
10. Dhyandchand Carr, "God and People in Liturgies," in *Vazhipaduvom (Dalit Liturgies)* (Madurai: Dalit Resource Centre, 2000), x.
11. Ibid., xii.
12. Joerg Rieger, "Liberating God Talk," in *Postcolonial Theologies: Divinity and Empire*, ed. Catherine Keller, Michael Nausner, and Mayra Rivera (St. Louis, Mo.: Chalice Press, 204), 219.
13. Cited in Sherinian, "The Indigenization of Tamil Christian Music," 638, cf. 643.
14. Carr, "God and People in Liturgies," xiii.
15. Dalit Resource Centre, *Vazhipaduvom (Dalit Liturgies)*, 39–51.
16. Sherinian, "The Indigenization of Tamil Christian Music," 583.
17. Sherinian, "Dalit Theology in Tamil Christian Folk Music," 241.
18. Sherinian, "The Indigenization of Tamil Christian Music," 585–598.
19. David Blumenthal, "Liturgies of Anger," *Crosscurrents* 52.2 (2002): 186, cf. 196–197.
20. *karacaraṇavepathustambhagātrasaṅkocahṛdayaprakampena | śuṣkauṣṭhatālukaṇṭhair-bhayānako nityamabhineyaḥ* || (*NŚ* VI.72, p. 265).

21. Mark Juergensmeyer, *Terror in the Mind of God: The Global Rise of Religious Violence* (Berkeley: University of California Press, 2000), 145–148.
22. Juergensmeyer, *Terror in the Mind of God,* 156. Cf. Natalie Zemon Davis, "The Rites of Violence," *Past and Present* 59.1 (1973).
23. Wendy Farley, *The Wounding and Healing of Desire: Weaving Heaven and Earth* (Louisville: Westminster John Knox, 2005), 60; cf. 58–60.
24. Nirmal, "Towards a Christian Dalit Theology," 62.
25. Rainer Maria Rilke, *Duino Elegies*, cited in Don Saliers, "Beauty and Terror," *Spiritus* 2.2 (2002): 181.
26. Saliers, "Beauty and Terror," 181.
27. Ibid., 184.
28. Richard Beck, Dan McGregor, Brooke Woodrow, Andrea Haugen, and Kyna Killion, "Death, Art and the Fall: A Terror Management View of Christian Aesthetic Judgments," *Journal of Psychology and Christianity* 29.4 (2010): 303.
29. Saliers, "Beauty and Terror," 185, 187.
30. NBCLC, *The Navarasa of Jesus.*
31. Raj, *Dalithink*, 216–217.
32. Michael Rowe, "What it Says About Us When a 17-Month-Old Boy Is Beaten to Death for 'Acting Like a Girl,'" *Huffington Post*, August 5, 2010. http://www.huffingtonpost.com/michael-rowe/what-it-says-about-us-whe_b_671373.html.
33. Martha C. Nussbaum, *From Disgust to Humanity: Sexual Orientation and Constitutional Law* (Oxford: Oxford University Press, 2010), 13. Disgust's ambivalent moral function is also treated in William Ian Miller, *The Anatomy of Disgust* (Cambridge, Mass.: Harvard University Press, 1997), chapters 8–9.
34. Nussbaum, *From Disgust to Humanity*, 16–17, 23.
35. Ibid., chapter 1.
36. Marchand, *The Yoga of the Nine Emotions*, 103–104.
37. In his ecological ethics, James Gustafson views "revulsions of feelings that motivate concerns for the environment as clues to what we value about it." James M. Gustafson, *A Sense of the Divine: The Natural Environment from a Theocentric Perspective* (Cleveland, Ohio: Pilgrim Press, 1994), 35.
38. *sa ca śāpakleśavinipāteṣṭajanaviprayogavibhavanāśavadhabandhavidravopadhātavyasan asaṃyogādibhirvibhāvaiḥ samupajāyate* | (*NŚ* prose after VI.61, p. 258).
39. Sahi, "Compassionate Teacher," *Jyoti Art Ashram* (blog), June 1, 2011, http://jyotiartashram.blogspot.com/2011/06/compassionate-teacher.html.
40. Sahi, "Relating Art to Compassion," *Jyoti Art Ashram* (blog), June 1, 2011, http://jyotiartashram.blogspot.com/2011/06/relating-art-to-compassion.html.
41. Nirmal, "Towards a Christian Dalit Theology," 62.
42. Sarah McNamer, *Affective Meditation and the Invention of Medieval Compassion* (Philadelphia: University of Pennsylvania Press, 2010), 9–10.
43. Ibid., 11.
44. Wendy Farley, *Tragic Vision and Divine Compassion: A Contemporary Theodicy* (Louisville: Westminster John Knox, 1990), 110.
45. Ibid., 117.
46. Mohan Larbeer, personal conversation with the author, Tamilnadu Theological Seminary, May 22, 2010.

47. James D. Whitehead and Evelyn Eaton Whitehead, *Shadows of the Heart: A Spirituality of the Negative Emotions* (New York: Crossroad, 1994), 56, cf. 53–57.
48. See Sherinian, "The Indigenization of Tamil Christian Music," 636–724.
49. The Kabir Project, http://www.kabirproject.org/.
50. Gabriella Eichinger Ferro-Luzzi, *The Taste of Laughter: Aspects of Tamil Humour* (Wiesbaden: Otto Harrassowitz, 1992), 134–135. Other works on the importance of play in Hindu traditions include Sax, ed., *The Gods at Play*; and David Kinsley, *The Divine Player*.
51. Landmark works in this field include: Johan Huizinga, *Homo Ludens: A Study of the Play-Element in Culture* (New York: Roy Publishers, 1950); Harvey Cox, *The Feast of Fools: A Theological Essay on Festivity and Fantasy* (New York: Harper & Row, 1969); Hugo Rahner, S.J., *Man at Play*, trans. Brian Battershaw and Edward Quinn (New York: Herder and Herder, 1967); Jürgen Moltmann, *Theology of Play*, trans. Reinhard Ulrich (New York: Harper & Row, 1971); and Mark C. Taylor, *Erring: A Postmodern A/theology* (Chicago: The University of Chicago Press, 1984). The implications of such works for the humorous sentiment, in particular, are highlighted in Doris Donnelly, "Divine Folly: Being Religious and the Exercise of Humor," *Theological Studies* 48.4 (1992): 385–398.
52. Lee Siegel, *Laughing Matters: Comic Tradition in India* (Chicago: The University of Chicago Press, 1987), 12.
53. Ibid., 50.
54. Gemma Tulud Cruz, "Weapons of the Weak: Cultural Forms of Resistance and Their Implications for Missionary Theology and Practice," *Missiology: An International Review* 38.4 (Oct. 2012): 388. Cf. Gerald A. Arbuckle, *Laughing with God: Humor, Culture, and Transformation* (Collegeville, Minn.: Liturgical Press, 2008), 12–13.
55. Selva J. Raj and Corinne G. Dempsey, Introduction to *Sacred Play: Ritual Levity and Humor in South Asian Religions*, ed. Selva J. Raj and Corinne G. Dempsey (Albany: State University of New York Press, 2010), 6–7.
56. A. Whitney Sanford, "Don't Take It Badly, It's Holi: Ritual Levity in Balarama's Holi," in *Sacred Play: Ritual Levity and Humor in South Asian Religions*, ed. Selva J. Raj and Corinne G. Dempsey (Albany: State University of New York Press, 2010), 54.
57. Kathleen M. Sands, "Ifs, Ands, and Butts: Theological Reflections on Humor," *Journal of the American Academy of Religion* 64.3 (1996): 502.
58. Ibid., 505.
59. Ibid., 516.
60. Ibid., 518.
61. Bhagavad Gītā 2.2. *The Bhagavad-Gita: Krishna's Counsel in Time of War*, trans. Barbara Stoler Miller (New York: Bantam Books, 1986), 29.
62. Jarrod Whitaker, *Strong Arms and Drinking Strength: Masculinity, Violence, and the Body in Ancient India* (Oxford: Oxford University Press, 2011), 59. Arguably, the epitome of the warrior ideal is the hero Karṇa, a key player in the epic battle of the *Mahābhārata* that frames Kṛṣṇa's discourse. Kevin McGrath regards Karṇa as an "unembellished" model of the hero: Though not elevated through worship to divine status, Karṇa "is the most heroic due to his lineage, his divine and intrinsic armor, and his complete devotion to the honor of kṣatriya [ruler/warrior caste] ideals" (Kevin McGrath, *The Sanskrit Hero: Karṇa in Epic Mahābhārata* [Leiden: Brill, 2004], 3–4).

63. McGrath, *The Sanskrit Hero*, 4.
64. Rūpa Gosvāmin finds examples of devotees with each of these traits in *BhRS* 4.3.
65. *sa ca asaṃmohādhyavasāyanayavinayabalaparākramaśaktipratāpaprabhāvādibhirvibhāvairutpadyate | tasya stairyaśauryadhairyatyāgavaiśāradyādibhiranubhāvairabhinayaḥ prayoktavyaḥ* | (*NŚ* prose after VI.66, p. 262).
66. Abhinavagupta, *Loc* 3.26b. The heroism of the ascetic mendicant is a point of comparison between Jain and medieval Franciscan monks. See Stephen R. Munzer, "Heroism, Spiritual Development, and Triadic Bonds in Jain and Christian Mendicancy and Almsgiving," *Numen* 48 (2001): 48–80.
67. M. C. Raj observes that the endemic violence in the media no longer arouses revulsion in its viewers but is "characterized as heroism and capacity of human being." "Shedding of innocent blood becomes achievement hitherto unknown. Killing of supposedly immoral beings becomes a true symbol of moral policing." Raj, *Dalithink*, 217.
68. Gail Streete explains how "*virtus* or *andreia*, often translated as courage but whose primary meaning is manliness," enabled early Christian female martyrs to overcome the "obstacles" of "female embodiment and sexuality." Gail Corrigan Streete, "Of Martyrs and Men: Perpetua, Thecla, and the Ambiguity of Female Heroism in Early Christianity," in *The Subjective Eye: Essays in Culture, Religion, and Gender in Honor of Margaret R. Miles*, ed. Richard Valantasis (Eugene, Oreg.: Pickwick Publications, 2006), 256.
69. Barbara Newman, *From Virile Woman to WomanChrist: Studies in Medieval Religion and Literature* (Philadelphia: University of Pennsylvania Press, 1995).
70. Brian S. Hook and R. R. Reno, *Heroism and the Christian Life: Reclaiming Excellence* (Louisville: Westminster John Knox Press, 2000), 9.
71. Ibid., 11.
72. Paul Tillich, *The Courage to Be* (New Haven, Conn.: Yale University Press, 1952), 157.
73. Paul G. King, Kent Maynard, and David O. Woodyard, *Risking Liberation: Middle Class Powerlessness and Social Heroism* (Atlanta: John Knox Press, 1988), 18.
74. Tillich, *On Art and Architecture*, 12.
75. Coomaraswamy, *The Dance of Śiva*, 9, 11.
76. Ibid., 10–11.
77. Each of these figures receives attention in Janet K. Ruffing, ed., *Mysticism and Social Transformation* (Syracuse, N.Y.: Syracuse University Press, 2001).
78. Robert J. Egan, "Foreword," in *Mysticism and Social Transformation*, ed. Janet K. Ruffing (Syracuse, N.Y.: Syracuse University Press, 2001), x.
79. NBCLC, "The Navarasa of Jesus."
80. Roland Faber, "The Sense of Peace: A Para-doxology of Divine Multiplicity," in *Polydoxy: Theology of Multiplicity and Relation*, ed. Catherine Keller and Laurel C. Schneider (London: Routledge, 2011), 40.
81. Raghavan, *The Number of Rasa-s*, 201.
82. Representative works include Rita Nakashima Brock, *Journeys By Heart: A Christology of Erotic Power* (New York: Crossroad, 1988); Virginia Burrus and Catherine Keller, eds., *Toward a Theology of Eros: Transfiguring Passion at the Limits of Discipline* (New York: Fordham University Press, 2006); Wendy Farley, *Eros for the Other: Retaining Truth in a Pluralistic World* (University Park: Pennsylvania State University Press, 1996); and

Margaret D. Kamitsuka, ed., *The Embrace of Eros: Bodies, Desires, and Sexuality in Christianity* (Minneapolis: Fortress Press, 2010).

83. Cf. Sallie McFague, *Models of God: Theology for an Ecological, Nuclear Age* (Minneapolis: Fortress Press, 1987).
84. W. Anne Joh, "The Transgressive Power of Jeong: A Postcolonial Hybridization of Christology," in *Postcolonial Theologies: Divinity and Empire*, ed. Catherine Keller, Michael Nausner, and Mayra Rivera (St. Louis, Mo.: Chalice Press, 2004), 157, cf. 161.
85. Rita Sherma posits that "*rasa* as *response of feeling* is eros in its deepest sense." Sherma, "Eros, Ethics, and Enlightenment."
86. Sherma, "Eros, Ethics, and Enlightenment."
87. Santosh Kumar analyzes the CSI's Eucharistic Liturgy in this vein. See Santosh Sathya Kumar, "Towards the Development of an Inculturated Eucharistic Liturgy for the Church of South India: A Liturgical Experiment Using the Ragas of Indian Classical Music," ThD diss., Melbourne College of Divinity, 2006, 260–283.

9. *Wonder*

1. Robert C. Fuller, *Wonder: From Emotion to Spirituality* (Chapel Hill: University of North Carolina Press, 2006), 10.
2. Ibid., 15.
3. Nussbaum, *Upheavals of Thought*, 54.
4. Fuller, *Wonder*, 68.
5. Ibid., 132, citing the research of Herbert Benson, Andrew Newberg, Eugene d'Aquili, Richard Davidson, and Dean Hamer.
6. Fuller, *Wonder*, 131.
7. Ibid., 117.
8. Ibid., 120.
9. "The depths and riches" of God (Rom. 11:33) are the basis for Mark Heim's search for the Trinitarian origins of religious diversity: Mark S. Heim, *The Depth of the Riches: A Trinitarian Theology of Religious Ends* (Grand Rapids: Eerdmans, 2000).
10. Francis X. Clooney, *Beyond Compare: St. Francis de Sales and Śrī Vedānta Deśika on Loving Surrender to God* (Washington: Georgetown University Press, 2008), 208.
11. Loriliai Biernacki, "Towards a Tantric Nondualist Ethics through Abhinavagupta's Notion of Rasa," *Journal of Hindu Studies* 4.3 (2011): 265. In place of Bharata's term for the *rasa* of wonder (*adbhuta*), Abhinavagupta employs a technical term in Kashmir Śaivism (*camatkāra*) for wonder as the peak of both religious and aesthetic experience.
12. Jeannine Hill Fletcher, "As Long as We Wonder: Possibilities in the Impossibility of Interreligious Dialogue," *Theological Studies* 68.3 (2007): 549.
13. Ibid., 551.
14. Following Bharata, Abhinavagupta calls this spectator *sumanas*, one possessing a well-disposed (*su*) mind (*manas*). Masson and Patwardhan, *Aesthetic Rapture*, 46, 68.
15. *dharmo 'dharmapravṛttānāṃ kāmaḥ kāmopasevinām | nigraho durvinītānāṃ vinītānāṃ damakriyā || klīvānāṃ dhārṣṭyakaraṇamutsāhaḥ śūramāninām | abudhānāṃ vibodhaśca vaiduṣyaṃ viduṣāmapi ||* (*NŚ* I.108–109, p. 31).

16. Masson and Patwardhan, *Śāntarasa and Abhinavagupta's Philosophy of Aesthetics*, 56–67.
17. Uttara Asha Coorlawala, "It Matters For Whom You Dance: Audience Participation in Rasa Theory," in *Audience Participation: Essays on Inclusion in Performance*, ed. Susan Kattwinkel (Westport, Conn.: Praeger, 2003), 48.
18. David Mason, *Theatre and Religion on Krishna's Stage*, 10, and chapter 6.
19. Schwartz, *Rasa*, 25.
20. Case, *Seeing Krishna*, 151.
21. See, for example, Shannon Craigo-Snell, "Command Performance: Rethinking Performance Interpretation in the Context of *Divine Discourse*," *Modern Theology* 16.4 (2000); and Todd Johnson and Dale Savidge, *Performing the Sacred: Theology and Theatre in Dialogue* (Grand Rapids, Mich.: Baker Academic, 2009).
22. Haberman, *Acting as a Way of Salvation*. Latina/o participation in theodramas might present a comparable phenomenon in Christian practice. See Nancy Pineda-Madrid, "On Mysticism, Latinas/os, and the Journey: A Reflection in Conversation with Mary Engel," *Journal of Feminist Studies in Religion* 24.2 (2008).
23. Fuller, *Wonder*, 86.
24. Clooney, *Beyond Compare*, 208.
25. Clooney, "Passionate Comparison," 383.
26. Ibid., 389.
27. Jon Paul Sydnor, "Shaivism's *Nataraja* and Picasso's *Crucifixion*: An Essay in Comparative Visual Theology," *Studies in Interreligious Dialogue* 15.1 (2005): 93.
28. Ibid., 98–99.
29. See, for example, Clooney, "Passionate Comparison"; and Catherine Cornille, ed., *Many Mansions: Multiple Religious Belonging and Christian Identity* (Maryknoll, N.Y.: Orbis, 2003).
30. Jon Paul Sydnor, "Complementarity Reasoning and Interreligious Dialogue: A Case Study in Interdisciplinary Reflection," *Studies in Interreligious Dialogue* 15.2 (2005): 169.
31. Raghavan, *The Number of Rasa-s*, 203–205.
32. Goebbels cited in Mary-Elizabeth O'Brien, *Nazi Cinema as Enchantment: The Politics of Entertainment in the Third Reich* (Rochester, N.Y.: Camden House, 2004), 8.
33. Michael H. Kater, *The Twisted Muse: Musicians and Their Music in the Third Reich* (New York: Oxford University Press, 1997), 3–4.
34. Rubenstein, *Strange Wonder*, 21.
35. Ibid., 10.
36. Ibid., 133.

GLOSSARY OF SANSKRIT TERMS

ābhasa: semblance (of *rasa*)

Abhinavabhāratī (ABh): Abhinavagupta's commentary on the *Nāṭya Śāstra*

Abhinavagupta: tenth-century philosopher and literary theorist

acintyabhedābheda: the Gauḍīya Vaiṣṇava doctrine of the interplay of unity and difference, which is beyond human comprehension

adbhuta: the marvelous sentiment, one of the aesthetic emotions enumerated in the *Nāṭya Śāstra*

adhikāra: qualification or preparation to study

advaita: nondual

Advaita Vedānta: philosophical school that teaches the nondual relationship between *ātman* and *brahman*

ahaṃkāra śṛṅgāra: self love, love related to the ego

aiśvarya: fear or awe, the form of devotional love experienced in the presence of Kṛṣṇa's majesty; synonym for *śānta bhakti rasa*

alaṃkāra: poetic ornament or figure of speech

alaukika: non-worldly, transcendent, sublime

ānanda: supreme joy, bliss

anaucitya: improper, inappropriate

anubhāva: indicator, a physical or emotional response to excitants (*vibhāvas*) of emotion, displayed by an actor; one of the three components that awaken *rasa* in an audience

anukāra: imitation

anurāga: the fifth stage of the development of *prema* for Kṛṣṇa, which aims to enhance his pleasure without concern for one's own pleasure

anurasa: a semblance of devotional love in which emotion arises without a connection to Kṛṣṇa

anusāra: "following after" an exemplar

aparasa: a semblance of devotional love which arises in an enemy of Kṛṣṇa

aprakaṭa: immaterial, lacking *prakṛti*

artha: wealth or material well-being, one of the four human ends of life

āśrama: one of the four stages of life; also a place of retreat

āśraya:	"vessel" of sentiment (i.e., the person in whom it appears)
asura:	anti-god, in Vedic literature
āsvādana:	enjoyment or relishing
ātman:	one's true self
aucitya:	appropriate, what may properly be depicted in art to evoke certain emotions
avatāra:	"descent," a bodily form taken by Viṣṇu or Kṛṣṇa on earth
bhakta:	devotee
bhakti:	devotion
bhakti rasa:	devotional sentiment, love for a personal deity
Bharata:	legendary author of the drama manual, the *Nāṭya Śāstra*
bhāva:	emotion; as contrasted to *rasa,* it denotes ordinary emotion; also, in devotional contexts, it denotes a state of religious ecstasy; the sixth and culminating stage of the development of *prema*
bhāva bhakti:	the second stage of devotional development for initiates of the *rāgānugā* path, which cultivates the foundational emotion of love
bhaya:	fear, the foundational emotional state of the terrible sentiment
bhayānaka:	the terrible sentiment, one of the aesthetic emotions enumerated in the *Nāṭya Śāstra*
bhuj:	to participate, enjoy
bhukti:	enjoyment; contrasted with *bhakti*, it denotes concern with one's own pleasure
bībhasta:	the odious or disgusting sentiment, one of the aesthetic emotions enumerated in the *Nāṭya Śāstra*
Brahmā:	the creator
brahman:	the ultimate; divinity beyond name and form, which is experienced as true being, consciousness, and bliss
brahmāsvāda:	taste or relishing of the ultimate
brahmin	a member of the priestly caste *(varṇa)* [sometimes spelled "brahman"]
Caitanya:	fifteenth-/sixteenth-century saint, said to be the incarnation of Rādhā and Kṛṣṇa in one body, inspiration for the Gauḍīya Vaiṣṇava tradition
camatkāra:	wonder or mystic delight
daivikī:	divine; in the context of drama, describes a supremely successful performance
dāna vīra:	heroism of generosity, one of the subtypes of heroic sentiment; the generous hero
darśana:	vision of divinity, especially in the presence of a temple image
dāsya bhakti rasa:	the devotional sentiment of respect, exemplified by Kṛṣṇa's servants and sons
dayā vira:	heroism of compassion, one of the subtypes of heroic sentiment; the compassionate hero
dharma:	duty, righteousness; one of the four ends of human life
dharma vīra:	heroism of religious duty, one of the subtypes of heroic sentiment; the righteous hero

dhvani: resonance or suggestion of meaning, which Ānandavardhana names the soul of poetry
dhyāna yoga: the spiritual practice of meditation
dīpti: excitement or flaring up; a technical term in aesthetic theory that denotes particular styles and emotions
garbha gṛha: the interior ("womb") of a Hindu temple where the image of the deity resides
Gauḍīya Vaiṣṇavism: tradition of Kṛṣṇa devotion inspired by the medieval saint Caitanya, codified in the teachings of Caitanya's followers, the Gosvāmins
gopīs: the women of the cow-herding community in Vrindavan where Kṛṣṇa resided in his youth, who exemplify the devotional sentiments of parental and erotic love
hāsa: laughter, the foundational emotional state of the humorous sentiment
hāsya: the humorous or comic sentiment, one of the aesthetic emotions enumerated in the *Nāṭya Śāstra*
hladinī śakti: Kṛṣṇa's power of pure bliss
hṛd: heart
jīva: the individual soul
Jīva Gosvāmin: one of Caitanya's chief disciples and author of several important religious commentaries
jīva śakti: Kṛṣṇa's power to manifest as individual persons
jñāna: wisdom, philosophical knowledge
jugupsā: disgust, the foundational emotional state of the odious sentiment
kāma: pleasure or desire, including sexual desire
Kāma: the god of erotic love
kāraṇa: (ordinary) cause; distinguished from *vibhāva* (aesthetic excitant of emotion)
karma: action, work
karma yoga: spiritual practice focused on righteous action and service
karuṇa: compassion; the pathetic sentiment, one of the aesthetic emotions enumerated in the *Nāṭya Śāstra*
kārya: (ordinary) effect; distinguished from *anubhāva* (aesthetic indicator of the presence of emotion)
kīrtana: devotional song of praise for the deity
krodha: anger, the foundational emotional state of the furious sentiment
Kṛṣṇa (Krishna): the *avatāra* of Viṣṇu who was a charming young man in Vrindavan and later a warrior and king; the supreme deity for Gauḍīya Vaiṣṇavas
laukika: ordinary, worldly
līlā: play, drama; especially the divine play of creating the world and taking form on earth
Locana (Loc): Abhinavagupta's commentary on Ānandavardhana's *Dhvanyāloka*
lokasvabhāva: the shared human nature to which Bharata attributes the human ability to experience emotions in common
madhura bhakti rasa: the sentiment of erotic devotional love, exemplified by Rādhā and the other *gopīs*

mahābhāva: the supreme emotion, love's culmination in the union of Rādhā and Kṛṣṇa
mamatā: "myness," personal investment
māna: the lover's jealous indignation; the second stage of the development of *prema* for Kṛṣṇa
manas: mind, the seat of thought and emotion
maṇḍapa: open-pillared courtyard in a temple complex
mañjarī: a friend or assistant to one of Kṛṣṇa's *gopī* lovers
mānuṣī: human; in the context of drama, describes a relatively successful performance
māyā: artifice or illusion
māyā śakti: Kṛṣṇa's power to create the external world
mokṣa: liberation; the highest of the four ends of human life
mudrā: hand signal used by actors and dancers to suggest an object or idea
mukti: synonym for *mokṣa*, liberation; contrasted with *bhakti*, it denotes a religious fulfillment in which one's individual identity is dissolved
mūrti: image of a deity
Nāṭarāja: Lord of the Dance, traditional epithet of Śiva
Nāṭya Śāstra (NŚ): a drama manual written between 200 BCE and 400 CE and attributed to Bharata
navarasa: the nine basic human emotions, savored aesthetically in art
nirveda: world-weariness, a foundational emotional state of the peaceful sentiment
ojas: vital energy; in literary theory, a style of writing that is strong and energetic
pañcama: fifth
parakīya: love for the spouse of another; adulterous love
paramātman: the supreme Self or spirit
prakaṭa: material
prakṛti: matter
praṇaya: the lover's deep longing and assurance; the third stage of the development of *prema* for Kṛṣṇa
pratyāhāra: withdrawal of the senses, one of the eight limbs of yoga
prema: the pure love of Kṛṣṇa
prema bhakti: the third and highest stage of the development of Gauḍīya Vaiṣṇava devotees on the *rāgānugā* path, characterized by the full flowering of devotional love
preman: self love; a synonym of *ahaṃkāra śṛṅgāra*, which for Bhoja is the emotion at the base of all aesthetic feeling
prīti: synonym for *dāsya bhakti rasa*, respectful love
pūjā: worship of an image with chanting, flowers, flame, and other substances
puruṣa: the primal person
puruṣārthas: the four ends of human life
Rādhā: Kṛṣṇa's favorite lover

rāga: the fourth stage of the development of *prema* for Kṛṣṇa; one becomes "colored" by his love

rāgānugā: the path in Gauḍīya Vaiṣṇava devotion that develops a spiritual identity following one of the emotional relationships to Kṛṣṇa in scripture

rākṣasas: ogres or demons in the Hindu epics

rasa: aesthetic emotion, emotion as "tasted" in art

rasa dhvani: suggestion of emotion

rāsa līlā: the round dance of Kṛṣṇa with the *gopīs*; also a style of drama that depicts stories from Kṛṣṇa's life

rasa sūtra: the aphorism from *Nāṭya Śāstra* VI.31, which states that *rasa* arises from the combination of excitants, indicators, and transitory emotional states

rasābhasa: semblance of *rasa*

rasāsvāda: aesthetic relishing, taste of *rasa*

rati: affection or love, the foundational emotion of the erotic sentiment

raudra: the furious sentiment, one of the aesthetic emotions enumerated in the *Nāṭya Śāstra*

rūpa: body, form

Rūpa Gosvāmin: one of Caitanya's chief disciples and the principal theologian of the Gauḍīya Vaiṣṇava tradition

sādhaka rūpa: the body of the practitioner in the world

sādhana: religious practice or path

sādhāranīkaraṇa: the generalization or universalization (of emotion) that happens in aesthetic experience; an abstraction of emotion that is not individual or inflected by personal experiences

sādhāranīkṛta: generalized, universalized

sahṛdaya: the sympathetic spectator or ideal audience member, whose heart (*hṛd*) is fully attuned to the range of emotion

sakhī: friend of Rādhā, who enjoys the love of Kṛṣṇa and Rādhā as a bystander or spectator

sakhya bhakti rasa: the *rasa* of companionable devotion, exemplified by Kṛṣṇa's friends

śakti: divine power

śāma: pacification, a foundational emotion of the peaceful sentiment

sambhoga śṛṅgāra: love in union

saṃsāra: the cycle of rebirth

sañcāribhāva: emotion that nurtures or complements the main sentiment; synonym for *vyabhicāribhāva*

sannyāsa: the renouncer stage of life

sannyāsin: renouncer

śānta: peace; the peaceful sentiment, the ninth aesthetic emotion that was added to those enumerated in the *Nāṭya Śāstra*

śānta bhakti rasa: the *rasa* of peaceful devotion, characterized by yogis and people who worship Kṛṣṇa with awe

sāttvikabhāva: involuntary state experienced with emotion, such as blushing, sweating, goose bumps, and tears

siddha rūpa: a devotee's perfected form in Kṛṣṇa's realm

sneha: the first stage of the development of *prema* for Kṛṣṇa; has a "melting" quality

śoka: sorrow, the foundational emotion of the pathetic sentiment

śṛṅgāra: love; the erotic sentiment, one of the aesthetic emotions enumerated in the *Nāṭya Śāstra*

śṛṅgāra bhakti rasa: sentiment of devotional love

sthāyibhāva, sthāyin: the ordinary foundational emotion that underlies each of the corresponding aesthetic emotions

śūdra: the lowest of the four *varṇas*

śūnya: the void, unity of consciousness

svadharma: the idea that each person must do the things dictated by their own social and spiritual status

svakīya: married love, love of one's own spouse

svarūpa śakti: Kṛṣṇa's own form

tattva: gradations or levels of cosmic manifestation, also levels of consciousness

tattvajñāna: knowledge of the truth, a foundation of the peaceful sentiment

upanāyana: initiation ceremony, investment of the sacred thread for an upper-caste Hindu male

utsāha: energy, the foundational emotion of the heroic sentiment

vaidhī bhakti: the introductory path in Gauḍīya Vaiṣṇavism, which involves following sixty-four practices enjoined in scripture

vairagya: world-weariness, indifference to worldly things, a foundational emotion of the peaceful sentiment; synonym of *nirveda*

varṇa: class of society; caste

vāsanā: a mental impression or trace carried from one life to the next

vastu: a bare fact or idea

vatsalya bhakti rasa: parentally affectionate devotion, exemplified by Kṛṣṇa's parents and elders

vibhāva: excitant; contextual factor in a drama; one of the three components that give rise to *rasa*

vighna: obstacle (to *rasa*)

vipralambha śṛṅgāra: love in absence

vīra: the heroic sentiment, one of the aesthetic emotions enumerated in the *Nāṭya Śāstra*

vismaya: astonishment, the foundational emotion of the marvelous sentiment

vyabhicāribhāva: a transitory emotional state; one of the three components that give rise to *rasa*

yoga: spiritual practice

yogamāyā: Kṛṣṇa's divine power to create, to veil

yuddha vīra: heroism in battle, one of the subtypes of the heroic sentiment; the heroic warrior

BIBLIOGRAPHY

Abhinavagupta. *The Doctrine of Divine Recognition (Īśvara Pratyabhijñā Vimarśinī of Abhinavagupta)*, 3 vols. Edited by R. C. Dwivedi, K. A. Subramania Iyer, and K. C. Pandey. Delhi: Motilal Banarsidass, 1986.

Altieri, Charles. *The Particulars of Rapture: An Aesthetics of the Affects*. Ithaca, N.Y.: Cornell University Press, 2003.

Amaladass, Anand, S.J. "'Dhvani' Theory in Sanskrit Poetics." *Biblebhashyam* 5.4 (1979): 261–275.

———. *Philosophical Implications of Dhvani: Experience of Symbol Language in Indian Aesthetics*. Vienna: De Nobili Research Library, 1984.

Amaladoss, Michael, S.J., *Beyond Inculturation: Can the Many Be One?* Delhi: Vidyajyoti Education and Welfare Society/ISPCK, 1998.

Amalorananda, Swami (D. S. Amalorpavadass). *Integration and Interiorization*. Mysore: Anjali Ashram, 1990.

———. *Inculturation Realizes the Church's Universality, Fulness [sic] and Unity*. Inculturation Pamphlet Series, no. 7. Bangalore: NBCLC, n.d.

Appavoo, James Theophilus (Parattai). *Folklore for Change*. Madurai: TTS Publications, 1986.

———. "Communication for Dalit Liberation." In *Frontiers of Dalit Theology*, edited by V. Devasahayam, 363–372. Gurukul: ISPCK, 1997.

———. "Dalit Way of Theological Expression." In *Frontiers of Dalit Theology*, edited by V. Devasahayam, 283–289. Gurukul: ISPCK, 1997.

Arbuckle, Gerald A. *Laughing with God: Humor, Culture, and Transformation*. Collegeville, Minn.: Liturgical Press, 2008.

Arun, C. Joe. *Constructing Dalit Identity*. Jaipur: Rawat Publications, 2007.

Ashcroft, Bill, Gareth Griffiths, and Helen Tiffin. *The Empire Writes Back: Theory and Practice in Post-Colonial Literatures*. London: Routledge, 1991.

Astell, Ann W. *The Song of Songs in the Middle Ages*. Ithaca, N.Y.: Cornell University Press, 1990.

Baloian, Bruce Edward. *Anger in the Old Testament*. New York: Peter Lang, 1992.

Bäumer, Bettina. "Aesthetics of Mysticism or Mysticism of Aesthetics? The Approach of Kashmir Śaivism." In *Mysticism in Shaivism and Christianity*, edited by Bettina Bäumer, 329–349. New Delhi: D. K. Printworld, 1997.

Beck, Richard, Dan McGregor, Brooke Woodrow, Andrea Haugen, and Kyna Killion. "Death, Art and the Fall: A Terror Management View of Christian Aesthetic Judgments." *Journal of Psychology and Christianity* 29.4 (2011): 301–307.

Bernard of Clairvaux. *On the Song of Songs I*. Translated by Kilian Walsh. Cistercian Fathers Series 4. Kalamazoo, Mich.: Cistercian Publications, 1971.

———. *On the Song of Songs II*. Translated by Kilian Walsh. Cistercian Fathers Series 7. Kalamazoo, Mich.: Cistercian Publications, 1976.

———. *On the Song of Songs III*. Translated by Kilian Walsh and Irene M. Edmonds. Cistercian Fathers Series 31. Kalamazoo, Mich.: Cistercian Publications, 1979.

———. *On the Song of Songs IV*. Translated by Irene Edmonds. Cistercian Fathers Series 40. Kalamazoo, Mich.: Cistercian Publications, 1980.

Bharata. *Nāṭyaśāstra of Bharatamuṇi, Vol. I, Bare Text of Chs. I–VII (with Commentary Abhinavabhāratī on Adhyāya VI only)*. Edited by M. Ramakrishna Kavi and K. S. Ramaswami Sastri. Baroda: Oriental Institute, 1980.

———. *Nāṭyaśāstra of Bharatamuni: Text, Commentary of Abhinava Bhāratī by Abhinavaguptācārya and English Translation*. Vol. 1. Translated by M. M. Ghosh, edited by Pushpendra Kumar. Delhi: New Bharatiya Book Company, 2006.

Bhattacharyya-Panda, Nandini. *Appropriation and Invention of Tradition: The East India Company and Hindu Law in Early Colonial Bengal*. Oxford: Oxford University Press, 2008.

Biernacki, Loriliai. "Towards a Tantric Nondualist Ethics through Abhinavagupta's Notion of Rasa." *Journal of Hindu Studies* 4.3 (2011): 258–273.

Blumenthal, David. "Liturgies of Anger." *Crosscurrents* 52.2 (2002): 178–199.

Brock, Rita Nakashima. *Journeys By Heart: A Christology of Erotic Power*. New York: Crossroad, 1988.

Brunetti, Claire F. "Songs of Silence: The Affection for Bride and Body in the Rhetoric of Bernard of Clairvaux, Margery Kempe, and Teresa of Jesus." PhD diss., University of Florida, 1991.

Bryant, Edwin F. Introduction to *Krishna: The Beautiful Legend of God: Śrīmad Bhāgavata Purāṇa, Book X, With Chapters 1, 6, and 29–31 from Book XI*. Translated by Edwin F. Bryant. New York: Penguin, 2003.

———, trans. *Krishna: The Beautiful Legend of God: Śrīmad Bhāgavata Purāṇa, Book X, With Chapters 1, 6, and 29–31 from Book XI*. New York: Penguin, 2003.

Burrows, Mark S. "Foundations for an Erotic Christology: Bernard of Clairvaux on Jesus as 'Tender Lover.'" *Anglican Theological Review* 80.4 (1998): 477–494.

Burrus, Virginia, and Catherine Keller, eds. *Toward a Theology of Eros: Transfiguring Passion at the Limits of Discipline*. New York: Fordham University Press, 2006.

Butler, Judith. *Precarious Life: The Powers of Mourning and Violence*. London: Verso, 2004.

———. "Performativity, Precarity and Sexual Politics." *Revista de Antropologia Iberoamericana* 4.3 (2009): i–xiii. www.aibr.org.

———. "New Thoughts on Solidarity." Unpublished speech at the annual meeting of the American Academy of Religion, San Francisco, Calif., November 19, 2011.

Bynum, Carolyn Walker. *Jesus as Mother: Studies in the Spirituality of the High Middle Ages*. Berkeley: University of California Press, 1982.

Cabezón, José Ignacio. "The Discipline and Its Other: The Dialectic of Alterity in the Study of Religion." *Journal of the Academy of Religion* 74.1 (March 2006): 21–38.

Carr, Dhyandchand. "God and People in Liturgies." In *Vazhipaduvom (Dalit Liturgies)*, ix–xiv. Madurai: Dalit Resource Centre, 2000.

Carroll, David. *Paraesthetics: Foucault, Lyotard, Derrida*. New York: Methuen, 1987.

Case, Margaret H. *Seeing Krishna: The Religious World of a Brahman Family in Vrindaban*. Oxford: Oxford University Press, 2000.

Casey, Michael. *Athirst for God: Spiritual Desire in Bernard of Clairvaux's Sermons on the Song of Songs*. Kalamazoo, Mich.: Cistercian Publications, 1988.

Clarke, Sathianathan. *Dalits and Christianity: Subaltern Religion and Liberation Theology in India*. New York: Oxford University Press, 1998.

Clooney, Francis X. *Theology after Vedanta: An Experiment in Comparative Theology*. Albany: State University of New York Press, 1993.

———. "Passionate Comparison: The Intensification of Affect in Interreligious Reading of Hindu and Christian Texts." *Harvard Theological Review* 98.4 (2005): 367–390.

———. *Beyond Compare: St. Francis de Sales and Śrī Vedānta Deśika on Loving Surrender to God*. Washington: Georgetown University Press, 2008.

———. *Comparative Theology: Deep Learning Across Religious Borders*. West Sussex: Wiley-Blackwell, 2010.

———, ed. *The New Comparative Theology: Interreligious Insights from the Next Generation*. London: T&T Clark, 2010.

———. *His Hiding Place is Darkness: A Hindu-Catholic Theopoetics of Divine Absence*. Stanford, Calif.: Stanford University Press, 2013.

Collins, Paul M. *Christian Inculturation in India*. Burlington, Vt.: Ashgate, 2007.

Coomaraswamy, Ananda K. *Christian and Oriental Philosophy of Art*. New York: Dover Publications, 1956.

———. *The Dance of Śiva: Essays on Indian Art and Culture*. New York: Dover Publications, 1985.

———. *The Mirror of Gesture: Abhinaya Darpana of Nandikeśvara*. 4th ed. New Delhi: Munshiram Manoharlal Publishers, 1987.

Coorlawala, Uttara Asha. "It Matters For Whom You Dance: Audience Participation in Rasa Theory." In *Audience Participation: Essays on Inclusion in Performance*, edited by Susan Kattwinkel, 37–53. Westport, Conn.: Praeger, 2003.

Cornille, Catherine, ed. *Many Mansions: Multiple Religious Belonging and Christian Identity*. Maryknoll, N.Y.: Orbis, 2003.

Corrigan, John. "Introduction: A Critical Assessment of Scholarly Literature in Religion and Emotion." In *Emotion and Religion: A Critical Assessment and Annotated Bibliography*, edited by John Corrigan, Eric Crump, and John Kloos, 1–19. Westport, Conn: Greenwood Press, 2000.

———. "Introduction: Emotions Research and the Academic Study of Religion." In *Religion and Emotion: Approaches and Interpretations*, edited by John Corrigan, 3–31. Oxford: Oxford University Press, 2004.

———. "Introduction: The Study of Religion and Emotion." In *The Oxford Handbook of Religion and Emotion*, edited by John Corrigan, 3–16. Oxford: Oxford University Press, 2008.

———, ed. *The Oxford Handbook of Religion and Emotion*. Oxford: Oxford University Press, 2008.

Cose, Ellis. *The Rage of a Privileged Class*. New York: HarperPerennial, 1993.

Cox, Harvey. *The Feast of Fools: A Theological Essay on Festivity and Fantasy*. New York: Harper & Row, 1969.

Craigo-Snell, Shannon. "Command Performance: Rethinking Performance Interpretation in the Context of *Divine Discourse*." *Modern Theology* 16.4 (2000): 475–494.

Cruz, Gemma Tulud. "Weapons of the Weak: Cultural Forms of Resistance and Their Implications for Missionary Theology and Practice." *Missiology: An International Review* 38.4 (Oct. 2012): 383–394.

D'Sa, Francis X., S.J. "'Dhvani' as a Method of Interpretation." *Biblebhashyam* 5.4 (1979): 276–294.

D'Souza, Dinesh. *The Roots of Obama's Rage*. Washington: Regnery, 2010.

Dalit Resource Centre. *Vazhipaduvom (Dalit Liturgies)*. Madurai: Dalit Resource Centre, 2000.

———. Accessed December 24, 2011. http://www.drctts.com/DRC_htm/Dalit_Arts.htm.

Damrosch, David. "*Non Alia Sed Aliter*: The Hermeneutics of Gender in Bernard of Clairvaux." In *Images of Sainthood in Medieval Europe*, edited by Renate Blumenfeld-Kosinski and Timea Szell, 181–195. Ithaca, N.Y.: Cornell University Press, 1991.

Davis, Natalie Zemon. "The Rites of Violence." *Past and Present* 59.1 (1973): 51–91.

De, Sushil Kumar. "The Bhakti-Rasa-Sastra of Bengal Vaisnavism." *The Indian Historical Quarterly* 8 (1932): 643–688.

———. *Some Problems of Sanskrit Poetics*. Calcutta: Firma K. L. Mukhopadhyay, 1959.

Delmonico, Neal G. *Sacred Rapture: A Study of the Religious Aesthetic of Rupa Gosvamin*. PhD diss., The University of Chicago, 1990.

Deshpande, J. V. "Behind Dalit Anger." *Economic and Political Weekly*, August 16–23, 1997, 2090–2091.

Dimock Jr., Edward C. *The Place of the Hidden Moon: Erotic Mysticism in the Vaiṣṇava-Sahajiyā Cult of Bengal*. Chicago: The University of Chicago Press, 1966.

Dimock Jr., Edward C., and Denise Levertov. *In Praise of Krishna: Songs from the Bengali*. New York: Anchor Books, 1967.

Dimock Jr., Edward C., and Tony K. Stewart. Introduction to *Caitanya Caritāmṛta of Kṛṣṇadāsa Kavirāja*. Edited by Tony K. Stewart. Cambridge, Mass.: Harvard University Press, 1999.

Doniger, Wendy. *The Hindus: An Alternative History*. New York: Penguin, 2009.

Donnelly, Doris. "Divine Folly: Being Religious and the Exercise of Humor." *Theological Studies* 48.4 (1992): 385–398.

Dunne, John S., C.S.C. *A Search for God in Time and Memory*. London: MacMillan, 1967, 1969.

Dyczkowski, Mark S. G. *The Doctrine of Vibration: An Analysis of the Doctrines and Practices of Kashmir Shaivism*. Delhi: Motilal Banarsidass, 1989.

———, trans. *The Stanzas on Vibration: The Spandakārikā with Four Commentaries*. Varanasi: Dilip Kumar Publishers, 1994.

Edwards, Jonathan. *Religious Affections*. Edited by John E. Smith. Works of Jonathan Edwards 2. New Haven, Conn.: Yale University Press, 1959.

———. *Treatise Concerning Religious Affections*. Edited by John E. Smith. New Haven, Conn.: Yale University Press, 1959.

Egan, Robert J. Foreword to *Mysticism and Social Transformation,* edited by Janet K. Ruffing, ix–xi. Syracuse, N.Y.: Syracuse University Press, 2001.

Ekka, Manmasih. "Liberation Theme in Tana Bhagat Prayers." In *Doing Theology with the Poetic Traditions of India: Focus on Dalit and Tribal Poems*, edited by Joseph Patmury, 182–192. Bangalore: PTCA/Sathri, 1996.

Endean, Philip. "The Ignatian Prayer of the Senses." *The Heythrop Journal* 31 (1990): 391–418.

Faber, Roland. "The Sense of Peace: A Para-doxology of Divine Multiplicity." In *Polydoxy: Theology of Multiplicity and Relation*, edited by Catherine Keller and Laurel C. Schneider, 36–56. London: Routledge, 2011.

Farley, Wendy. *Tragic Vision and Divine Compassion: A Contemporary Theodicy.* Louisville: Westminster John Knox, 1990.

———. *Eros for the Other: Retaining Truth in a Pluralistic World.* University Park: Pennsylvania State University Press, 1996.

———. *The Wounding and Healing of Desire: Weaving Heaven and Earth.* Louisville: Westminster John Knox, 2005.

Ferro-Luzzi, Gabriella Eichinger. *The Taste of Laughter: Aspects of Tamil Humour.* Wiesbaden: Otto Harrassowitz, 1992.

Fields, Stephen, S.J. "Balthasar and Rahner on the Spiritual Senses." *Theological Studies* 57 (1996): 224–241.

Fishbane, Michael. "Biblical Hermeneutics and Philosophical Theology." Paper delivered at "The *Song of Songs*: Translation, Reception, Reconfiguration" Spring Conference, Center for the Study of World Religions, Harvard University, April 14, 2013.

Fredericks, James L. *Faith among Faiths: Christian Theology and Non-Christian Religions.* Mahwah, N.J.: Paulist Press, 1999.

Fuller, Robert C. *Wonder: From Emotion to Spirituality.* Chapel Hill: University of North Carolina Press, 2006.

Gaston, Anne-Marie. "Dance and the Hindu Woman: Bharatanāṭyam Re-ritualized." In *Roles and Rituals for Hindu Women*, edited by Julie Leslie, 149–172. Rutherford, N.J.: Fairleigh Dickinson University Press, 1991.

George, Kuruvilla. *From People's Theatre to People's Eucharist: Recovering the Drama of Christian Worship.* Delhi: ISPCK, 2002.

Gerow, Edwin. "Abhinavagupta's Aesthetics as a Speculative Paradigm." *Journal of the American Oriental Society* 114.2 (1994): 193–208.

Gerow, Edwin, and Ashok Aklujkar. "On *Śānta Rasa* in Sanskrit Poetics." *Journal of the American Oriental Society* 92.1 (1972): 80–87.

Ghosh, Manomohan. Introduction to *The Nāṭyaśāstra: A Treatise on Ancient Indian Dramaturgy and Histrionics ascribed to Bharata-Muni.* Vol. 1. 2nd ed. Edited by Manomohan Ghosh, xxv–lxix. Calcutta: Manisha, 1967.

Gnoli, R. *The Aesthetic Experience According to Abhinavagupta.* Varanasi: Chowkhamba Sanskrit Series, 1985.

Goldman, Robert P., and Sally J. Sutherland Goldman. *Devavāṇīpraveśikā: An Introduction to the Sanskrit Language.* 3rd ed. Berkeley: University of California Center for South Asia Studies, 1999.

Gosvāmī, Jīva. *Śrī Kṛṣṇa-sandarbha.* Vol. 3. Translated by Kuśakratha Dāsa, edited by Pūrṇaprajña Dāsa. Vrindaban: Ras Bihari Lal and Sons, 2006.

———. *Śrī Prīti-sandarbha.* 2 vols. Translated by Kuśakratha Dāsa, edited by Pūrṇaprajña Dāsa. Vrindaban: Ras Bihari Lal and Sons, 2007.

Gosvāmin, Rūpa. *Bhaktirasāmṛtasindhu.* Translated by Swami B. H. Bon Maharaj. Vrindavan: Institute of Oriental Philosophy, 1965.

———. *The Bhaktirasāmṛtasindhu of Rūpa Gosvāmin.* Translated by David L. Haberman. Delhi: IGNCA and Motilal Banarsidass, 2003.

———. *Ujjvalanīlamaṇiḥ.* Vrindavan: Gauḍīya Vedānta, 2003.

———. *Śrī Ujjvala-nīlamaṇi*. Translated by Kuśakratha Dāsa, edited by Pūrṇaprajña Dāsa. Vrindavan: Rasbihari Lal and Sons, 2006.

Goswamy, B. N. *Essence of Indian Art*. San Francisco: Asian Art Museum of San Francisco, 1986.

Gustafson, James M. *A Sense of the Divine: The Natural Environment from a Theocentric Perspective*. Cleveland, Ohio: Pilgrim Press, 1994.

Haberman, David L. *Acting as a Way of Salvation: A Study of Rāgānugā Bhakti Sādhana*. Delhi: Motilal Banarsidass, 1988.

———. Introduction to *The Bhaktirasāmṛtasindhu of Rūpa Gosvāmin*, translated by David L. Haberman, xxix–lxxiv. Delhi: IGNCA and Motilal Banarsidass, 2003.

Harris-Perry, Melissa V. *Sister Citizen: Shame, Stereotypes, and Black Women in America*. New Haven, Conn.: Yale University Press, 2011.

Hawley, John Stratton. *At Play with Krishna: Pilgrimage Dramas from Brindavan*. Princeton, N.J.: Princeton University Press, 1981.

———. *Songs of the Saints of India*. New York: Oxford University Press, 1988.

Hedges, Paul. *Controversies in Interreligious Dialogue and Theology of Religions*. London: SCM Press, 2010.

Heim, Mark S. *The Depth of the Riches: A Trinitarian Theology of Religious Ends*. Grand Rapids: Eerdmans, 2000.

Hernández, Gloria M. "'Where Did You Hide?' Locating the Divine in the *Cántico Spiritual* and *Rāsa Līlā*." *Journal of Hindu-Christian Studies* 25 (2012): 35–42.

Hill Fletcher, Jeannine. "As Long as We Wonder: Possibilities in the Impossibility of Interreligious Dialogue." *Theological Studies* 68.3 (2007): 531–554.

Hiltebeitel, Alf, and Kathleen M. Erndl, ed. *Is the Goddess a Feminist? The Politics of South Asian Goddesses*. New York: New York University Press, 2000.

Holdrege, Barbara A. "Body Connections: Hindu Discourses of the Body and the Study of Religion." *International Journal of Hindu Studies* 2.3 (1998): 341–386.

———. *Bhakti and Embodiment: Fashioning Divine Bodies and Devotional Bodies in Kṛṣṇa Bhakti*. London: Routlege, 2013.

Hollywood, Amy. *Sensible Ecstasy: Mysticism, Sexual Difference, and the Demands of History*. Chicago: The University of Chicago Press, 2002.

Holsinger, Bruce. "The Color of Salvation: Desire, Death, and the Second Crusade in Bernard of Clairvaux's *Sermons on the Song of Songs*." In *The Tongue of the Fathers: Gender and Identity in Twelfth-Century Latin*, edited by David Townsend and Andrew Taylor, 156–186. Philadelphia: University of Pennsylvania Press, 1998.

Hook, Brian S., and R. R. Reno. *Heroism and the Christian Life: Reclaiming Excellence*. Louisville: Westminster John Knox Press, 2000.

Huizinga, Johan. *Homo Ludens: A Study of the Play-Element in Culture*. New York: Roy Publishers, 1950.

Inden, Ronald. *Imagining India*. Oxford: Basil Blackwell, 1990.

Ingalls, Daniel H. H., Jeffrey Moussaieff Masson, and M. V. Patwardhan. *The* Dhvanyāloka *of Ānandavardhana with the* Locana of Abhinavagupta. Cambridge, Mass.: Harvard University Press, 1990.

Isaac, A. Royapan, and S. Selvaraj. *The Beginning of Our Rural Journey*. Madurai: Tamilnadu Theological Seminary, 2009.

Jantzen, Grace. *Power, Gender, and Christian Mysticism*. Cambridge: Cambridge University Press, 1995.

Jhanji, Rekha. *The Sensuous in Art: Reflections on Indian Aesthetics*. Shimla: Indian Institute of Advanced Study, 1989.

Joh, W. Anne. "The Transgressive Power of Jeong: A Postcolonial Hybridization of Christology." In *Postcolonial Theologies: Divinity and Empire*, edited by Catherine Keller, Michael Nausner, and Mayra Rivera, 149–163. St. Louis, Mo.: Chalice Press, 2004.

Johnson, Todd, and Dale Savidge. *Performing the Sacred: Theology and Theatre in Dialogue*. Grand Rapids, Mich.: Baker Academic, 2009.

Juergensmeyer, Mark. *Terror in the Mind of God: The Global Rise of Religious Violence*. Berkeley: University of California Press, 2000.

Kabir Project, The. http://www.kabirproject.org/.

Kamitsuka, Margaret D. ed., *The Embrace of Eros: Bodies, Desires, and Sexuality in Christianity*. Minneapolis: Fortress Press, 2010.

Kämpchen, Martin, and Jyoti Sahi. *The Holy Waters: Indian Psalm-Meditations*. Bangalore: Asian Trading Corporation, 1984.

Kang, Namsoon. "Who/What Is Asian?" In *Postcolonial Theologies: Divinity and Empire*, edited by Catherine Keller, Michel Nausner, and Mayra Rivera, 100–117. St. Louis, Mo.: Chalice Press, 2004.

Kater, Michael H. *The Twisted Muse: Musicians and Their Music in the Third Reich*. New York: Oxford University Press, 1997.

Kavirāja, Kṛṣṇadāsa. *Caitanya Caritāmṛta of Kṛṣṇadāsa Kavirāja*. Edited by Tony K. Stewart. Cambridge, Mass.: Harvard University Press, 1999.

Keller, Catherine, Michael Nausner, and Mayra Rivera. Introduction to *Postcolonial Theologies: Divinity and Empire*, edited by Catherine Keller, Michael Nausner, and Mayra Rivera, 1–19. St. Louis, Mo.: Chalice Press, 2004.

Kienzle, Beverly M. "Tending the Lord's Vineyard: Cistercians, Rhetoric, and Heresy, 1143–1229. Part I: Bernard of Clairvaux, the 1143 Sermons and the 1145 Preaching Mission." *Heresis* 25 (1995): 29–61.

King, Paul G., Kent Maynard, and David O. Woodyard. *Risking Liberation: Middle Class Powerlessness and Social Heroism*. Atlanta: John Knox Press, 1988.

Kinsley, David R. *The Divine Player: A Study of Kṛṣṇa Līlā*. Delhi: Motilal Banarsidass, 1979.

Knitter, Paul. "Toward a Liberation Theology of Religions." In *The Myth of Christian Uniqueness: Toward a Pluralistic Theology of Religions*, edited by John Hick and Paul Knitter, 178–202. Maryknoll, N.Y.: Orbis, 1987.

———. *Introducing Theologies of Religions*. Maryknoll, N.Y.: Orbis, 2002.

Kobialka, Michal. *This is My Body: Representational Practices in the Early Middle Ages*. Ann Arbor: University of Michigan Press, 1999.

Krahmer, Shawn M. "The Virile Bride of Bernard of Clairvaux." *Church History* 69.2 (2000): 304–327.

Krishnamoorthy, K. "The Relevance of RASA Theory to Modern Literature." In *Some Aspects of the Rasa Theory*, edited by V. M. Kulkarni, 81–96. Delhi: B. L. Institute of Indology, 1986.

Kristeva, Julia. *Tales of Love*. Translated by Leon S. Roudiez. New York: Columbia University Press, 1987.

Kulkarni, V. M. *Outline of Abhinavagupta's Aesthetics*. Ahmedabad: Saraswati Pustak Bhandar, 1998.

Kumar, Santosh Sathya. "Towards the Development of an Inculturated Eucharistic Liturgy for the Church of South India: A Liturgical Experiment Using the Ragas of Indian Classical Music." ThD diss., Melbourne College of Divinity, 2006.

LaCocque, André, and Paul Ricouer. *Thinking Biblically: Exegetical and Hermeneutical Studies.* Chicago: The University of Chicago Press, 1998.

Larbeer, P. Mohan. "Dalit Identity—A Theological Reflection." In *Frontiers of Dalit Theology*, edited by V. Devasahayam, 375–391. Madras: ISPCK/Gurukul, 1997.

Larbeer, P. Mohan, and V. Alexander. Introduction to *The Colours of Liberation*, edited by P. Mohan Larbeer and V. Alexander, i–xii. Madurai: Dalit Resource Centre, 2000.

Leclerq, Jean. *Monks and Love in Twelfth-Century France.* Oxford: Clarendon Press, 1979.

———. *Women and St. Bernard of Clairvaux.* Cistercian Studies Series 104. Kalamazoo, Mich.: Cistercian Publications, 1989.

———. *A Second Look at Bernard of Clairvaux.* Translated by Marie-Bernard Saïd. Kalamazoo, Mich.: Cistercian Publications, 1990.

Lester, Andrew D. "Why Hast Thou Forsaken Me! Anger at God." *The Journal of Pastoral Theology* 16:1 (2006): 53–70.

Lobo, Lancy. "Christianization, Hinduization and Indigenous Revivalism among the Tribals of Gujarat." In *Margins of Faith: Dalit and Tribal Christianity in India*, edited by Rowena Robinson and Joseph Marianus Kujur, 211–234. New Delhi: Sage Publications, 2010.

Locklin, Reid B., and Hugh Nicholson. "The Return of Comparative Theology." *Journal of the American Academy of Religion* 78.2 (2010): 477–514.

Lorde, Audre. *Sister Outsider: Essays and Speeches.* Berkeley, Calif.: Crossing Press, 1984.

Lott, Eric, and Jyoti Sahi. *Faces of Vision: Images of Life and Faith.* Leicester, UK: Christians Aware, 2008.

Lutz, Catherine A., and Lila Abu-Lughod, eds. *Language and the Politics of Emotion.* Cambridge: Cambridge University Press, 1990.

Lytje, Maren. "The Interior and the Abject: Uses and Abuses of the Female in the Middle Ages." *Culture and Religion* 5.3 (2004): 287–319.

MacKenzie, Caroline. "Art and Architecture as Locus for Dialogue: Inter-Religious Dialogue through Art." *Hindu-Christian Studies Bulletin* 4 (1991): 31–34.

———. "Liberation and Imagination: Art, Theology and Women's Experience." *Feminist Theology* 8 (1995): 9–19.

Madison, D. Soyini. "Crazy Patriotism and Angry (Post)Black Women." *Communication and Critical/Cultural Studies* 6.3 (2009): 321–326.

Mahārāja, Bhaktivedānta Nārāyaṇa. "Four Classes on *Rāga Vartma Candrikā*." In *Rāga Vartma Candrikā: A Moonbeam to Illuminate the Path of Spontaneous Devotion*, Viśvanātha Cakravartī Ṭhākura, translated with commentary by Bhaktivedānta Nārāyaṇa Mahārāja, 107–175. New Delhi: Gauḍīya Vedānta Samiti, 2001.

Malhotra, Rajiv, and Aravindan Neelakandan. *Breaking India: Western Interventions in Dravidian and Dalit Faultlines.* Delhi: Amaryllis Publishers, 2011.

Marchand, Peter. *The Yoga of the Nine Emotions: The Tantric Practice of Rasa Sadhana, Based on the Teachings of Harish Johari.* Rochester, Vt.: Destiny Books, 2006.

Mason, David V. *Theatre and Religion on Krishna's Stage: Performing in Vrindavan.* New York: Palgrave MacMillan, 2009.

Masson, J. L., and M. V. Patwardhan. *Śāntarasa and Abhinavagupta's Philosophy of Aesthetics.* Pune: Bhandarkar Oriental Research Institute, 1969.

———. *Aesthetic Rapture: The Rasādhyāya of the Nāṭyaśāstra*. 2 Vols. Poona: Deccan College Postgraduate and Research Institute, 1970.

Mattison III, William C. "Jesus' Prohibition of Anger (Mt. 5:22): The Person/Sin Distinction from Augustine to Aquinas." *Theological Studies* 68 (2007): 839–864.

McCarthy, Michael C. "Divine Wrath and Human Anger: Embarrassment Ancient and New." *Theological Studies* 70 (2009): 845–874.

McDaniel, June. "Blue Lotuses Everywhere: Divine Love in Gauḍīya Vaiṣṇava and Catholic Mysticism." *Journal of Vaishnava Studies* 5 (1996–1997): 83–102.

———. "Emotion in Bengali Religious Thought: Substance and Metaphor." In *Religion and Emotion: Approaches and Interpretations*, edited by John Corrigan, 249–270. Oxford: Oxford University Press, 2004.

McFague, Sallie. *Models of God: Theology for an Ecological, Nuclear Age*. Philadelphia: Fortress Press, 1987.

McGrath, Kevin. *The Sanskrit Hero: Karṇa in Epic Mahābhārata*. Leiden: Brill, 2004.

McNamer, Sarah. *Affective Meditation and the Invention of Medieval Compassion*. Philadelphia: University of Pennsylvania Press, 2010.

Miller, Barbara Stoler, trans. *Love Song of the Dark Lord: Jayadeva's Gītagovinda*. New York: Columbia University Press, 1977.

———. *The Bhagavad-Gita: Krishna's Counsel in Time of War*. New York: Bantam Books, 1986.

Miller, William Ian. *The Anatomy of Disgust*. Cambridge, Mass.: Harvard University Press, 1997.

Moltmann, Jürgen. *Theology of Play*. Translated by Reinhard Ulrich. New York: Harper & Row, 1971.

Moore, Stephen D. "The Song of Songs in the History of Sexuality." *Church History* 69.2 (2000): 328–349.

Mosse, David. "The Catholic Church and Dalit Christian Activism in Contemporary Tamil Nadu." In *Margins of Faith: Dalit and Tribal Christianity in India*, edited by Rowena Robinson and Joseph Marianus Kujur, 235–262. New Delhi: Sage Publications, 2010.

Mukerjee, Radhakamal. *The Cosmic Art of India: Symbol* (Mūrti), *Sentiment* (Rasa) *and Silence* (Yoga). Bombay: Allied Publishers Private Limited, 1965.

Müller, Max, trans. *Taittiriya Upanishad*. 1884. http://en.wikisource.org/wiki/Taittiriya_Upanishad.

Munzer, Stephen R. "Heroism, Spiritual Development, and Triadic Bonds in Jain and Christian Mendicancy and Almsgiving." *Numen* 48 (2001): 48–80.

Nandi, T. S. "Worldly Nature of Rasa." In *Some Aspects of the Rasa Theory*, edited by V. M. Kulkarni. Delhi: B. L. Institute of Indology, 1986.

Naravane, Vishwanath S. *Ananda K. Coomaraswamy*. Boston: Twayne Publishers, 1977.

National Biblical Catechetical and Liturgical Centre. *The Navarasa of Jesus*. VCD. Bangalore: NBCLC, n.d.

National Biblical Catechetical and Liturgical Centre. Accessed September 1, 2011. http://nbclc.in/nri.html.

Newman, Barbara. *From Virile Woman to WomanChrist: Studies in Medieval Religion and Literature*. Philadelphia: University of Pennsylvania Press, 1995.

Nicholson, Hugh. "The Reunification of Theology and Comparison in the New Comparative Theology." *Journal of the American Academy of Religion* 77.3 (2009): 609–646.

———. *Comparative Theology and the Problem of Religious Rivalry*. Oxford: Oxford University Press, 2011.

Nirmal, Arvind P. "Towards a Christian Dalit Theology." In *A Reader in Dalit Theology*, edited by Arvind P. Nirmal, 53–70. Madras: Gurukul, 1991.

Nussbaum, Martha C. *Upheavals of Thought: The Intelligence of the Emotions.* Cambridge: Cambridge University Press, 2001.

———. *From Disgust to Humanity: Sexual Orientation and Constitutional Law.* Oxford: Oxford University Press, 2010.

O'Brien, Mary-Elizabeth. *Nazi Cinema as Enchantment: The Politics of Entertainment in the Third Reich*. Rochester, N.Y.: Camden House, 2004.

Omvedt, Gail. *Dalit Visions: The Anti-caste Movement and the Construction of an Indian Identity.* Hyderabad: Orient Longman, 1995.

Origen. *De Principiis.* Translated by Frederick Crombie. Revised and edited by Kevin Knight. Ante-Nicene Fathers 4. Buffalo, N.Y.: Christian Literature Publishing Co., 1885. http://www.newadvent.org/fathers/0412.htm.

———. *The Song of Songs: Commentary and Homilies.* Translated by R. P. Lawson. Ancient Christian Writers Series 26. New York: Newman Press, 1956.

Panda, P. K. *Concept of Dhvani in Sanskrit Poetics: Indian Theory of Suggestion and Principles of Literary Criticism in the Light of Ānandavardhana's Dhvanyāloka and Its Commentator Madhusudan Miśra's Avadhāna Commentary.* Delhi: Penman Publishers, 1988.

Pandit, B. N. *Aspects of Kashmir Śaivism.* Srinagar: Utpal Publications, 1977.

Patankar, R. B. "Does the Rasa Theory Have Any Modern Relevance?" In *Some Aspects of the Rasa Theory*, edited by V. M. Kulkarni, 110–120. Delhi: B. L. Institute of Indology, 1986.

Pathak, Acharya Jagannath. *Dhvanyaloka of Sri Anandavardhanacharya with the Lochana Sanskrit Commentary of Sri Abhinavagupta.* Varanasi: Chowkhamba Vidyabhawan, 2003.

Paulsell, Stephanie, and Harvey Cox. *Lamentations and the Song of Songs.* Louisville: Westminster John Knox, 2012.

Petroff, Elizabeth Alvida. *Body and Soul: Essays on Medieval Women and Mysticism.* Oxford: Oxford University Press, 1994.

Pineda-Madrid, Nancy. "On Mysticism, Latinas/os, and the Journey: A Reflection in Conversation with Mary Engel." *Journal of Feminist Studies in Religion* 24.2 (2008): 178–183.

Plamper, Jan. "The History of Emotions: An Interview with William Reddy, Barbara Rosenwein, and Peter Stearns." *History and Theory* 49 (2010): 237–265.

Prabhu, George M. Soares. "And There Was a Great Calm: A 'Dhvani' Reading of the Stilling of the Storm (Mk. 4, 35–41)." *Biblebhashyam* 5.4 (1979): 295–308.

Pramuk, Christopher. "Sexuality, Spirituality and the 'Song of Songs.'" *America* 193.13 (2005): 8–12.

Raghavan, V. *Studies on Some Concepts of the Alaṃkāra Śāstra.* 2nd ed. Madras: Adyar Library and Research Center, 1973 [1942].

———. *The Number of Rasa-s.* 3rd ed. Madras: The Adyar Library and Research Centre, 1975.

Rahner, Hugo, S.J. *Man at Play*. Translated by Brian Battershaw and Edward Quinn. New York: Herder and Herder, 1967.

Rahner, Karl. "The Religious Meaning of Images." In *Theological Investigations,* vol. XXIII, translated by Joseph Donceel, S.J., and Hugh M. Riley. New York: Crossroad, 1992.

Raj, M. C. *Dalithink: An Adventure into Dalit Philosophy*. Tumkur: Ambedkar Resource Center, 2006.

———. "Dalit Spirituality." February 5, 2011. http://dalitreds.org/2011/02/05/dalit-spirituality-by-m-c-raj/.

Raj, Selva J. "Adapting Hindu Imagery: A Critical Look at Ritual Experiments in an Indian Catholic Ashram." *Journal of Ecumenical Studies* 37 (2000): 333–353.

Raj, Selva J., and Corinne G. Dempsey. Introduction to *Sacred Play: Ritual Levity and Humor in South Asian Religions*, edited by Selva J. Raj and Corinne G. Dempsey, 1–18. Albany: State University of New York Press, 2010.

Rajkumar, N. D. "Neeli Suria: A Dalit Dance and Drama Programme." Video CD. Tumkur: Booshakthi Kendra, n.d.

Rieger, Joerg. "Liberating God Talk." In *Postcolonial Theologies: Divinity and Empire*, edited by Catherine Keller, Michael Nausner, and Mayra Rivera, 204–220. St. Louis, Mo.: Chalice Press, 2004.

Rivera, Mayra. *The Touch of Transcendence: A Postcolonial Theology of God.* Louisville: Westminster John Knox, 2007.

Roberts, Robert C. "Emotions Research and Religious Experience." In *The Oxford Handbook of Religion and Emotion*, edited by John Corrigan, 490–506. Oxford: Oxford University Press, 2008.

Rosenwein, Barbara H. *Emotional Communities in the Early Middle Ages.* Ithaca, N.Y.: Cornell University Press, 2006.

Rothermindt, Gottfried. "Umstrittene Indische Christliche Kunst." *Zeitschrift für missionswissenschaft und Religionswissenschaft*, January 1982.

Rowe, Michael. "What it Says About Us When a 17-Month-Old Boy Is Beaten to Death for 'Acting Like a Girl.'" *Huffington Post*, August 5, 2010. http://www.huffingtonpost.com/michael-rowe/what-it-says-about-us-whe_b_671373.html.

Rubenstein, Mary-Jane. *Strange Wonder: The Closure of Metaphysics and the Opening of Awe.* New York: Columbia University Press, 2008.

Ruffing, Janet K., ed. *Mysticism and Social Transformation.* Syracuse, N.Y.: Syracuse University Press, 2001.

Sahi, Jyoti. *Stepping Stones: Reflections on the Theology of Indian Christian Culture.* Bangalore: Asian Trading Corporation, 1986.

———. *Kristo Jyoti Chapel: Notes and Sketches by Jyoti Sahi.* Sambalpur, Orisa: Kristo Jyoti Mohavidyaloyo, 1993.

———. *The Child and the Serpent: Reflections on Popular Indian Symbols.* Bangalore: Asian Trading Corporation, 1994.

———. *Holy Ground: A New Approach to the Mission of the Church in India.* Auckland: Pace Publishing, 1998.

———. "Dalit as a Cultural Memory: The Creative Language of the 'Panchama.'" In *The Colours of Liberation*, edited by Larbeer, P. Mohan, and V. Alexander, 1–8. Madurai: Dalit Resource Centre, 2000.

———. "School of Storytelling and Seeing." *Jyoti Art Ashram* (blog). February 25, 2007. http://jyotiartashram.blogspot.com/2007_02_01_archive.html.

———. "Some Reflections on Yoga and Jesus." *Jyoti Art Ashram* (blog). June 29, 2007. http://jyotiartashram.blogspot.com/2007_06_01_archive.html.

———. "Transforming the Heart." *Jyoti Art Ashram* (blog). July 20, 2007. http://jyotiartashram.blogspot.com/2007/07/transforming-heart.html.

———. "The Yoga of the Heart in Relation to a Vision of Reality." *Jyoti Art Ashram* (blog). July 20, 2007. http://jyotiartashram.blogspot.com/2007/07/yoga-of-heart-in-relation-to-vision-of.html.

———. "The Yoga of the Heart in Relation to Eastern Practices of Meditation." *Jyoti Art Ashram* (blog). July 20, 2007. http://jyotiartashram.blogspot.com/2007/07/yoga-of-heart-in-relation-to-eastern.html.

———. "The Yoga of Art." *Jyoti Art Ashram* (blog). July 22, 2007. http://jyotiartashram.blogspot.com/2007/07/yoga-of-art-relation-of-art-to-yoga-has.html.

———. "Mandala of the Kingdom of Heaven." *Jyoti Art Ashram* (blog). October 2, 2007. http://jyotiartashram.blogspot.com/2007/10/mandala-of-kingdom-of-heaven.html.

———. "Dancer on the Cross." *Jyoti Art Ashram* (blog). October 7, 2007. http://jyotiartashram.blogspot.com/2007/10/dancer-on-cross.html.

———. "Jesus Dies on the Tree." *Jyoti Art Ashram* (blog). October 8, 2007. http://jyotiartashram.blogspot.com/2007/10/jesus-dies-on-tree.html.

———. "The Way of the Cross as Dreaming the Mandala." *Jyoti Art Ashram* (blog). April 20, 2009. http://jyotiartashram.blogspot.com/2009_04_01_archive.html.

———. "Dalit and Tribal Theologies." *Jyoti Art Ashram* (blog). September 29, 2009. http://jyotiartashram.blogspot.com/2009_09_01_archive.html.

———. "Wayanad: A Land of Ancient Forests." *Jyoti Art Ashram* (blog). February 5, 2010. http://jyotiartashram.blogspot.com/2010_02_01_archive.html.

———. "Cultural Patchworks: A *Dhvani* Understanding of Art and Secularism. Part I: Outline of the Position of Art within the Secular Space of the Modern State." *Jyoti Art Ashram* (blog). April 20, 2010. http://jyotiartashram.blogspot.com/2010/04/cultural-patchwork-part-1.html.

———. "Cultural Patchworks: A *Dhvani* Understanding of Art and Secularism. Part II: Towards a Spirituality of Art within Secular Society." *Jyoti Art Ashram* (blog). April 20, 2010. http://jyotiartashram.blogspot.com/2010/04/cultural-patchwork-part-ii.html.

———. "Cultural Patchworks: A *Dhvani* Understanding of Art and Secularism. Part III: Indian Art and the Representation of a Secular Christ." *Jyoti Art Ashram* (blog). April 20, 2010. http://jyotiartashram.blogspot.com/2010/04/cultural-patchwork-part-iii.html.

———. "The Cosmic Cross." *Jyoti Art Ashram* (blog). October 23, 2010. http://jyotiartashram.blogspot.com/2010/10/cosmic-cross.html.

———. "The Cross of Light." *Jyoti Art Ashram* (blog). October 23, 2010. http://jyotiartashram.blogspot.com/2010/10/cross-of-light.html.

———. "Compassionate Teacher." *Jyoti Art Ashram* (blog). June 1, 2011. http://jyotiartashram.blogspot.com/2011/06/compassionate-teacher.html.

———. "Relating Art to Compassion." *Jyoti Art Ashram* (blog). June 1, 2011. http://jyotiartashram.blogspot.com/2011/06/relating-art-to-compassion.html.

———. "Towards a Spiritual Understanding of Dance." Unpublished manuscript, e-mail to the author, June 20, 2011.

———. "The Drum and the Dancer in Adivasi Culture." Unpublished manuscript, e-mail to the author, November 20, 2011.

———. "The Drum and the Dance in Adivasi Culture." In *Silver Jubilee Souvenir (1987–2012) of the Interdiocesan Regional Theologat of Odisha*, 54–57. Sambalpur, Orisa: Khristo Jyoti Mohavidyaloyo, 2012.

Said, Edward W. *Orientalism*. New York: Vintage Books, 1978.

Saliers, Don S. "Sound Spirituality: On the Formative Expressive Power of Music for Christian Spirituality." *Christian Spirituality Bulletin* 8.1 (2000): 1–5.

———. "Beauty and Terror." *Spiritus* 2.2 (2002): 181–191.

———. *Music and Theology*. Nashville: Abingdon Press, 2007.

Sambamurthy, P. *A Dictionary of South Indian Music and Musicians.* 3 vols. Madras: Indian Music Publishing House, 1984 [1952].

Sands, Kathleen M. "Ifs, Ands, and Butts: Theological Reflections on Humor." *Journal of the American Academy of Religion* 64.3 (1996): 499–523.

Sanford, A. Whitney. "Painting Words, Tasting Sound: Visions of Krishna in Paramānand's Sixteenth-Century Devotional Poetry." *Journal of the American Academy of Religion* 70.1 (2002): 55–81.

———. "Don't Take It Badly, It's Holi: Ritual Levity in Balarama's Holi." In *Sacred Play: Ritual Levity and Humor in South Asian Religions*, edited by Selva J. Raj and Corinne G. Dempsey, 37–56. Albany: State University of New York Press, 2010.

Sastri, K. S. Ramaswami. *Indian Aesthetics.* Srirangam: Sri Vani Vilas Press, 1928.

———. "Preface to the Second Edition." In *Nāṭyaśāstra of Bharatamuni*, edited by M. Ramakrishna Kavi, 1–54. Baroda: Oriental Institute, 1980 [1956].

Saussy, Carroll. *The Gift of Anger: A Call to Faithful Action.* Louisville: Westminster John Knox, 1995.

Sax, William S., ed. *The Gods at Play: Līlā in South Asia.* New York: Oxford University Press, 1995.

Schwartz, Susan L. *Rasa: Performing the Divine in India.* New York: Columbia University Press, 2004.

Schweig, Graham M. *Dance of Divine Love: The Rāsa Līlā of Krishna from the Bhāgavata Purāṇa, India's Classic Sacred Love Story.* Delhi: Motilal Banarsidass, 2007 [2005].

Sharma, Arvind. *Religious Studies and Comparative Methodology: The Case for Reciprocal Illumination.* Albany: State University of New York Press, 2005.

Sherinian, Zoe. "The Indigenization of Tamil Christian Music: Folk Music as Liberative Transmission System." PhD diss., Wesleyan University, 1998.

———. "Dalit Theology in Tamil Christian Folk Music: A Transformed Liturgy by James Theophilus Appavoo." In *Popular Christianity in India: Riting Between the Lines*, edited by Selva J. Raj and Corinne G. Dempsey, 233–253. Albany: State University of New York Press, 2002.

———. "Musical Style and the Changing Social Identity of Tamil Christians." *Journal of Ethnomusicology* 51.2 (2007): 238–280.

Sherma, Rita Dasgupta. "Eros, Ethics, and Enlightenment: Towards a Reconstructive Approach to Ultimate and Penultimate Goals in Hindu Theology." Accessed April 25, 2012. http://www.infinityfoundation.com/mandala/s_es/s_es_sherm_eros_frameset.htm.

Siegel, Lee. *Laughing Matters: Comic Tradition in India.* Chicago: The University of Chicago Press, 1987.

Singh, Jaideva. Introduction to *Vijñānabhairava or Divine Consciousness: A Treasury of 112 Types of Yoga*, translated by Jaideva Singh. Delhi: Motilal Banarsidass, 1979.

———. "Exposition." In Abhinavagupta, *Parā-trīśikā-Vivaraṇa: The Secret of Tantric Mysticism*, translated with notes by Jaideva Singh, corrected by Swami Lakshmanjee, edited by Bettina Bäumer. Delhi: Motilal Banarsidass, 1988.

Smith, Jonathan Z. "The 'End' of Comparison." In *A Magic Still Dwells: Comparative Religion in the Postmodern Age*, edited by Kimberley C. Patton and Benjamin C. Ray, 237–241. Berkeley: University of California Press, 2000.

Spivak, Gayatri Chakravorty. "Strategy, Identity, Writing." In *The Postcolonial Critic*, edited by Sarah Harasym, 35–49. New York: Routledge, 1990.

Streete, Gail Corrigan. "Of Martyrs and Men: Perpetua, Thecla, and the Ambiguity of Female Heroism in Early Christianity." In *The Subjective Eye: Essays in Culture, Religion, and Gender in Honor of Margaret R. Miles*, edited by Richard Valantasis, 254–264. Eugene, Oreg.: Pickwick Publications, 2006.

Sugiharto, Bambang. "Javanese Epistemology Revisited." Unpublished paper presented to the Institute for Advanced Study in Asian Cultures and Theologies, Hong Kong, 2007.

Sydnor, John Paul. "Complementarity Reasoning and Interreligious Dialogue: A Case Study in Interdisciplinary Reflection." *Studies in Interreligious Dialogue* 15.2 (2005): 165–181.

———. "Shaivism's *Nataraja* and Picasso's *Crucifixion*: An Essay in Comparative Visual Theology." *Studies in Interreligious Dialogue* 15.1 (2005): 86–100.

Tagore, Rabindranath. *Gitanjali*. Translated by Rabindranath Tagore. http://www.sacred-texts.com/hin/tagore/gitnjali.htm.

Taneja, Leena. "Tracing the Absence of Faith: Hermeneutics, Deconstruction, and the School of Gauḍīya Vaiṣṇavism." PhD diss., George Washington University, 2005.

Tanner, Kathryn. *Theories of Culture: A New Agenda for Theology*. Minneapolis: Fortress Press, 1997.

Taves, Ann. *Fits, Trances and Visions: Experiencing Religion and Explaining Experience from Wesley to James*. Princeton, N.J.: Princeton University Press, 1999.

———. *Religious Experience Reconsidered: A Building-Block Approach to the Study of Religion and Other Special Things*. Princeton, N.J.: Princeton University Press, 2009.

Tavris, Carol. *Anger: The Misunderstood Emotion*. New York: Simon and Schuster, 1982.

Taylor, Mark C. *Erring: A Postmodern A/theology*. Chicago: The University of Chicago Press, 1984.

Taylor, Richard W. "From Khadi to Kavi: Toward a Typology of Christian Ashrams." *Religion and Society* 24.4 (1977): 19–37.

Thangaraj, M. Thomas. "Indian Christian Tradition." In *Religions of South Asia: An Introduction*, edited by Sushil Mittal and Gene Thursby, 185–200. London: Routledge, 2006.

Tillich, Paul. *The Courage to Be*. New Haven, Conn.: Yale University Press, 1952.

———. *On Art and Architecture*. Edited by John Dillenberger and Jane Dillenberger, translated by Robert P. Scharlemann. New York: Crossroad, 1989.

Toomey, Paul M. "Krishna's Consuming Passions: Food as Metaphor and Metonym for Emotion at Mount Govardhan." In *Divine Passions: The Social Construction of Emotion in India*, edited by Owen M. Lynch, 157–181. Berkeley: University of California Press, 1990.

Trinh T. Minh-ha. *When the Moon Waxes Red: Representation, Gender, and Cultural Politics*. London: Routledge, 1991.

Tripathi, K. D. "From Sensuous to Supersensuous: An Inquiry into Some Terms of Indian Aesthetics." In *Prakrti III: The Agamic Tradition and the Arts*, edited by Bettina Bäumer, 67–77. New Delhi: IGNCA and D.K. Printworld, 1994.

Tuhiwai Smith, Linda. *Decolonizing Methodologies: Research and Indigenous Peoples*. New York: Zed Books, 1999.

Turner, Denys. *Eros and Allegory: Medieval Exegesis of the Song of Songs*. Kalamazoo, Mich.: Cistercian Publications, 1995.

van Wolde, Ellen. "Sentiments as Culturally Constructed Emotions: Anger and Love in the Hebrew Bible." *Biblical Interpretation* 16 (2008): 1–24.

Vatsyayan, Kapila. *Bharata: The Nāṭyaśāstra*. New Delhi: Sahitya Akademi, 1996.

Vellanickal, Matthew. "Drink from the Source of the Living Water." *Biblebhashyam* 5.4 (1979): 309–318.

Viśvanātha Cakravartī Ṭhākura. *Śrī Bhakti-rasāmṛta-sindhu-bindu: A Drop of the Nectarine Ocean of Bhakti-rasa*. Translated with commentary by Bhaktivedānta Nārāyaṇa Mahārāja. Mathurā: Gauḍīya Vedānta Publications, 1996.

———. *Rāga Vartma Candrikā: A Moonbeam to Illuminate the Path of Spontaneous Devotion*. Translated with commentary by Bhaktivedānta Nārāyaṇa Mahārāja. New Delhi: Gauḍīya Vedānta Samiti, 2001.

von Balthasar, Hans Urs. *Heart of the World*. Translated by Erasmo S. Leiva. San Francisco: Ignatius Press, 1979.

———. *The Glory of the Lord: A Theological Aesthetics, Volume I: Seeing the Form*. Translated by Erasmo Leiva-Merikakis, edited by Joseph Fessio, S.J., and John Riches. San Francisco: Ignatius Press, 1982.

Voss Roberts, Michelle. "Neither *Bhukti* nor *Mukti*: The New Sensorium in Devotional Practice." *Practical Matters* (Spring 2009): http://www.practicalmattersjournal.org/issue/1/analyzing-matters/neither-bhukti-nor-mukti.

———. "Power, Gender, and the Construction of a Kashmir Śaiva Mystic." *Journal of Hindu Studies* 3.3 (2010): 279–297.

———. "Tasting the Divine: The Aesthetics of Religious Emotion in Indian Christianity." *Religion* 42.4 (2012): 575–595.

Whitaker, Jarrod. *Strong Arms and Drinking Strength: Masculinity, Violence, and the Body in Ancient India*. Oxford: Oxford University Press, 2011.

Whitehead, James D., and Evelyn Eaton Whitehead. *Shadows of the Heart: A Spirituality of the Negative Emotions*. New York: Crossroad, 1994.

Wulff, Donna M. *Drama as a Mode of Religious Realization: The Vidagdhamādhava of Rūpa Gosvāmin*. Chico, Calif.: Scholars Press, 1984.

———. "Religion in a New Mode: The Convergence of the Aesthetic and the Religious in Medieval India." *Journal of the American Academy of Religion* 54.4 (1986): 673–688.

Yancey, Phillip. *Prayer: Does It Make Any Difference?* Grand Rapids, Mich.: Zondervan, 2010.

INDEX

COMPARATIVE THEOLOGY: THINKING ACROSS TRADITIONS

Loye Ashton and John J. Thatamanil, *Series Editors*

Hyo-Dong Lee, ***Spirit, Qi, and the Multitude: A Comparative Theology for the Democracy of Creation***

Michelle Voss Roberts, ***Tastes of the Divine: Hindu and Christian Theologies of Emotion***